Serving Military Families in the 21st Century

Textbooks in Family Studies Series

The *Textbooks in Family Studies Series* is an interdisciplinary series that offers cutting edge textbooks in family studies and family psychology. Volumes can be complete textbooks and/or supplementary texts for the undergraduate and/or graduate markets. Both authored and edited volumes are welcome. Please contact the series editor, Robert Milardo at rhd360@maine.edu, for details in preparing a proposal that should include the goal of the book, table of contents, an overview of competing texts, the intended market including course name(s) and level, and suggested reviewers.

These are the books currently in the series:

Serving Military Families in the 21st Century written by Karen Rose Blaisure, Tara Saathoff-Wells, Angela Pereira, Shelley MacDermid Wadsworth, and Amy Laura Dombro (2012)

Father–Daughter Relationships: Contemporary Research and Issues written by Linda Nielsen (2012)

Serving Military Families in the 21st Century

Karen Rose Blaisure
Western Michigan University

Tara Saathoff-Wells
University of Central Florida

Angela Pereira
Colonel, U.S. Army, Retired

Shelley MacDermid Wadsworth
Military Family Research Institute at Purdue University

Amy Laura Dombro

Routledge
Taylor & Francis Group
New York   London

Routledge
Taylor & Francis Group
711 Third Avenue
New York, NY 10017

Routledge
Taylor & Francis Group
27 Church Road
Hove, East Sussex BN3 2FA

© 2012 by Taylor & Francis Group, LLC
Routledge is an imprint of Taylor & Francis Group, an Informa business

Version Date: 20120227

International Standard Book Number: 978-0-415-88065-7 (Hardback) 978-0-415-88066-4 (Paperback)

Visit the Taylor & Francis Web site at
http://www.taylorandfrancis.com

and the Psychology Press Web site at
http://www.psypress.com

To all members and veterans of the U.S. military and their families for their personal sacrifices, their dedication to duty, and their patriotism.

Contents

Foreword

Serving Military Families, written by an extraordinary team of talented scholars and practitioners, is one of the inaugural books in the *Textbooks in Family Studies Series*. In each book, our purpose is to pair leading experts with important topics in the field of family studies that are underrepresented in standard textbooks. These experts are active researchers, practitioners, and talented teachers who can write engaging books that can be used in the classroom as standalone textbooks or paired with additional books.

This book serves as an introduction to military families and the effects of military service on adults, their relationships, and their children. Relatively few individuals served on active duty in the last decade, that is, much less than 1 percent of the U.S. population.* Perhaps not surprisingly, about 8 in 10 veterans say the American public does not understand the problems faced by those in the military or their families. By and large the public agrees they do not understand. This book aims to close the gap in understanding families with active military members as well as families with recent veterans. There is good reason to do so.

The experience of veterans commands our attention as many of them, but not all, report considerable difficulty in readjusting to civilian life following military service. Nearly half of veterans report experiencing strains in family life after leaving the military, 47% say they have frequent outbursts of anger, and nearly a third (32%) report there are times they do not care about anything. For those who experience combat, the array of psychological and relational problems reported is disconcerting, with over half reporting emotional trauma and many reporting reliving distressing experiences in the form of flashbacks or sleep disturbances. About one in six recent veterans reports experiencing serious injuries while serving in the military and most such injuries are combat related. Nearly half report knowing someone who was killed while in the military.

Coupled with these statistics is the changing face of the military over recent decades. Service members are far more likely to be married (about 53%) than was the case in the recent past (about 41% in 1973), and they are more likely to be married than civilians of comparable ages. These are sobering statistics, and they challenge students of families to enrich our understanding of those who serve in the military and their relationships with intimate partners, children and extended kin.

The 13 chapters in this book provide an extensive primer on military culture and family life, essential background for chapters that address a variety of core issues including detailed descriptions of the many programs developed for individuals and families. The presentation spans an array of ordinary challenges facing all families in their development and maintenance, as well as challenges that are unique to military families. The unique challenges of military families include frequent relocations, separations and long deployments in difficult conditions, combat injury, and violent death, all of which can have profound effects on children, spouses, parents, and extended

---

* Taylor, P. (Ed). (2011). The military-civilian gap: War and sacrifice in the post-9/11 era. Pew Social & Demographic Trends. Washington, D. C.

kin. While many current and former soldiers experience difficulties, many do not and clearly demonstrate resilience in their personal and family lives. Recent veterans, for instance, report levels of personal happiness and satisfaction in their family lives comparable to those of the general public. In this book, the authors wisely present a balanced perspective that neither omits addressing the challenges of military life nor fails to appreciate resiliency and the benefits of participation in a culture of service.

Robert M. Milardo, PhD
Professor of Family Studies
University of Maine
Series Editor

Preface

Being in the military is not just a job. There is a sense of calling, a depth of feeling that service and family members have, often for generations. As Lieutenant Colonel Jessica Milam, Deputy Chief, Air Force Diversity Operations explains, "The military culture has a core value of service before self. When the nation calls, we understand it is an honor to serve. This shared value creates a strong bond and culture within the military and places a unique responsibility on military families. Understanding these and other realities of military life and acknowledging them to service members and their families are essential in supporting military families in your personal life and professional life."

People supporting military families often share a sense of calling too. You may be a college student preparing to work with military families. Or you may already be established in your career as a teacher, child care provider, nurse or physician, lawyer, counselor, law enforcement officer, writer, or researcher. You may work in a university setting or a civilian social services agency where you sometimes meet and work with military family members, perhaps more often than you used to. Or you may work in an organization with the mission to serve military families. Perhaps you are a member of a military family or a veteran. When we consider there are 30 million veterans and 2.2 million service members and their families in the United States, the chances are that whatever you do or will do, and wherever you do it, you will end up serving members of military families. That means each day you have an opportunity to make a difference in the lives of those who sacrifice so much for the rest of us.

In this book, you will find information and research about military families that you can use to build your knowledge base about military culture. You will learn about how much military families have in common with civilian families as well as issues specific to military families.

You will have the chance to meet people who study and work with military families, as well as those who make policy, design programs, and of course family members themselves. As so many of them have said to us: no one can ever know it all when it comes to military families, but if you can listen and ask questions with respect, families will help fill in the gaps of what you need to know.

In addition, you will also learn about services available to military families from both the military and civilian sectors. There comes a time when every family needs support of one kind or another. Yet, just because services exist and you may be there committed to supporting families does not mean that families are being served or that they are receiving the support they need when they do connect with a program or service provider.

To take advantage of the support offered, a person must know about and understand the services being offered. Yet, the wide array of services offered by the military and community, in person and online, can be overwhelming to negotiate at the best of times. When a family is experiencing stress, no matter the reason, it can be even more of a challenge.

If and how one begins to search for support can depend on a variety of factors including one's culture, personal style, mental health, access to a computer and/or transportation, and past experiences with seeking support. In military families, stigma may be an obstacle as seeking help can be viewed as a weakness and a potential threat to one's career.

This text is designed as a primary text for courses on military families and as a supplemental text for courses on family relationships, stress and coping, social work, family therapy, counseling, clinical and counseling psychology, human development, sociology, nursing, and education. We believe that this text will provide readers, whether students or professionals in the field, with fundamental knowledge to appreciate the strengths of military families and respond with insight to support families with the challenges of military life.

LEARNING TOOLS

Creating positive change for military families means building bridges between families and the support they need. It means building bridges between what we know and what we do. To these ends, throughout this book you will find a series of features filled with information you can tailor to the unique strengths and needs of the diverse families you work with. These include

- **Spotlight on research:** Here you will find the work of researchers who are learning more about military families with the goal of informing and enriching the work of practitioners like you. As you will see, there are many areas such as how families deal with a service member's death due to combat that we still have much to learn about.
- **Best practices:** This feature includes accepted strategies from the field.
- **Voices from the frontline:** In this feature, you will find stories of support program leaders, practitioners, researchers, policy makers, and, most importantly, service members and their families. Each has generously shared their personal experiences, successes, challenges, and insights from a moment in time. By the time you are reading this book, their stories will have taken new paths. Like the family members you will (or already do) work with—and members of your family and ours—each is a unique individual in a unique family constellation.
- **Tips from the frontline:** In these sections, you will find concrete, hands-on suggestions based on the experiences and wisdom of people you have met in this book.
- **Objectives and chapter summaries:** To encourage recall of content, each chapter begins with a list of objectives and ends with a summary of content.
- **Key terms and glossary:** Key terms are bolded and defined the first time they are used to help readers build a military vocabulary. A glossary of terms provides easy access to definitions.
- **Tables and figures:** Tables and figures are used to convey demographic and other statistical information. Figures are used to display conceptual models.
- **Exercises:** Each chapter ends with exercises, including web-based exercises, to actively engage readers in examining primary source material, reflecting on their own experiences, and applying chapter content to "real-life" situations.

As you read, we predict that you will not only learn about military families, but like some of the people you meet in the following pages (including the authors), you will learn something about yourself, and your assumptions and stereotypes about the military and our country. Being open to learning, not only about others but about yourself, is a key ingredient to being an effective provider of family support no matter your role.

We think you will be inspired too by the other professionals you meet as Shelley was the day she walked into a small office at the Pentagon: "The walls were covered with sheets filled with writing. I asked a senior-level person what was going on. The Secretary of Defense had given a small team three weeks to figure out how to get every child in Iraq back to school. They were busy solving a problem no one had ever tackled before." Like these professionals, every day military family members are faced with problems they may have never tackled before.

The Department of Defense needs a workforce of people to support military families and veterans. As a country, we need a sustainable support network for military families long after the troops come home. We hope this book will help you make a difference in that regard.

CONTENT OVERVIEW

In Chapter 1, you will be introduced to the military culture and military families. You will meet Colonel Angela Pereira, U.S. Army, Retired, one of the coauthors of this book who grew up in a military family and provided mental health support to troops in Iraq before retiring. This chapter discusses the role of the military in our country and the strengths and challenges of military families.

Chapter 2 describes requirements to join the military and factors that lead people to do so. It will paint pictures for you of service personnel, active duty, and selected reserve by branch and discuss what we know and do not know about military families.

Chapter 3 describes features of military life including a sense of community, priority of the mission, relocation, spouse employment and education, separation due to temporary duty, deployment, and death of the service member.

In Chapter 4, we take a closer look at children and youth in military families. Among the people you will meet is Connery Otto, a high school senior, who talks about "growing up military." This chapter looks at young peoples' experiences of moving and going to child care and school. It then turns its focus to the impact of parental deployment on children's behavior and psychological well-being and ways to support children with parental deployment, injury, and death.

Chapter 5 will ground you in theories about stress and resilience providing you with a framework to shape your attitudes and approach to your work with military families. You will see that yes, at times, families are suffering and may need specialized intervention. But, you will also see that dealing with challenging times can be an opportunity for families to recognize and draw upon their strengths. In the words of Froma Walsh, PhD, whom you will meet: "What is remarkable is the potential for individual and family resilience—the capacity to rebound—and even grow stronger—when family members pull together as a team to master their challenges. Families hold the keys to resilience."

Chapter 6 focuses on common individual and family milestones that service members experience during their career and how the military, as an organization, has developed support structures and programs to help service members through significant life transitions. There is also discussion of the limits of the military to meet every individual and family need.

In Chapter 7, you will meet Colonel Rick L. Campise who describes his work as a psychologist in a combat zone supporting service members with issues from trauma over the horrors of war to everyday life issues including finances and relationships with their significant others and their children. A discussion of the physical and psychological effects of war ends with good news: exposure to stress and involvement in traumatic events can lead to positive changes in relationships and to philosophical, physical, and spiritual growth.

Chapter 8 discusses research focused on risk and resilience experienced in family systems and familial roles in relation to war and deployment experiences. There is a particular focus on marital relationships, combat injured families, and emerging research with parents of service members. You will hear voices of service members and spouses and meet researchers who focus on military family relationships. Each of these areas of research addresses assumptions and clarifies strengths and concerns for military family well-being. In turn, these findings inform policies that are directed toward these families.

Chapter 9 discusses resources provided by the military as well as special programs and policies to support families with a variety of issues including deployment, health care, education, child care and youth programs, and other services to promote quality of life.

Chapter 10 describes federal policies that address military families and highlights examples of civilian organizations that serve military families. This chapter ends with a review of services on college and university campuses for veterans and military service members.

In Chapter 11, you will meet Barbara Purinton who is a Family Readiness Assistant in Vermont as well as the wife and mother of service members who have recently returned home from deployments in both Iraq and Afghanistan. Barbara describes her work in a program recently developed to support National Guard and Reserve members and their families. In the rest of the chapter, you will learn about other programs developed to support military members and families with reintegration and reunification and service members' injuries. You will also be introduced to programs that reflect a new resilience-based view of psychological health.

In Chapter 12, we discuss innovations in promoting a culture of resilience within the military and families; provide direction for working with those who have experienced traumatic events and injuries, such as TBI and PTSD, and their families; and give information pertaining to families who have experienced the death of their service member.

Finally, Chapter 13 looks ahead with you to serving military families. We examine some of the obvious and not-so-obvious careers that offer a way to serve military families, either directly or indirectly. These career paths are illustrated through stories shared by working professionals. This chapter concludes with a discussion about compassion satisfaction and its role in providing highly competent and compassionate support to military families.

Acknowledgments

We owe thanks to the many individuals and organizations who made this textbook possible. We would like to recognize the pivotal role of the Military Family Research Institute (MFRI) at Purdue University in the development of this book. MFRI staff and students helped with this effort in a myriad of ways, including answering many questions, designing the cover, and providing many materials in addition to doing the high-quality work they complete every day.

Stories form the heart of this book. These stories come from nearly 50 military family members, service members, veterans, researchers, clinicians, writers, film producers, students, university staff, and experts from military and civilian family support organizations who agreed to share their experiences and reflections. We are grateful, as we know readers will be, for their generosity.

We would like to recognize the following persons for their assistance in locating or confirming the status of public information: Captain Lori Laraway, Nurse Corps, U.S. Navy; Lieutenant Colonel Laurel Devine, U.S. Army; Aggie Byers; Marianne Coates; and Kirsten Woodward, MSW, LCSW.

Many thanks to Pat Chandler for insight into the Reserve Component; to Jackie Chandler for reading and responding to early versions of the chapters; to students enrolled in *Military Family Life* and *Family Life and the Military* courses taught during fall 2010 for their feedback on selected chapters; to Diana Boulin for preparing figures and tables; to Andreza Mancuso Schaden for assistance with the reference list, figures, and tables; to the Department of Family and Consumer Sciences and the College of Education and Human Development at Western Michigan University for administrative and travel support; to Cheryl Wellman for her assistance in manuscript preparation; to Richard J. Westphal, RN, Ph.D. Captain (Retired), Nurse Corps, U.S. Navy for guidance on the use of the Stress Continuum; to Sandra K. Dye, Ph.D., Chief Master Sergeant, U.S. Air Force Reserve for loaning her boots to be photographed; and to our colleagues, friends, and family for their encouragement.

We appreciate the guidance provided by Robert Milardo, editor of the *Textbooks in Family Studies Series*, and reviewers Adrian Blow (Michigan State University), Whitney A. Brosi (Oklahoma State University), Elizabeth O. Carroll (East Carolina University), Lynn K. Hall (University of Phoenix), Angela Huebner (Virginia Tech), James A. Martin (Bryn Mawr College), and David Rohall (Western Illinois University). We also want to express our gratitude for the editorial expertise of Debra Riegert and Andrea Zekus at Routledge.

Finally, for sustaining us through multiple weeklong writing sessions we would like to recognize Tony Vargas for his generous hospitality, Jerry Strouse and Ed Silverman for their homemade treats, and Patch (otherwise known as the Perfect Army Trained Canine Helper) for being sweet and playing fetch.

Authors

Karen Rose Blaisure, PhD, a licensed marriage and family therapist and a certified family life educator, is a professor of family studies in the Department of Family and Consumer Sciences at Western Michigan University in Kalamazoo. Her research focuses on education and policy initiatives for families experiencing separation and divorce. She regularly teaches a graduate course, *Family Life and the Military*, for students in the helping professions. From 1986 through 1989, she worked as a program specialist and an education services supervisor and, in 1992, as a special project consultant at the Navy Family Services Center in Norfolk, Virginia (renamed the Naval Station Norfolk Fleet and Family Support Center). In these roles, she regularly facilitated programs on deployment, reunion, children, and parenting. She has presented on military families to many professional groups and has written about the Navy's Return and Reunion program.

Tara Saathoff-Wells, PhD, is a faculty member in the Department of Child, Family and Community Sciences at the University of Central Florida in Orlando and a certified family life educator. From 1989 through 1994, she worked in Kenya and Mozambique with both indigenous and U.S. expatriate populations. As a doctoral student, she completed an internship with the U.S. Department of State in the Family Liaison Office, the primary family and child resource and support office for U.S. diplomatic families. From 2000 through 2010, Dr. Saathoff-Wells was a faculty member in Human Development and Family Studies at Central Michigan University in Mount Pleasant, where she taught a human development and family studies course on military family life and served as the director of the Women's Studies Program. In fall 2010, Dr. Blaisure and Dr. Saathoff-Wells team-taught their respective courses coordinating lectures, videos, guest speakers, class discussions, and field trips. The classes were linked by compressed video interactive technology.

Colonel Angela Pereira, PhD, U.S. Army, Retired, is a consultant and an educator on psychological health and military life issues, having completed a distinguished career in the military. She is a member of the External Advisory Council of the Military Family Research Institute at Purdue University in West Lafayette, Indiana. She previously served as the U.S. Army's regional mental health consultant and director of the U.S. Army Europe Regional Medical Command's Solider and Family Support Services in Heidelberg, Germany; as a member of the Department of Defense Task Force on Mental Health; as the director of the Combat Stress Control/Mental Health Clinic in Abu Ghraib, Iraq; as the director of education and training on health and wellness at the U.S. Army Center for Health Promotion and Preventive Medicine; and as a division social worker for the Third Armored Division during Operations Desert Shield/Storm. Board certified in clinical social work, she earned her PhD from the University of South Carolina in Columbia and her master's and bachelor's degrees from the University of California, Berkeley. Dr. Pereira's many honors include the Legion of Merit, the Bronze Star Medal, and the Order of Military Medical Merit.

Shelley M. MacDermid Wadsworth, PhD, is a professor in the Department of Human Development and Family Studies at Purdue University in West Lafayette, Indiana, where she also directs the Military Family Research Institute and the Center for Families and serves as an associate dean in the College of Health and Human Sciences. Her research focuses on relationships between job conditions and family life, with special focus on military families and organizational policies, programs, and practices. Dr. MacDermid Wadsworth is a fellow of the National Council on Family Relations and a recipient of the Work Life Legacy Award from the Families and Work Institute. Dr. MacDermid Wadsworth served as a civilian co-chair of the Department of Defense Task Force on Mental Health and currently serves on the Psychological Health External Advisory Committee of the Defense Health Board and the Returning Veterans Committee of the Institute of Medicine.

Amy Laura Dombro, MS, develops resources to assist teachers, family support professionals, and community leaders in making positive change for children and families. As former head of the Bank Street Infant and Family Center, Amy works with and for organizations including the Military Family Research Institute, ZERO TO THREE, The What to Expect Foundation, and Families and Work Institute to translate information so that it is engaging and easy to use. In addition, she often documents stories of successes, challenges, and lessons learned so that readers can benefit from the experiences of others. Her recent publications include *Honoring Our Babies and Toddlers: Supporting Young Children Affected by a Military Parent's Deployment, Injury or Death* (ZERO TO THREE, 2009) and *Powerful Interactions: How to Connect with Children to Extend Their Learning* (NAEYC, 2011).

1

An Introduction to Military Culture and Military Families

In Chapter 1, you will

- Meet retired Army Colonel Angela Pereira, one of the coauthors of this book
- Review the role of the military in the United States
- Gain insights into military culture
- Learn basic military terms
- Consider the strengths and challenges faced by military families
- Understand why helping professionals should learn about military families

Meet

Coauthor Angela Pereira, Colonel, U.S. Army, Retired

People join the military for many different reasons: education benefits, the camaraderie and sense of belonging, the travel, the challenge, following a family member's footsteps. My father was in the Army for 27 years. When I was growing up, we moved every 3 years in the United States and Germany. I went to eight different schools between the first and twelfth grade. After graduating college, I realized how much I wanted to join those doing the important work of watching over our nation.

Recently retired, I was an Army social worker for 25 years. I did just about every kind of job a social worker can do in the Army. I worked in community mental health and in the exceptional family member program with families who have children with special needs. I worked in corrections. I provided services on the ground to soldiers of an armored division during the Gulf War. I've been a policymaker and worked on program development. And I've been in management roles—first serving as a regional chief of domestic violence for one-third of the Army family advocacy programs in Europe and later as the consultant and program director for mental health services for Army soldiers and families in Europe. During my Army career, I served in Fort Riley, Kansas; San Antonio, Texas; Frankfurt, Germany; Saudi Arabia; Iraq (twice); Kuwait; Fort Jackson, South Carolina; Aberdeen Proving Ground, Maryland; and Heidelberg, Germany (twice). In 15 years of marriage, my husband, who also served in the Army, and I were apart for a total of 6 years due to our work.

INTRODUCTION

Like Colonel Pereira, you may have grown up in a military family. Perhaps you are a service member, planning to become one, or a veteran. Or you may have never thought much about the military and could never see yourself signing up. Perhaps someone very dear to you is serving in the military or has served. You may be a student considering entering a helping profession. Perhaps you are already out in the field working with children and families. You may be a first responder, a law enforcement agent, or a public health worker. You may be working with military families. This book is for you.

We, the authors, bring to this book a wide range of experience and knowledge about the military. As you will see, some of us were born into the military and made it our life's work. Some of us worked as civilians with a branch of the military or have family members who are serving. Others of us are relatively new to the military and have had to confront and lay aside misperceptions as we got to know service members and their families and learned more about military life. Throughout this book, we look forward to sharing some of our experiences, questions, and lessons learned about the military and military families.

WHY FOCUS ON MILITARY FAMILIES?

Military service members are members of your families and neighborhoods. They are your work colleagues and schoolmates, little league coaches, teachers, firefighters, bank tellers, and insurance agents. They are parents, children, uncles, aunts, and grandparents—people you have known all your lives as well as people you have never met. Relationships with service members and their loved ones are embedded into your communities in many different ways, as noted in Box 1.1.

Military families offer you, as a current or future human service professional, a unique opportunity to learn about and work with individual and family capacities, strengths, and challenges within distinctive cultural and sociohistorical contexts. The military is often described as having a culture of its own, "a military culture." As a workplace organization, it has no rival among other career paths in terms of the number of individuals and families who are systematically affected by U.S. international diplomatic relations and policy.

For the past two decades, U.S. military engagements have been conducted with a volunteer military. Major engagements during this time have been **Gulf War I** (1990–1991), **Operation Enduring Freedom** (OEF; the name given to the U.S. military actions in Afghanistan that began in October 2001), **Operation Iraqi Freedom** (OIF; the name given to the U.S. military actions in Iraq that began in March 2003 and ended in August 2010), and **Operation New Dawn** (OND; the name given to the U.S. military action in Iraq that began in September 2010). At this time in our history, operations in both Afghanistan and Iraq have been underway for nearly a decade. If you,

---

BOX 1.1   TIPS FROM THE FRONTLINE

Military families want what every family wants. Just as all Americans are concerned about quality education for their children and work and career opportunities for both spouses, so are military families. Families bring issues from the civilian world with them, such as issues around money, parenting, caring for elderly parents, and raising children.

Today many military families are living out in their communities and may never live or work on a military installation. They are learning what a military family is while their service member is serving in a war zone. They need a targeted support system that includes support from their families, friends, and community. We are all in this together.

Joyce Wessel Raezer
Executive Director, National Military Family Association

the reader, are within the typical age range of today's college student (18–24 years old), this current effort has been ongoing for about one-half of your life. If you are older, you may remember other conflicts and/or peacekeeping missions involving U.S. military personnel. Regardless of your age, however, you, your friends, family, colleagues, and clients will be affected directly or indirectly by these military engagements and the impact of them for the foreseeable future.

UNDERSTANDING THE ROLE OF THE MILITARY

This section addresses the historical roots of the U.S. Armed Forces, the civilian control of the military, the relatively new use of an all-volunteer force, the concept of total—both active and reserve—force, and the branches of the military. The information below will help to clarify misconceptions and promote greater understanding of the structure and function of the military.

History

The roots of today's U.S. Armed Forces extend from 1636 when the English colonists brought the tradition of militias, where citizens organized themselves into military units for the purpose of defense. This tradition of the "citizen-soldier" is now called the National Guard (National Guard, 2009). Then, nearly 150 years later, in 1775, the Continental Congress established the Continental Army (initially formed from militia members), the Continental Navy, and the Continental Marines in order to defend the colonies and fight for their independence from Great Britain. When the War of American Independence ended with the signing of the Treaty of Paris in 1783 and its ratification the following year, Congress disbanded the Continental Navy, the Continental Marines, and the Continental Army although it did maintain a small number of soldiers at a few critical forts. In a few years, however, Congress established the War Department in 1789 and the Department of the Navy in 1798 to defend the country and protect the merchant fleet at sea (Cooper, 1999; Goodspeed, 2003).

Central to democracy is the civilian control of the military, in contrast to a **military dictatorship** in which a leader, who may be from the military or who assumes military rank once in power, or a **military junta** (a group of military leaders) rules a country without the consent of the people and often through oppressive means. In countries where the military is in control of the nation, it is free to take any action it deems appropriate, without input from the citizens of that nation, and that is, in effect, an authoritarian government instead of a democracy.

In the United States, civilian control of the military is established in the U.S. Constitution and is divided between the U.S. President (see Article II of the U.S. Constitution) and members of Congress who are elected by U.S. citizens (see Article 1 of the U.S. Constitution). In the United States, the military follows civilian leadership and carries out the policies of the United States as directed by the President. The military is one of many tools used to carry out U.S. policy. Another tool is the U.S. State Department's Diplomatic Corps.

The current Armed Forces reflect changes that occurred following the end of World War II. Today, the **Department of Defense** (DoD; the federal department tasked with national security and supervising the U.S. Armed Forces) is led by the **Secretary of Defense**, a cabinet post, who oversees national security agencies and the Department of the Army, the Department of the Air Force (created from the World War II Army Air Forces), and the Department of the Navy (which also includes the Marine Corps).

Each service has a **Chief of Staff**, the most senior ranking officer, who is responsible for the readiness of personnel, among numerous other responsibilities, and who serves on the **Joint Chiefs of Staff** (JCS), an advisory body to the President and the Secretary of Defense. The operational **chain of command** (the highly structured line of authority and responsibility that designates who is in charge of what and whom and along which orders are passed) begins with the President of the United States and continues down to the Secretary of Defense and then to the commanders of the unified combatant commands (DoD, 2009).

Between the War of American Independence and 1973, the United States relied periodically on conscription or a draft to acquire the service personnel needed to engage in wars or conflicts. In 1973, however, the military became an all-volunteer force. The following list summarizes the history of conscription in the United States, ending with the current policy of registration of males 18–25 years of age with the Selective Service (Chambers, 1999; Hansen, 2000; Perri, 2008).

- 1792—Congress passed an act requiring all able-bodied male citizens to have a gun and join the state militia. No penalty for noncompliance.
- War of 1812—The war ended before conscription was enacted.
- 1862—The government of the Confederate South initiated a compulsory military draft.
- 1863—The first wartime conscription passed by the U.S. Congress required male citizens, ages 20–45, and aliens seeking citizenship to enroll. Exemptions were made for only sons and some occupations. Enrollment quotas for each congressional district were filled first by selectees from Class 1 (all men 20–35 and single men 35–45) and then by Class 2 (married men 35–45). Conscription was controversial because of substitutions and exemptions that could be bought for $300.
- 1898 (Spanish–American War)—Congress declared men 18–45 years of age were subject to military service.
- 1917–1918 (World War I)—The Selective Service Act of 1917 prohibited substitutions; allowed for conscientious objectors due to religion; and established boards to register, induct, or defer men 21–30. Opposition to conscription was strong.
- 1940–1946 (World War II)—The Selective Training and Service Act was passed by Congress in 1940. Males 21–35 were required to register and a lottery was held. As the war progressed, the age was lowered to 18 and the selection was changed from lottery to age, with the oldest called up first.
- 1950–1953 (Korea)—Men between 18½ and 35 were drafted for an average of 2 years. World War II veterans were exempted from the draft. The Universal Military Training and Service Act of 1951 required males 18–26 to register.
- 1964–1973 (Vietnam)—The first lottery since 1942 was held in 1969 for men born between 1944 and 1950, replacing the "oldest first" practice. Exemptions and deferments for college students were established. Some joined Reserve or National Guard units that were less likely to be deployed.
- 1973—The draft ended with the expiration of the 1967 Selective Service Act (extended by Congress in 1971); registration with the Selective Service continued until 1975. Initiation of the all-volunteer force.
- 1980 to present—Congress reinstated registration with the Selective Service System for most male U.S. citizens and male aliens living in the United States between 18 and 25.

Registration with the Selective Service does not mean a man will be inducted into the military. If a draft were instituted "men would be called in sequence determined by random lottery number and year of birth [and] examined for mental, physical and moral fitness by the military before being deferred or exempted from military service or inducted into the Armed Forces" (Selective Service System, 2009, para. 1).

Along with an all-volunteer force, another important shift emerged in the 1970s with the implementation of the "total force" policy. With this policy, the total force is considered to be the combination of **Active Component** members (who work full time in the Army, Navy, Marine Corps, and Air Force), and **Reserve Component** members (comprised of the Ready Reserve, Standby Reserve, and Retired Reserve, which are defined and described below), and key government civilian employees. However, it was not until the beginning of the Gulf War in 1990 when Americans began to feel the practical implications of a total force policy. At this time, the total force policy, coupled with the downsizing of the Active Component, meant large numbers of reservists and members of the National Guard were called to active service (Knox & Price, 1999). More recently, the total force policy has guided the mobilization of service personnel for OEF, OIF, and OND.

Downsize in Active Force and Increase in Military Operational Tempo

At the end of the 1980s, after the fall of the communist system in the Soviet Union and its satellite Eastern European nations, the Union of Soviet Socialist Republics (the USSR or Soviet Union, for short) was no longer seen as a threat to the United States. By 1991, the Soviet Union had collapsed into independent nations. The **Cold War**—the ongoing political, military, and economic tension between the Soviet Union and its satellites and the United States and other powers of the western world that had existed since the end of World War II—was over. Because the largest threat against the United States no longer existed, military planners and Congress reduced the size of the U.S. military. The number of military combat divisions and the total number of active duty military were significantly reduced. The downsizing continued after the Persian Gulf War. Combat forces were reduced from 18 to 13 active duty divisions (self-sustaining Army and Marine military units consisting of 10,000–30,000 combat and support service members) by 1993 (Bruner, 2005; Global Security, 2005).

Today the size of the military is 30% smaller than that in 1990. Although the past few years have shown slight increases for the Active Army and Marine Corps, they remain below their 1990 strength. Since 1990, the Navy has steadily declined in numbers, as has the Air Force until 2009 when it showed an increase, bringing its strength to nearly 7000 members more than that in 1990. All branches of the **Selected Reserve** (reservists in the Army, Navy, Marine Corps, Air Force, and Coast Guard, and members of each state's Air and Army National Guard) had fewer members in 2009 than in 1990 although there were recent slight increases in the number of Army Reserve, Marine Corps Reserve, Air National Guard, and Air Force Reserve members (Office of the Deputy Under Secretary of Defense (Military Community and Family Policy) [DUSD], 2010).

While the size of the U.S. military has decreased, the military **operational tempo or optempo** (i.e., the frequency and intensity of military operations or missions) has greatly increased since September 11, 2001. In addition to combat **deployments** (moving people and material to an area of military operation), thousands of U.S. military personnel continue to be deployed in peacekeeping operations throughout the world, although the number of U.S. military members serving in United Nations peacekeeping missions has decreased dramatically since the mid-1990s (Serafino, 2004). Recent peacekeeping missions have included those in Kuwait, Bosnia, the Balkans, Kosovo, South Korea, the Sinai, Haiti, Georgia, Ethiopia/Eritrea, and Liberia.

The right size and structure for the military depends primarily on the kinds of missions that it will be given. Since the early 1990s, many defense analysts, military leaders, and policymakers have debated the appropriate size and structure of the military and whether the United States should continue to participate in so many peacekeeping missions, especially during periods when it is also heavily involved in armed conflicts (Bruner, 2005). More than two decades after the end of the Cold War, U.S. policymakers are still trying to determine how best to configure the U.S. military force.

Today, active duty and selected reserve total approximately 2.3 million service members compared with 3.2 million in 1990 (DUSD, 2010). Throughout the Cold War, U.S. active duty forces alone were over 2 million personnel, with over 3.5 million serving during the Korean and Vietnam Wars (Bruner, 2005). From 1989 to 2009, the active duty force was reduced from approximately 2.1 million to a current level of 1.4 million and the selected reserve was reduced from approximately 1.2 million to 846,000 (DUSD, 2010).

The term **Armed Forces of the United States** refers to all of the components of the Army, Navy, Air Force, Marine Corps, and Coast Guard, when it augments the Navy. The Coast Guard's main missions are maritime law enforcement and safety, maritime homeland security, and search and rescue (U.S. Coast Guard, 2010). It normally operates under the Department of Homeland Security but can be transferred to the Department of the Navy during time of war or national emergencies to provide naval support. Because its structure, policies, and missions are distinct from those of the other four branches of the Uniformed Services, the Coast Guard will not be a focus of this textbook.

Uniformed Services include the Army, Navy, Air Force, Marine Corps, Coast Guard, Public Health Service Commissioned Corps, and the National Oceanic and Atmospheric Administration Commissioned Officer Corps. The first five are Armed Forces and the last two are Noncombatant Uniformed Services.

Branches of the U.S. Armed Forces

The branches of the Armed Forces depend upon one another, yet their missions and traditions make each unique. The Army, Navy, Marine Corps, and Air Force each has a long military history and distinct customs that differ from its sister services. Each branch of the military has its own language, character, and terminology. For example, the Navy and Air Force call their **military installations** (i.e., facilities owned or leased and operated by the military) "**bases**," the Army refers to them as "**posts**," and the Marine Corps uses the term "**camps**." Even rank structures are not completely consistent from branch to branch. The differences in character, customs, and language are often the basis of much banter and competition between the services. However, what stays constant across the services is a commitment to the country and to the other members of the greater military community, as illustrated by their core values (U.S. Army, n.d.; U.S. Air Force, n.d.; U.S. Navy, n.d.-b; U.S. Marine Corps, n.d.-b).

Army—loyalty, duty, respect, selfless service, honor, integrity, and personal courage
Air Force—integrity first, service before self, excellence in all we do
Navy—honor, courage, and commitment
Marine Corps—honor, courage, and commitment

Collectively the U.S. Armed Forces, under the direction of the Commander-in-Chief, engage in fighting wars, humanitarian efforts, peacekeeping, evacuations, and protecting the security of the United States. Each force has its specific mission. The Army defends the United States, its territories, commonwealths, and possessions. Army units are deployed to combat zones and to locations such as South Korea to help secure borders or to Kosovo to participate in peacekeeping. The Navy provides combat-ready naval forces. Navy carrier groups and vessels are stationed around the world to provide a deterrent and a quick response to crises and humanitarian emergencies. The Marine Corps, under the authority of the Navy, maintains a ready expeditionary force. Along with the Army, the Marine Corps provides ground troops in combat and humanitarian efforts. The Air Force provides air and space defense and is involved in peacekeeping, humanitarian, and aeromedical evacuation missions. It provides air cover for ground troops.

Generally, we think of the services in terms of their missions to defend separate domains: air space by the Air Force, ground by the Army and Marine Corps, and seas by the Navy. Despite the distinct missions of each of the services, however, they may use similar processes or use similar equipment to accomplish their missions. Both the Army and the Marine Corps are equipped with tanks; the Air Force, Navy, Army, and Marine Corps all use aircraft to accomplish their missions; and both the Army and the Marine Corps are trained in close-range and hand-to-hand combat.

The Reserve Component contains three categories: the Standby Reserve, the Retired Reserve, and the Ready Reserve (see Table 1.1). The **Standby Reserve** personnel are temporarily not in the Ready Reserves due to a hardship or disability, or due to being designated as having civilian employment critical to national security. The **Retired Reserve** personnel are those reserve officers and enlisted who receive retired pay or are eligible for retired pay but are not 60 years old or over, not members of the Ready or Standby Reserves, and have not chosen to be discharged. The **Ready Reserve** consists of the selected reserve, the **Individual Ready Reserve** (personnel who have served as active duty or in the selected reserve and still have time remaining on their military service obligation), and the **Inactive National Guard** (required only to muster once a year with their unit) (Office of the Assistant Secretary of Defense for Reserve Affairs, 2005).

TABLE 1.1   Reserve Component Categories

Ready Reserve	Active status	Selected Reserve	Selected reserve units Individual mobilization augmentees Active guard or reserve members of the selected reserve
	May be called to active duty	Individual Ready Reserve	Completing military service obligation Officer training programs/health scholarship programs
		Inactive National Guard	Inactive ready reserve Muster once a year, do not need to train
Standby Reserve	May be mobilized involuntarily	Active status list	Maintain affiliation with military Key employees (e.g., removed from ready reserve because critical to national security in their civilian job) Other active status members place here due to hardship/physical disability
		Inactive status list	Retain reserve affiliation in a nonparticipating status May have skills which may be useful to armed forces
Retired Reserve	May be called to active duty	Reserve officers and enlisted retired and drawing or not drawing pay Reserve officers/enlisted eligible for retired pay but have not reached 60 Reserve physical disability retirees Other reserve retirees	

Source: Information compiled from Office of the Assistant Secretary of Defense for Reserve Affairs (2005). *Reserve component categories of the reserve components of the Armed Forces.* Washington, DC: Author. Retrieved from http:// ra.defense.gov/documents/publications/RC101%20Handbook-updated%2020%20Sep%2005.pdf.

The selected reserve consists primarily of the following: the Army, Navy, Marine Corps, and Air Force Reserves, a federal force that is under the control of the President; and the Army and Air National Guard, which is a state force under the control of a state's Governor unless released by the Governor to the President at the latter's request. The National Guard has limited law enforcement power during crises. Reservists and National Guard members of the selected reserve typically drill one weekend a month and two weeks or more a year.

For decades, individuals in the selected reserve were known as "weekend warriors," typically responding to natural disasters within the United States. Many families needed to know very little about the military culture in order to support their loved one as a member of the National Guard or Reserves. Also, families usually did not worry about their loved ones being activated to full-time service and sent to combat zones. However, with the advent of the Gulf War (1990–1991), reliance on the Reserve Component rose sharply. The total force concept emphasized the increased reliance on reservists for combat and peacekeeping missions (Knox & Price, 1999). As operational tempo has increased, reservists have continued to be vital to U.S. military capabilities. Nearly 30% of deployed forces for OEF and OIF have come from the Reserve Component (Institute of Medicine, 2010), requiring many family members, with little or no prior identity as a military family, to quickly learn a new culture and respond to new stressors.

THE CULTURE OF THE MILITARY

Successfully working and living within the military culture requires fluency in a new language; knowledge of the chain of command; comfort on military installations; respect for those who serve; appreciation of the strengths of and challenges faced by military families; and knowledge of the steps taken by the DoD and each branch of the military to make military life more family-friendly. Each branch has developed its own subculture based on its specializations and missions. The cultural nuances can be as simple as the difference between the Army battle cry "Hooah!" (which has come to stand for "heard, understood and acknowledged" or HUA, but is more often use to show motivation or to motivate other soldiers), the Marine Corps battle cry, "Oorah!" (also used to show spirit or enthusiasm), and the Marine Corps motto, "Semper Fi," which is short for the Latin *Semper Fidelis* or "Always Faithful."

As you learn about the military as a culture, consider the following questions: What are its rituals and what meaning do these rituals hold? What are the rules for social interaction in this culture? What expectations do you have of yourself and others? Anthropologist and scholar Ward Goodenough (1981) defines culture as "a system of standards or rules for perceiving, believing, evaluating, and acting" (p. 110). For many of you, the military is a new culture to get to know. If you are part of the military, this book is an opportunity for you to step back and gain new insights into a familiar culture and perhaps yourself. As you study the military in the weeks to come, here are a few tips to keep in mind:

- Be aware of what you bring to your classroom or workplace. We each have expectations, values, biases, and prejudices that often are based in past experiences. These are part of being human. They may assist or interfere with knowing and understanding others. Being aware of them can help you remain open to learning more about another culture.
- Adopt the stance of being a learner. Listen. Observe. Ask questions of yourself, your classmates and colleagues, and military families.
- Be open. Try to withhold judgment. If something you hear stirs up feelings, ask yourself "why?" Continue to listen, observe, and ask questions.
- Remember, every family, every parent and child, is both unique and part of multiple cultures.

Language

Every occupation has specialized terminology, and the military is no different. Military language is replete with acronyms and abbreviations that can overwhelm civilian workers and family members new to military service. For example, what does an "E-5" refer to? What does an E-5 mean when he tells his family "In today's brief, my CO said even though my MOS is needed downrange, I'll probably be TDY to another post first. Tomorrow I'm going to the PX for an ACU. Remember my Navy buddy who was sent as an IA? Well, he went outside the wire and was injured by an IED but his IBA protected him pretty well. He was MEDEVAC'd to an OCONUS base and is expected to be fine." The translation: "In our meeting today, my boss said that even though people who do my job are needed in the combat zone, I'll probably be temporarily sent to another location first. Tomorrow I'm going to the store for a combat uniform. Remember my friend who is in the Navy who was the only one sent from his ship to the combat zone? Well, he was outside of his work group's camp and was injured by a homemade terrorist bomb, but his body armor protected him pretty well. He was flown to a military base somewhere outside of the United States and is expected to be fine."

Most people pick up military language quickly when they are exposed to it in daily life. It helps to have a patient interpreter or a military-civilian "dictionary." Box 1.2 lists a few common terms and their definitions. The glossary at the end of this book includes military terms used in this textbook. Throughout this book, we will define many terms that you can use to build your military vocabulary.

BOX 1.2   TIPS FROM THE FRONTLINE

A "POCKET" MILITARY-CIVILIAN DICTIONARY

OIF—Operation Iraqi Freedom; the war in Iraq that began with in 2003

OEF—Operation Enduring Freedom; the term used to refer to the conflict that began in Afghanistan in 2001 and includes operations in other countries (e.g., Pakistan, Uzbekistan, Djibouti, Turkey and Tajikistan) (DoD, 2010n)

FOB—Forward Operating Base; a stand-alone military camp in a combat location where service members live and work

IA—Individual Augmentee(s); a service member or small group of service members who are assigned to a unit going to combat during or just prior to the unit's deployment to a combat zone

PX or BX—Post Exchange or Base Exchange; a tax-free department store on a military installation and reserved for use by military beneficiaries

Commissary—a tax-free grocery store located on a military installation and reserved for use by military beneficiaries

CO—Commanding Officer; the officer responsible for the welfare of the service members assigned to his/her unit and for the accomplishment of that unit's missions

MOS—Military Occupational Specialty; a job title and code used by the Army and Marines; similarly the Air Force uses Air Force Specialty Codes (AFSC) and the Navy uses a Navy Enlisted Classification (NEC) system

TDY or TAD—temporary duty; a short-term assignment to another installation or unit

ACU—Army Combat Uniform

IED—improvised explosive device; an unconventional bomb often used in terrorist attacks

Battle Rattle—military slang for protective armor used in combat; also referred to as IBA or Interceptor Body Armor

MEDEVAC or MEDIVAC—Medical evacuation; the quick transfer of wounded service members from the battlefield to the medical facility that can provide the specialized care needed, while providing professional medical care en route

OCONUS—Outside of the continental or contiguous United States (CONUS)

To continue building a military vocabulary, visit the DoD Dictionary of Military Terms (http://www.dtic.mil/doctrine/dod_dictionary).

As in civilian life, a word may have multiple meanings in the military depending upon the context. For example, family members typically use the term **separation** to refer to time apart from their service member (although spouses may also use the word to indicate a break in a romantic relationship). However, **separation from the military** can refer being released from active duty, discharged from military obligations, and transferred to the reserves or retired list (Naval Inspector General, n.d.). The word separation also appears in the term **family separation allowance** that may be paid to service members when required to be away from their permanent duty station for more than 30 continuous days.

Chain of Command

We live within a society that recognizes authority, such as the authority of employers, experts, and the legal system. The military's authority and structure permeates the daily lives of service members and their families. While civilians can quit their jobs, service members cannot. They must serve out their contracts. For active duty service members, contracts include a set number of years of "24-7-365" (24 hours a day, 7 days a week, for 365 days a year) active duty service, and additional years in the individual ready reserve during which time they could be called back to active service. The contracts of members who join the Reserve Component (i.e., the Air or Army National Guard or the Reserves) stipulate they can be called to active service at the direction of the state's Governor (National Guard) or the President (the Reserves and National Guard).

The military chain of command is highly structured and begins with a civilian: the President of the United States who serves as the Commander in Chief of the U.S. Armed Forces. As noted earlier, civilian control of a nation's military is a significant feature of a democracy, and the U.S. Constitution divides responsibility for the military between the President and Congress. The chain of command designates who is in charge of what and whom at each link in the chain and ensures an efficient means of carrying out orders. Service members know who is in their chain of command, up to the President. Each service member must follow the orders given by those of higher rank in their chain of command unless the order is unlawful; military personnel have an obligation to disobey orders that do not comply with the U.S. Constitution or the Uniformed Code of Military Justice, the judicial code that pertains to members of the United States military.

As Figure 1.1 illustrates, the President directs the Secretary of Defense who, under the direction of the President, directs and has authority and control over the JCS; the unified commands; and the departments of the Army, Navy (including the Marine Corps), and Air Force. The President chairs the National Security Council (NSC), which advises and assists the President on national security issues and foreign policy. The core NSC meeting attendees include the Vice President, the Secretary of State, the Secretary of the Treasury, the Secretary of Defense, the Assistant to the President

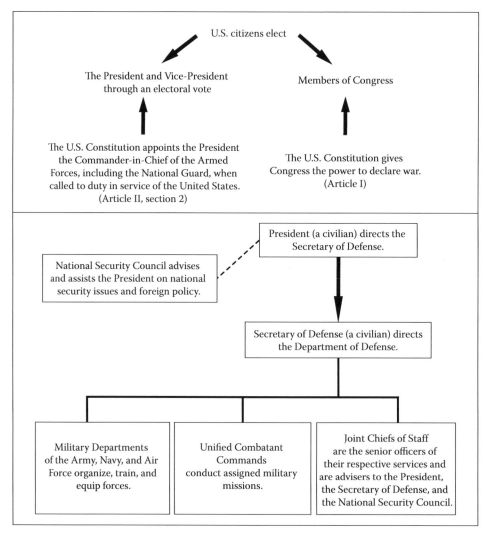

Figure 1.1 The chain of command. (Information compiled from Joint Chiefs of Staff (n.d.). *Joint Chiefs of Staff*. Retrieved November 29, 2011 from http://www.jcs.mil/; National Security Council (n.d.). Retrieved November 29, 2011 from http://www.whitehouse.gov/administration/eop/nsc; Department of Defense. (n.d.). Organizational Chart. Retrieved from http://www.defense.gov/orgchart.)

for National Security Affairs, the Chairman of the JCS, and the Director of National Intelligence (National Security Council, n.d.; Department of Defense Organizational Structure, n.d.).

The JCS are the senior officers of their respective services, who are military advisors to the President, the Secretary of Defense, and the NSC. Through the Chairman of the JCS, they respond to requests for and may voluntarily offer advice or opinions. Members of the JCS are the Chairman of the JCS, the Vice Chairman of the JCS, the Army Chief of Staff, the Marine Corps Commandant, the Chief of Naval Operations, and the Air Force Chief of Staff (Department of Defense Organizational Structure, n.d.; Joint Chiefs of Staff, n.d.).

The JCS transmit orders of the President or Secretary to Commanders (either an Admiral or four-star General) of the Unified Commands. **Unified Commands** are composed of units from two or more military departments working under a single commander to conduct operations in support of a continuing defense or combat mission in a region (e.g., U.S. European Command or USEUCOM) or an ongoing functional mission (e.g., U.S. Special Operations Command or USSOCOM). The Unified Commands are established by the President, with input from the JCS, and report to the Chairman of the JCS.

On April 6, 2011, President Obama signed a new **Unified Command Plan** (an annual review with possible modification of the Unified Commands) designating six unified combatant commands (DoD, 2011a). They are listed here along with their acronyms: U.S. Pacific Command (USPACOM), U.S. European Command (USEUCOM), U.S. Northern Command (USNORTHCOM), U.S. Southern Command (USSOUTHCOM), U.S. Central Command (USCENTCOM), and U.S. Africa Command (USAFRICOM). The USCENTCOM, or CENTCOM as it is usually referred to in the media, oversees many of the OEF, OIF, and OND and related operations. It consists of 20 countries, including Afghanistan and Iraq. The four unified functional commands are U.S. Transportation Command (USTRANSCOM), U.S. Special Operations Command (USSOCOM), U.S. Strategic Command (USSTRATCOM), and the Joint Forces Command (USJFCOM) approved for dissolution (DoD, 2011b).

The Department of the Army, the Department of the Navy (which includes the Marine Corps), and the Department of the Air Force are **military departments**. Each department is responsible for organizing, training, and equipping its personnel.

A service member's **rank** is an achieved status, representing a level of responsibility and attainment of knowledge, expertise, and leadership skills. Rank is displayed on military uniforms through insignias to facilitate identification of rank. Those with higher rank have greater responsibilities and can issue orders to those of lower rank in their chain of command. If you are unfamiliar with how rank is displayed on uniforms, visit one of the numerous websites that show ranks for enlisted personnel and officers by branches of the military.

"E" refers to enlisted service members (i.e., pay grades or ranks E-1 to E-9). They typically join (i.e., enlist) in the military after high school and sign the enlisted document DoD Form 4/1 that states the required number of years in active duty and the required number of years in the Reserve Component. In total, these years equal the Military Service Obligation, typically 8 years for the initial enlistment (e.g., 3 years on active duty and 5 years in the inactive ready reserve). Enlisted service members first go through basic training (Army and Air Force) or boot camp (Navy and Marine Corps) and then to advanced training (called Military Occupational Speciality, or MOS, in the Army and Marine Corps). The service obligation is the length of time that must be served before the service member can voluntarily separate (leave) the military or retire if 20 or more years were served.

"O" refers to officers (i.e., pay grades or ranks O-1 to O-10). They join the military by attending one of the military academies, after college by being accepted into the officer's candidate school, or by participating in the Reserve Officers' Training Corps (ROTC) during college. Upon successful completion of their training, they are issued their commission, that is, their appointment as an officer, in the name of the President of the United States. Commissioned officers must complete 8 years of military service obligation, either in Active or Reserve Components or a combination of both. The length of the active duty service obligation varies by branch and by whether the officer attended ROTC, a military academy, or Officer Candidate School.

"W" refers to **Warrant Officers** (i.e., pay grades W-1 to W-5). They are designated an officer through a warrant (a specific authorization) as opposed to an officer who is designated through a commission. Warrant officers usually are technical experts or specialists with a specific set of skills. The Navy, Marines Corps, and Army have Warrant Officers while the Air Force does not. Active duty service members authorized as a Warrant Officer must complete 6 years of active duty service obligation.

Pay grades are equivalent across the military and are used to determine basic pay and allowances due to a service member. While titles of ranks may differ across branches of the military, pay grades do not and thus offer the way to tell who is the higher-ranking service member. For example, a Private First Class in the Army, a Seaman in the Navy, a Lance Corporal in the Marine Corps, and an Airman First Class in the Air Force are all E-3s, even though they have different titles. Also, while an O-3 in the Army, Marine Corps, and Air Force has the rank of Captain, in the Navy an O-3 is a Lieutenant, and a Navy Captain is an O-6.

The title associated with a rank may differ from branch to branch. Recognizing and addressing service members by the correct rank are important skills for civilians working with the military. The service member's last name is typically found above the right breast pocket of the uniform. It is best to address someone with the rank and last name, such as Private First Class Smith, Master Sergeant Mancuso, or Commander Rodriguez. However, last names are not found on dress uniforms, so it is also polite to refer only to the rank if the person's name is unknown, such as "Hello, Private," "Good evening, Master Sergeant," or "Thank you, Commander." Even though chaplains hold officer rank, it is common to address them as "Chaplain" rather than by their rank.

Rank structure and the use of military rank when addressing service members is very important to most military members, who would rather that you ask them how they should be addressed than to be addressed by a civilian title (e.g., "Mr." or "Ms."). In fact, if you inadvertently address an enlisted service member by an officer's rank or address them as "Sir," or "Ma'am," you may receive a response similar to, "I work for a living!" This quip is a reference to a long-standing military joke that officers do little work and that enlisted service members really run the military. Conversely, since officers of all branches are typically addressed as "Sir" and "Ma'am," using these honorifics is appropriate when speaking to officers.

The average military career lasts less than 10 years; most military service members do not serve the 20 years necessary for retirement. Fewer than a third of separations from the military for whatever reason each year are due to retirements. The "up or out" policy in which service members must earn promotion within a specified time or exit active duty service is designed to maintain a force that is young and avoid too many personnel at higher ranks. For example, most service members in the Marine Corps leave after fulfilling one 4-year enlistment contract. Still, a greater percent of personnel remain in the military until retirement now as part of an all-volunteer force than during the era of conscription (Segal & Segal, 2004).

Military Installations

The DoD operates more than 30 million acres of property in over 5000 locations around the world and operates or controls hundreds of military installations (DoD, 2009). Installations include the National Guard armories found in local communities across the United States and the forts, bases, camps, or other installations in approximately 63 countries. The DoD operates Naval Station Norfolk in Virginia, the world's largest naval base, and the National Training Center in Fort Irwin, California, a world-class training center that specializes in desert combat, counterinsurgency operations, and urban terrain training (DoD, 2009).

American military installations overseas differ significantly from those in the continental United States in several ways that impact the military unit, service members, and their families. Installations located in the United States can include schools, recreational and health-care facilities, and department and grocery stores for use only by military beneficiaries. (A **beneficiary** is someone who is eligible for a military-related benefit, in this case, shopping at the stores on military installations.) Commonly, installations overseas are broken up into smaller areas of land with fewer services and organizations on each installation. Other agencies and services are often located on one installation some distance from the installation on which the service or family member works or lives. This distance can be inconvenient for service and family members who tend to rely on these services and facilities even more overseas than at installations located in the United States. There may be fewer options for some services in the local community requiring the service member or family member to travel to the more distant installation for services. This situation requires coordinating time and travel, both of which may be limited. Cultural differences, language barriers, and unfavorable local currency exchange rates might provide additional obstacles to getting services (Burrell, 2006).

Just as laws, regulations, and customs differ from country to country, they differ from civilian communities to military installations. Working or living on a military installation requires knowing and following regulations about appropriate conduct. Regulations and laws on military installations are strictly enforced and are often more stringent than those in civilian communities. For example, although wearing a helmet while riding bicycles or motorcycles is not required by law in all states, all military installations mandate that helmets be worn. Similarly, not all states require the use of a "hands-free" device while driving and using a mobile phone, but they are required when driving and telephoning on military installations. Traffic regulations and laws, such as speed limits and the use of seat belts, are generally much more strictly enforced. In addition, service members who live on military installations are required to maintain their residences to a certain standard and can lose their "on base" or "on post" housing privileges if they fail to do so or if they or a family member conduct themselves inappropriately. Standards of politeness may also be higher than civilians are accustomed to. Courteous and respectful language (e.g., "please," "thank you," "pardon me," "excuse me," "Ma'am," and "Sir") and polite behavior (e.g., holding a door for someone, placing trash in correct receptacles) are expected.

Respect for Those Who Serve

Respecting those who serve in the military includes acknowledging the ramifications of service and of having an all-volunteer force: some citizens must voluntarily decide to allow their country to determine what job they will do, where they will live, and if they will go into combat. Joining the military also means conducting oneself according to the values noted above. These values require "service before self," that is, a commitment to serve the country even to the point of sacrificing one's own life.

Voices From the Frontline

GOING TO IRAQ

When I put on the uniform, I made the decision I would do whatever my country decided was appropriate for me to do. My last deployment before retiring was to Iraq. How could I not go? It was my turn to hold the baton. To say to those who were there, "Let me take it now. You need a rest." I knew I was putting my life at risk and it was scary. I got my life in order at home—preparing for the worst—and headed off for a year.

It was a horrible year. We were under daily mortar attacks and experienced three very major coordinated attacks by insurgents. Sometimes people are afraid to ask me about my experience, and it's not easy for me to talk about. But I had a job to do, and I did it.

Angela Pereira
Colonel, U.S. Army, Retired

Many **military operational specialties** (MOS; jobs or occupations) place personnel in danger not only during operations but also during training. Military personnel often work with highly specialized equipment that costs millions of dollars and in environments in which a mistake can cost one's own life or the lives of others. Military members often advance more quickly in their military career path than their age counterparts in their civilian career path (Duckworth, 2003). With this acceleration comes responsibility for the well-being of others in the unit and their families that extends well beyond an eight-to-five workday. Active duty means that service members are available 24 hours a day, 7 days a week, for 365 days a year. For example, they can be called into work early or kept late; they can be sent on temporary or extended assignments with only a few hours notice; and even though service members are granted leave (i.e., time off), it can be revoked regardless of the plans made or family members disappointed.

Personal Sacrifice and Discipline

When civilians join the military, they voluntarily give up many privileges, much of their autonomy, and many rights that they had as civilians. As an example, one of the rights that they are relinquishing is their right to privacy. A military supervisor can enter a service member's quarters (residence) at any time to monitor the service member's behavior or inspect his or her living conditions when he or she lives on a military installation (e.g., U.S. Army Garrison Baumholder, 2008). The supervisor can look for contraband items, ensure that the quarters are clean, or check if the service member is conducting himself or herself in a manner that represents the U.S. military positively. As another example, a supervisor can forbid a service member from taking a second job.

Military members also give up some political rights. The political election ballots of military voters are very often not counted because the mail delivery system delivers them to election officials after the deadline required for those ballots to be counted, or they vote absentee in states that routinely do not count absentee ballots unless election results are very close (Roff, 2009). Military members serving overseas are also not able to participate in the voting process for presidential delegates in any state that requires that participants appear in person to have their votes counted.

There are also military regulations that restrict how service members can participate in political activities (Office of the Law Revision Counsel, 2008). Military members are allowed to vote for and support any political party or candidate they choose but cannot do so in uniform. They cannot attend political rallies in uniform either because that might suggest that the military or one of its branches endorses that particular candidate or party. Service members cannot use their workplaces or any other government facility to engage in political activities, such as gathering votes and gaining support for a candidate or political party. Service members are also not permitted to strike for higher wages.

Service members can be required to spend weeks or months of training away from their homes and families to ensure that they can perform their jobs well in spite of intense pressure. Military units often conduct grueling military training in extreme, sometimes very uncomfortable, conditions that approximate war and require that service members perform their jobs flawlessly.

The military services place the accomplishments of their assigned missions before everything else, including individual needs and family concerns. Service members are required to accept and comply with this priority. They know that they can be sent to new locations, either temporarily or permanently, to work or train with no advance notice to them or to their families. The instability they live with can be very disruptive to their or their family members' activities or personal goals. For example, the military services will not ask a service member if there is a reason that he or she cannot be sent to a new unit, such as a daughter's involvement in an upcoming soccer tournament or the service member's own enrollment in a college course.

Accomplishing the tasks and living the lifestyle required of the military demands a focus on the mission and a personal discipline to keep physically, emotionally, and mentally fit. To be certain that service members are physically fit, each service has a periodic physical fitness test that the service member must pass. This physical fitness test usually includes a weigh-in, to ensure that a member's weight falls within what is considered appropriate limits for someone who may have to run, jump, and carry heavy equipment in combat. In addition, the physical fitness test includes a demonstration by each member that he or she is in good physical condition. In the Army, for example, every 6 months a soldier must complete a 2-mile run within a certain time and complete a specified minimum number of push-ups and sit-ups within 2 minutes. Failing to pass the weigh-in or the fitness test results in administrative actions against the service member and can result in disciplinary action or the end of his or her military career. To avoid this, service members are required to participate in unit physical fitness training, often early in the morning while it is still dark and most civilians are still in their beds, or to conduct regular physical training on their own before or after work. Not all persons who seek to enter the military are accepted. In Chapter 2, we will address the entrance standards.

Military Laws and Discipline   Service members are subject to the **Uniform Code of Military Justice** (UCMJ; part of the U.S. Code of law that regulates the conduct of the Uniformed Services) and to the *Manual for Courts-Martial* (MCM), an executive order that contains detailed instructions for implementing military law for the U.S. military. Under the UCMJ (Office of the Law Revision Counsel, 2008), service members can be charged, tried, and convicted of a range of crimes, including assault or robbery and military-specific crimes like desertion. The MCM (Joint Service Committee on Military Justice, 2008) specifies the procedures used in courts-martial. These documents are designed to balance the need for individual rights with the need for a system of justice that accommodates the discipline requirements of the military.

Under the UCMJ, military commanders have the authority to administer disciplinary actions or punishment for minor offenses, which can be addressed through nonjudicial punishment. Examples of these offenses are disobeying an order, showing up late for a formation (i.e., a gathering of military members for an inspection, physical training, or some other purpose), improperly wearing a military uniform, and showing disrespect to a higher-ranking service member. These kinds of offenses do not require a formal hearing with judicial due process protection that a regular civilian court must provide. The kinds of punishments commanders are able to administer are based on the rank of the commander. These usually include restriction, extra duty, and forfeiture of up to half the service member's pay. A court-martial usually takes place when there is a more serious crime that requires that the service member receives **judicial due process**. Judicial due process, or due process of law, is the principle that the government must respect all of the legal rights that are owed to a person, including witnesses, a jury, a pre-trial hearing, formal notification of the charges, free legal representation, and a speedy trial. These processes are necessary in order to protect the service member when the punishment could potentially be severe, such as involuntary separation from the military or imprisonment (Library of Congress, 2009).

APPRECIATION FOR THE STRENGTHS OF AND CHALLENGES FACED BY MILITARY FAMILIES

Most military families adjust well to the challenges that come with military life. They demonstrate numerous strengths while responding to frequent moves, separations from extended family, deployments, and living in other counties (Wiens & Boss, 2006). The resilience of military families is highlighted throughout this book.

Research on military families has moved beyond **deficits models** (i.e., identifying the factors families lack that are associated with unhealthy development) to **strengths-based models** that identify and build on families' existing strengths to encourage healthy development (MacDermid, Samper, Schwarz, Nishida, & Nyaronga, 2008). Military families share with civilian families the **normative stressors** of family life, that is, stressors that occur for most families and at expected times, such as life cycle transitions (e.g., birth of a child, death of an aged grandparent) and developmental changes (e.g., children going to school). However, military families experience additional stressors that are normative for them: lengthy work hours, frequent moves, separations, deployments, **unaccompanied tours** (i.e., assignments to overseas locations where the family is not authorized to travel with and remain with the service member), dangerous work settings, and combat-related activities. Active duty and selected reserve members differ somewhat in the types of stressors they experience.

For example, while active duty members move many times throughout their careers as they are assigned to different military installations, members of the National Guard and Reserves could serve their whole careers at one installation. National Guard and Reserve members work at and advance in their civilian job or career and their military career, while active duty members typically focus on their military career.

Families, military and civilian, also experience **nonnormative stressors**. Nonnormative stressors are ones that do not occur to most families and are unexpected (e.g., a child with a terminal illness). Examples of nonnormative stressors unique to military families would be injury or death of their service member by friendly fire or their service member missing in action. However, worry about service members' safety during deployment would be considered normative (Blaisure & Arnold-Mann, 1992; MacDermid et al., 2008).

Research on military families has identified many strengths associated with positive adjustment to the challenges of military life (e.g., flexibility, strong family relationships, social support) (Wiens & Boss, 2006). This research and lessons learned from those who work with military families will be shared in upcoming chapters.

STEPS TAKEN TO MAKE MILITARY LIFE MORE FAMILY-FRIENDLY

The welfare and success of military families are crucial to the accomplishment of the mission of the DoD. Therefore, the DoD has developed and funded numerous programs and services to help military families adapt to and thrive within the military community and to assist them in dealing with challenges that come with a military life. However, this approach has not always been the case. Until the advent of the all-volunteer force, only the service member himself or herself was of concern to the DoD. Basic needs such as schools, housing, recreation, health care, and shopping facilities have historically been provided for military families, but the specialized programs that have been developed and funded to meet many needs that military families may have were instituted within the past 30 years (MacDermid Wadsworth & Southwell, 2011). In fact, until recently a standing military joke was that, "If the military wanted you to have a spouse, it would have issued one to you!"

In recent decades, the DoD has begun to view spouses and other family members as vital to the success of an all-volunteer force (MacDermid Wadsworth & Southwell, 2011). If family members are well cared for and doing well in the military community, the service member is more likely to consider staying in the military; and civilians who know that spouses and children will be supported are more likely to join the military. The DoD also realizes that service members who know that their families are taken care of will not need to spend as much time and energy worrying about them, especially during times when they cannot physically be with their families, such as during combat deployments.

Most civilians do not know that the DoD manages the largest school and child development center systems in the United States. The Department of Defense Education Activity (DoDEA, 2009) operates 191 schools in 12 foreign countries, seven states, Guam, and Puerto Rico. There are over 8700 DoDEA educators who serve more than 77,000 DoDEA students. The DoD also oversees approximately 800 Child Development Centers located on 300 military installations worldwide and caring for approximately 200,000 military and DoD civilian children each day (Military Community & Family Policy, 2009).

There are numerous other examples of the ways in which the DoD has tried to improve family life for the military. For example, the Departments of the Air Force and Army now have a dual-military program that tries, when possible, to assign service members who are married to service members to the same location so that they can live together (Department of the Army, 2006a, 2009). The Army also has an assignment stabilization program for keeping service members from having to change assignments during the child's senior year in high school because changing high schools, especially during the final year, is a significant stressor for teenage family members. Each branch of the military has extensive family support that sponsors programs affecting almost every aspect of family life. These range from social services programs, such as domestic abuse and violence programs that work to prevent, identify, and treat child and spouse abuse and neglect; to medical programs, such as those identifying family members with special medical and/or educational requirements and then ensuring that those families are assigned to locations where the services they require are available; to programs that encourage mutual support of families, such as family social support and recreation groups that help service members and their families offer each other social and emotional support and exchange information.

While the service branches have different titles for their programs and may manage and deliver the services differently, each places great emphasis on the successful and appropriate delivery of all of its family services and programs. All of the programs for military families are regulated extensively, and they are overseen and enforced by the very top leadership of each of the services. These programs are monitored very closely and constantly evaluated and modified, as part of the DoD's effort to ensure that military families thrive. These programs and services will be introduced and discussed at length in later chapters of this textbook.

APPLYING WHAT YOU LEARN

There are both civilian and military career paths where people can work with members of the military community. In upcoming chapters, you will become familiar with programs and services for military families. In Chapter 13, you will learn where to apply for jobs working in the military community. There is also a possibility that you may choose a career path where interaction with military families is only occasional or unexpected. No matter where your choices may lead you in life, having a better understanding of military families and the contexts that shape their lives, give them strength, and challenge them will help you become a better neighbor, family member, and community member.

SUMMARY

- Service members and their loved ones live in communities throughout the United States.
- Civilian control of the military is a central feature of democracy in the United States.
- The military has a distinctive culture and a history that begins prior to the formation of the country. The military culture is exhibited through language, a chain of command, location (e.g., military installations), respect for service, personal sacrifice and discipline, and military laws.
- The Active and Reserve Components combined total approximately 2.3 million service members, approximately a 30% decline in numbers since the end of the Cold War.
- The branches of the U.S. Armed Forces depend upon one another, yet their missions and traditions make each unique. Under the direction of the Commander in Chief, the Armed Forces engage in fighting wars, humanitarian efforts, peacekeeping, evacuations, and protecting the security of the United States.
- The total force concept emphasizes reliance on the Reserve Component for combat and peacekeeping missions. Families of Reserve Component service members, with little or no prior identification as a military family, suddenly have been required to learn a new culture and respond to new stressors.
- Most military families demonstrate numerous family strengths while responding to frequent moves, separations from extended family, deployments, and living in other counties. The resilience of military families is highlighted throughout this book.
- The DoD has developed and funded programs and services to help military families adapt to and thrive within the military community and to assist them in dealing with challenges that come with a military life.

EXERCISES

To become aware of military links in your own community and your own preconceptions and depth of knowledge, answer the following questions:

1. Go to the Department of Defense website (http://www.defense.gov). Find the links to the military branches and explore their websites to learn more. How do they each contribute to national security and how do they coordinate with one another?
2. Learn about the military links and relationships in your local community:
   a. Campus—is there a military science program (often a Reserve Officer Training Corps or ROTC) at your university or college? If so, what branches are represented and how many students are involved? Who are the instructors for this program? How many students of your university have served in or been wounded or killed in recent conflicts?
   b. Is there a military installation near you? If so, what kind of installation is it? How many service members and civilians are part of the installation?
   c. Is there an Armory in your town or county?
   d. Is there a Veterans Affairs (VA) health-care facility in your community? If so, what services do they provide?
   e. Is there a Veterans of Foreign Wars (VFW) and/or American Legion hall in your community? What purpose do these organizations serve?
3. Consider the history of military service in the United States. From the beginning of the country, arguments have been made that those with more money and more power have been able to sidestep military service, even when there has been conscription. Respond to these questions:
   a. The current law in the United States requires its male citizens and aliens living in the United States to register with the Selective Service. Do you agree with this policy? Should female citizens and aliens living in the United States be required to register?
   b. Should the United States require its citizens, upon reaching the age of 18, to engage in military service? Public service? Would you prefer the United States to require military service of everyone, use a lottery and only draft some persons, or continue with an all-volunteer policy? What are the possible consequences of each option?
   c. Do you prefer that the country continue with the practice of the all-volunteer force even if it means multiple deployments for the same individuals and families?
4. Think about your experience with the military.
   a. Are you part of a military family? Do you know anyone serving in the military? Are you or have you been a member of the military? Have you ever considering joining? Why or why not?
   b. How many service members or military family members do you think you encounter in an average week or average day and where in your school or community, maybe even without being aware they are in the military?
   c. What are your views about war? About the wars in Iraq and Afghanistan?
   d. If you could ask a service member who just returned home from war a question what would it be? How would you feel asking the question? How do you think he or she would feel about your question?
   e. If you could ask a family member a question, what would it be? How do you think you would each feel?
   f. How might your political or religious views influence your thoughts and feelings about the military, service members, or family members you might meet in your work?
   g. Do you know someone who has been injured or killed while serving in the military?
   h. How do you think the military impacts your everyday life?
   i. What else do you want to learn about the military? How will you go about learning it?

An Overview of Military Personnel and Their Families

In Chapter 2, you will

- Meet Lisa Drew and her husband, Captain PC Drew, who discuss the decision to become a military family
- Examine demographic characteristics of recruits and service members and how they compare to civilians
- Understand the variety of family structures found in the military
- Identify limitations in the data about military family demographics
- Gain insights into how military families do—and do not—reflect the larger population
- Consider how this information will be useful to working with military families

Meet

Captain PC Drew, U.S. Marine Corps, and Lisa Drew

Captain Drew begins: *I grew up in a military family but my wife, Lisa, did not. After Lisa and I married, I was working in the financial services industry where people were totally focused on money. Lisa and I wondered if this was the environment we wanted to raise our children in. Then came 9/11. We asked ourselves: What do we need to do for ourselves and our kids? We started talking about joining the military for real.*

Lisa continues: But no way was I going to do the military: too scary, too much worry, too little pay, moving around all the time and the biggest one for me—being by myself if and when he deployed.

We visited PC's sister, Campbell, then in the military too, and her husband, an Air Force Captain at the time. I envied what they had: they were living overseas, Sam had a guaranteed paycheck, a secure job, 30 days vacation, and health insurance. Of course "The Question" loomed in my mind: What if PC gets sent to war and killed? PC's sister helped me get my arms around all the unknowns and worry. They are something every military family experiences.

We did it. We took a big pay cut. PC joined. It was the best decision for our family at the time; we couldn't have been happier. Since then we've lived in Japan for 5 years, spent a lot of time apart while PC was deployed, and now we're back in the States.

Here's what I've learned about the military: I'm lucky to be surrounded by such brave, amazing, selfless people. There is always someone to help if you need it. I think about my friend who took our toddler for the whole day when I caught his stomach bug (while PC was deployed and I was pregnant!). She brought him back at night, bathed, fed, and with his jammies on. We're lucky our kids are growing up surrounded by these people.

Our family is just like any other family. We want the best for our kids. I'm not sure how much they will remember as they grow up, but I hope being surrounded by so many diverse people in the military and our travels around Asia have at least shown them different cultures and different ways of doing things. As for whether or not they choose to join the military, that's up to them, but thankfully it's a long way down the road.

INTRODUCTION

Lisa Drew and her husband Captain PC Drew describe a process shared by many who consider joining the military: the decision is a family one, influenced by experiences and reactions of family and friends (Laurence, 2006). Across the country individuals and couples weigh the benefits of a secure income against raising children with regular separations from a parent; adults who have worked in the civilian sector reassess their career goals; parents and teenagers discuss the pros and cons of enlisting; and older siblings join and introduce brothers and sisters to the possibility of serving. In some families, military service is passed along from one generation to the next; military service is the largest parental occupational pool from which recruits come (Ender, 2006).

This chapter provides a demographic overview of military recruits, military service personnel, and their families. As you read the descriptions of military personnel and their family members, consider how civilian and military families share many characteristics. As Lisa says, her family is like any family. She and PC make decisions about what is a rewarding life, they rely on the support of family members and friends, and they wonder about their children's future.

The DoD gathers data about several characteristics of active duty and reserve component service members to better understand their needs and strengths. Data are also gathered about family members—spouses, children, and other dependents—in order to better understand the needs that stem from having one or more service members within a family system. These data inform the policies and programs that are intended to enhance quality of life for both service members and their families.

Four main sources of publicly available data and reports describe military service members and their families. Each source contributes to our understanding of the larger military family community. At times numbers presented for the same year that come from different sources may vary because of slight differences in definitions used by services. Yet, the overall picture each creates is similar.

The first source of public data comes from the Defense Manpower Data Center (DMDC), which publishes tables monthly and yearly that show the number of active duty personnel by rank and location. Data specifically highlighting female service members are published each September, and data on casualties are updated periodically (web addresses for casualty tables found in the reference list of this book link to the most recent data). These tables can be accessed at http://siadapp.dmdc.osd.mil/personnel/MMIDHOME.HTM. A second source of public data is the annual *Demographics: Profile of the Military Community* (DUSD, 2010). Third, DoD publishes the *Population Representation in the Military Services: Fiscal Year Report* (Office of the Under Secretary of Defense, Personnel and Readiness, n.d.) annually as required by the Senate Committee on Armed Services (Report 93–884, May 1974). Finally, the *Quadrennial Quality of Life Review* (DUSD, 2009b) reports the programming for and identified needs of military families. Some data are reported by fiscal year (FY) rather than by calendar year. The military's FY is the same as the U.S. federal government's: October 1 through September 30. For example, FY 2011 began October 1, 2010, and ended September 30, 2011.

This chapter continues building your foundational knowledge of military families and their service members. It may be tempting to skim through paragraphs with statistics and skip looking at tables and figures. To make it easier to think about the significance of the data, we include comparisons with civilian populations when possible. For example, how many military service personnel are there? Do you think it is the same, less than, or greater than the number of employees of Walmart, the largest retailer and private employer in the U.S.? Moreover, we expect that you are curious about a number of details, such as who joins the military and why, which branch of the service is the largest, what percentage of service members have children, or if more military couples are divorcing. These and other details are highlighted in this chapter. We encourage you to take time to think about the numbers, because they provide a picture of the military community. Knowing more about the larger community will help you better understand military families that you meet.

JOINING, STAYING IN, AND SEPARATING FROM THE MILITARY

While we commonly say that individuals joined the military, actually they must apply and be accepted into one of the branches of service. The DoD uses the terms **applicants** (those who apply to enter the military) and **accessions** (those accepted into the military, also called recruits) to differentiate between these groups. For example, in 2009, of the 374,368 active duty enlisted applicants, only 45% became active duty enlisted accessions. You may also encounter the term **endstrength**, which refers to the total number of military personnel required by the Armed Forces or a branch of the Armed Forces, taking into account recruitment, retention, death, and retirements and other separations (Office of the Under Secretary of Defense, Personnel and Readiness, n.d.).

Of the 340,000 individuals who joined the U.S. military in FY 2009, 55% joined the Active Component, and 45% joined the Reserve Component. Ninety percent became enlisted personnel, 10% were commissioned as officers, and 1% became warrant officers (Office of the Under Secretary of Defense, Personnel and Readiness, n.d.).

Every year some individuals who have left the military decide to rejoin. Veterans with prior service may apply to either the Active or Reserve Component and to another service branch. A majority of accessions are individuals who never were in the military prior to joining, referred to as nonprior service. However, a larger percent of accessions in the Reserve Component are prior service than in the Active Component. In FY 2009, 46% of enlisted reserve accessions were prior service compared with only 5% of active duty enlisted accessions (Office of the Under Secretary of Defense, Personnel and Readiness, n.d.).

Who joins the military and why became very important questions to answer when conscription ended and the all-volunteer force began in the 1970s. Given that the average stay in the military is just under 10 years, the DoD must continually attract and accept into its ranks the best candidates possible. The following sections address the requirements for joining, demographic descriptions of recruits, reasons for joining and remaining in military service, and factors that may lead to ineligibility to serve.

Aptitude and Education Requirements

Critical thinking and analytical abilities are both important characteristics to consider when reviewing qualifications of applicants for a job or a profession. The DoD uses two measures for these characteristics: the Armed Forces Qualifying Test (AFQT), and educational credentials (i.e., high school diploma, adult education, college credit, General Education Certificate). Among recent nonprior service accessions, 72% scored above the 50th percentile on the AFQT and 92% had earned a high school diploma. Accessions in FY 2009 showed significant improvements in overall quality over the four prior FYs, due, in part, to a rise in unemployment (Office of the Under Secretary of Defense, Personnel and Readiness, n.d.).

Race, Ethnicity, Geographic Region, Median Household Income, and Gender

To examine the extent to which racial or ethnic groups are represented in new military recruits, we can compare the number of active duty, nonprior service recruits identifying with a race or an ethnicity with the percent of 18–24-year-old civilians who also identify with the same group. This comparison results in a recruit/civilian comparison ratio. For example, a 1.0 ratio means that the percent is the same in the military and civilian population. A 1.1 ratio means that for every one person in the military there are 1.1 persons in the 18–24-year-old population, or a 10% overrepresentation. A 0.95 ratio means there is a 5% underrepresentation.

TABLE 2.1   Comparison of the Percent and Proportion of Recruits and 18–24 Year-Old Civilians by Race and Ethnicity FY 2009

Racial and Ethnic Groups	Recruit/Civilian Comparison Ratio[a]	Percent of Military Nonprior Service Active Component Enlisted Accessions	Percent of 18–24 Year-Old Civilians
Native Hawaiian or other Pacific Islander	3.45	1.31	0.38
American Indian/Alaska Native	2.19	2.50	1.14
Combination of two or more races	1.87	3.97	2.12
Black or African American	1.05	15.36	14.68
White	0.92	71.44	77.68
Asian	0.67	2.68	4.01
Unknown	NA	2.74	0.00
Hispanic	0.88	15.76	17.89
Non-Hispanic	1.03	84.24	82.11

Source: Data compiled from Office of the Under Secretary of Defense, Personnel and Readiness (n.d.). *Population representation in the military services: Fiscal year 2009 report.* Table B-3. Retrieved from http://prhome.defense.gov/MPP/ACCESSION%20POLICY/poprep.aspx.
[a]   Ratio calculated by authors.

Table 2.1 shows that in FY 2009, four racial groups were overrepresented and two racial groups were underrepresented in recruitment numbers. Regarding ethnicity, Hispanics were underrepresented and non-Hispanics were represented nearly proportionally (Office of the Under Secretary of Defense, Personnel and Readiness, n.d.).

The same recruit/civilian comparison ratio can be used to consider the proportional representation of regions of the county. In FY 2009, the South (1.19) was overrepresented, and the West (0.99) was represented proportionally. The Northeast (0.71) and the North Central regions (0.94) of the United States were underrepresented. The representation reflects those areas of the country seeing the greatest increase in population: the South and the West (Office of the Under Secretary of Defense, Personnel and Readiness, n.d.).

Using data on 2006 and 2007 recruits, Watkins and Sherk (2008) examined the median household income of the census tract in which recruits lived, in order to estimate the economic status of the recruits' parents. Recruits were overrepresented from areas in which the median income was more than $42,000 and underrepresented from lower income areas.

Of the nonprior service accessions in 2009, 16% were women. Although women continue to be underrepresented in the military services, the 2009 accessions increased the overall percent of women in the enlisted force to 14% (Office of the Under Secretary of Defense, Personnel and Readiness, n.d.).

Propensity to Serve and Motivation to Join

Voices From the Frontline

ON JOINING THE MILITARY

I always ask the people under my command: Why did you join the military? Everyone has a crazy and entertaining story, but they all seem to fall into one of the categories below:

- It's a chance to protect and serve my country.
- It's what my family does.

- It's a steady paycheck.
- The educational benefits are amazing.
- I needed to get away from my family, town, or circumstances.
- I wanted to see the world.

Captain PC Drew
U.S. Marine Corps

Throughout the history of the United States, many considered military service to be a duty of citizenship. That perspective changed for many during the Vietnam era when mistakes and misinformation by government and high-ranking military leaders led to a mistrust of the military. More recently, however, the American public has shown an increase in its confidence in the military and in support for those in uniform (Laurence, 2006).

Researchers studying those who join the military typically examine **propensity to serve** (interest or plans to serve) and **motivation to serve** (reasons for serving). These concepts become important for predicting who will join and remain in an all-volunteer military. The propensity to serve increased in the first years of the all-volunteer force but has been declining for 30 years. This decline is assumed to reflect economic conditions, educational opportunities, and combat deployments (Woodruff, Kelty, & Segal, 2006). Regarding motivation for joining, as Captain Drew noted, military service members vary. Woodruff et al. (2006) have categorized these reasons as

- Institutional (i.e., patriotism, desire to serve, adventure/challenge, desire to be a soldier, "After 9/11, I wanted to serve my country.")
- Future-oriented (i.e., desire military career, money for college, "Being in the military gives me something I can be proud of for my whole life.")
- Occupational (i.e., support of one's family, crisis, lack of better options, best available option, "I got laid off from the factory where I was working. Signing up for the military meant I'd have a job and could support my girls.")
- Pecuniary (i.e., financial incentives such as enlistment bonuses, steady income, health care, "The money looked good.")

Voices From the Frontline

WHO IS THE NATIONAL GUARD?

The National Guard is made up of an amazing array of people, each with his or her own reasons for serving. Most of our National Guard are civilian soldiers and airmen who have other jobs. They are teachers, mechanics, ministers, contractors, policemen and women, emergency medical technicians, nurses, physician assistants, artists, and students. They are moms and dads, (sometimes single moms and dads), grandparents, sisters, and brothers. They may leave elderly parents and young children when they deploy. They have chosen to serve because they want to give back to our country; they like the camaraderie of those they train with; and they appreciate the extra job, training, and achievement they can obtain. They are all ages: close to retirement, in the middle of their careers, and young men and women still in college or just out of high school.

Barbara Purinton
Vermont Family Readiness Support Assistant

To examine motivating factors for joining and staying in the Army National Guard, Griffith (2009) examined survey data about recruitment and retention gathered from over 22,000 first-time junior-ranking soldiers (E-1 to E-4) during three time periods occurring between 2002 and 2006. Because units could choose whether to administer the surveys, results cannot be generalized to all Army National Guard service personnel. Educational benefits and service to country were the top two reasons for *joining* the Army National Guard across the three time periods. The top reason for *remaining* in the military across all time periods was education benefits (e.g., tuition assistance while on active duty, GI bills for veterans). While in the first time period, money and a sense of fulfillment were tied for second as reasons for remaining, by the third time period in 2006, money dropped to sixth, replaced by belongingness/camaraderie.

This study also noted that demands of serving during wartime influenced junior enlisted personnel's reported intentions of serving. Those who planned on leaving the Army National Guard after completing their current obligation increased from 40% prior to OIF to 57% in 2006. However, the percentage of respondents indicating they wanted to leave the Army National Guard prior to the end of their current obligation dropped from 8% prior to OIF to 2% in 2006, reflecting higher levels of belongingness, camaraderie, and wanting to serve the country. These results are consistent with another study of E-1 to E-6 Army reservists from a reserve combat division, 23% of whom had deployed in the past year. This study also noted that institutionally oriented soldiers reported stronger intentions to stay in the reserves than occupationally oriented soldiers (Griffith, 2008).

As well as the factors noted above, service members' decisions to remain in the military are influenced by a sense of job satisfaction (Griffith, 2008). Those with greater job satisfaction are more likely to remain or indicate intentions to remain in the military. In a study of nearly 25,000 military members in the 1990s, Reserve Component respondents reported higher levels of military job satisfaction than Active Component respondents, perhaps reflecting differing work experiences (Sanchez, Bray, Vincus, & Bann, 2004). However, both active duty and reserve respondents who indicated higher job pressure and who saw their biggest life problem resulting from job issues rather than nonjob issues such as family or individual stressors reported lower job satisfaction. Greater job satisfaction was reported by older members and by officers. Older members were probably satisfied enough to continue to serve past their initial time period. Higher job satisfaction among officers may be explained by the varying duties, responsibilities, and privileges associated with a higher ranks and pay grade. Married respondents also reported greater job satisfaction than nonmarried. Active duty Black respondents and reserve Black and Hispanic respondents reported lower job satisfaction than White respondents. Finally, a greater number of pleasant life changes (e.g., marriage, birth of a child, promotion) were associated with lower levels of job satisfaction, perhaps reflecting that even positive life changes may add to work-family stress (Sanchez et al., 2004).

Factors That May Lead to Ineligibility

Multiple situations may make a potential recruit ineligible for service: medical or physical conditions (e.g., obesity, asthma); illegal substance use; failure of the AFQT; prior felony or serious misdemeanor convictions; and too many dependents under the age of 18 (Bicksler & Nolan, 2009; Christenson, Taggart, & Messner-Zidell, 2009). Depending upon their needs, the military services may provide waivers for certain conditions or situations. In 2009, however, both active duty and reserve components met or exceeded recruiting goals with respect to numbers and high quality of recruits, an achievement attributed to challenging economic conditions in the country, increasing bonuses for enlistment, spending more on recruiting, and declining violence in Iraq (Bicksler & Nolan, 2009).

DESCRIPTION OF SERVICE PERSONNEL

The United States has 1.4 million active duty and nearly 850,000 selected reserve personnel, totaling more than 2.2 million members (DUSD, 2010). In comparison, Walmart has nearly the same number of employees worldwide: 2.1 million (*Corporate Facts: Walmart by the Numbers*, 2010). In this section, Description of Service Personnel, we will consider the number of service personnel by branch of service, age, education, gender, and ethnicity.

Active Duty and Selected Reserve by Branch of Service

The Army has the largest percentage of active duty members and the Marine Corps has the smallest. Table 2.2 shows the distribution of active duty personnel across branches of the service as of March 31, 2011 (DMDC, 2011a). Of the active duty component, 84% are enlisted members and 16% are officers. For every active duty officer, there are approximately five enlisted service members (DUSD, 2010).

Table 2.3 shows the distribution of selected reserve personnel across branches of the service for FY 2009. Recall that the selected reserve includes both federal reservists and state Army and Air National Guard personnel. The Army has the majority of selected reserve members (66.7%), followed by the Air Force (20.9%). For every selected reserve officer, there are about six enlisted service members (DUSD, 2010).

When compared with the overall civilian population in the United States, service personnel on average are younger. The difference is because the maximum age in the military is much lower than in the civilian work force. Enlisted service members and officers in the selected reserve are on average older than their active duty counterparts. In 2009, the average age of active duty enlisted personnel was 27 and officers was 35; the average age of selected reserve enlisted personnel was 31 and officers was 40 (DUSD, 2010).

TABLE 2.2   Number and Percent of Active Duty Personnel by Branch of Service as of March 2011

Service	Cadets/Midshipmen	Enlisted	Officer[a]	Total	Percent[b]
Army	4,581	470,885	95,253	570,719	39.8
Air Force	4,430	265,507	65,101	335,038	23.3
Navy	4,454	271,492	52,281	328,227	22.9
Marine Corps	NA	179,410	22,056	201,466	14.0
Total	13,465	1,187,294	234,691	1,435,450	100

Source: Data compiled from Defense Manpower Data Center (2011a). *Active duty military strength report for March 31, 2011.* Retrieved from http://siadapp.dmdc.osd.mil/personnel/MILITARY/miltop.htm.
[a] Includes Warrant Officers.
[b] Percent calculated by authors.

TABLE 2.3   Number and Percent of Selected Reserve Personnel by Branch FY 2009

Service	Enlisted	Officer[a]	Total	Percent[b]
Army National Guard	317,725	40,666	358,391	42.4
Army Reserve	169,317	35,980	205,297	24.3
Air National Guard	94,870	14,326	109,196	12.9
Air Force Reserve	53,233	14,753	67,986	8.0
Navy Reserve	51,999	14,509	66,508	7.9
Marine Corps Reserve	34,814	3,696	38,510	4.5
Total Selected Reserve	721,958	123,930	845,888	100

Source: Data compiled from Office of the Deputy Under Secretary of Defense (Military Community and Family Policy) (2010). *2009 demographics: Profile of the military community.* Exhibit 4.02 (p. 69). Washington, DC: Author. Retrieved from http://www.militaryhomefront.dod.mil/portal/page/mhf/MHF/MHF_DETAIL_0?current_id=20.20.60.70.0.0.0.0.0.
[a] Includes Warrant Officers.
[b] Percent calculated by authors.

Education

A COLLEGE STUDENT AND MEMBER OF ROTC

I always wanted to have the military and college life together. ROTC allows me to do both and helps pay for college. When I graduate, I will have my B.S. and be commissioned as a junior officer. Then I'll start specialized training.

I did it a little differently than most. When I got out of high school, I went into the Army Reserves and found that the military is a good fit for me. I contracted with the ROTC for 4 years of active duty or reserves because I enjoyed it.

To be a student and a cadet, I have to be organized. I get up each day at 6:00 AM for PT, then go to classes. Like everyone else, I take courses for my major but I also take an additional two or three ROTC credits. Our classes cover various military topics like running a mission and first aid. In my program, every now and then we have a formal dinner in our dress uniforms. Once a semester we have a two-to-three day field training exercise where we set up a base and learn skills like **land navigation** (using a map and compass to travel from one place to another) and **squad tactics** (strategies used by a small unit of service members to achieve a goal). I will also have a month of training during the summer after my junior year.

Being in the military is like being part of a family. We have about 317 cadets in our battalion. These are the people I mostly hang out with. There are no respect issues with other students when we wear our uniforms to class once a week. I tend to get questions from my professors about the military perspective. Other students seem to pretty much ignore the uniform. I look forward to being a leader and making a difference in the military.

Kendra Beth Klinger
College student and member of ROTC

Compared with the civilian population aged 25 and older, the active duty population (enlisted and officer) has a higher level of formal education. In FY 2009, 87% of the civilian population aged 25 and over had a high school diploma or more education, while 99% of active duty and 96% of selected reserve enlisted did so. In addition, 86% of active duty and selected reserve officers had a bachelor's or an advanced degree compared to 30% of the civilian population aged 25 and over. The Air Force (24%) had the highest percentage of active duty members with a bachelor's or an advanced degree and the Marine Corps (10%) had the lowest (DUSD, 2010).

Gender

While 54% of the U.S. civilian workforce is made up of women aged 16 and over, women make up only one-seventh of the active duty military. In FY 2009, 14% of active duty and 18% of the selected reserve were women. As noted in Table 2.4, a slightly greater percent of active duty officers than active duty enlisted personnel were women, while the percent of selected reserve officers and enlisted personnel who were women was nearly the same. The Navy Reserve showed the greatest percentage difference between active duty and enlisted women (DUSD, 2010).

The Air Force had the greatest *percentage* of women of the active duty branches, and the Army had the largest *number* of women. Likewise, among the branches in the selected reserve, the Air Force Reserve had the greatest *percentage* of women, and the Army National Guard had the largest *number* of women (DUSD, 2010).

Most military occupational specialties are open to women. They serve on combat ships and fly aircraft on combat missions, but ground combat specialties (e.g., armor, infantry, Special Forces) in

TABLE 2.4   Percent of Active Duty and Selected Reserve Who Are Women FY 2009[a]

	Percent of Active Duty				Percent of Selected Reserve		
	Enlisted	**Officer**	**Total**		**Enlisted**	**Officer**	**Total**
Air Force	20	18	20	Air Force Reserve	25	25	25
Navy	16	15	15	Army Reserve	24	24	24
Army	13	16	13	Navy Reserve	21	16	20
Marine Corps	6	6	6	Air National Guard	19	17	18
				Army National Guard	14	12	14
				Marine Corps Reserve	5	7	5
Total	14	16	14		18	18	18

Source: Data compiled from Office of the Deputy Under Secretary of Defense (Military Community and Family Policy) (2010). *2009 demographics: Profile of the military community*. Exhibits 2.11 (p. 17) and 4.14 (p. 77). Washington, DC: Author. Retrieved from http://www.militaryhomefront.dod.mil/portal/page/mhf/MHF/MHF_DETAIL_0?current_id=20.20.60.70.0.0.0.0.0.

[a] Percents are rounded.

the Army and Marine Corps are still closed to women. Although they may not serve in combat specialties, it does not mean they do not face combat situations, as experiences in OEF and OIF have shown. A greater percent of female than male officers and enlisted personnel are found in health care and administration specialties. About the same percentage of female as male officers serve in engineering and maintenance, and enlisted women are as likely as men to serve in communications, intelligence, and service and supply specialties (Segal & Segal, 2004).

Ethnicity and Race

In 1948, President Harry S. Truman signed Executive Order 998 requiring racial equality among service members. Today, the DoD understands that ethnic and racial diversity of the services creates a force with broader skills and experiences and a stronger force.

Beginning in 2009 and per directives from the Office of Management and Budget, "Hispanic" was no longer considered a minority race designation, and so the number and percent of service personnel counted as racial minorities showed a decrease from 2008 (36% active duty; 30% selected reserve) to 2009 (30% active duty; 24% selected reserve) as a result. Even with this change, the military shows a trend of increasing racial diversity over the past 20 years. From 1990 to 2009, the racial diversity of active duty enlisted personnel increased from 28% to 31%, active duty officers increased from 9% to 22%, selected reserve enlisted personnel increased from 24% to 25%, and selected reserve officers increased from 12% to 18% (DUSD, 2010).

In general, enlisted personnel are more racially diverse than officers, and active duty personnel are more diverse than selected reserve personnel as shown in Table 2.5. It also shows the extent of diversity by branch of service (DUSD, 2010).

Table 2.6 shows the percentage of service members on active duty and in the selected reserve by race in FY 2009. Eleven percent of active duty and 9% of selected reserve members reported Hispanic ethnicity in FY 2009 (DUSD, 2010).

As Dr. Jennifer Lundquist explains in Voices From the Frontline, the military provides a location to study the impact of policies and practices that integrate work and housing, enforce equal employment opportunities, and reflect a social hierarchy built on rank and not class or race. As a result, service personnel report much better race relations in the military than in the civilian world, and Black and Latino service personnel report high satisfaction with the quality of life and employment opportunities afforded by the military (Lundquist, 2008).

TABLE 2.5   Percent of Military Members Who Identify as a Racial Minority by Branch FY 2009

Percent of Active Duty Who Identify as a Racial Minority				Percent of Selected Reserve Who Identify as a Racial Minority			
	Enlisted	Officer	Total[a]		Enlisted	Officer	Total[a]
Navy	40	19	37	Navy Reserve	36	20	33
Army	31	27	30	Army Reserve	33	27	32
Air Force	28	19	27	Air Force Reserve	30	15	27
Marine Corps	22	18	22	Marine Corps Reserve	22	18	22
				Army National Guard	20	14	20
				Air National Guard	18	12	18
Total DoD	31	22	30		25	18	24

Source: Data compiled from Office of the Deputy Under Secretary of Defense (Military Community and Family Policy) (2010). *2009 demographics: Profile of the military community*. Exhibits 2.02, 2.18, 2.21, 2.22, and 2.24 (pp. 11, 21–24), and 4.04, 4.23, 4.24, 4.25 (p. 70, 83–85). Washington, DC: Author. Retrieved from http://www.militaryhomefront.dod.mil/portal/page/mhf/MHF/MHF_DETAIL_0?current_id=20.20.60.70.0.0.0.0.0.
[a] Percents calculated by authors.

TABLE 2.6   Percent of Active Duty and Selected Reserve Personnel by Race FY 2009

	Active Duty (%)	Selected Reserve (%)
White	70.3	76.0
Black or African American	17.0	14.9
Asian	3.6	2.7
American Indian or Alaska Native	1.7	0.9
Multiracial	1.6	0.6
Native Hawaiian or other Pacific Islander	0.6	0.5
Other or unknown	5.2	4.4

Source: Data compiled from Office of the Deputy Under Secretary of Defense (Military Community and Family Policy) (2010). *2009 demographics: Profile of the military community*. Exhibits 2.16 (p. 20) and 4.19 (p. 81). Washington, DC: Author. Retrieved from http://www.militaryhomefront.dod.mil/portal/page/mhf/MHF/MHF_DETAIL_0?current_id=20.20.60.70.0.0.0.0.0.

Voices From the Frontline

RACE AND THE MILITARY

I grew up in Annapolis, Maryland, home to the U.S. Naval Academy, curious about what happened behind the Academy gates. When working on my Ph.D. in Sociology and Demography, I became interested in understanding how the economic, social, and cultural conditions experienced by military families differ from those faced by civilian families and have pursued this line of research. In doing so, I discovered that racial differences found in U.S. society are not evident in the military. Why? The military is one of the few places in U.S. society where interracial contact is high and where full racial equality comes closest to realization. It was among the first U.S. institutions to become racially integrated. There is a notably greater degree of African American job mobility and superior opportunities for advancement in the military relative to the civilian labor force. On-base housing is explicitly racially integrated, and there is evidence that off-base housing is also highly racially integrated. The high prevalence of interracial marriage in the military (at more than twice that of civilian rates) could be interpreted as an indicator of the quality of Black–White relations. Moreover, African American soldiers and their spouses report overall higher quality of life than any other group in the service, civilian race differences in divorce and marriage rates (e.g., lower rate of marriage and higher rate of divorce in the African American community) do not apply to those in the military service, and the racial gap in preterm birth is substantially reduced in the military setting.

Jennifer Lundquist, Ph.D.
Associate Professor, University of Massachusetts, Department of Sociology
Associate Director, Social and Demographic Research Institute, University of Massachusetts

DESCRIPTION OF MILITARY FAMILIES

This section summarizes demographic data about those whom the DoD has traditionally recognized as family members and dependents of service members. Knowing the target population is necessary for creating or updating programs designed to build strengths, meet particular needs, and improve overall quality of life. For example, what decisions would you make about designing or funding parenting programs if you know that children under the age of five represent a large proportion of active duty military children? While reading this section, consider the gaps in our knowledge of characteristics and categories of family members and how these gaps might affect our understanding of the familial support systems and their connections to programming available for these service members.

DoD-Recognized Family Members

In FY 2009, there were 2.2 million military service personnel with over 3 million associated family members. The DoD defines a family member as a spouse, child, or another person who meets certain legal definitions (e.g., guardianship of sibling). Given the definition, 58% of active duty personnel and 56% of selected reserve personnel had family responsibilities. Approximately 63% of family members were children, 37% were spouses, and less than 1% were other dependents (DUSD, 2010).

The DoD keeps a record of all dependents of a service member through the **Defense Enrollment and Eligibility Reporting System** (DEERS; a system that verifies those who are eligible for military-based services and benefits). Each eligible person is enrolled into this system so that he/she can be identified as a family member or legal dependent when interacting with the military community. In addition to spouses and children, service members may be the primary or legal caregiver for children who are not their own and who are under the age of 22. To qualify as an eligible family member, children who are 21 or 22 must be full-time students. Additionally, service members may care for one or more adult dependents, including disabled older children, siblings, former spouses, parents, or grandparents. Each of these persons, if claimed as a family member by the service member, will be enrolled in and acknowledged through DEERS (DUSD, 2010).

It is important to recognize that service members may likely feel emotionally or financially responsible for unmarried partners, parents, siblings, grandparents, aunts, uncles, cousins, and others who do not meet the DoD's definition of family member. As a human service professional, it is important to acknowledge all who play important roles in the lives of service members.

Number of Family Members

As noted in Chapter 1, the number of military members decreased once the Cold War ended. Most of the decrease in both the active duty and the selected reserve occurred between 1990 and 2000. In just the past two decades, the number of active duty members decreased by approximately 31%, from 2 million in 1990 to 1.4 million in 2009. However, even though the number of family members decreased approximately 28% from 2.6 million in 1990 to 1.9 million in 2009, they still outnumber active duty personnel; for every 1 active duty member, there are 1.4 family members. The same trend is seen in the selected reserve, which decreased approximately 27% during the same time period, from 1.2 million in 1990 to 853,581 in 2009. Selected reserve families decreased approximately 28%, from 1.5 million in 1990 to 1.1 million in 2009 (DUSD, 2010).

The active duty Army is the largest branch of the armed services, both in number of service personnel and in number of family members. In FY 2009, the Navy had slightly more active duty members than the Air Force, but the Air Force had more family members than the Navy. The Marine Corps had the fewest service personnel and family members. Across the branches in the selected reserves in FY 2009, the Army National Guard and Army Reserve had the greatest number of personnel and family members. The Air National Guard and Air Force Reserve were next in size, followed by the Navy and the Marine Corps (DUSD, 2010).

A Snapshot of Family Composition

This section provides a snapshot of the types of military families. Details about parenthood, marriage, divorce, children, ethnicity, race, and geographic location follow.

Across both Active and Reserve Components, junior enlisted members (E-1 to E-4) and junior officers (O-1 to O-3) are most likely to be single with no children; senior enlisted members, senior officers, and senior warrant officers are most likely to be married with children. This difference in family status is largely due to age differences as junior military personnel are younger on average than senior personnel. The military includes in the "single/never-married" category military personnel who have never married, who are divorced or widowed, or whose marriage was annulled (DUSD, 2010).

Figure 2.1 shows that in 2009 approximately 39% of active duty members and nearly 43% of selected reserve members were single with no children. The remaining members were married or had children or both. Among active duty personnel, nearly 56% were married (with or without children) compared with 48% of selected reserve personnel. Slightly more married and single active duty personnel, 44%, had children than their counterparts in the selected reserve, 43% of who had children.

Mid-level enlisted (E-5 to E-6) active duty and selected reserve personnel comprise the largest segment of the "single with children" category, followed closely by their entry-level (E-1 to E-4)

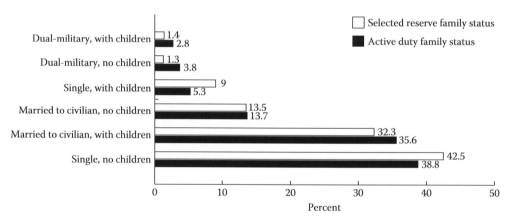

Figure 2.1 Active duty and selected reserve military family status FY 2009. (Data compiled from Office of the Deputy Under Secretary of Defense (Military Community and Family Policy) (2010). *2009 demographics: Profile of the military community.* Exhibits 3.09 (p. 53) and 5.09 (p. 117). Washington, DC: Author. Retrieved from http://www.militaryhomefront.dod.mil/portal/page/mhf/MHF/MHF_DETAIL_0?current_id=20.20.60.70.0.0.0.0.0.)

colleagues. For those who have achieved officer ranks, the entry (O-1 to O-3) and mid-level (O-4 to O-6) ranks represent the largest group of single members, in both the active duty and selected reserves (DUSD, 2010).

Marital Status

Fifty-six percent of active duty members and 48% of selected reserve members were married in FY 2009. In general, older and higher-ranking enlisted members and officers are more likely to be married than younger and entry-level personnel. This trend holds true across all branches for both active duty and selected reserve members (DUSD, 2010). It is not known what percent of married personnel are in remarriages; however, in 2008, 16% of military spouses reported that they were currently in a stepfamily (DMDC, 2009).

Table 2.7 shows the percent of women and men in the active duty and selected reserve components who were married in 2009; the Air Force had the highest percentage of married service personnel. Across all branches, men on active duty were more likely than women to be married. Likewise in the selected reserve, male service personnel were more likely than women to be married, across all branches except for the Marine Corps Reserve (DUSD, 2010).

Dual-military marriages are those in which a military member in one branch of service is married to a military member in the same or different branch of service. For example, active duty male and female Army sergeants could be married to one another, or an Air Force active duty officer could be married to a Marine Corps Reserve officer (DUSD, 2010).

Of all active duty members in FY 2009, 7% were in dual-military marriages, as were 3% of all selected reserve members. Of married members in 2009, 12% of married active duty and 5% of married selected reserve personnel were in dual-military marriages, while 88% and 95%, respectively, were in military–civilian marriages (DUSD, 2010).

Active duty and selected reserve female service members are more likely to be in dual-military marriages than their male counterparts. In 2009, 48% of married active duty females were in dual-military marriages: 66% of married active duty Marine Corps women, 57% of married Air Force women, 44% of married Navy women, and 39% of married Army women. The percentage of their married male counterparts who were in dual-military marriages ranged from 13% of married Air Force men to 5% of married Army and Marine Corps men (DUSD, 2010).

In FY 2009, 23% of married selected reserve women compared with 3% of married selected reserve men were in dual-military marriages. Specifically, 56% of married Marine Corps Reserve women, 39% of married Air Force women, 38% of Air National Guard women, 28% of married Army Reserve women, and 19% of married Navy Reserve women were in dual-military marriages

TABLE 2.7   Percent of Married Active Duty and Selected Reserve by Sex

Percent of Active Duty Married				Percent of Selected Reserve Married			
	Men	Women	Total		Men	Women	Total
Air Force	61	51	59	Air Force Reserve	63	48	60
Army	60	48	58	Navy Reserve	62	45	58
Navy	60	40	54	Air National Guard	60	46	57
Marine Corps	47	41	47	Army Reserve	48	36	45
				Army National Guard	48	30	45
				Marine Corps Reserve	33	38	33
Total DoD	57	46	56		51	38	48

Source: Data compiled from Office of the Deputy Under Secretary of Defense (Military Community and Family Policy) (2010). *2009 demographics: Profile of the military community.* Exhibits 2.53 (p. 38) and 4.55 (p. 102). Washington, DC: Author. Retrieved from http://www.militaryhomefront.dod.mil/portal/page/mhf/MHF/MHF_DETAIL_0?current_id=20.20.60.70.0.0.0.0.0.

(data on dual-military marriages in the Army National Guard were not available). The percent of their married male counterparts who were in dual-military marriages ranged from about 6% of married Air Force Reserve men to 2% of married Navy Reserve men (DUSD, 2010).

Divorce

Comparing divorce rates for those in the military to overall divorce rates in the United States is difficult as calculations are done differently and in both cases are done imperfectly. The U.S. divorce rate does not include data from six states (i.e., California, Georgia, Hawaii, Indiana, Louisiana, and Minnesota). Additionally, the U.S. divorce rate is reported as the number of divorces per 1000 total population, which is misleading because it includes children who cannot marry and, thus, cannot divorce. The 2009 U.S. divorce rate was 3.4 divorces per 1000 people, a decline from 3.5 in 2008 and 3.6 in 2007 (Tejada-Vera & Sutton, 2010).

Meanwhile, the DoD estimates the percentage of divorces each year by counting the number of service personnel who indicated that they were married 1 year but did not indicate that they were married a year later. This method can overlook those who divorce and remarry within the year because they would be listed as married at both data collection points. Also, the divorce figures include cases of those who were widowed although the DoD states the number of widowed cases is small and unlikely to affect the percent reported. Finally, the numbers and percents presented here indicate only those who divorced in 2009, not those who divorced in the years prior to 2009. According to this method, 3.6% of active duty personnel and 2.8% of reserve component personnel divorced in 2009 (DUSD, 2010).

Figures 2.2 and 2.3 show the percent of active duty and reserve component enlisted members and officers who divorced in FY 2000 and the percent who divorced in FY 2009. Across each branch of the service and in both years, the percent of enlisted members who divorced was higher than the percent of officers who divorced, except in the Navy Reserve. Overall, increases occurred for both enlisted and officer service members in the Active and Reserve Components. The greatest percent increase, from 1.3% to 6.5%, was seen among Navy Reserve officers between 2000 and 2009 (DUSD, 2010).

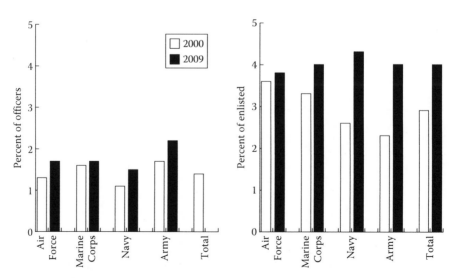

Figure 2.2   Estimated percent of active duty who divorced in 2000 and 2009. (Data compiled from Office of the Deputy Under Secretary of Defense (Military Community and Family Policy) (2010). *2009 demographics: Profile of the military community.* Exhibit 2.62 (p. 42). Washington, DC: Author. Retrieved from http://www.militaryhomefront.dod.mil/portal/page/mhf/MHF/MHF_DETAIL_0?current_id=20.20.60.70.0.0.0.0.0.)

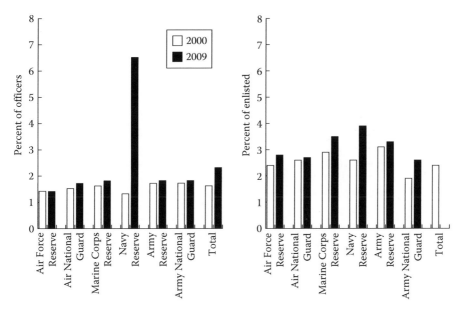

Figure 2.3   Estimated percent of selected reserve who divorced in 2000 and 2009. (Data compiled from Office of the Deputy Under Secretary of Defense (Military Community and Family Policy) (2010). *2009 demographics: Profile of the military community.* Exhibit 4.64 (p. 106). Washington, DC: Author. Retrieved from http://www.militaryhomefront.dod.mil/portal/page/mhf/MHF/MHF_DETAIL_0?current_id=20.20.60.70.0.0.0.0.0.)

Parenthood

In FY 2009, 44% of active duty and 43% of selected reserve service members had children, an average of two children per member. There are differences between the branches and between active duty and selected reserve in the average age of the service member at the time of their first child's birth. In general, active duty members in each branch become parents earlier than their corresponding selected reserve colleagues (DUSD, 2010).

Compared to civilians, military members are more likely to have their first child during their 20s and less likely to have them in their teens or 30s (MacDermid Wadsworth, 2010). In FY 2009, 57% of active duty members and 45% of selected reserve members were between the ages of 20 and 25 when their first child was born, and their average age was 24.8 and 26.4, respectively (DUSD, 2010).

Children

As a group, children of active duty members are younger than children of reserve component members. As Figure 2.4 illustrates, 42% of active duty component children in 2009 were age birth to 5 years, while only 27% of selected reserve component children were in this category (DUSD, 2010).

Spouses

Spouses of active duty members are younger on average than spouses of selected reserve members, reflecting the older average age of those in the reserves. Likewise, spouses married to enlisted personnel are younger than spouses of officers in both active duty and selected reserve (DUSD, 2010).

Information about race and ethnicity of dependents appears limited to survey information collected from active duty spouses. The following information on race and ethnicity of active spouses comes from the *2008 Survey of Active Duty Spouses* (DMDC, 2009) that used random sampling procedures. Service member pay grades represented in this study range from E-1 to E-9 and O-1 to O-6. Pay grades of the most senior officers (O-7 to O-9) were not included. The average age of

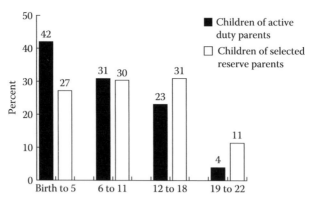

Figure 2.4   Percent of children by age groups FY 2009. (Data compiled from Office of the Deputy Under Secretary of Defense (Military Community and Family Policy) (2010). *2009 demographics: Profile of the military community.* Exhibits 3.23 (p. 61) and 5.21 (p. 125). Washington, DC: Author. Retrieved from http://www.militaryhomefront.dod.mil/portal/page/mhf/MHF/MHF_DETAIL_0?current_id=20.20.60.70.0.0.0.0.0.)

the respondents was 32, with those married to enlisted younger on average (31 years old) than those married to officers (36 years old). Forty-seven percent of the sample was 30 years old or younger.

In this survey, 12% of the spouses indicated they were Hispanic, and nearly one-third were 25 years old or younger. A greater percentage of spouses married to enlisted personnel (13%) than to officers (7%) were Hispanic (DMDC, 2009). Overall, 78% of this sample indicated they were White, with a greater percentage of diversity found in Navy (26%) and Army (25%) spouses than in the Marine Corps (16%) and Air Force (16%). A greater percentage of spouses of enlisted personnel (24%) than of officers (14%) indicated they were a race other than White. The percentage of spouses reporting they were Black or African American ranged from 9% of Marine Corps spouses to 17% of Army spouses. The second more commonly reported race was Asian, ranging from 6% of Army and Marine Corps spouses to 14% of Navy spouses. The racial diversity of spouses increased by age category. Whereas only 9% of spouses who were 21 years old or younger reported a race other than White, over a quarter of responding spouses 31 years old and older did so (DMDC, 2009).

Location of Military Families

Although military personnel are deployed to countries throughout the world, most active duty and selected reserve personnel and their families live within the United States. Spouses and children tend to live where their service member is stationed although there are exceptions (e.g., unaccompanied tours, choose to live apart to pursue a career or education).

In 2009, 86% of active duty personnel were assigned within the United States and its territories, and approximately 6% were assigned within Europe and in East Asia. Fifty percent of the active duty component were stationed in five U.S. states: California, Texas, Virginia, North Carolina, and Georgia. Twenty-nine states had less than 1% of the active duty component (DUSD, 2010).

As with the active duty component, the majority of the selected reserve was located in the U.S. or its territories in FY 2009. Only about 1% of the selected reserve were located at permanent duty stations outside of the United States, including North Africa, Europe, and East Asia. The Navy Reserve had the largest contingent of internationally located personnel (DUSD, 2010).

In 2009, 50% of the selected reserve lived in 13 states: California, Texas, Florida, Pennsylvania, New York, Georgia, Ohio, Virginia, Illinois, Missouri, North Carolina, Alabama, and Indiana (DUSD, 2010).

In approximately 30 local labor markets, the military plays a significant role in the regional economy. For example, in Virginia Beach, Virginia, Jacksonville, North Carolina, and Killeen, Texas, more than 15% of employed people are active duty service personnel. Moreover, communities with significant military presence are among the least residentially and racially segregated in the United States (Segal & Segal, 2004).

Both active duty and reserve service members may be stationed outside the United States and its territories. Whether the DoD infrastructure at the military facility is sufficient to support families usually determines whether a tour is accompanied or unaccompanied.

An **accompanied tour** is an assignment to an overseas location that includes the service member's family. This type of tour is "command sponsored," meaning that the service member's new command is responsible for the support and welfare of the service member's family. Transportation of family members and household goods, housing, commissary and exchange privileges, medical care, child care, and schools are some of the services provided to command-sponsored families.

For families with Army or Air Force active duty members, the most common stations outside the United States currently are in Europe, with the most populous installations in Germany, Italy, the United Kingdom, Turkey, Spain, and Belgium. For Navy families, the most common stations outside the United States are in Italy, Greece, and Japan. The Marine Corps has a large, accompanied installation in Japan. Germany is usually an accompanied tour of 3 years but Army personnel can choose to go unaccompanied for 2 years.

Unaccompanied tours overseas occur when areas are deemed to be politically unstable, dangerous, or lacking in support services for families. No services are provided to families through the DoD in these locations; however, service members might elect to bring their families at their own expense and request support services.

South Korea may be accompanied or unaccompanied. For single service members, the length of military assignments to South Korea is generally 12 months although service members can request an extension of their overseas assignments. Married service members have the option of accepting a 1-year unaccompanied assignment or bringing their family members for a 2- or 3-year tour. Married military members assigned to installations in the northern part of South Korea, near the **Demilitarized Zone** (a buffer zone between North Korea and South Korea), can opt to accept a 2-year accompanied tour or a 1-year unaccompanied tour (McMichael, 2008).

Limitations in Our Knowledge about Family Structures

Voices From the Frontline

BEING A FORMER SPOUSE OF A SERVICE MEMBER

I think it is so great that service members and their families are being supported. But when you are no longer an "official family member," you are out there floating around. As a former spouse, I have this different perspective on life, and it's hard to find a place to fit in.

I'm 23 but I am so different than other 23 year olds. I know the value of money and hard work. My former husband was in the infantry. I was preparing for his possible death since I was 17. Most people my age never think about such a thing, but you can't help whom you fall in love with.

In some ways, being a military family member is like being a service member, even if you never saw combat. You come home and your family expects you to be the same but you are changed. Marines give 110%. The mission always has to be completed. And now here I am in college where people slack off and I ask myself, "Is it worth it?" But I'm going to stick with it, work hard and do it for me. The military is still part of who I am.

Sonia Santamaria
College student, former spouse of a Marine

Data about families are not gathered the same way across the service branches even though the DoD works to learn more about the total force under its command. In terms of data about families, several limitations impact the state of our knowledge about family diversity, support systems, needs, and strengths.

As an organization, the military focuses on the **family of creation** (the family system created through partnering and/or parenting). These are the relationships that have implications for legal responsibilities of service members and are most commonly reported in DoD publications. However, these reports do not include data on adopted children. Likewise, most reports do not address service members' **family-of-origin relationships** (e.g., relationships with parents or siblings or others one grew up with) unless they are identified as an adult dependent of a service member. As a result, little is known about the extended families of service members, including cohabiting relationships.

The different branches offer slightly different responses in reporting marital status, in that the Navy only offers "Married" or "Never Married" as choices while other branches include "Divorced" and "Other" as choices (DUSD, 2010). The married category includes first-time marriages as well as remarriages. These data allow for a very broad categorization of marital status but may frustrate both research and policy/program professionals who would like to better understand marital relationship development, strengths and challenges, as well as marital programming within the larger military community.

In addition to the challenges of accessing more detailed data about divorces and remarriages and extended families, knowledge is lacking about families of lesbian, gay, and bisexual (LGB) military service members. The DoD Directive 1304.26, commonly referred to as **Don't Ask, Don't Tell** (DADT), was issued by President Clinton in 1993 in response to the passage of a federal law prohibiting gay and lesbians from serving in the U.S. Armed Forces. Under this directive, the military could not ask recruits about their sexual orientation, and military members were not to disclose if they were gay or lesbian because they would be discharged from the military. As a result, survey data about family structures with same-sex partners, with or without children, are lacking.

One recent study has estimated the percentage of service members who identify as lesbian, gay, or bisexual by using data from the American Community Survey and the General Social Survey (Gates, 2010). Gates estimated that LGB people constituted 0.9% of the active duty force and 3.4% of the National Guard and Reserve, including the ready reserve, the standby reserve, and the retired reserve.

On December 22, 2010, President Barack Obama signed legislation to repeal "DADT" (Parrish, 2010), and the DoD began a certification process that included reviewing regulations, policies, and eligibility for benefits (e.g., designated beneficiary for benefits); preparing training materials for use by family support staff, military chaplains, personnel specialists, commands, and others; and carrying out training (Pellerin, 2011). On July 22, 2011, President Obama announced that the required certification process was completed. Repeal of DADT went into effect September 20, 2011, after a 60-day waiting period (Marshall, 2011).

As part of the required certification process leading up to the repeal, the DoD, through an independent research agency, Westat, issued a survey to a random selection of 200,000 military members in July 2010 and a similar survey to 150,000 randomly selected spouses of military members in August 2010. The purpose of the surveys was to obtain opinions from service members and family members about the impact on unit cohesion, retention, privacy, and family life of repealing the law restricting lesbians, gay men, and bisexuals from serving openly.

The results of both surveys indicated that the majority of military personnel and spouses believe repeal of DADT will have a neutral effect. Military personnel indicated an overall neutral effect on unit cohesion, readiness, effectiveness, and morale. Two-thirds to three-quarters of spouses indicated repeal would have a neutral effect on family readiness, retention, referral, and attendance at social events and family and deployment support programs (Westat, 2010).

SUMMARY

- This chapter provided a demographic picture of military recruits, military service personnel, and their families.
- Four main sources of publicly available data and reports describe military service members and their families: DMDC's monthly and yearly reports on the number of active duty personnel; the annual publication, *Demographics: Profile of the Military Community*; the annual *Population Representation in the Military Services* report; and the *Quadrennial Quality of Life Review*.
- As a group, Active and Reserve Component recruits typically exceed the performance of their civilian counterparts on measures of aptitude in math and reading, educational attainment, and health.
- Those who join the military report various reasons for joining: institutional, occupational, future-oriented, and financial.
- Military personnel as a group are younger than the civilian population. They reflect ethnic and racial diversity found in the United States. However, the military is largely male and does not reflect the U.S. workforce that is just over half female.
- Compared with the civilian population aged 25 and older, the active duty population, enlisted and officer, has a higher level of formal education.
- In FY 2009, there were over 2.2 million military members who had over 3 million family members.
- The Army has the largest percentage of active duty members, and the Marine Corps has the smallest. For every active duty officer, there are approximately five enlisted service members.
- The Army has the majority of selected reserve members, followed by the Air Force. For every selected reserve officer, there are about six enlisted service members.
- In FY 2009, 14% of active duty and 18% of selected reserve personnel were women. The Air Force had the greatest percentage of women of the active duty branches, and the Army had the largest number of women. Likewise, among the branches in the selected reserve component, the Air Force Reserves had the greatest percent of women, and the Army National Guard had the largest number of women.
- In FY 2009, 30% of active duty members and 24% of selected reserve members reported their race as something other than White; and 11% of active duty and 9% of selected reserve reported Hispanic ethnicity.
- In 2009, there were 3 million family members of service personnel, and a majority of these family members were children. The largest group of reserve component children was 12–18 years old, whereas for active duty the largest group was birth to 5 years old. Approximately 39% of active duty members and nearly 43% of selected reserve members were single with no children.
- Fifty-six percent of active duty personnel and 48% of selected reserve personnel were married in FY 2009. Of active duty members, 4% were in dual-military marriages, as were 3% of selected reserve members.
- In FY 2009, 44% of active duty and 43% of selected reserve service members had children, and they had an average of two children.
- Military spouses and children are likely to live with the service member, and most are located within the United States.
- More research on military families is needed, particularly in the areas of divorce, remarriage, stepfamilies, families of LGB service members, and extended families of service personnel.
- Repeal of DADT is scheduled to go into effect September 20, 2011. The results of surveys indicated that the majority of military personnel and spouses believe the repeal will have a neutral effect.

EXERCISES

1. Of those motivating factors discussed in this chapter (institutional, occupational, future-oriented, and pecuniary), which ones would most likely motivate you to join the military? Why? Which ones are most likely to motivate you to seek another career path? Why?

2. If possible, ask an active duty member and a member of the Reserve Component what motivated them to join the military and what has motivated them to remain. You may wish to share the four motivating factors with the service members and ask them to reflect on how much each factor played into their decision to join and into their decision to remain in the military.

3. Estimate the number of family members a service member might have. Write down the family members you are including in your estimate (e.g., parents, children, grandparents, cousins, nieces, nephews, aunts, uncles).

4. If you were designing family life education (e.g., workshops, web-based information, social networking sites) or recreational services, how would you use the demographics shared in this chapter to guide your work for active duty service personnel and their family members? For reserve component service members and their family members? What additional demographic information would you like to have about military families in order to better design programs and services?

5. What differences, if any, will repeal of DADT make in the design and presentation of family programs and information conveyed through various media?

6. Go to the DoD Personnel and Military Casualty Statistics website at http://siadapp.dmdc.osd.mil/personnel/MMIDHOME.HTM. Choose military personnel and compare the latest report on *Active Duty Military Strength by Service*. Compare the totals by branch of service with the totals reported in this chapter.

7. Examine the website for Reserve Affairs at http://ra.defense.gov/index.html. Describe what you learned about families of those service personnel in the reserve component.

8. Choose one of the multiple reports found on the website for the DoD's Military Community and Family Policy at http://prhome.defense.gov/MCFP/Reports.aspx to examine. What additional information about military families did you learn?

3

Defining Features of Military Family Life

In Chapter 3, you will

- Meet Rhonda Thomlinson, spouse of a Navy Chaplain
- Discover normative stressors in the lives of military families
- Consider the importance of spouse education and employment
- Understand how moving, separations, and deployments influence family life
- Gain insights into the factors that promote resilience in military families

Meet

Rhonda Thomlinson, Spouse of a Navy Chaplain

My husband and I were married for a good 20 years before he joined the Navy as a chaplain. A lot of spouses are 18 to early 20s and I really respect them. My husband had the advantage that his father was retired Air Force, so he understood the military environment. However, it was quite the shock for me. I knew nothing coming to it outside of a few times way back in college going to a PX. That was my total experience. I was surprised at how much I didn't know.

I meet new people and do new things, from making new friends to living on a beautiful island. I'm not saying there aren't days I don't think, "What did I get into?" especially at the beginning. But with a positive attitude there are many new and amazing opportunities.

I was surprised at how unique and strong the ties are between people. In the military, we can share things with one another; we have common experiences.

It's not always easy. When our spouses are deployed, there are times we may be out of communication, and there's a lot to handle at home. I've become a firm believer that anything that can go wrong will go wrong during a deployment. Once the water heater started leaking right over my electric dryer and my husband's ship still hadn't left the harbor.

There are times it is virtually impossible to continue a career path. Sometimes spouses may not be able to work or need special qualifications depending on where they are. A friend of mine has started a career online doing medical transcription.

You have to keep your mind open. I couldn't find a good job that paid me enough to make it worth my while. Luckily with the cost of living where my husband is stationed now, we're okay. I'm hoping to become a Family Readiness Officer, hired by the command as a liaison with families to coordinate communication.

They say you can't understand someone until you walk a mile in their shoes. Sometimes service members and families have experiences and civilians can't follow in their footsteps, no matter whose shoes are worn. But we can be open and respectful, listen, and begin to understand the culture.

INTRODUCTION

The military and families have both been called "greedy institutions" because they demand an individual's loyalty, commitment, time, and energy (Segal, 1986). Institutions influence and structure, in varying degrees, social life through sets of norms and roles (Parsons & Bales, 1956). **Norms** are expectations about how to act in a situation. Norms can be explicitly stated or implicitly understood. For example, an **explicit norm**, or overtly stated expectation, in the military is wearing a uniform on duty, while in a family an explicit norm may be a set bedtime for children. An **implicit norm**, or implied expectation, in the military is showing respect for all military service members and veterans, while in a family an implicit norm is how affection is shown. **Roles** consist of a group of norms that govern a situation. These are similar to "parts" played by actors who assume characters to play on stage or in a movie (Goffman, 1959). The military has numerous roles, such as noncommissioned officers, commanders, platoon leaders, and command financial specialists. Likewise, families are comprised of numerous roles, such as parents, daughters, sons, cousins, grandparents, aunts, and uncles. Whether in the military or in families, each role carries expectations about how to act.

Both families and the military exert normative pressures on their members. Families feel the pressure of *military* norms and roles through the demands made on the service member's loyalty (e.g., service before self even when in danger), commitment (e.g., signing a contract to work for the military for 4, 6, or 8 years), time (e.g., always available), and energy (e.g., focus on the mission). Spouses and children may feel pressure to regulate their behavior so it does not negatively affect the service member's career. Likewise, service members may worry a superior in their unit will see family problems as indication of their inability to lead others competently.

In turn, however, the military feels the pressure of *families'* norms and roles through the demands made on service members' loyalty, commitment, time, and energy to be with and care for family members. As a result of this pressure, the military in recent years has responded to the importance of families in the lives of its members by improving access to and quality of services, such as child development centers and online information (e.g., http://www.militaryonesource.com), to support families.

Military life includes many defining characteristics, such as those noted by Rhonda Thomlinson above and those highlighted in Chapter 1 (e.g., living within a chain of command, placing service to others before self, being part of a community). It may also bring periodic separation from family, geographic mobility and residence in foreign countries, and risk of injury and death (Segal, 1986). With the advent of the all-volunteer force, the numbers of spouses and children have increased and so has the importance of spouse employment and raising children. This chapter will address characteristics of military life that affect many families: a sense of community; the priority of the mission (i.e., "duty first"); relocation, including mobility and living outside of the United States; spouse employment challenges; separation, including deployment; and risk of injury or death. Issues specific to military children are addressed in Chapter 4.

Military families, as all families, face stressors that may be developmental (e.g., birth of a child, aging, death of a parent) or related to a family member's occupation. Occupations usually bring normative stressors that are experienced by most workers in that occupation. The normative stressors of military life such as relocation, separation, and risk of injury or death are shared by families with members in some other occupations (Orthner & Rose, 2009). For example, many dual-earner couples in business or the diplomatic corps move to support the job or career advancement of one spouse while the job or career of the "trailing spouse" is secondary. Migrant workers move regularly for work, and their children change schools accordingly; if parents and children are separated, they may use technology to stay involved in each other's lives. Commercial fishermen, who often describe their occupation as central to their identity, engage in a dangerous and unpredictable occupation (Zvonkovic, Solomon, Humble, & Manoogian, 2005). As you read about the characteristics of military families, imagine other occupations that may place similar demands on civilian family life. Think about the strengths individuals, families, and communities have to cope with these demands (see Box 3.1).

BOX 3.1   TIPS FROM THE FRONTLINE

ON NORMALIZING STRESS

We can support military families by recognizing their strengths and celebrating their resilience.

There's a lot of stress in our country experienced by everyone. Not just our military families. Look at the Gulf Coast. Fishing is a dangerous, unpredictable, stressful occupation, and in most cases not lucrative. Think about the families of firefighters and police officers. People who choose these occupations risk their lives everyday. Is this any different than the military? How do we support these families?

I would suggest that one way is to normalize stress, that is, to recognize that military families, and other families, face challenges everyday, yet they have strengths as individuals, families, and a community to cope with these challenges. We can support military families by recognizing their strengths and celebrating their resilience.

Evonne Carawan, Director
Personnel Readiness and Community Support Office of the
Deputy Assistant Secretary of the Navy (Military Personnel Policy)

THE SENSE OF COMMUNITY

Many military family members comment on the sense of belonging to a community that comes from living among others who share similar challenges and experiences. Throughout this book you will find firsthand accounts of the importance of this sense of community to the well-being of families. They rely on each other to understand what it is like to relocate, worry about a loved one's safety, and keep a home functioning and children cared for when the military parent is frequently away.

Sharing in a sense of community bolsters positive family adaptation (Bowen, Mancini, Martin, Ware, & Nelson, 2003). We can think of families experiencing support within the military community in three ways: informal, formal, and unit level (Rosen, Durand, & Martin, 2000). As with civilian families, military families are likely to seek interpersonal connection and assistance from informal support systems, such as community groups (e.g., church, work, clubs), friends, neighbors, and family (Martin & McClure, 2000). Military families take care of one another through such acts as giving and receiving of emotional support (e.g., listening, understanding) and practical help (e.g., child care, help around the house and yard, car rides). Such support and help are important in adjusting well to challenges such as deployments and relocations (Bowen et al., 2003).

Formal support can be considered the family programs and services available to service members and their families by each branch of the military. In upcoming chapters, you will read more about military family support centers, Military OneSource, and programs such as the Exceptional Family Member Program, the Family Advocacy Program, the New Parent Support Program, Spouse Employment Assistance, and financial literacy programs. These programs and services have expanded since the introduction of the all-volunteer force in 1973 and reflect the DoD's recognition that recruitment, retention, and mission readiness are affected by the quality of life offered in the military (MacDermid Wadsworth & Southwell, 2011).

Unit-level support is offered through the unit commander and unit leaders, including a family readiness group or key volunteer network. Each branch of the military emphasizes "we take care of our own," and this attitude is perhaps most keenly put into action at the unit level. Unit support includes information and social–emotional support (e.g., social events, deployment programming) through which families can strengthen their informal networks of support. Units that support families positively influence their sense of community and thereby affect their adaptation to military life (Bowen et al., 2003).

Spouses and children of active duty service members are likely to live near or on military installations and have opportunities to interact with other military families on a daily basis as they shop, go to the movies, exercise, attend religious activities, and attend school and community events. A built-in support system arises when a group of people who live close to one another experience similar day-to-day lives. They can empathize and share their insights and advice. A sense of community is more difficult to cultivate if military families are not located near one another. For example, National Guard or Reserve unit's families are spread across a state or region, and family members do not necessarily identify with being a military family when their loved one joins.

DUTY FIRST

From the first day when a loved one puts on a uniform, families experience the consequences of "duty first," that is, the priority of a mission over family events or needs. Military service is an obligation—an obligation to fulfill regardless of other competing demands. The mission may include deploying, training, standing watch, or just staying late to complete a task. To accomplish the mission of the military, its leaders must be able to send its members wherever they are needed, whenever they are needed. As a result, service members may miss the birth of a baby, a significant birthday, significant milestones in a child's life, funerals of close loved ones, and the list goes on.

Duty first means more workload for family members at home as they pick up the roles and tasks the service member would perform if at home. They can also feel under scrutiny within a military community as they are expected to follow codes of conduct when on base doing everyday tasks (e.g., shopping, going to school), when living in military housing, and when their loved one has leadership responsibilities (MacDermid Wadsworth & Southwell, 2011). At the same time that the mission takes priority, many military families find pride in also "serving" the country through their daily support of their loved one and the sacrifice of family time.

Many military leaders recognize that the more reasonable and predictable the demands, the more likely they are to retain families (Martin & McClure, 2000). For example, service members have access to types of leave not "charged" against their paid leave time. Leaders may authorize a leave for morale or rest and recuperation, or emergency unpaid leave; they can also grant special liberty of a short period of time to an individual or unit in recognition of their superior work. They can also let a service member off to attend a program or special event (MacDermid Wadsworth & Southwell, 2011).

RELOCATIONS

Issues related to moving differ for Active and Reserve Components. Moving is a hallmark of military life for many active duty members (Burrell, 2006). If the new duty station is of significant distance from the old one, family members typically move. However, members of the Reserve Component who wish to move a great distance from their current unit because of personal or professional reasons (e.g., taking a job elsewhere to advance their civilian career) cannot assume that they will find a new unit with which to drill. They will need to return to the initial unit to drill in order to meet their obligation to the National Guard until they serve out their contract or locate a unit closer to their new residence that will accept them.

Active Duty

The active duty military lifestyle is a mobile lifestyle. Often for those who join the military, the adventure of "seeing the world" is part of the motivation. Family members, too, can appreciate the allure of living in a variety of locations, learning to adapt to new cultures, picking up another language, acquiring a larger vision of the world and its inhabitants, and becoming more culturally competent through living daily life in another country. Successfully navigating these challenges can help to develop self-confidence and maturity among service members, spouses, and children. A move can also provide adults and children the opportunity to start over at school or work, to shed negative behaviors, and to apply new coping skills (Burrell, Adams, Durand, & Castro, 2006).

When the military directs the active duty service member to change duty location, it issues a **Permanent Change of Station (PCS)** order that relocates the member's work affiliation from one duty station to another. Service members may submit a duty preference form, indicating where they would prefer to be stationed. However, the PCS order may or may not assign the member to any of the preferred stations. In the end, where a service member is assigned is determined by the needs of the Army, Air Force, Navy, or Marine Corps. In the Army, junior enlisted and command level officers are the most frequent movers (Burrell et al., 2006).

Whether it is called PCSing, moving, or relocating, active duty military families do so often. For example, Army families average a move every 2–3 years (Burrell, 2006). Military families move more often than their civilian counterparts and move longer distances, including outside of the United States (Booth, Segal, & Bell, 2007). In 2009, approximately 13% of military members were stationed overseas (DUSD, 2010).

If a new duty station is close to the former one, families may choose to stay in their current residence, if they live off base, and may be able to stay in the current on-base housing. For example, numerous ships, submarines, air commands, and shore commands are located in the Hampton Roads area of Virginia. A service member completing a rotation on a ship whose homeport is Naval Station Norfolk could receive PCS orders to another ship there or to a command located at a nearby base, allowing the member and her or his family to remain where they are living. However, if the new installation is a significant distance away from the current one, perhaps in another state or country, then the PCS orders will often result in a move for the whole family. At times, spouses and children may remain near the old duty station while the service member relocates because of schooling for the children or a delay in selling a house. In other situations, families have a multiple-hop move during which they relocate first to temporary housing and then to permanent housing on the installation when it becomes available or to housing in the local civilian community. In these cases, children may attend a temporary school before moving to the permanent one.

Although studies on military families and relocation are limited, they suggest that a majority of military families adjust well to relocation. However, the preparation for the move, the actual move, and the first year following a move can include challenges and stresses for both adults and children. Relocation can be considered a process rather than an event, beginning with the anticipation of moving and ending months after the physical move, only to be reexperienced when the anticipation begins again with the expected next PCS (MacDermid, Weiss, Green, & Schwarz, 2007).

There are many challenges inherent in a move. On the practical side, families must decide whether to request a government move or a **Personally Procured Transportation Move** (i.e., a "do it your-self" move) and then proceed with the corresponding tasks. Other practical matters include understanding qualifications for moving allowances (i.e., money for a special need, in this case, relocation) and ensuring the total weight of household goods does not exceed the amount allowed. Parents must arrange for schooling at the new location and obtain or update copies of school and health records.

Meanwhile, adults and children are saying good-bye to friends and family and perhaps beginning to grieve over the loss of daily connection to these important people or to worry about making friends in the new location. An employed spouse may be ending a favorite job and despairing over finding another at the next duty station as frequent relocations can hinder the ability to build a career (Booth et al., 2007).

Families must accomplish many tasks before moving day arrives. To facilitate the process of moving, families are encouraged to use online tools and to visit the installation's relocation office, transportation office, and housing office. The *Plan My Move* tools found online at http://www .militaryhomefront.dod.mil enable service members and their families to prepare a customized calendar of tasks to accomplish, to learn about allowances associated with the move, and to obtain information about the new installation and its surrounding community.

In addition to online resources, each service branch has a Relocation Program located in the respective family center: Army Community Services (ACS), Marine Corps Community Services

(MCCS), Navy Fleet and Family Support Services (FFSP), and the Airman and Family Readiness Centers (A&FRC). A relocation office can assist in determining PCS allowances, using *Plan My Move*, connecting with resources at the new installation, and accessing a loan closet (i.e., basic household goods to use until a shipment of personal belongings arrive). Many military installations have a housing office where service and family members can receive assistance to determine housing allowances and the availability of family, unaccompanied, and off-base housing and to arrange for temporary lodging.

In quality of life studies, Army soldiers have reported between moderate to very large problems with relocation, decreasing their satisfaction with military life. In a 2003 Army study, 36% of those surveyed had to wait for permanent housing to become available after they had arrived at the new duty station; 47% perceived they did not have enough preparation time before the move; 43% had delays in and 40% had problems with the accuracy of reimbursements for costs incurred while traveling from the old duty station to the new one; 46% experienced a reduction in spouse income; and 38% encountered problems changing dependents' schools (Booth et al., 2007).

Personal, social, and financial supports are central to adjusting positively to relocations (Orthner, 2002). A conceptual model of resilience and risk provides some insight into how adults and children can cope with relocation challenges (MacDermid, Samper, Schwartz, Nishida, & Nyaronga, 2008). In this model, resilience and risk are measured at the level of the individual (e.g., social skills, coping style), the family (e.g., parental warmth), and community (e.g., social supports). This model guided researchers at the Military Family Research Institute who conducted a study of 608 randomly selected premove and postmove married families with one or more children from the Army and Air Force in 2004–05 (MacDermid et al., 2007). The service member, spouse, and one child between the ages of 10 and 17 completed a survey for a total number of 1083 participants.

Families reported an average of 4.9 changes in duty station prior to their current one and received an average of 83 days notice of the move. Less than half (48%) received a PCS order similar to what they had requested, and 13% experienced a change in PCS orders after receiving an earlier set of orders. Parents considered moving more difficult when it occurred during the summer, when they experienced more severe daily hassles (i.e., general household stress), when service members lacked confidence in their ability to handle the move and found adjustment to new work situation more difficult, and when spouses were dissatisfied with services on the military installation. Those persons who reported an **external locus of control** (i.e., assuming they have little or no control over events that are affecting them) or high negative emotion appeared at risk for experiencing negative events and evaluating events more negatively.

In this study, multiple resilience factors were associated with positive coping and enhanced psychological well-being, resulting in the expectation of and the actual experience of easier moves. Human capital factors included "positive self-evaluations, sense of mastery, optimism, good physical and psychological health … [and] skills acquired from education, training, and experiences, high role balance, [and] life satisfaction." Social capital factors included "marital satisfaction, better family functioning, responsive and effective parenting, social competence and involvement in group activities" (MacDermid et al., 2008, p. 16–17). For the adults and children in this study, important positive coping strategies included positivity, balancing family and work, and using formal (e.g., religious organizations) and informal (e.g., support from friends, family, coworkers, unit leaders, children's teachers) support.

Reserve Component

Air and Army National Guard

As you will recall from Chapter 1, the Air National Guard and Army National Guard are state forces under the control of the Governor unless released to the U.S. President. Members of the Guard typically serve their service obligation with units close to where they live. However, they may accept assignment at a unit within the state that requires significant travel. Reasons for doing so may be prompted by an opportunity for promotion or a change in MOS. For Guard members who wish to move out of state, they must fulfill their contract either by (1) returning to drill with their unit, or (2) identifying a Guard unit in the new state that will accept them and obtaining the agreement of the first unit to release them to the new unit. Finding a new unit may be a challenge as it is up to the Guard members to locate a new unit in need of their occupational specialty or willing to accept them and send them to a school to learn a new one. The same tasks are required of those who wish to transfer to another unit within a state. An interstate transfer refers to changing units across state lines, whereas an intrastate transfer refers to changing units within a state.

For those who remain with a unit that is far away from their home, the time away from family will be increased. They have to allow for substantial travel time to and from their drill weekend. To remain in the Guard and in their specialty, some members may choose not to move their households as it would be too difficult to return for drill once a month or to find a new unit. Also, some specialties are only found in a few units across the country. In these cases, for example explosive ordinance disposal units, members may need to fly in from multiple states.

Army, Navy, Air Force, and Marine Corps Reserves   As a federal force, the Army, Air Force, Navy, and Marine Force Reserves may be reassigned to another duty station but typically only within a region. Regions may encompass many states, so PCS orders may mean having significant travel demands in order to drill or may prompt reserve members to move their households to be nearer to their new unit.

SPOUSE EDUCATION AND EMPLOYMENT

Education

Education is important to military spouses. Of those responding to the *2008 Survey of Active Duty Spouses*, over 80% had at least some college education, and over a third had earned a bachelor's or graduate degree (DMDC, 2009). While 21% of spouses had achieved their educational goals, a majority were or wanted to be enrolled in higher education. Of these spouses, 35% wanted to earn a bachelor's degree, 28% wanted to earn a graduate or professional school degree, and 12% wanted to earn certification or a license. Those who were not in school but wish to be cited cost, family responsibilities, and child care needs as barriers (DMDC, 2009).

Guidance and support are available to military spouses who wish to pursue education. Spouses may use the services of the Education Center found on most military installations but may not know they can. Spouses can access assistance finding educational opportunities, financial aid, on-base courses, distance education courses, career counseling, and testing services (National Military Family Association, 2007). In addition, a majority of states offer spouses in-state tuition when the spouse is part of the service member's orders (National Military Family Association, 2007). Some institutions of higher education will honor in-state tuition rates for military spouses even if they move out of state and wish to continue taking distance education courses.

The Military Spouse Career Advancement Accounts (MyCAA) program funds education for an associate's degree or training leading to certifications and licensure. This program is open to spouses of active duty personnel or activated personnel in the Reserve Component in the following pay grades: E1-E5, W1-W2, or O1-O2. The maximum benefit is $4,000 with a $2,000 cap per fiscal year. A spouse has 3 years to complete the education or training (see http://www.usa4militaryfamilies. dod.mil).

Employment

Data on spouse employment and education are available for spouses of service members in the Active Component but not for spouses of those in the Reserve Component. Data often are divided into spouses of officers and of enlisted members (DUSD, 2010). Comparing military spouses to civilian spouses has focused primarily on wives (Harrell, Lim, Castaneda, & Golinelle, 2005) as the vast majority of active duty spouses across all branches are female, ranging from 90% of Air Force spouses to 98% of Marine Corps spouses (DUSD, 2010). The number of male spouses has been increasing so future analyses will be able to include comparisons of male civilian and military spouse employment (Little & Hisnanick, 2007). No data are available to discern part-time/full-time work status or possible underemployment (DMDC, 2009).

According to the *2008 Survey of Active Duty Spouses* (DMDC, 2009), 77% of responding spouses wanted to or needed to work. Of those who responded, 57% were employed, either in civilian jobs (44%) or the Armed Forces (13%); 34% were not in the labor force; and 9% were unemployed. Their most recent employment was likely to have been in health-care/health services (17%), retail (15%), and education (14%). Preferred career fields were health-care/health services (29%), education (14%), and business (9%). Five percent indicated they owned their own business, and 62% reported that they would like to own their own business.

The pursuit of employment or a career is a major component of military spouses' assessment of their quality of life (Castaneda & Harrell, 2008), and they experience factors that both help and hinder securing employment. In comparison to civilian counterparts, military spouses are more likely to reside in metropolitan areas, have graduated from high school, and have some college education—factors that enhance the possibility of obtaining employment. They also are more likely to be younger and have young children are home—factors that are barriers to employment (Harrell et al., 2005). For example, in 2009 just over half (54%) of active duty spouses were 30 years old or younger, and an additional 18% were between ages 31 and 35 (DUSD, 2010).

Compared with civilian spouses, military spouses have a lower rate of employment, earn less, work fewer weeks in a year, and are more likely to be looking for a job (Harrell et al., 2005). They report frequent relocations, deployments, being the primary caregiver to children due to the long and/or unpredictable hours worked by the military member, accessing reliable and affordable child care, and living in difficult labor markets as significant sources of stress and frustration in achieving steady employment (Castaneda & Harrell, 2008). Needing further education or certification can also hurt military spouses' employment opportunities (National Military Family Association, 2007). However, deployment appears not to affect their desire or need to work (DMDC, 2009).

Military spouses come from a society in which dual incomes are often needed, expected, and prepared for through education. For example, studies have found that a majority of spouses report a second income to pay bills and cover basic living expenses as an important or a very important reason to be employed (DMDC, 2009; Harrell et al., 2005). Spouses with less education, married to junior enlisted service members, and experiencing financial challenges were more likely to report working because of financial necessity (Harrell et al., 2005).

The desire for employment goes beyond financial needs. While 85% of spouses responding to the *2008 Survey of Active Duty Spouses* were intensely proud of being married to a service member, only 25% consider being a military spouse fulfilling personal needs. Regardless of their employment status, a majority considered a career as an important or very important reason to work (DMDC, 2009).

Military spouses who must leave their employment because of a PCS move are eligible for unemployment compensation in 38 states. Some states' laws are written to block increases in businesses' individual unemployment compensation premiums so to avoid disadvantaging employers of military spouses. Spouses are also eligible to use the Employment Assistance Program available in each service branch: the Army's Employment Readiness Program, the Navy's Spouse Employment Assistance Program, the Air Force's Career Focus Program, and the Marine Corps' Family Member Employment Assistance. These programs offer skill assessments, career counseling, and guidance on resume and cover letter preparation, local job leads, and encouragement (see http://www.usa4militaryfamilies.dod.mil).

For those spouses who live at a distance from a military installation or wish additional services, Military OneSource can locate local career resources, assist in locating local employment agencies specializing in specific career fields, and find local newspapers and websites that list job opportunities. For more tips and guidance (e.g., how to avoid employment scams), family members may subscribe to the Military OneSource Spouse Employment and Education Newsletter (see http://www.militaryonesource.com).

SEPARATION FROM FAMILY

In addition to frequent relocations, another normative stressor for military families is separation from the military member. Families report such separations as one of the most stressful parts of military life, particularly when the service member is deployed in dangerous situations. Separations occur when service members are ordered to go on temporary duty (TDY) to a temporary duty station (TDS) or on an unaccompanied tour (i.e., families are not allowed to accompany the service member). They can also be sent for schooling and on training exercises. However, the most well-known type of separation from family is deployment.

Regardless of the reason for separation, family members typically want to know the expected length of a separation. Deployment lengths are different among the services. Historically, Air Force personnel generally deployed for 4 months, Marine and Navy personnel for 6–7 months, and Army personnel for 1 year. Because the Marine Corps is dependent upon the Navy for transportation and logistical support while deployed, it uses the same deployment length as the Navy. Deployment lengths are the same for activated reserve units as for the respective active duty branch. Deployment lengths have generally remained the same during OEF/OIF, with a few exceptions. In 2007, the length of an Army deployment was increased to 15 months, with some units being extended up to 18 months. The Army deployment length was reduced back to 12 months in 2008. In addition, service members who are not deployed with their units but as individual augmentees (IAs) can find themselves deploying with a unit from a different branch; they then may be subject to the same length of deployment as that branch (i.e., an airman deploying with an Army unit may be sent home after the usual 4-month deployment or might be deployed with that unit for the entire 12-month period). IAs are most often Army personnel deploying with another Army unit; however, many Air Force and Navy personnel have deployed with Army units.

Temporary Duty or TDY

Military life is known for separating active duty service members from their families for periods of time. They are separated when they go to boot camp, join officer's candidate school, attend one of the military academies, or begin college where they might participate in ROTC. They are separated when they go to additional schools to learn their MOS. Once assigned to a duty station and for the rest of their career, service members may still be sent for a brief amount of time to another duty station. TDY orders reassign military members to another station where they will undergo additional training or attend an advanced school in their MOS. TDY can range in length from one week to several months. During this time, the service member may or may not be able to return home because of the type of duty required, the location, or the cost of transportation.

Although TDYs typically are shorter than 4–18-month combat deployments, they can disrupt family life. Schedules are reorganized and family members readjust each time the service member leaves and returns, which could be multiple times in the span of a few months or one year.

Deployments

According to the Deployment Health Clinical Center (n.d.), "military members meet deployment criteria anytime they leave the physical locale of the parent command and enter an environment for operational deployment or are stationed in a hostile territory" (para. 2). Service members may be deployed to established military installations in the United States or in another country, to an urban or a rural "field setting" in another country, or on a ship. Deployment typically refers to being sent to engage in military action that includes combat, peacekeeping, or humanitarian missions. Navy families may refer to a ship or submarine that is out to sea on a 2-week training exercise as being deployed or being on a cruise.

Deployments span all branches of the military and both the Active and Reserve Components. Deployments may be for a week (e.g., operational exercises) to 12 or 18 months or longer. Deployments may be planned for months (e.g., troop rotations to serve in war zones) or may be ordered with only the briefest of notification, as in conducting a mission of humanitarian assistance in response to a natural disaster (Deployment Health Clinical Center, n.d.). For example, multiple units from the Air Force, Army, Marines, and Navy were deployed to Haiti in Humanitarian Assistance/Disaster Response (HA/DR) missions in response to the January 12, 2010 earthquake.

Voices From the Frontline

A military spouse never exactly knows what to expect before the first deployment. I thought it was going to be a piece of cake. Families don't realize the stress on a partner when your Soldier, Marine, Airman, or Seaman is deployed. Not only are you mother and father, you are the fix-it person. I've changed a tire, fixed a garage door, while worrying about my husband. Where is he? Is he safe?

As each deployment progresses, it can wear you down. We spouses help each other a lot. Family Readiness Groups made up of volunteers keep families informed, provide resources, and help guide new military families. Yes, it's hard when my husband has to be away from our family for so long. Then he tells me about little girls in Afghanistan who are going to school now or how we helped to build a new school or hospital over there, and it makes me proud. He told me about the locals who come on base to sell things to the U.S. service members. I ended up sending boxes of clothes to an Afghani man who runs the bazaar. You realize the difference you are making. It really is worth it to be a part—if you can help someone.

Sabrina Beharie
Military spouse and mom

Military families have helped one another for centuries by sharing experiences and coping strategies. Emerging from experiences and studies of Navy families is the **emotional cycle of deployment model** that was first introduced by Logan (1987), a former Navy officer and spouse of a career Navy officer. This model, used by the United Nations as well as those working with Navy families (United Nations, 1995), identified six stages as noted in Table 3.1.

This model has been adjusted slightly over the past two decades (Morse, 2006; Pincus, House, Christenson, & Adler, 2001). Although this model and its more recent versions are used extensively throughout the military, we lack validation studies of it and so cannot claim it as evidence-based practice. The model does highlight structural issues that families typically encounter during predeployment (e.g., preparing financially and legally), deployment (e.g., redistributing responsibilities), and postdeployment (e.g., family roles). However, the emotional and stress reactions listed in the model may differ from family to family. No studies have been done on cycles of deployment models to know whether they approximate the experiences of families with one exception. Researchers from the Military Family Research Institute at Purdue University examined the reintegration phase. In this study of reservists, three reintegration patterns were identified. Some families adapted well, some experienced a decrease in well-being and then recovered, and some experienced variations in well-being throughout the reintegration period (MacDermid Wadsworth, Pagnan, & Seidel, 2010).

The predeployment, during deployment, and postdeployment timeline resonates with families and is easy to present during briefing and educational programs and through written materials. Although initially developed during a time when female sailors did not deploy, staff at Navy Fleet and Family Support Centers have found the module useful for male and female service members.

TABLE 3.1   Logan's (1987) Proposed Emotional Cycle of Deployment

Adjustment Stages		Possible Feelings and Actions
Predeployment	Anticipation of loss	Sadness, anger, irritability, worry, bickering, restlessness, focused on completing the "to do" list
	Detachment and withdrawal	Discomfort, distancing from one another, wanting the departure day to arrive so the deployment can begin
During deployment	Emotional disorganization	Pain from saying good-bye, guilt for feeling relief the deployment has started, routines disrupted, withdrawal from family and friends, sleep disturbances, restless, indecisive
	Recovery and stabilization	New patterns established, adapted to new roles and responsibilities, increased confidence, may feel stressed
	Anticipation of homecoming	Excited, nervous, tense, apprehensive, making emotional room for the returning spouse
Postdeployment	Renegotiation of relationships	Joy, relief, annoyance, adapt to changes in roles and responsibilities
	Reintegration and stabilization	Relaxed, comfortable with one another, enjoyment, new routines established

Source: Adapted from Logan, K. V. (1987). The emotional cycle of deployment. *U.S. Naval Proceedings, 113,* 43–47, Copyright © (1987) U.S. Naval Institute / http://www.usni.org.

their partners, and children (Navy Personnel Command, n.d.). Sharing one or more models of a deployment cycle with families may provide them information they can use to develop their own meaning of their separation and reintegration experience, according to their own timelines (Wiens & Boss, 2006).

The emotional cycle of deployment model was developed during a time of relative predictability of deployments. With the downsizing of the military in the 1990s and the advent of OEF and OIF, the tempo of rotations significantly changed. The time between deployments shortened at the same time that deployments lengthened and return dates became less certain (Lincoln, Swift, & Shorteno-Fraser, 2008). This accelerated optempo has meant that for many military families the stage of "reintegration and stabilization" quickly is overtaken by the "anticipation of loss" stage. In recognition of this optempo and multiple deployments, the National Military Family Association suggested that "cycle of deployment" should be replaced by "spiral of deployment." A spiral suggests not returning back to the beginning, but carrying experiences, feelings, attitudes, and lessons learned forward to the next separation (National Military Family Association, 2006).

A feature of a cycle, or a spiral, of deployment, particularly an extended one, is **boundary ambiguity**, that is, having a family member "present" physically but not psychologically or present psychologically but not physically (Faber, Willerton, Clymer, MacDermid, & Weiss, 2008). Under great stress, such boundary ambiguity may be experienced as an **ambiguous loss** (Boss, 2006). As you read more about the stages of deployment below, consider conditions under which boundary ambiguity may result in families experiencing an ambiguous loss.

Predeployment   Reservists and active duty members may spend months and perhaps a year **gearing up** for the deployment during which time their unit is focused on preparing personnel and accompanying gear (the type of gear depends upon the mission of the unit, e.g., civil engineering, infantry, medical). Small subgroups or an individual from the unit may be selected to deploy. Regardless if it is one person or the whole unit, military members need to acquire gear, obtain and prepare uniforms, go to medical appointments, complete legal and financial paperwork, and, if they have leadership responsibilities, ensure others in their unit are prepared. During this gear-up time, individuals or whole units often spend weeks, if not months, away from home obtaining additional training.

This preparation is vital to the conduct of the mission, including the safety of everyone in the unit. The focus on preparation often means service members have less time than they would like with their family, just when family members want extra time with them. Families count all of this preparation and training time as separation, that is as "boots away from home" time, rather than counting as separation just the "boots on the ground" time once the unit has reached its deployment location (Castaneda et al., 2008, p. 251). Even when at home, however, service members may be thinking and worrying about unit preparations. When service members are physically present yet psychologically absent from family life, families can experience increased stress (Boss, 2006).

At times, individuals or units are given only a week or as little as 6 hours to pack and report at the designated area for deployment. These short-notice deployments emphasize the need for military families always to be prepared for separation.

National Guard and Reserve families have additional steps to take when preparing for deployment when the service member also has a civilian job. Service members must continue to meet the obligations of their civilian employment and may even be asked to train another employee to do the job they have been doing (Griffith, 2005). Families need to prepare for a possible period of time when income from the civilian job has ended and income from the military has yet to begin. For a first deployment, families of a member of the National Guard or Reserves may find themselves quickly becoming a "military family" as they obtain ID cards, learn about military benefits, and seek information on services on installations.

Active and Reserve Component families who are well-prepared for deployment are more likely to "weather deployments more successfully" than those who are less prepared (Booth et al., 2007, p. 31). As noted above, units follow a general deployment schedule, but they or individual service members may be called to deploy with only hours or a few days notice. Given the likelihood of emergencies requiring deployment with little warning, the military's goal is for families to be prepared, that is, to "think about deployments as a condition of [military] life rather than as atypical events" (Booth et al., 2007, p. 31).

One major step in preparation for military parents is making arrangements for the care of their children during deployment. Most service members who are parents know the civilian parent will care for their children during deployment. Other service members who are in dual-military marriages, are single parents with custody or joint custody, or are legally responsible for a child or an adult member unable to care for themselves in the absences of the service member are required to submit a **Family Care Plan** to their command. A Family Care Plan must indicate: who will care for the member's child or children during deployment and other absences (e.g., training, temporary duty); arrangements to provide financial, medical, and logistical support (e.g., housing, transportation, food, clothing) for the children's well-being; name and consent to the plan of any noncustodial parent who will not be the caregiver during the service member's absence; and who will be the temporary caregiver in case of incapacity or death of the service member while permanent custody is established. The caregiver must be nonmilitary, and the service member must indicate that the caregiver has agreed to the arrangements and has received copies of relevant documents (e.g., power of attorney). Typically extended family members (e.g., the service member's parent or parents, a sibling, an aunt or an uncle) are appointed caregivers or guardians, but friends and the spouse of another military member have fulfilled these roles. Caregivers will need to show a power of attorney and the children's ID card to use military medical treatment facilities and a letter from the commanding officer of a military installation to use the commissaries and exchanges on behalf of the children (DoD, 2011b).

Military families need to prepare financially, legally, psychologically, and relationally. The increased stress that occurs during this phase is fueled by anticipation of a separation—a separation that has inherent risks and dangers. In response to the stress, family members may find themselves arguing more or feeling more tense. Some report they wish the deployment would "just begin" and then may feel guilty about having such thoughts. However, these reactions are common and families benefit from anticipating stages of deployment and from avoiding becoming overly worried about the significance of these reactions (Wiens & Boss, 2006). Meanwhile, couples experiencing more severe relationship conflict may try to ignore it before deployment and hope that disagreements will be resolved by the imposed separation (Drummet, Coleman, & Cable, 2003).

During Deployment   Multiple factors related to deployment can result in stress for military families. Renegotiation of boundaries is one of them. Military families often spend great effort maintaining their loved one's psychological presence in the family when the physical presence is not possible. Additional stressors include maintaining a relationship while apart and caring for children (Drummet et al., 2003).

Deployments call for family reorganization and adaptation as roles and responsibilities in the family are redistributed (Faber et al., 2008). As a stone thrown into a pond produces ripples, so does the deployment of a spouse, boyfriend, parent, adult child, sibling, niece, or nephew produce ripples throughout a family. For example, imagine the shifts and changes in roles and responsibilities among family members when the parent who helps with homework, the spouse who maintains connections with the extended family, the daughter who assists parents with investments, or the older brother who guides younger siblings is now deployed. This reorganization and adaptation may be challenging as family members unfamiliar with certain tasks become responsible for them but may be unclear if they will remain responsible for them when the deployed family member returns (Boss, 2006).

Postdeployment   During World War II and immediately following the end of the war, Reuben Hill (1949) conducted one of the first studies of military families, focusing on their adaptation during deployment and when service members returned. He noted that adjustment to both deployment and reintegration included a process of disorganization, recovery, and achievement of reorganization. The families who "closed ranks" during deployment faced more difficulty adjusting during reintegration even though they had functioned well while separated from the service member. By closing ranks, the family left the returning family member with a limited or even no role to assume. However, those families who adapted roles to accommodate the absence and then return of the member adjusted well to separation and reunion (MacDermid Wadsworth, 2010).

Adaptability continues to be a key component of family adjustment during reintegration. Upon return from deployment, the service member may again be physically but not psychologically present. It takes time to adjust to coming back from days spent inside and outside the wire, days spent inside a ship or submarine, or days flying missions. Service members may do highly dangerous jobs and may have experienced frightening and sad events and situations. While happy to be home and with their families, they may be thinking about the deployment, their buddies, and their shared experiences. Returned service members may spend significant time with buddies and talking with them because they know "what it was like." Service members may worry civilians, even family members, will be judgmental or repelled by their stories, or may wish not to burden their family members with vivid images and horrific situations. Family members who consider these buddies as support systems may find it easier to accept the time needed to transition psychologically from a combat, humanitarian, or routine deployment to daily life at home.

Returning from deployment also brings another reorganization of family roles and responsibilities, as illustrated by the story in Box 3.2. Family members may have grown comfortable and confident in their roles and may not wish to relinquish their responsibilities. Service members may or may not want to assume their old roles. One study of reservists and their families suggest that returning to civilian work assisted in dissipating perceived boundary ambiguity as routines were established. However, life events such as health problems or job changes were added stressors that prolonged the boundary ambiguity and made adjustment more difficult (Faber et al., 2008). During reintegration families must establish what many military families call "a new normal." Family life will not be the same as it was prior to deployment. People grow and change, especially children, and the goal is to mesh this growth and these changes into a mutually satisfactory and supportive family life.

BOX 3.2   TIPS FROM THE FRONTLINE

REFLECTIONS OF A FAMILY LIFE EDUCATOR

I worked at the Navy Family Services Center (now called Fleet and Family Support Center) in Norfolk, Virginia, and was part of three Return and Reunion Program teams. After deploying to the Mediterranean or elsewhere, Captains of ships in an aircraft carrier or a battleship group could request visits by Return and Reunion teams. The teams flew to Spain and joined the ships just before they began crossing the Atlantic on their way home. Team members would visit each ship for 1–3 days, transported between ships by helicopters or a whale boat. (A whale boat appears to be an oversized row boat, at least when sitting in one as it approaches a large supply ship.)

One popular presentation was on returning to a spouse and a new baby. During my first trip, a sailor asked to speak with me after attending this presentation. With a troubled look, he whispered, "My wife had our first baby while I was away. When we pull into port, do I hug my wife or my baby first?"

Looking at this sailor, who was probably in his early 20s, and recalling reunions where I had seen fathers envelope wives and infants in huge bear hugs, I responded, "It's obvious you love your wife and your new baby very much. I think you will know the right thing to do when you see them together."

He grinned. "Ahhh. Thank you!" All he needed to hear was reassurance that he had the wisdom to know what to do in this important moment.

Karen Blaisure
Coauthor of this textbook and Professor of Family Studies at Western Michigan University

Coping with Deployments   Service members and their spouses realize that separations are part of military life, as data from the *2008 Survey of Active Duty Spouses* illustrate. In this sample, 75% of Army, 73% of Navy and Marine, and 56% of Air Force spouses reported that their spouse had been deployed at least once in the past 3 years (DMDC, 2009). Of those who had deployed, over half had deployed more than once and nearly two-thirds had deployed to a combat zone. Half of the Army, Navy, and Marine Corps and 35% of Air Force spouses reported that their spouse was currently deployed or had been away from home because of a deployment during the past 12 months (DMDC, 2009).

If married or in a significant relationship other than marriage, service members and their partners face maintaining their relationship during challenging circumstances, including multiple deployments. One analysis of research on Army families concluded, "family members … expect their Soldiers to be deployed but become increasingly dissatisfied as the length, frequency, and unpredictability of deployments increase" (Booth et al., 2007, p. 30). Military spouses find deployments stressful, particularly combat, longer, and extended deployments. Being pregnant and having children increases spouses' risk of stress and depression, as does having a returning military spouse who is experiencing posttraumatic stress disorder (PTSD) (de Burgh, White, Fear, & Iversen, 2011). Extensions of deployments often spark anger and stress, particularly when they occur just before the expected time of return (Hosek, Kavanagh, & Miller, 2006).

It appears that experiencing one deployment may not facilitate coping with subsequent deployments for many spouses. Forty-four percent of spouses responding to the 2008 survey found coping more difficult with multiple deployments, 39% found it neither more nor less difficult, and 18% found it less difficult (DMDC, 2009).

As Table 3.2 illustrates, spouses reported experiencing problems during deployments. The most common were worrying about their spouse's safety and feeling lonely.

TABLE 3.2   Percentage of Spouses at Home Reporting Problems Experienced to a Large or a Very Large Extent during the Most Recent Deployment

Safety of deployer	49%	No time for recreation, fitness, or entertainment	23%
Loneliness	47%	Technical difficulties communicating with deployer	22%
Anxiety or depression	36%	Serious emotional problems in the family	18%
Difficulty sleeping	36%	Child care when not previously needed	18%
Being a "single" parent	32%	Managing expenses and bills	15%
Accurate information about return date	31%	Safety of family in the community	13%
House/car repairs, yard	28%	Serious health problems in the family	13%
Job/education demands	26%	Marital problems	13%
Maintaining emotional connection with deployer	25%	Not feeling part of civilian community	13%
Managing child care/child schedules	23%	Other	10%
Weight loss/gain	23%	Major financial hardship or bankruptcy	4%
Not feeling part of military community	23%	Loss of income from deployer's part-time job	3%

Source: Data compiled from Defense Manpower Data Center (2009). *2008 Survey of active duty spouses: Tabulation of responses (Report No. 2008-041).* Tables 19a–19x (p. 74–121). Arlington, VA: DMDC. Retrieved from http://prhome.defense.gov/MCFP/docs/2008%20Military%20Spouse%20Survey.pdf.

The military responds to situations that are dynamic, meaning that deployment schedules can and sometimes are expected to change. Family members are called upon to be flexible and to adapt personal and family plans to changes in military schedules. For example, imagine the changes in personal schedules that would occur if a reunion date was moved 1 week earlier or later than expected. Family members who had arranged time off from work would need to renegotiate time off, if possible, and revise transportation plans, perhaps at great expense.

Throughout the deployment cycle, it is common for family members to want and to request information. Prior to deployment, families want to know such information as deployment and return dates, the status of communication options down range, and where their loved one will be. During deployment families want reliable and timely information about their service member's well-being and safety (Faber et al., 2008). After reunion, families want to know that their service member is adjusting well and, if not, how to obtain help. Knowing the facts of a situation, the availability of help, and how to obtain help can reduce the experience of stress (Boss, 2006). However, some information cannot be told to family members or shared over the phone or in e-mail with family members who live at a distance. Sometimes service members withhold information from families out of the mistaken belief that the less families know the easier it will be for them.

Irregular communication and long separations stress relationships. Spouses report access to means of communication with a deployed service member as important or very important as a way to cope with a deployment (DMDC, 2009). Table 3.3 lists other items that spouses at home report as helping them cope with a deployment.

The research on deployment and families has primarily focused on active duty. Due to demographic (e.g, age and sex) and geographical differences between the Active and Reserve Components, more research on National Guard and Reserve families is necessary. In a 2006 study of deployment experiences of National Guard and Reserve members and their families, researchers interviewed military family experts from each of the six Reserve Components (i.e., Army National Guard, Air National Guard, Army Reserve, Air Force Reserve, Navy Reserve, and Marine Forces Reserve) and interviewed by telephone service members and family members from 653 families from four of the Reserve Components (i.e., Army National Guard, Army Reserve, Air Force Reserve, and Marine Forces Reserve) (Castaneda et al., 2008).

Most families in this study indicated their families were *ready* or *very ready* for deployment. Approximately 17% of service members and family members indicated their families were *somewhat ready*, and the same percentage indicated their families were *not ready at all*. Approximately 40% of respondents indicated readiness referred to financial matters, household responsibilities, and

TABLE 3.3   Percentage of Spouses at Home Reporting Item as Important or Very Important to Coping with the Most Recent Deployment

E-mail to and from deployer	95%	Understanding why deployment is important/necessary	66%
Telephone calls	93%	Support from civilian community	60%
Knowing length of deployment	93%	Contact with someone in deployer's unit	60%
No changes in length of deployment	84%	Family readiness/support group	57%
Temporary reunions with spouse	83%	Instant/text messaging with deployer	55%
Deployment pay	82%	Reunion planning information or classes	50%
Predeployment information	76%	Local counseling/support services	50%
Recreation, fitness, and entertainment activities	71%	Telephonic counseling/support services (i.e., Military OneSource)	42%
Support from the military community	69%		

Source: Data compiled from Defense Manpower Data Center (2009). *2008 Survey of active duty spouses: Tabulation of responses (Report No. 2008-041).* Tables 22a–22q (p. 138–171). Arlington, VA: DMDC. Retrieved from http://prhome.defense.gov/MCFP/docs/2008%20Military%20Spouse%20Survey.pdf.

emotional or mental preparation. A quarter indicated readiness referred to legal preparation. Ten percent indicated readiness referred to learning about military programs and benefits; addressing employment-related issues; finding information about the deployment; determining how to communicate during deployment; canceling classes or vacation plans; and preparing the service member to deploy. Almost two-thirds of service members and spouses indicated they coped well or very well with deployment, and 16% of service members and 20% of spouses indicated they coped moderately well. Less than 10% of service members and spouses indicated they coped poorly. The remaining respondents indicated they did not know how well they coped or did not answer (Castaneda et al., 2008).

A majority of service members and spouses reported at least one problem faced by their families because of the deployment or activation. Over a third of spouses reported emotional and household problems, and a quarter reported children's issues. In comparison, fewer service members than spouses reported their families experiencing these problems although more service members than spouses reported problems related to employment. Service members and their spouses were more in agreement on whether the family experienced financial or legal problems, and education. Approximately 10% of service members and spouses reported marital and health-care problems (Castaneda et al., 2008).

Those service members and spouses reporting *no* problems were more financially comfortable, felt they had received sufficient notice, and believed their families were ready or very ready for the deployment. Army reservists were *least likely* to report *no* problems. Husbands of service members, spouses with no children, and spouses married to Air Force reservists were *most likely* to report *no* problems (Castaneda et al., 2008).

The top three formal military supports service members and spouses reported using during deployment were Tricare, Family Readiness Groups or Key Volunteers, and MilitaryOneSource.com. The top three informal resources reported used were family, religious institutions, and friends and neighbors (Castaneda et al., 2008).

Perhaps startling to those not connected to the military, service members and military families may speak of the benefits and positive outcomes of deployments. Benefits of deployments for service members include using their skills and training, gaining experience vital to advancing in their career, additional money, assisting the nation, and time to think (Booth et al., 2007; Newby, McCarroll, et al., 2005). Partners may also derive benefits from deployments: having time to focus on career advancement or educational goals, gaining confidence and independence, and developing new interests.

A majority of service members and spouses in the 2006 study of National Guard and Reserves reported at least one positive development in their lives as a result of the deployment or activation.

For service members, these positives included financial gain; family closeness; patriotism, pride, or civic responsibility; independence, confidence, or resilience; and employment and education. Spouses reported the following positives: family closeness; patriotism, pride, or civic responsibility; financial gain and independence, confidence, or resilience; and employment or education. Service members who were likely to report no positives reported receiving less or insufficient notice, and spouses who were likely to report no positives were male spouses, Army Reserve spouses, prior military, and those who described employers as not supportive (Castaneda et al., 2008).

RISK OF INJURY OR DEATH

The military calls on its personnel to engage in training, conduct operations, and deploy on missions that are inherently dangerous during both peacetime and time of war. Military work is physical work even during peacetime, and workplace injuries and deaths occur. During time of war, going outside the wire on patrol, landing and guiding in an F-18 on the deck of an aircraft carrier, diving into deep waters in a submarine, loading bombs and missiles, and flying helicopters during a firefight to pick up the wounded are only a few examples of the dangers.

Injury and death of a service member are realities faced by military families. Since 9/11 and the beginning of OEF/OIF, military families have faced even greater possibility of their service member risking injury and death. Since September 2001, approximately 2 million service personnel have deployed (Institute of Medicine, 2010). During this time, a majority of deployers went to a combat zone, and family members worried about their loved one's safety (DMDC, 2009).

Research is limited on what helps family members cope with the fear that injury and death may occur. As noted in the section on deployment, communicating with the military member helps. Other coping strategies include contact with family, friends, and support groups; involvement with work or volunteer activities to provide social contact and benefits from positively contributing to society; self-awareness of stress levels and seeking assistance when appropriate; engaging in healthy behaviors (e.g., exercise, nutritional eating, adequate sleep); limiting time spent listening to or watching media accounts about the military; and recognizing that daily life may feel overwhelming at times (Wright, Burrell, Schroeder, & Thomas, 2006).

The military refers collectively to those who have died or have been wounded while serving as **casualties**. As of May 31, 2011, 43,822 service members had been wounded in action and 6,034 have died during OEF, OIF, and OND (DMDC, 2011b). Improvised explosive devices (IEDs) attacks and direct combat have produced the majority of casualties. Other reasons include noncombat helicopter/aircraft accidents, medical (e.g., heart attack), and vehicle accidents. *The Washington Post* newspaper publishes data based on military press releases and hosts an interactive website, "Faces of the Fallen" (http://projects.washingtonpost.com/fallen), where service members are listed by name, branch of service, state of residence, and date of death.

Combat and operational stress injuries include such wounds as **traumatic brain injury** (TBI; a blow or jolt to or penetration of the head), amputations, spinal cord injuries, chronic pain associated with musculoskeletal conditions, depression, anxiety, and **posttraumatic stress disorder** (an anxiety disorder that may occur following a traumatic event). An injury can disrupt family functioning. Lives are changed, not only for those wounded but also for families and loved ones. Changes can include short-term disruptions in routine until the service member recovers or major reorganizations of roles so family members can provide daily care for a son, daughter, spouse, mother, father, niece, or nephew. As we will see in other chapters, a constellation of protective factors available within and for the family can promote resilience in the service member and family.

With injuries come many challenges for military families. Upon notification of their service member being wounded, families are thrown into uncertainty as initial communication can be brief and lack the details family members want to know: how bad is the injury, where is the service member, can we talk to her or him? Sometimes service members find a way to call home before the official notification occurs in an attempt to reassure their families. If the service member is being transported to the United States, family members usually will travel to the military hospital and remain for weeks and even months as treatment and recovery progress. Longer-term challenges include ongoing health decisions, financial concerns, whether the service member can continue in the military, employment decisions for a spouse or parents providing care, and disruptions in children's lives (Cozza, 2009b).

When there is a death, the military notifies the next of kin in person. The Army sends a **Casualty Notification Officer** (CNO), often accompanied by a military chaplain and/or organization commander to notify a service member's designated next of kin. In cases of a death by a hostile action (e.g., combat) or terrorist attack, the secondary next of kin will also be notified in person. The Army assigns a **Casualty Assistance Officer** (CAO) to be with the family through the transition to provide information and assistance with funeral or memorial services, filing paperwork for benefits and entitlements, and relocation. If the next of kin lives geographically far from an Army installation or an Army National Guard or Reserve unit, the CNO and CAO may be the same soldier.

The Navy and Marine Corps **Casualty Assistance Calls Officer** (CACO) and the Air Force **Casualty Assistance Representative** (CAR) serve both functions: to notify next of kin and to be with the family through the transition to provide information and assistance. Service members assigned as a CNO, CAO, CACO, or CAR are senior enlisted personnel or commissioned officers who receive initial and ongoing training specifically for this position. When assigned a family, the CAO, CACO, and CAR serve as the official liaison between the family and the Army, Air Force, Marine Corps, or Navy and assist the family for as long as necessary (U.S. Army Human Resources Command, 2010; Willerton, Samper, & MacDermid, 2008).

Family members enrolled in the military sponsorship system (i.e., DEERS) may remain in military housing for up to 365 days after the death of a service member and retain some privileges until remarriage, such as shopping the base or post exchange. They also may use Morale, Welfare, and Recreation programs. Children in the Department of Defense Domestic Dependent Elementary and Secondary Schools (DDESS) may remain enrolled until graduation unless they move to another school system (DoD, 2011a).

Military families face challenges associated with frequent relocation and separation and with the risk of injury and death. Knowing about these normative stressors of military life can sensitize you to how stressors may pile up and to strengths of military families such as family role flexibility, active coping strategies, and sense of community that bolsters positive family adaptation (Wiens & Boss, 2006). As you continue learning more about military life, consider how this knowledge and sensitivity can guide you in interactions with individual military families who are both unique from and similar to other military families.

SUMMARY

- The normative stressors associated with the military lifestyle (e.g., relocation, separation, risk of injury or death) are shared by other occupations.
- Sharing in a sense of community encourages positive adaptation to military family life. Military families benefit from informal, formal, and unit-level support.
- The mission of a military unit takes priority over family events or needs. This "duty first" means more workload for family members at home as they pick up the roles and tasks the service member would perform if at home.
- Moving every few years is a hallmark of military life for active duty members, as they are relocated many times during a career. Problems with relocation can decrease family satisfaction with military life. Positive coping strategies such as positivity, balancing family and work, and using formal and informal support can enhance psychological well-being, resulting in the expectation of and the actual experience of easier moves.
- A majority of military spouses are seeking additional education and are or wish to be employed. Employment or a career is a major factor for military spouses' assessment of their quality of life.
- Families report separation as one of the most stressful parts of military life, even more so when the service member is deployed in dangerous situations. A feature of a deployment

cycle is boundary ambiguity, that is, having a family member "present" physically but not psychologically or present psychologically but not physically.

- Deployments span all branches of the military and both the Active and Reserve Components. Deployments may be for a week to 12 or 18 months or longer. Deployments may be planned for months or may be ordered with only the briefest of notification, as in the case of humanitarian assistance.
- A majority of Reserve Component families who were part of a 2006 study reported that they were ready or very ready for deployment. Military families who are well-prepared financially, legally, psychologically, and relationally are more likely to cope well with deployment than those who are less prepared. A majority of these Reserve families reported at least one positive outcome of the deployment.
- Military parents must make arrangements for the care of their children during deployment. Service members who are in dual-military marriages, are single parents with custody or joint custody, or are legally responsible for a child or an adult member unable to care for themselves in the absence of the service member are required to submit a Family Care Plan to their command.
- Adaptability is a key component of family adjustment during deployment and afterwards.
- The most common concerns during deployment reported by military spouses in a 2008 study were worrying about their spouse's safety and feeling lonely.
- Military work is physical work even during peacetime, and workplace injuries and deaths occur.
- The military refers collectively to those who have died or have been wounded while serving as "casualties."
- When there is a death, a military representative notifies the next of kin in person. The representative stays with the family through the transition to provide information and assistance with funeral or memorial services, filing paperwork for benefits and entitlements, and relocation.

EXERCISES

To gain insight into the characteristics of military family life, answer the following questions:

1. If you knew you had to move your entire household every 2–3 years, how would you live your life differently than you do now? How do you think this might impact your relationships with your family members? Friends? New people you meet?

2. Imagine you had 90 days to move your entire household to another country. What steps would be involved in not only moving items but also ending a job, and saying good-bye to friends and extended family? What steps would you also have to take to ensure a place to stay in the new location, daycare or a school for children, and a new job? What other steps would you need to take to facilitate a positive adjustment? What would you look forward to the most? The least?

3. Download one of the following major studies of military family life and examine a few research questions in detail. What information helps you better understand the stressors faced by family members? Is any of this information a surprise to you? How might this information inform your practice as a helping professional supporting military families?
   a. *What We Know About Army Families: 2007 Update.* http://www.army.mil/cfsc/research.htm
   b. *2008 Survey of Active Duty Spouses.* http://prhome.defense.gov/mcfp.html
   c. *Deployment Experiences of Guard and Reserve Families: Implications for Support and Retention.* http://www.rand.org/pubs/monographs/2008/RAND_MG645.pdf

4. Read first-person accounts of deployment experiences and discuss the extent to which they address boundary ambiguity and relationship maintenance.

5. Compare and contrast Pincus et al.'s (2001) Emotional Cycle of Deployment, Morse's (2006) New Emotional Cycles of Deployment, and Logan's (1987) Emotional Cycle of Deployment. How has the model evolved over time? How might you use a model to help families understand and cope with their experience of deployment?
6. Put together a welcome kit for military families moving into your hometown. Include in this kit the information a family would need to know and the community resources that might be of interest to military families.

4

Children and Youth in Military Families

In Chapter 4, you will

- Meet Connery, a high school senior, who has been raised in a military family
- Learn about military children's experiences of moving and going to school
- Discover the impact of parental deployments on children's adjustment
- Consider how to support children during parental deployment, injury, or death

Meet

Connery, A High School Senior

"We've had it good for us."

    A military family is different from civilian families. Being an active-duty son, I had to get used to moving around every 4 years. That's good because you are going to have to move anyway when you go to college or get a job. If you aren't the coolest guy in one state, you can have a fresh start. Here a lot of people know me. I call it home. I was 10 when we moved here and now I'm 18. It's the longest I've lived anywhere.

    When I was born, we moved to Germany. I just remember my grandmother coming, and mom and I traveled around with her. I have experienced different cultures and know lots of people not like me. I'm open to new ideas.

    The benefits are a huge plus. I am under my dad's health insurance, auto insurance, and dental insurance while I'm living with him.

    As a military kid, you have more respect for authority. Having a commanding officer for a dad, I feel you have to say, "Sir, yes, sir" and get on with it. It helps when you have procrastination issues like me.

    You see and do neat things. I got to sit in the cockpit of an A-10. My dad flies it. The A-10 is a close air support for troops on the ground that sticks with the soldiers and keeps our guys alive. There's a lot of buttons. It's a safe plane. You can take a hit and go back in.

    When my dad goes off to missions, he's fulfilling a commitment he has made. I've experienced his leaving many times. Maybe his discipline has rubbed off on me. I want to go into the Air Force Reserve or Air National Guard. The benefits are good. I want to follow my dad's footsteps and serve my country. I'd like to fly a helicopter. I hear stories that being a pilot is all it is cracked up to be. It's like being on a roller coaster all the time. I want to have a civilian job, too, in architecture. My parents are behind it as long as I finish college first, but I always planned to do that. I'm aware of the danger, and I still want to do my part.

I don't recommend military life for everyone. It was hard to leave my really good friends when we moved. We talk on Facebook sometimes, but now my life has moved on. You can have friends but not a huge bond.

The most important thing is to be on good terms with your family. Talk. Hang out together. My brothers and I are good friends. We always had each other every time we moved. We hold a lot of respect for our parents. They put us first. If you don't have a close-knit family, you kick yourself in the butt. We've had it good for us.

INTRODUCTION

Nearly two million children in the United States have at least one parent serving in the military. In 2009, there were approximately 1.2 million children of active duty personnel and over 700,000 children of selected reserve personnel (DUSD, 2010). Many of these children have only known military family life, while some recall a prior civilian life. Others transitioned through a parent leaving active duty and joining the National Guard or Reserve, or vice versa. The number of studies on these military children has increased greatly over the last decade, and results of these studies are just beginning to be published. Much more will be learned in the coming years.

In addition to those children with a parent currently in the military, there are children who experience military family life while at least one parent was in the Active or Reserve Component for some years but now are living a civilian life because their parent separated from the military. Finally, there are adults who, as military children, grew up in the military culture. We are learning more about their perspectives of life as they share their stories with the media and researchers (Martin, Rosen, & Sparacino, 2000).

Of course not all children with a parent in the military experience the same type of "military family life." For example, those children whose parents are in the Active Component may experience separations, relocations including overseas, and life on or near a major military installation. These children usually are familiar and comfortable with military culture and being on military bases or posts. They typically attend either DoDEA schools or civilian schools with a high population of military children. However, children of parents who are in the Air or Army National Guard or the Reserves may never experience relocating to a new community or know many children like themselves. Although they may visit an Armory or an Air National Guard base, their daily lives are lived in the civilian rather than a military world.

In this chapter, we examine the influence of military culture, relocation, child care, education, and deployment on children. Connery, the 18-year-old high school senior you met at the beginning of this chapter, shares some of his perceptions of life in a military family. He emphasizes being close to his brother and parents as a key component of living in a military family. As you read, notice how many of Connery's points are highlighted in what we know about military children. The experiences of military children vary, and not all may have such positive responses as Connery.

Military children face relocations, separations, and risks of parental injury. The studies we have of military children suggest that most adapt well to military life (Chandra et al., 2011; MacDermid et al., 2008). However, some military children experience more extensive and intensive stressors when parents deploy multiple times over the course of a few years, are injured, or die. These events and a pile-up of stressors (e.g., combat deployment followed by a PCS move and extended work hours at the new duty station and another combat deployment) can immobilize individual family members, including children, and wear away or overwhelm families' coping skills. Even then we know that protective factors such as positive family dynamics, social support, and finding meaning from such adversities can make a difference in the resilience of children and families (Boss, 2006; Park, 2011; Walsh, 2002; Wiens & Boss, 2006).

RELOCATION

As noted in Chapter 3, relocation is a well-known feature of active duty military life. If raised their whole life in an active duty family, military children will have moved an average of six to nine times between kindergarten and graduating from high school (Department of Defense-State

Liaison Office, 2010), or every 2–3 years (Finkel, Kelley, & Ashby, 2003). Military children have reported traveling and meeting new people as benefits of military life. Yet, both of these benefits occur because of one of the "toughest" parts of military life for children: moving (Ender, 2002, 2006; National Military Family Association, 2010).

Moving can seem to be a perpetual process for some active duty military children and teens. They are preparing to move, physically moving, settling in, or wondering where the next move will be. Prior to the physical move, they are saying good-bye to friends and family and perhaps beginning to grieve over the loss of daily connection to these important people. Little is known about military children under the age of 5 and relocation. However, as with any move or transition, infants, toddlers, and preschoolers are greatly influenced by the prevalent emotions of their caregivers and consistency in routine.

For school-age children and teens, a move usually means changing schools, rejoining sports teams and interest groups, and finding new friends. They may be concerned about whether they will be "behind" or "ahead" others in their grade. However, they also report liking the opportunity to start over at a new school that a relocation offers (Finkel et al., 2003).

The website *Military Youth on the Move* includes information for children, teens, and parents on transitioning to a new location and school. Some military installations have a youth sponsorship program that will match a new child to a child approximately of the same age who is living in the new location in order to assist with integration into the new installation, surrounding community, and school.

Although research has given us some insight into the experiences of military children with moves, our knowledge is still limited. For example, few studies have followed children longitudinally as they go through the process of a move or followed up with them for a period of time afterward to determine the longer-term consequences. Most studies ask children about their experiences only after the fact. Most studies are relatively small, and as noted above, there is little information about preschool children (Weber & Weber, 2005). To better understand how relocation affects military children, we need representative samples across age ranges and branches of service and more focus on what factors are associated with positive adjustment.

Relocation often means changing schools for military children. The *Military Families on the Move* study (MacDermid et al., 2007) introduced in Chapter 3 offers some insight into what can make transitioning to a new school easier or more difficult for youth. The study included collecting data from one child, age 10–17; the service member; and the spouse from 608 Army and Air Force families. The average number of schools attended by these youth since the age of 5 was 4.08. Children reported experiencing school transitions as more difficult when they were female, had social anxiety (i.e., fear of negative evaluation), had negative attitudes about moving, and had negative perceptions of their own academic competence. They also indicated moves during the school year as more difficult. However, summer moves may also result in challenges for teens who, without the interaction with peers that comes with attending school, may not be able to identify potential friends and create friendships (Tyler, 2002).

Evidence suggests that the number of moves is not what predicts children's adjustment (Finkel et al., 2003). Although teens report loss of friends, maneuvering in new surroundings, and changing schools as stressful, factors such as maternal functioning (or the functioning of the major caregiver), family cohesiveness, and time at a current residence appear to be more important than the rate of mobility (i.e., dividing the number of moves a child experiences by the child's age) in predicting children's psychosocial adjustment (Finkel et al., 2003). In a nonrepresentative sample of 86 mother–child pairs, children, whose average age was 12, reported less loneliness and more positive relationships with peers when they lived longer at the current residence. Trusting relationships with mothers, cohesive family ties, and longer time at the current residence reduced children's concern about others evaluating them negatively and predicted children's self-esteem. Mothers' self-reports of depressive symptoms were associated with children's sadness, anxiety, and withdrawal. The number of moves did not predict children's adjustment in these areas (Finkel et al., 2003).

Military children may learn positive coping skills when faced with multiple relocations. A study examined 179 military parents' perceptions of teens' adjustment to multiple relocations. The average number of moves was 4.89, with a range of 1–18 moves. Military parents, from the four military branches, were recruited from four secondary schools with a large proportion of military teens. Seventy-five percent of parents considered relocations to have positively influenced their children's development, and parental perception of this positive influence increased as the number of moves increased. Also, parents perceived improved behavior as the frequency of moves (i.e., number of relocations per year of life) increased (Weber & Weber, 2005).

The education of children can affect whether and when military families move to a new location. If service members are scheduled to deploy soon after arriving at a new duty station, families may choose to remain where they are currently living or move to be close to extended family. If the date for the permanent change of duty station occurs after the beginning of the school year, families may choose to remain in their current location to allow children to complete the academic year at the same school. Finally, if the quality of education is better at the current location, families may remain in order not to negatively affect the education of their children (Department of Defense, 2011c).

Military teens perceive themselves as adaptable and comfortable talking with others because of frequent relocations, including moves outside of the United States (National Military Family Association, 2010). In some ways, military children share these and other characteristics with children of missionaries, business executives, and diplomats who live years in cultures outside of their "passport country" (Ender, 2002). They are often identified as "third culture kids" because they spend a significant number of their developmental years outside of their parents' culture(s) (Pollock & Van Reken, 2001).

Raised within the military community on self-sufficient bases and posts, whether the installations are in or outside of the United States, military children can feel in a world apart from their civilian cousins and peers. Then, upon adulthood or when their parent leaves the military, they are no longer officially part of the military community (unless they join themselves as an adult) and may not feel in synch with the larger civilian population. As a result, they can feel between cultures and may enter adulthood feeling in "a world between worlds" (Pollock & Van Reken, 2001, p. 29).

The Internet has facilitated the connection of military children, including those who are now adults, with others who have shared experiences. A quick search of the Internet for the term **military brat** (or Air Force brat, Army brat, Navy brat, or Marine Corps brat), a positive and affectionate term claimed by military children to refer to themselves and others growing up in the military (Wertsch, 1991), will show social networking and informational sites. Some military brats hold reunions based on the DoDEA school attended (Martin et al., 2000). Although the origin of the term is disputed, military children use "backronyms" including "'brave, resilient, adaptable, and trustworthy'" to describe the meaning of BRAT (Park, 2011, p. 67).

CHILD CARE

Provision of child care is an important daily issue that affects a large number of military families with children. In 2009, 42% of children of active duty parents and 27% of children of selected reserve parents were age 5 or under (DUSD, 2010).

In particular, dual-military, single parents, and those with children under the age of 6 have indicated that the availability of child care that is responsive to a parent's work schedule (e.g., overnight duty, early morning hours, evening hours) influences their decision to remain in the military. Child care is also important to military families with a civilian spouse who is or wants to be employed (Zellman, Gates, Moini, & Suttorp, 2009). Box 4.1 highlights how child care providers play an important role in supporting military families.

Found on most military installations, **child development centers (CDCs)** serve infants to 5-year-olds, and **family child care (FCC) providers** (called child development providers in the Navy) serve children from infancy to 12 years of age. CDC hours of operation are typically 6:00 AM to 6:30 PM (or 0600 to 1830 in military time). FCC homes may offer even longer hours as well as evening, nighttime, and weekend hours. Both CDCs and FCC providers may offer care on an hourly

---

BOX 4.1   BEST PRACTICES

Military parents have a wide array of strengths and skills and want the best for their children. However, corrosive stress, the experience of combat, and injuries (visible and invisible) can make it difficult for parents to function as they did before. Service members and spouses may feel overwhelmed or distracted. A parent may become depressed—unable to access feelings of competence or hope. Family life may become disorganized.

All these are natural responses to difficult situations. However, these changes can disrupt family relationships and a baby or toddler's sense of safety, security, and self.

For children under age 3, whose brains are literally being wired cognitively and emotionally, early relationships with parents and other caregivers are laying the foundation for the future. This is where you come in.

You may provide child care, health care, mental health services, or family support. This guide will support you in building respectful, responsive relationships with family members.

As you will see, the little things you say and do matter. When you genuinely listen, family members are less alone. When you reflect back their strengths, there is hope. When you play a game of peek-a-boo or sing a silly song with a child, you remind families (and yourself) of the joy babies and toddlers feel and give. As you build trust with family members, they are more likely to get the support and information they need to be more available to their babies and toddlers. The positive cycle continues. (ZERO TO THREE, 2009, p. 6)

---

basis (Zellman et al., 2009). **School-age care (SAC) programs**, along with resource and referral services, are also available to families. A military installation's website typically includes information about local CDCs, FCC providers, and SAC programs.

The military's systematic and multipronged approach to delivering child care has been lauded as a model for the nation, although that was not always the case (Pomper, Blank, Duff Campbell, & Schulman, 2005). The Military Child Care Act of 1989 is credited for drastically improving the quality of child care and its affordability (Zellman et al., 2009). As a result, all child care that comes under the purview of the DoD is subject to DoD and national accreditation standards. Ninety-eight percent of military CDCs have earned accreditation by the National Academy of Early Childhood Programs, a division of the National Association for the Education of Young Children, compared with 8–10% of community child care centers (Graham, 2010). It is estimated that military parents pay 25% less in child care fees than civilian parents (Castaneda & Harrell, 2008).

FCC providers also must meet DoD guidelines for certification (e.g., background check; certification in CPR and First Aid; an initial training that includes child abuse protection; fire, medicine, and program inspection; health screening), participate in ongoing training, and meet recertification requirements. In addition, home visits are conducted to ensure the safety and well-being of children. FCCs may be required to meet state licensing requirements and accreditation with the National Association for Family Child Care (Commander, Navy Region Mid Atlantic. n.d.). Nationally, only 1% of civilian FCC homes are accredited (Smith & Sarkar, 2008).

Care for school-age children is offered through before- and after-school school-age and youth programs (Zellman et al., 2009). Children can participate in physical activities and sports, complete homework, do arts and crafts, or access computers. Programs may be accredited through the National AfterSchool Association.

Single parents and dual-military parents have priority in accessing care by DoD policy. Most CDCs have waiting lists, and these families are given priority on them. Care for infants is the longest wait list, and infant care is the most expensive for centers although not for families. Fees are based on income, not on the cost of care, and so benefit most those in the junior ranks with the youngest children (Zellman et al., 2009). As of fall 2010, fees ranged from $56 to $137 per week for full-day care (Daniel, 2010).

Military spouses have raised concern about the limited capacity, limited hours, high costs of child care, and use of multiple types of child care (Castaneda & Harrell, 2008; Smith & Sarkar, 2008; Zellman et al., 2009). A study with a random, stratified sample of active duty, single parent, dual-military, and civilian-spouse families with children from infancy to age 12 found that parents of children under the age of 5 face a number of difficulties related to child care (Zellman et al., 2009). In this sample, more than 50% of parents had irregular work hours, forcing them to rely on multiple arrangements to meet their child care needs. Although single parents and dual-military parents received priority at CDCs, with their lack of evening, overnight, holiday, and weekend care, these facilities were the option least likely to fit military schedules. Military parents in this and other studies found child care too expensive (Castaneda & Harrell, 2008). Most parents did not know that their child care was subsidized, and some believed CDCs make a profit for the DoD, which they do not (Zellman et al., 2009).

FCC homes provide, at least in theory, longer hours of care and more flexible scheduling than CDCs. However, in practice, these benefits are unstable because if the provider becomes ill or has a family emergency, child care is compromised. Even a provider's back-up plan can be uncertain as it usually involves other FCC providers who may be at capacity and cannot accommodate an additional child (Zellman et al., 2009).

The DoD has initiated two programs, *Operation: Military Child Care* and *Military Child Care in Your Neighborhood*, to assist active duty, Reserve, and National Guard parents in locating child care when they live at a distance from military installations. The DoD partnered with the National Association of Child Care Resources and Referral Agencies (NACCRRA), a national organization for agencies that offer child care resources and referrals (http://www.naccrra.org), to offer these programs. Continued attention is needed, however, to examine more policy alternatives to meet the needs of families. Suggestions include offering subsidized slots at community centers, developing wraparound care, and partnering with community after-school programs (Zellman et al., 2009).

EDUCATION

In addition to child care, other concerns of military families are access to a quality education for their children and availability of regular after-school and summer activities.

A majority of school-age military children attend private or public civilian schools in the communities where they live or are home-schooled (DoDEA, 2011). Many attend school with other military children in a community near a military installation. However, a family may move in order to be closer to extended families during deployment. Going back home to be near grandparents or other extended family may result in a military child attending a school with students and staff unfamiliar with military life. Likewise, children of Reserve Component personnel typically attend civilian schools, many of which are located far from major military installations. They too may feel isolated from other children who do not have a parent serving in the military.

Military children may experience physical disruptions in their formal education, reflecting the high mobility of these military families. A parent's change of duty station may mean a change of schools for military children. Relocations can take families to military installations across the country. International moves may take children to countries where they do not speak the language and/or are unfamiliar with the local customs and culture.

Approximately 7% or 80,000 of the 1.2 million military children attend schools established specifically for DoD family members (DoDEA, 2011). The DoDEA, a DoD organization that falls under the direction of the Under Secretary of Defense for Personnel and Readiness and the Deputy Under Secretary of Defense for Military Community and Family Policy, manages these schools and the education programs for family members of U.S. military personnel and civilian DoD employees. The DoDEA consists of two separate school systems: the DoD Dependents Schools (DoDDS) overseas (located in Europe, Guam, and the Pacific) and the DoD DDESS in the United States.

The DoDEA schools provide students with a standardized curriculum that makes it easier for students of military families to move from school to school, particularly from a domestic school to an overseas school or vice versa. The DoDEA schools provide resources and support to help students cope with the stress of frequent moves and other stressors that come with being a military family member.

The DoD also provides resources to civilian schools relied on by military families so students not in a location with a DoD school can receive support coping with the challenges associated with military life. In recent years, the DoDEA has granted public schools throughout the nation grants for improving the education for military students and for providing professional development for educators in schools that serve military students (Department of Defense, 2011c).

Military children show academic strengths. In 2010, children in DoDEA schools, grades 3–11, exceeded national averages on standardized testing in math, science, language arts, social studies, and reading (DoDEA, 2010a, 2010c). In 2010, 68% of DoDEA students took the SAT test (a college admissions test), compared with a national rate of 47%. DoDEA students' average critical reading score exceeded and writing scores were slightly above the national average scores although the DoDEA math score was lower than the national average. African American and Hispanic DoDEA students continued to score higher (10–49 points out of a possible 800 points, or 1–6% higher) in each section of the SAT than their stateside civilian peers in 2010, continuing a multiyear trend (DoDEA, 2010b). Reasons for this difference in performance are not clear but may reflect the fact that military children avoid some of the hardships that disproportionately affect ethnic minority families in the civilian population: parental unemployment, limited parental education, extreme poverty, lack of access to health care, poor-quality schools, discrimination, and/or disadvantaged or dangerous neighborhoods.

In addition to the process of saying good-bye to friends and making new ones because of relocation, children and their parents have had to contend with differences in education policy across states. However, the recent Interstate Compact on Educational Opportunities for Military Children is beginning to establish continuity in many education policies and practices across the 39 participating states (Military Interstate Children's Compact Commission, 2011; see Chapter 10 for more information on this compact).

Teachers and other school staff members play an important role in the lives of children. Learning provides a positive focus, and the school day provides a structure and a routine that can benefit children. School teachers, counselors, and administrators may find the following recommendations (Chandra et al., 2010; DoDEA, 2011; "Educator's Guide to the Military Child During Deployment," n.d.; Harrison & Vannest, 2008) helpful in creating a school environment that supports military children and their families:

- Know which students have a parent or parents serving in the military.
- Talk with parents to learn about past, current, or future deployments and relocations. Let parents know you appreciate their service and are there to support their children during any transitions.
- Recognize that adjusting to transitions throughout the cycle of deployment take time and patience.
- Recognize signs when students are having difficulty adjusting.
  - Extensive clinginess
  - Disruptions in eating and sleeping patterns
  - Misbehavior
  - Headaches, stomachaches, other unexplained pains
  - Difficulties in speech
  - Withdrawn or aggressive behavior
  - Excessively active
- Recognize more serious signs of difficulty coping.
  - Not resuming typical levels of academic engagement
  - Continuing intense emotional responses

- Continuing depression, withdrawal, noncommunication
- Disturbing drawings or writings
- Hurting themselves intentionally or appearing likely to hurt others
- Significant weight loss or gain
- Poor hygiene or personal care
- Symptoms of alcohol or drug use
- Anxious or aggressive
- Act.
  - Speak with parents about observations.
  - Consult with administrators and knowledgeable community supports.
  - Be sensitive to students' needs.
  - Provide structure in the classroom and offer time to listen to students.
  - Use objectivity about war and conflict, setting aside personal beliefs in order to help students.
  - Focus on safety and security of students and parents.
  - Use patience, consider briefly reducing workload for students, and offer tutoring or mentoring support.
  - Be approachable, attentive, and knowledgeable about children, relocation, and deployment; acknowledge and normalize their feelings.
  - Be culturally sensitive.
  - Encourage appropriate ways to handle feelings such as anger.
  - Weave deployments into subjects (e.g., geography, social studies, cultures).
- Ensure school is a safe place for military children: maintain routines, be sensitive, and encourage all staff to be aware of needs of military children.
- Encourage parents to visit the classroom. Military parents could discuss their jobs or their knowledge of another culture.
- If feasible, invite the deployed parent to communicate with the class. If not possible, encourage the class to write a letter to the parent.
- Maintain communication, to the extent possible, with the nondeployed parent about the student's class work.
- If concerned about the nondeployed parent's adjustment to the deployment, encourage his or her use of resources.
- Encourage parents to attend school activities and parent–teacher conferences.

Box 4.2 lists resources for school staff about military children and support for military families.

BOX 4.2   BEST PRACTICES

RESOURCES FOR SCHOOL STAFF

Learn More about Military Families

Access the DoDEA's *Students at the Center* website for information and resources for school leaders, military families, and military leaders: http://www.militaryk12partners.dodea.edu/studentsAtTheCenter/

Building Resilient Kids, developed and offered through the Military Child Initiative at Johns Hopkins School of Public Health: http://www.jhsph.edu/mci

Stay Updated

Military Child Education Coalition: http://www.militarychild.org

Military Impacted Schools Association: http://www.militaryimpactedschoolsassociation.org

Department of Defense Education Activity: http://www.dodea.edu
Military Homefront: http://www.militaryhomefront.dod.mil

Direct Students and Families to Resources

Military OneSource: http://www.militaryonesource.com
Military Youth on the Move: http://apps.mhf.dod.mil/pls/psgprod/f?p=MYOM:HOME:
    1177610008336629
Student Online Achievement Resources: http://www.soarathome.org
Tutor.com for U.S. military families: http://www.tutor.com/military

DEPLOYMENT

Since 9/11, the optempo of the military has increased significantly compared with the prior decade, particularly for the National Guard and Reserves. As a result, the number of children affected is larger than in prior conflicts since World War II (Committee on the Initial Assessment of Readjustment Needs of Military Personnel, Veterans, and Their Families; Board on the Health of Selected Populations; Institute of Medicine [Committee on the Initial Assessment of Readjustment Needs], 2010).

Over a million U.S. military children have experienced separation from their parents because of wars since 2001 (MacDermid Wadsworth, 2010). Combat deployment and the possibility of multiple deployments have been continuous factors in the lives of many military children, complicated by uncertainty of length and by parental injury or death or the threat of them (Cozza, 2009b). Box 4.3 illustrates that deployed parents, and grandparents, worry about maintaining their relationships with their children and their grandchildren.

Research on the implications of these factors is limited although we will learn more as studies undertaken during OEF/OIF/OND are completed and results published. Evidence prior to and since OEF/OIF suggests that deployments influence children's academic functioning, behavior, and psychological well-being (Sheppard, Malatras, & Israel, 2010). Studies on children and deployment undertaken in the 1990s suggested that symptoms of distress exhibited by children did not meet clinical significance (Committee on the Initial Assessment of Readjustment Needs, 2010). In many studies, the impact of deployment was small on the variables measured, yet statistically significant. Results of studies conducted in the last decade are noting possible effects on children of multiple parental deployments and total number of months of deployment. Woven throughout studies is the recognition of the important roles parents and parental adjustment have on children's well-being.

BOX 4.3   VOICES FROM THE FRONTLINE

REFLECTIONS OF A MILITARY GRANDPARENT

When I was in Iraq I held a monthly parent forum. Parents were worried their kids didn't know them. For some it's true. When a child is 5 and his mom or dad has been deployed three times that doesn't leave much time to spend together. Our grandchildren were ages 10, 4, and 2 when I deployed. I went from being active in their lives to talking with them during occasional calls and the mail. I worried, too.

Colonel Rick Campise, Col, USAF, BSC
Commander, 559th Medical Group

Academics

Prior to OEF/OIF, studies of the effect of deployment on children's academic functioning either showed no effect or a slight decrease (Sheppard et al., 2010). For example, the math scores of children of deployed Army enlisted and officers showed a small 1–2 point decrease compared to scores of children whose military parent had not deployed. The largest decrease occurred for children who experience parental deployments over 3 months, total parental deployment of 7 or more months within the last 4 years, maternal deployment, and total maternal deployment of 7 or more months (Lyle, 2006).

Since the beginning of OEF/OIF, three known published studies have looked at military children's academic functioning during parental deployment. A study of academic achievement of children in DoD schools from 2002 to 2006 whose active duty parent was in the Army (Engel, Gallagher, & Lyle, 2010) found similar effects as the study noted above (Lyle, 2006). The decreases in academic achievement were small, from less than 1% to 1.5% points, but significant. Decreases in test scores in math and science were greater than those for language, arts, social studies, and reading.

A second study, sponsored by the National Military Family Association, considered the academic engagement (e.g., arrive at school on time, complete homework) of 11- to 17-year-olds. Academic engagement was more problematic as children aged, when there was poorer quality of communication between the caregiver and youth, and when the caregiver reported poorer mental health (Chandra et al., 2011).

Finally, in 2008, Chandra and colleagues conducted 24 focus groups of teachers, counselors, and administrative staff at 12 schools that served a high concentration of Army families assigned to one of two installations with high deployment rates (Chandra, Martin, Hawkins, & Richardson, 2010). They also conducted telephone interviews with 16 school staff members (i.e., teachers, counselors, and administrative staff) who worked in areas with higher numbers of National Guard and Reservists. What follows are themes from the interviews, although not every focus group or interviewee mentioned each theme.

Overall, school personnel noted that many military children were able to handle the stress of deployment well, yet some children had difficulty with functioning well at school. School personnel thought three points contributed to military children experiencing difficulty with deployment: when they were unsure of the length of the deployment, when they experienced increased stress at home, and when they perceived the parent at home had difficulty adjusting (Chandra et al., 2010). Moreover, school personnel concluded that parental deployment isolates children of National Guard and Reservists who may know few, if any, other children in their school with a deployed military parent. Some children's sadness and anger were apparent in classroom and peer interactions. Increased number of chores at home (e.g., helping with younger siblings more) and taking care of the nondeployed parent emotionally at times interfered with children's functioning at school. School personnel noted that depressed adult caregivers at home did not attend school activities, did not assist children with homework, and at times kept children at home "as a source of comfort" rather than sending them to school (p. 221). Although school personnel recognized the resilience of some children to do well in school after an initial adjustment period, they noted the toll multiple and extended deployments were having even on these children. In subsequent deployments children who demonstrated resilience during the first deployment became "less engaged in school work" and engaged in more risk-taking behaviors (p. 221). During the reintegration phase when the deployed parent returned, school personnel noticed that some children had difficulties in adjusting. Finally, school personnel saw school as a safe haven for those military children who experienced instability at home (Chandra et al., 2010).

Behavior and Psychological Well-Being

Studies of military children and deployment conducted during OEF/OIF have focused on preschool children (Chartrand, Frank, White, & Shope, 2008), school-age children, and teens (Chandra et al., 2011; Huebner & Mancini, 2005; Huebner, Mancini, Wilcox, Grass, & Grass, 2007) but not on infants and toddlers (Cozza, 2009a). The following sections address children's worry about parental safety during deployment, psychological distress and behavioral problems, parental factors influencing child adjustment during deployment, child maltreatment, and evidence of resilience and maturity.

Children's Worry about Parental Safety

Children under the age of 10 in the United States have lived during an era in which their country has been responding to terrorism and using its military on extended combat operations. Likewise, youth, who now are between the ages of 11 and 18, were toddlers, preschoolers, or first and second graders when the World Trade Center was attacked and the United States launched OEF and OIF. These events prompted, and may continue to prompt, civilian and military children to worry about their own and their loved ones' safety.

Military children worry about their parent's well-being when they are apart. Worry can be evident even during the predeployment phase. Very young children may show their stress by clinging more to parents, crying more, and resisting engaging in their daily eating and sleeping routines. Preschoolers often are concerned about practical matters such as where will mommy sleep or what will daddy eat and may become confused, angry, or sad when they ask their parents to stay home but their parents leave on deployment anyway. Their stress is manifested in regression to earlier behaviors, becoming aggressive or demanding, and behaving in attention-seeking ways (Lincoln, Swift, & Shorteno-Fraser, 2008).

School-age children can become very concerned about their parent's physical safety when "going to war." They may express volatile emotions, have trouble sleeping, be distracted by worry, and have difficulty focusing on school work (Lincoln et al., 2008).

Teens are clearly knowledgeable about the possible injury and death of a parent deployed to a combat zone and media accounts of combat and danger in theater sustain this awareness (Huebner & Mancini, 2005). They may act out, play "cool," and stop activities they once enjoyed (Lincoln et al., 2008). Although phone calls, e-mails, and face-to-face video calls can momentarily reassure children, once contact ends, uncertainty can reappear (Huebner et al., 2007).

How worries about parental safety can influence adolescents' psychological well-being and behaviors is illustrated in two studies. One study engaged teens in focus groups (Huebner et al., 2007), and the other used a telephone interview design (Chandra et al., 2011).

In the first study, 107 adolescents between the ages 12 and 18, attending a free camp for military children experiencing parental deployment, participated in focus groups to discuss their experiences. About a third of the teens described signs consistent with depression (e.g., losing interest in activities, isolation, changes in eating and sleeping) and higher anxiety (e.g., ruminating on the deployed parent's safety and daily life). These signs, along with changes in roles and responsibilities and increased emotionality in the family added up to stressful situations for these youth. The 27 youth who described getting angry and lashing out often also described trying to hide their emotions in order to protect the nondeployed parent, siblings, or friends (Huebner et al., 2007).

The second study likewise found evidence of increased anxiety among 1507 military adolescents who were between 11 and 17 years old. Of these adolescents 30% reported symptoms of anxiety, a higher percent than what has been found in another, albeit somewhat younger, youth sample (Chandra et al., 2011).

In Box 4.4, Dr. Patricia Lester notes the importance of parents being tuned into the concerns and worries of their children. Rather than diminishing children's fears, avoiding discussions of children's possible worries and questions can actually magnify fear and feed anxiety. For example, one of the authors of this textbook recalls a situation during peacetime in which a mother sought guidance because her 6-year-old sobbed and would not be consoled whenever the family discussed the upcoming, routine deployment. She was encouraged to ask her son what he thought deployment meant. After listening to their son, the mother and father realized that he had heard the family and neighbors talk about a recent accident aboard a deployed ship in which dozens of sailors had died. As a result, their son equated deployment with ships exploding and sailors dying. Given this understanding of deployment, his reactions were justified and warranted, particularly when the adults

BOX 4.4   BEST PRACTICES

SUPPORTING CHILDREN BY SUPPORTING THEIR FAMILIES

Creating a shared story about deployment experiences and having that story to share builds resilience of families and their children.

Today's military families are experiencing understandable reactions to the challenges they face. The stress of wartime and multiple deployments reverberates within families.

We created FOCUS to support children and teens by enhancing the strengths of families in areas of emotional regulation (identifying and understanding emotions, communication, problem solving, goal setting, and managing reminders of deployment and combat stress). Families talk, play, and work with resiliency trainers to create their family's unique story of deployment experiences, challenges, and successes.

One of our challenges is always how to make concepts concrete and specific that children at different ages can understand. For example, there is a lot of discussion in sessions about how to use a calendar so deployment isn't one big overwhelming chunk of time for children. It's complicated because there is often uncertainty about return dates. So our resiliency trainers work together with families to come up with ideas that are not linked to a specific day.

A little boy with a Marine Corps dad liked to wear his dad's boots. At one session, the family brought in Dad's boots and outlined them. They then made a map from their home to Iraq. Each month the little boy put down the outline of his dad's boots on a path showing Dad coming home. It allowed him to mark time and see it pass concretely.

Children have questions about danger and risk. When a child asks, "Will my dad (or mom) die?" it can be hard to know what to say. Many parents—like most of us—try to avoid questions like this. So we do lots of talking together with families to help parents know what to say. A family with a younger child (age 3–7) might bring in their service member's flak vest and helmet and talk about training and how the deployed parents' buddies will help keep him safe.

As a child gets to be older, the conversation shifts. The parent who is at home might acknowledge, "I get worried, too," then share ideas of what helps them when they are worried and suggest, "Let's make a plan together about what we can do when we get worried."

Over the years, we've learned a lot about resilience from military families. One of my favorite stories is about a family in Okinawa who came in with a 4-year-old. When the child was 2, his dad deployed. It was a tough time, in part because Dad had always given him his "special good-night kiss." Mom couldn't do it right. This time the family came in advance of Dad's next deployment saying, "We want to make this transition smoother."

Dr. Patricia Lester
Director of Family Resiliency Training for Military Families (FOCUS)

around him seemed nonchalant about what he perceived to be a clear possibility of his father dying at sea. Once the parents realized what their son thought and feared, they explained what deployment was, that the explosion on the other ship was atypical, and the ways in which the ship's Captain and crew made sure everyone aboard was safe during deployment. The parents reported that after this conversation their son no longer displayed signs of panic when discussing the upcoming deployment and, when the deployment began, displayed an appropriate level of sadness.

Psychological Distress and Behavioral Problems   Studies of children who experienced parental deployment in peacetime and wartime prior to OEF/OIF indicated that children exhibited increases in externalizing and internalizing symptoms, including depression and anxiety, but that they typically did not need clinical assistance (Cozza, Chun, & Polo, 2005). Studies of children since OEF and OIF are, as of yet, limited in number; however, their findings are consistent with those prior to the recent conflict (MacDermid Wadsworth, 2010).

Young children, who could be separated from a deployed parent for a length of time that represents one-third or half of their lives, may exhibit confusion, fear, anxiety, and clinginess (Barker & Berry, 2009). In a study focused on the adjustment of preschoolers (Chartrand et al., 2008), researchers examined parent and teacher reports about children, ages 1.5–5, enrolled in Marine Corps CDC. They found that 3- to 5-year-olds with a deployed parent (but not 1.5- to 3-year-olds) displayed more behavioral problems than those of the same age whose parent was not deployed. In another study of 57 Army families with children under the age of 4, parents reported an increase in behavioral problems during deployment. Although young children showed confusion and distress when the deployed parent returned home, the majority of parents indicated that problematic behaviors disappeared within 3 weeks; however, 31% of children showed continuing attachment problems past this time. Parents of these children listed only one or two behaviors that persisted, such as children not staying in their own bed, not wanting comfort from the returning parent, not wanting the returning parent to leave the home, or preferring the other parent or caregiver in lieu of the returning parent (Barker & Berry, 2009).

Deployment is associated with an increase in the number of outpatient medical visits for mental and behavioral health care for military children. A study of medical records of over 642,000 3- to 8-year-old children of active duty personnel during fiscal years 2006 and 2007 indicated that there was an 11% increase in outpatient medical visits during a parental deployment. Diagnoses of behavioral disorders increased 18% and stress disorders increased 19% with a deployed parent. During the same time, however, there was an 11% decrease in outpatient visits for routine care or for physical complaints such as colds. Rates were increased for children of male service members compared with children of female service members, for children of married parents compared with children of single parents, and for older than younger children. Researchers suggest that these results may be explained by mothers being more familiar with children's typical behaviors versus fathers or extended family members in the case of single parents, and by older children having a greater range of emotional and behavioral responses. Girls and boys did not differ in the number of visits (Gorman, Eide, & Hisle-Gorman, 2010).

Voices From the Frontline

DISENTANGLING THE IMPACT OF DEPLOYMENT

I've been a youth and family researcher for years. I started studying military youth and families 5 years ago. Lots of what I'd learned over the years about children and families was transferrable. Although military youth have some unique experiences, it is also important to remember that they are children and youth first and follow the same developmental milestones. That information can help any researcher or provider in working with these families.

Visiting military families on installations and talking with them by phone gave me insight into their experiences. Aside from deployment and reintegration, these include frequent moves and transitions to new homes, schools, and communities that can be a source of difficulty but also a source of strength.

We still have relatively little information on the experiences of military families. Our first project at RAND [a nonprofit institution focused on research and analysis] was Children on the Home Front. The National Military Family Association funded us to explore the lives of military youth. In the summer and fall of 2007, we did a pilot study in which we surveyed youth attending the association's Operation Purple summer camps and their parent or primary caregiver at home. The next year, we conducted a larger study, with 1500 families, to assess the impact of parental deployment and reintegration and followed youth and families over a year.

We've also worked with the U.S. Army to learn what teachers and other school staff see in the many hours they spend each day with military and other youth. Recently, the Department of Defense has funded us to look at how families from all services and components fare before, during, and after a specific period of deployment. Unlike studies before, this research will allow us to disentangle the specific effect of deployment from other life experiences and to surface the factors that contribute to family resilience.

As we've been studying the functioning and well-being of military youth and teens, we have learned a lot about how they are handling deployment. We assessed youth anxiety symptom levels and found that one-third reported symptoms in the moderate or elevated range as opposed to 15% of civilian kids. Colleagues working with younger children have found the same thing. The more months a parent was deployed, the more symptoms of anxiety were reported.

We've also found a strong relationship between the mental health of the nondeployed parent and child. This is true in the literature about civilian families, too. In military families, we see that parents (or other caregivers) at home often put themselves last. The fact that the challenges of the parents impact children has led us to recommend that the at-home parent also receive support throughout deployment. We also recommend that we continue to study military families as systems and examine how the experiences of each family member influence others in the family.

If you are going to work with military families:

- Bring the principles and knowledge you have gained working with other families.
- Consider the strengths that each family brings and try to build on these assets to help families confront the stress of deployment.
- Get a little smart about resources available to families. If you work in a community with an installation, don't be intimidated. Make a connection and learn what resources are available. And remember that most families don't live on installations—they live in the community. They are your neighbors, and your support means a lot.

To work with or study military youth and families you don't have to know the entire lexicon or military structure. You do have to listen, learn about, and understand their experience.

Anita Chandra, Dr.PH, Behavioral Scientist
Manager, Behavioral and Social Sciences Group, RAND Corporation

Chandra and colleagues, who conducted the telephone interview study of military adolescents referred to earlier, asked both adolescents and their nondeployed caregivers questions about challenges, behaviors, and emotional responses. The researchers found more reported difficulties and problematic behavior during deployment and reintegration among the middle and older adolescence groups compared to the younger youth in the sample and among girls (Chandra et al., 2011). According to caregivers, youth experienced more challenges during deployment and reintegration as the total number of parental deployments increased; however, data provided by the youth did not show this outcome. Caregivers who reported poorer mental health also indicated more child emotional difficulties and family functioning problems; youth of these caregivers reported greater anxiety and emotional difficulties. Finally, compared with a 2001 national sample of children in the United States, military children in this sample exhibited significantly more emotional and behavioral difficulties.

A study of Army and Marine Corps families explored the link between parent combat deployment and parental distress on the behavioral and emotional adjustment of their school-aged children who were between 6 and 12 years old (Lester et al., 2010). The children either had a currently deployed parent or a recently returned parent. The military children in this sample did not differ from community norms for girls and boys in depression scores or in internalizing or externalizing symptoms. They did, however, show significantly higher levels of anxiety; 32% of children with a recently returned parent and 25% of children with a currently deployed parent had anxiety symptoms in the clinical range. Girls whose active duty parent was currently deployed had a higher externalizing score than girls with a recently returned parent, whereas boys were opposite. Boys with a recently returned parent showed higher externalizing scores than boys with a currently deployed parent. The total number of combat months predicted depression and externalizing behaviors, but not internalizing behaviors, in children.

Sixty-five youths from grades 4–8 who attended a charter school for military children located near a Naval Air Stations-Joint Reserve Base and their parents participated in a study on adjustment and coping strategies (Morris & Age, 2009). Better adjustment was associated with higher levels of effortful control (i.e., being able to pay attention and inhibit or use behavioral responses as strategies to regulate emotions and behavior) and perceived maternal support. The study also indicated that compared to a community sample, military youth, at least during an extended period of wartime, are at risk for conduct problems (Morris & Age, 2009).

Military spouses who participated in the 2008 *Survey of Active Duty Spouses* were asked to choose two of their children most impacted by deployment and answer questions about them. Over half of spouses reported their first and second child most impacted by deployment respectively coped well or very well with the deployment. Yet, 23% reported their most impacted children coped poorly or very poorly (DMDC, 2009). Sixty percent of spouses described their most impacted child as showing increased fear/anxiety, 57% reported increases in problem behaviors at home, and 41% reported increased anger about the deployed parent's military duty. However, children also showed growth in closeness to family members (47%), responsibility and independence (approximately one-third), and closeness to friends (29%). Box 4.5 lists ideas to help children and parents maintain their relationship during deployment.

Parental Factors   Family and parental factors influence children's lives and how they cope with the stress of deployment (Sheppard et al., 2010). How well children adjust to the stressor of deployment and to many other stressors depends to a great extent upon the responses of their parents. Parents who respond with an attitude that conveys a sense of security and confidence and

---

BOX 4.5   TIPS FROM THE FRONTLINE

MAINTAINING THE PSYCHOLOGICAL PRESENCE OF THE MILITARY PARENT FOR CHILDREN

- Phone calls, webcams, e-mails, and letters are important in maintaining psychological presence and emotional connection among family members. However, they are not always possible, particularly according to a child's schedule. So, children need other ways to maintain connection that they can access when they feel a need to be close to the deployed parent.
- Children benefit from concrete items such as photographs, videos, and audio messages that can be prepared before the deployment. Some children like deployment dolls that have a clear plastic cover on the head where a photo of a parent can be placed, a life-sized poster board photo of a parent, or a stuffed toy replica of their deployed parent.
- Younger children can watch a video, DVD, or digital movie of the deployed parent reading their favorite books and doing everyday tasks such as shaving, putting on makeup, washing dishes, helping to pick up toys, and mowing the yard.
- Smell can also bring a person to mind; service members can give their child a T-shirt, hat, or scarf behind that "smells like" mom or dad. This article of clothing could be placed on a stuffed animal for younger children to cuddle.
- Family and service members can share an activity while apart, such as reading the same book or doing the same puzzle book.
- The deployed parent can leave "surprises" for children to find throughout the deployment.

with effective coping strategies serve as "a powerful protective factor" in the lives of their children. Parents who cope with the stressor and feel able to cope transmit to their children a repertoire of effective coping behaviors (MacDermid et al., 2008; Walsh, 2007).

Voices From the Frontline

FACILITATING A PREDEPLOYMENT PROGRAM FOR FAMILIES

"I love you."

When I worked at a Navy Family Services Center (now called a Fleet and Family Support Center), predeployment programs for families often occurred aboard ships so children would know where their mother or father was going to live during the deployment. The families toured the ship to see where the deploying parent would sleep, eat, and work. They often had dinner aboard ship for children to feel reassured that their parent would be cared for while they were separated. Afterward, while parents remained on the mess deck (i.e., the cafeteria) to discuss typical reactions of children to deployment and ways to support children during deployment, we divided the children and teens into small groups by ages and took them to different areas of the ship for their own age-appropriate program centered around normalizing feelings and identifying positive steps to take to when feeling sad or lonely during deployment.

I remember facilitating a group of 6- and 7-year-olds. During one activity in which the children were drawing pictures of feelings we asked them, "What would you like your dad to know or do with you before he leaves on deployment?" (At this time, this ship only accommodated male service members.) Children often said play a game, go to an amusement park, go swimming, or see a movie as did these children, except one. One 7-year-old boy said nothing. About 20 minutes later after the group was involved in another activity, he motioned to me with his finger to lean over to him. He whispered in my ear, "I want my daddy to tell me he loves me."

During the final part of the program, the children and children's group facilitators returned to the mess deck. The children sat with their parents and the facilitators reported back to the large group parents, in general and using no names, what the children did and said during their group time. When we reported that the 6- and 7-year-olds wanted to hear their fathers say, "I love you" to them, the mess deck went silent. The wisdom and the need of a Navy child for his daddy to "tell me that he loves me," educated all of us. From then on, "say 'I love you'" became my first message from children to deploying parents.

Karen Blaisure
Coauthor of this textbook and Professor of Family Studies at Western Michigan University

Positive parent–child relationships and family adjustment influence child adjustment (Lincoln et al., 2008). Studies conducted during OEF and OIF have demonstrated the close association between maternal or caregiver adjustment and children and youth adjustment to deployment (Chandra et al., 2011).

The study of Army and Marine Corps children and parents described earlier found that parental distress and children's level of distress were linked. The at-home mothers and the active duty parents (primarily fathers) had clinically significant differences in global distress, anxiety, and depression compared with community norms. At-home civilian mother distress predicted depression and externalizing and internalizing behaviors in children. PTSD symptoms in active duty parents predicted depression and internalizing and externalizing symptoms in children; and the greater the symptoms in the parent, the greater the symptoms in the child. Depression and anxiety symptoms in active duty parents predicted internalizing symptoms in children (Lester et al., 2010).

Multiple and dangerous deployments and the stress associated with them can result in the reduction of **parental efficacy**, that is parents' availability and effectiveness in caring for their children. One way this stress can be exhibited in some military families is in child maltreatment (Cozza, 2009a).

Since 2001, studies have found an increase in child maltreatment of military children during deployment. A state-level study of military families in Texas where there are numerous military installations showed an increased rate of child maltreatment before and after the first large-scale deployment after 9/11 (Rentz et al., 2007). Research on Army families with one or more instances of substantiated child maltreatment found the overall rate of child maltreatment was 42% greater during combat deployments compared to periods of time when soldiers were not deployed (Gibbs, Martin, Kupper, & Johnson, 2007). Of the types of substantiated child maltreatment, child neglect was the most common (Gibbs et al., 2007; McCarroll, Fan, Newby, & Ursano, 2008). In the 1990s, Army families experienced a decline in substantiated child neglect; however, the rate in 2004, after the initiation of OEF/OIF, approximated 1991 rates (McCarroll et al., 2008). Although researchers have not reached a consensus on how rates of child maltreatment in military families compare with nonmilitary families, the study of military families in Texas from 2000 to 2003 showed the rate of child maltreatment was higher for nonmilitary families (Rentz et al., 2007).

A major way to promote children's positive adjustment to deployment then is to support parents in acquisition and use of positive coping strategies themselves. Given the knowledge that deployment and reintegration are stressful times for families, additional prevention efforts should be focused on increasing positive parent–child relationships and family adjustment all along the deployment cycle (Chandra et al., 2011).

Results of focus groups with 71 military fathers from 14 military installations across the world suggest multiple messages to share with military families about father involvement. Leaving most of the parenting to wives, some military fathers become visitors in their children's lives by pulling back and having a "softened" role as a parent (Willerton, Schwarz, MacDermid Wadsworth, & Oglesby, 2011). Others, feeling guilty over not being the ideal involved father, may use permissive parenting practices. However, fathers can expand their ideas on involvement in their children's lives by not equating "good fathering" only with a physical presence but by focusing on quality time and managing their time well to facilitate involvement with children when home; planning and thinking creatively before deployment about ways to be psychologically present when deployed; and considering how to best reunite and resume day-to-day parenting with their children after deployment (Willerton, Schwarz, et al., 2011).

Overall   The research on deployment and children suggests that as a group military children are resilient; studies are not finding a majority of them having academic, behavioral problems, or psychological symptoms rising to clinical levels. However, for some military children, parental deployments, particularly combat deployment and multiple deployments, appear to be taking a toll in terms of academic outcomes, worry, internalizing and externalizing symptoms, anxiety, and depression. In summary, risk factors for problematic adjustment to deployment include combat deployments; multiple deployments; total number of deployed months (Chandra et al., 2011; Engel et al., 2010; and Lester et al., 2010; Lyle, 2006); nondeployed caregiver distress (Chandra et al., 2011); deployed parent post-traumatic stress symptoms, PTSD, and other mental health problems (Lester, Leskin, et al., 2011; Lester, Mogil, et al., 2011); and caregiver–youth communication (Chandra et al., 2011). Factors that promote resilience include positive parent–child relationships and communication, social support, overall family adjustment, parental emotional well-being, and effective parental coping skills (Lester et al., 2010; MacDermid et al., 2008).

It is important for service providers to be sensitive to the experience of multiple deployments and address all phases of deployment and to encourage development of capabilities and processes associated with resilience (Lester, Leskin, et al., 2011; Lester, Mogil, et al., 2011; Walsh, 2002). For example, providers can and do offer online, group education, family support groups, and one-on-one counseling to families in order for them to prepare for both the emotional side of deployment and reintegration and the practical side (e.g., financial and legal documents, communication plans, budgets); gain information and guidance on parenting; address family stress and find help for overwhelming emotions such as sadness, depression, anxiety, or anger; develop a shared meaning of deployments; promote close family relationships, goal setting, and problem solving; enhance family communication and address family conflict; and develop strong social support systems for all family members, including children and adolescents (Chandra et al., 2011; Gewirtz, Erbes, Polusny, Forgatch, & DeGarmo, 2011; Lester, Leskin, et al., 2011; MacDermid et al., 2008; Morris & Age, 2009). Service providers can identify and encourage parents to provide social support for one another. Those who work with children can notice changes in their appearance, attitude, or behaviors and then talk with parents to determine if they need assistance with self-care or with obtaining help for their children.

PARENTAL INJURY AND DEATH

As noted earlier, reintegration with a parent returning from deployment can be stressful for children. Combat-related injuries, both physical and psychological, pose additional challenges for family members, including children who must adapt to a new understanding of their parent (Gorman, Fitzgerald, & Blow, 2010).

Although few studies exist that examine children's adjustment to parental injury, medical and social service professionals who work with families of injured service members indicate that children will take their cue from their parents (Cozza, Chun, & Polo, 2005). Children benefit from developmentally appropriate information about the injury whether visible or invisible, reassurance of the parent's love for the child, encouragement to ask questions, and guidance on how to interact with the parent (e.g., "Mommy cannot give you a piggyback ride because she hurt her back, but she can play frisbee with you," or "sometimes Daddy forgets things so we write down what we will do tomorrow to help Daddy remember"). Parents may benefit from learning how to communicate with their children about injuries, particularly if the injury has interfered with the ability to interact sensitively. Resources for families can be found in Chapters 9 through 12.

Nonvisible injuries such as depression, anxiety, and posttraumatic stress symptoms may be particularly challenging for children. For example, a study of National Guard fathers demonstrated a link between increases in postdeployment PTSD symptoms and lower levels of effective parenting as reported by the service members (Gewirtz, Polusny, DeGarmo, Khaylis, & Erbes, 2010). Evidence points to PTSD negatively affecting parent–child relationship parenting through emotional numbing/avoidance (Ruscio, Weathers, King, & King, 2002). The symptom of hyperarousal may also play a factor. For example, service members or veterans with PTSD symptoms may withdraw from family interactions, do less monitoring of children, be less involved with children, and exhibit volatile emotions when stressed and when in conflict with children members (Gewirtz et al., 2010).

When a parent is injured, the parent–child attachment may be challenged by separations due to hospitalizations perhaps at great distances from the child's home, medical treatments, doctor and therapy visits, and rehabilitation. The child's developmental needs may be overlooked to a small or large degree, and may place the child at risk for psychological distress, and problems with attachment, regulation of emotions, behavior, health, and well-being. Social support for the family improves the quality of life for its members and supports child development. Training, resources, and support can increase rehabilitation professionals' ability to involve children in the rehabilitation process (Gorman, Fitzgerald, & Blow, 2010).

Service members, veterans, and families may benefit from education on how to help children adjust well to a parent's injury. As Dr. Lynette Fraga explains in Box 4.6, even very young children

BOX 4.6   BEST PRACTICES

BEGINNING MILITARY PROJECTS AT ZERO TO THREE

Even the youngest baby is affected by deployment, illness, injury, and loss.

My work creating and directing Military Projects at Zero to Three began from a personal perspective. I'm from a military family. After 9/11, I knew from my personal and professional experience that we had something important to offer families and their young children experiencing separation and loss.

As we started Military Projects, we went to Fort Riley, Kansas, where up to 80% of service members were being deployed, so we could listen and learn from families. Many people we talked with believed children under 3 are too young to notice when a parent is deployed.

Our first projects focused on communicating the message that even the youngest children are impacted by separation and supporting families around deployment. The Department of Defense was a strong and welcome partner.

Fairly quickly, within a year or two, our focus shifted to injury, illness, and loss due to deployment and what these might mean for young children. We had to be both proactive and reactive as families experienced multiple deployments and reintegrations. Coming Together Around Military Families (CTAMF) continues to be a growing initiative at Zero to Three. We are developing products including written materials, videos, and online training to help parents and professionals be able to recognize and respond to the impact of trauma, grief, and loss on very young children. A core part of this work is our Duty to Care (DTC) training that brings together professionals from a variety of disciplines including health, mental health, family support, and early childhood professionals to create collaborations with the goal of supporting families as they support their young children.

This has been uncharted territory for our organization and our field. My hope is that as we support the resilience of the next generation of military families, we can use what we are learning to support other populations experiencing great stress such as foster care families and those in which a parent is incarcerated. There are many families in our country under stress who need support.

Lynette Fraga, PhD
Former Chief Program Officer, ZERO TO THREE

are affected by deployment, parental injury, and loss. Resources and training such as those offered by Zero to Three will continued to be needed into the foreseeable future.

Approximately 6000 service members have died since 9/11 (DMDC, 2011d, 2011e, 2011f). We know very little about how children adjust to the death of a military parent. In general, however, bereavement is a risk factor for children developing emotional or behavior problems (Cozza et al., 2005).

The National Child Traumatic Stress Network (2008a, 2008b) has published a series of manuals for medical providers, educators, and parents on traumatic grief in children. These publications remind us that children may show grief in different and multiple ways. They may regress in behaviors, show sadness, become fearful, develop problems in school, notice "aches and pains," be moody, show anger and irritation, withdraw, and/or isolate themselves. They may "not be themselves" as they do uncharacteristic behaviors.

Young children whose parents die while deployed may not initially understand the permanence of death. They often seek the comfort of their closest caregivers and need extra attention and reassurance. School-age children may ask lots of questions about their parent's death and about death in general. Teens may try to hide their emotions (National Child Traumatic Stress Network, 2008a, 2008b).

Some children may develop traumatic grief, that is, exhibiting symptoms of posttraumatic stress whether initially or months following a parent's death, given it is unexpected, sudden, or traumatic. These symptoms can include children experiencing intrusive thoughts about the death or reliving the details of the death, if known; avoiding conversation, activities, or reminders of the parent or the parent's death; and startling easily, being "on alert," and becoming nervous, jumpy, distracted, and angry. If symptoms persist, appear after an initial stable period, or they disrupt daily life (e.g., attending school, playing with friends, participating in or enjoying activities), counseling may be appropriate (National Child Traumatic Stress Network, 2008a, 2008b).

Given the public nature of a military death during wartime, children and other family members may experience unexpected or unwanted intrusions while they are mourning. Families have a right to as much privacy as they wish, including privacy from the media. Children who hear someone say that their "parent died 'needlessly' in an 'unnecessary' war may find it much harder to accept and integrate that death than [children] whose parent's death is considered 'noble' or 'heroic.'…[O]lder teenagers may have their own opinions and feelings about the war, and these may either ease or complicate their grief" (National Child Traumatic Stress Network, 2008b, p. 4).

Following the death of a loved one, parents can assist their children by providing a sense of security by being physically and emotionally close and predictable; being patient; "listening" to what children's behaviors are saying they need; encouraging expression of feelings; knowing that grief and other feelings can get mixed up; and being aware of possible reminders of the death at unexpected times. Parents can also promote positive adjustment by supporting children's connection to the person who has died by talking and looking at photographs and videos; providing age-appropriate explanations; spending time with each child and considering their individual needs; and informing other adults about the children's experiences. Parents may need to advocate for children at school; encourage children's involvement in a project or organization, possibly one related to the interests of the person who died; and encourage bonds with other children by attending camps or support groups for children who are grieving (National Child Traumatic Stress Network, 2008a).

Death of a service member brings other changes in military children's lives. If living on a military installation, the family will need to move within a year and the move may also bring a change in schools. With a death of a parent comes a possibility of losing touch with that parent's side of the family. Finally, the remaining parent will need to support and guide children as they realize the loved one will not be there for small and major milestones in life (National Child Traumatic Stress Network, 2008a).

Adults are also encouraged to care for themselves by seeking social support; exercising, eating healthy foods, and sleeping adequately; showing feelings; and modeling healthy coping (e.g., "I miss Daddy right now, that's why I'm crying. Let's take a walk together because I like being with you."). They are also encouraged to seek professional support if necessary (National Child Traumatic Stress Network, 2008a).

The risk of injury and death of a parent is a stressor known by many military children. They may also experience changes brought about by relocation and separation from a parent due to long duty hours, TDYs, or deployments. Positive family dynamics, social support, and finding meaning from such adversities can make a difference in the resilience of children. If you work with children directly, you know the importance of acceptance, listening, and guidance in supporting them through life's minor and major stressors. Likewise, by building trusting, responsive relationships with adult family members, you may have a positive influence on their ability to support their children. As a helping professional, what you know and what you say and do matters to families.

SUMMARY

- Nearly two million children in the United States have a parent who is serving in the Active or Reserve Component of the military.
- Even in the face of relocations, separations, and risks of injury and death, the majority of military families adapt, and their resilience is evident.
- Studies are needed to identify the particular strengths families use to overcome stressful situations.
- Children who grow up in the military culture on average move every 2–3 years. Evidence suggests that children's adjustment to moving is influenced by family cohesiveness and time at a current residence.
- Military child care includes CDCs, FCC providers, SAC programs, and resource and referral services.
- Military children attend civilian schools with a small or large presence of other military children, and DoDEA schools. Overall, military children attending DoDEA schools compare very favorably to civilian children.

- Teachers and other school staff members play important roles in supporting military children during relocation and parental deployments.
- Combat deployment and multiple deployments have been continuous factors in the lives of many military children, complicated by uncertainty of length and by parental injury or death or the threat of them.
- Evidence exists of children's positive adjustment to deployment as well as evidence of the "wear and tear" of multiple deployments, complicated deployments, and compromised parenting.
- When a parent is injured, the parent–child attachment may be challenged and a child's developmental needs may be overlooked. Social support for the family can promote attachment and positive child development.
- Little is known about how children adjust to the death of a military parent. In general, bereavement is a risk factor for children developing emotional or behavior problems.
- A parent and close adults can provide important emotional support and guidance to children whose parent or other loved one has died.
- Professionals who work with military families can focus interventions and supports toward decreasing identified risk factors and enhancing protective factors related to children's adjustment.

EXERCISES

1. Investigate academic databases and websites for more information about third culture kids. For example, the U.S. Department of State's Family Liaison Office has a webpage on third culture kids, at http://www.state.gov/m/dghr/flo/c21995.htm.
2. If you live near a school district with a high percentage of military children or near a DoDEA school, interview two elementary or secondary teachers about their experiences with military children in their classes. How do their experiences compare or contrast with those described in this chapter? What tips do they have for supporting military children?
3. Prepare tip sheets for extended family members about children and deployment and how to support children of different ages when their parent or another loved one deploys. Be sure to include tips on how to support a child who lives at a distance from grandparents, aunts, uncles, and cousins.
4. Identify local programs and support systems for children whose parents serve in the Reserve Component (i.e., National Guard and Reserve).
5. Talk with a teenager who has grown up in the military culture. Prepare topics to discuss based on information presented in this chapter. For example, "many military teens will have attended multiple schools by your age. Tell me your experiences about attending school." Compare what you learned from this teenager with what you have studied.

5

Ways of Thinking About Family Stress and Resilience

In Chapter 5, you will

- Meet Froma Walsh, a clinical researcher and practitioner, who draws on stress and resilience theories in working with families
- Learn how individual and family stress, coping, and resilience are conceptualized
- Discover how stress theories and applied models of stress and resilience help us better understand and support military families
- Practice applying concepts to a case study example of a military family

Meet

Froma Walsh, MSW, PhD, Codirector, Chicago Center for Family Health, University of Chicago

All of my work has been directed to understand how families best support each other in overcoming adversity. My family resilience approach expands the mental health field's focus on symptomatic individuals to facilitate the family's powerful role in their recovery. In military families, like all families, serious crises or an overload of stress can break down their functioning. It can happen to any family in situations of trauma, tragic loss, disruptive transitions, or chronic disabling conditions. Although some individual lives and bonds are shattered, what is remarkable is the potential for individual and family resilience—the capacity to rebound—and even grow stronger—when family members pull together as a team to master their challenges. Families hold the keys to resilience.

My conviction in the potential for family resilience goes back to my own childhood experience. My parents faced devastating losses and ongoing financial hardship, yet they supported each other and loved me well, encouraging me always to reach for the best. My father had a disability and experienced crushing disappointments, yet he didn't lose his "can-do" spirit. When a fire destroyed our apartment building, we lost everything and were homeless for a time. The kindness and generosity of others were "lifelines" in our recovery. Our adversity taught us valuable lessons: that we may not be able to control bad things that happen in life, but our resilient response is what matters. And that resilience is nurtured by caring relationships—with our loved ones and with our communities.

As I grew up, people commented on my resilience, but assumed I was strong despite my troubled family situation. Our society has a myth of "the rugged individual." We tend to credit individuals for success and blame families for problems. Early resilience research focused on individual character traits for hardiness and assumed that distressed families were hopelessly dysfunctional. But my own resilience was due to the strength my family rallied through hard times. And as resilience research advanced, it became clear that a systemic perspective is required, recognizing family influences in resilience.

The family is the primary resource in the recovery when someone has suffered trauma, with physical and/or psychological wounds. By strengthening the family, we build "lifelines"—supportive bonds for healing and resilience. We tap positive resources in the kinship network, including children and grandparents, aunts and uncles, and godparents. We recruit positive role models and mentors, draw out stories of resilience in overcoming past adversity to inspire best efforts, and we encourage important family members to support each other. More than coping, or just surviving trauma or stressful conditions, gaining resilience enables families and their members to thrive. And they become more resourceful in meeting future challenges.

Most research funding is directed at problems—we need to redirect attention from how families fail to how they can succeed. It is important to see families not as damaged, but as challenged by adversity, with the potential to repair and rebuild their lives. We have much to learn from families that overcome adversity to inform our efforts to help those who are struggling. To understand military families—and all families—it takes both large-scale quantitative studies and small case studies in a mixed-methods approach. My research-informed Family Resilience Framework identifies nine key processes that practitioners can facilitate for family resilience. They can be applied to help families rebound from serious crises, to navigate disruptive transitions, and to cope effectively with prolonged hardship or disabling conditions. Our Center has developed a range of programs and modalities from brief counseling to multifamily groups.

I've learned the most in my career from the families I have worked with—seeing the extraordinary resilience of ordinary families when faced with adversity. This practice is about tapping into families' own potential for healing and positive growth. Through appreciative inquiry, we draw out their sparks of resilience. This approach doesn't ignore or minimizing difficulties or simply tell a family "don't worry; be happy." We start by listening to their stories to understand their struggle and bring out their best efforts and strengthen their bonds. When hopes and dreams have been shattered, we help them to envision new possibilities for personal and relational fulfillment. Helping professionals can benefit from this approach, too. Hernandez found that therapists who work this way gain "vicarious resilience" and are less likely to suffer burnout. Clients' stories and efforts, their hope, courage, endurance, and triumph of the human spirit can restore out spirit in our work and in our own lives.

INTRODUCTION

The goal of this chapter is to help students and new professionals in human services form a strong grounding in theories about stress and resilience that have clear connections to practice with military families and their individual members in multiple settings. As Dr. Walsh stated, the theories that guide our practice determine whether we look for and see only damage or if we see those "sparks of resilience" that propel families to overcome challenges.

You may have heard the descriptive proverb "Sometimes one can't see the forest for the trees," meaning that people sometimes get bogged down in details and lose sight of the larger picture that shapes, supports, and constrains those details. This chapter is designed to give you a good foundation of the quickly growing "forest" of stress and resilience research and to reinforce this knowledge through practice exercises where you can apply concepts of stress, coping, and resilience to examples of individuals and their families.

The field of stress and resilience research and theory spans multiple disciplines and has a strong connection to reflections on human reactions in war contexts during the nineteenth and twentieth centuries (Hobfoll, 1998). Indeed, two of the more familiar concepts derived from this connection are battle/combat fatigue and shell shock, which have, in turn, framed much of the present-day study of PTSD. But there is much more to the study of stress and resilience than a focus on psychosocial outcomes to traumatic events. Events and circumstances do not have to be traumatic to be stressful. As readers interested in gaining a deeper understanding of military family life, theories about stress and resilience are valuable tools for a variety of human service professions. These theories help us understand stress and resilience processes, assess individuals' or families' strengths and challenges in the face of adverse circumstances, and give us guidance as to best practices for intervention and prevention.

You can think of the forest as being the wide-ranging and multidisciplinary study of stress and resilience. Each discipline occupies space within the forest and may be thought of as groves or particular stands of trees that share a common focus in particular aspects of stress and resilience that help differentiate one discipline from the next. Yet, there is also shared ground where the borders of one discipline blend to some degree with neighboring disciplines and the opportunity to shape and be shaped by another discipline creates growth and change in our communal understanding of the larger forest. The study of stress and resilience is experiencing a time of interdisciplinary growth and change brought on, in part, by the continuing connection with the contexts of war and other human conflicts (Haglund, Nedstadt, Cooper, Southwick, & Charney, 2007; Hobfoll, Horsey, & Lamoureux, 2009; MacDermid Wadsworth, 2010; Walsh, 2003c), and we benefit from starting with a strong, basic foundation that draws from multiple sources.

This chapter first focuses on characteristics of "the forest" of stress and resilience literature. This section highlights common terms used in this area of research and how they are defined when applied to individuals and when applied to families, as well as their underlying assumptions about care and keys to well-being. A case study example of a military family is presented so that you can begin applying the concepts and then refer back to the case study as the chapter continues to present different theories and models that are useful in interpreting the needs, strengths, and challenges present in this family system.

The second section of this chapter explores a few of the "groves" of discipline-based stress theories and their usefulness in working with military families and their members. All the theories and models presented in this chapter have been selected due to a shared commitment to understanding how context shapes experiences of stress and resilience, but some focus primarily on individuals, while others focus primarily on family systems or particular relationships. We organize these theories by their primary focus and level of analysis. At the individual level, we review three lines of theory and research development. The first line of research focuses on learning how individuals think about and perceive stressful events (cognitions), how certain cognitive responses and patterns indicate types of coping strategies, and the circumstances (i.e., contexts) in which some strategies may be more or less effective for individuals trying to resolve their stress (Folkman & Moskowitz, 2007; Lazarus & Folkman, 1984). A second line of research brings together the rapidly expanding field of neurobiology with psychosocial research to better understand how hormonal and chemical influences on brain and body functioning are linked with both positive and negative psychosocial outcomes (Charney, 2004; Haglund et al., 2007; Sussman, 2006). The third line of individually focused research centers on the individual in context (Hobfoll, 1998) and concentrates on understanding the roles that resources (such as personal skills/abilities, social support, health, money, and community) play in coping with stressors and gaining/losing or maintaining one's optimal level of well-being.

As helpful as it is to gain a foundation in understanding individual stress, we realize that most people are connected to other people in meaningful ways as Dr. Walsh so eloquently stated at the beginning of this chapter. Military families are, after all, the focus of this text and much attention has been focused on the families—spouses, children, parents, and siblings—of the military personnel who are currently serving or have served in the theatres of the Global War on Terror, as well as ongoing humanitarian and peacekeeping missions where our troops are or have been called upon to provide help. At the family level, we also review three different branches of family stress theory. As mentioned earlier, there is a longstanding connection between the study of stress and military action. Reuben Hill's book, *Families Under Stress* (1949), is considered a landmark work that focused on deployment cycle issues of World War II veterans and their families. Hill's work established the basis of studying stress at the family level, and several researchers continue to refine and expand on his initial model of family stress (Malia, 2006; McCubbin et al., 1980). Each of the family stress theories reviewed in this chapter builds upon this and other writings as the researchers work to expand our understanding of families and the stress process.

We first review the contributions of McCubbin and Patterson (1983a, 1983b) who offered a significant expansion of Hill's model of family stress and explicated ways for researchers and practitioners to identify and measure adaptation processes and adjustment levels in family systems. The second line of family level work focuses on two particular circumstances that are stressful for families: ambiguous loss (not knowing what has happened to a family member or experiencing significant change in a family member, such as brain trauma) and boundary ambiguity (uncertainty in knowing if a person is psychologically and/or physically present in a family system, such as in different phases of deployment and reunion) (Boss, 1987, 2006, 2007; Wiens & Boss, 2003). The third branch of family level theory offers a practical framework for understanding and fostering family resilience and takes care to attend to the contextual details that both help and hinder family resilience (Walsh, 2003a, 2003c, 2007).

Each of these lines of research is part of the larger field of stress and resilience. Yet, because they focus on different concerns and questions, they offer unique pieces of information that can help human service professionals tailor their approaches to a variety of individual and family stress issues. At the end of this chapter, we developed exercises where you can practice the concepts and each theoretical focus with the example of the military family in this chapter's case study. You may find it useful to take short reading breaks between each theory and go to the exercises to practice what you just read. By applying each theoretical lens to the same case study, you will be able to see how having a solid grounding in the wide-ranging field of stress and resilience gives therapists and practitioners a flexible toolkit when working with a wide variety of family members and challenges.

CASE STUDY 5.1   Example of a Military Family

Joe Smith is the oldest of three boys raised by a single parent mom and her parents near Atlanta, GA. Joe enlisted in the U.S. Marine Corps after graduating from high school in 2001 and has supported his younger siblings as they have finished high school and entered into the workforce. Joe's youngest brother followed in Joe's footsteps and just enlisted in the Marines. Joe was deployed to Afghanistan soon after the terrorist attacks on the World Trade Center towers. This first deployment was 13 months long, after which he returned with his unit to Camp Legeune, NC. Joe met and married his wife, Jane, in 2004 and was deployed for a second time shortly thereafter. Jane was pregnant with their first child, and she moved back to her hometown and lived with her parents during her pregnancy and until Joe returned. Joe returned from his second deployment to his wife and 6-month-old baby daughter. Joe and Jane had applied for base housing during this separation and were able to move into housing within a week of Joe's return.

Jane has been working toward a college degree in nursing and is planning to transfer to a local college to finish her degree. Their baby girl is healthy, but developed colic and still cries from mid-afternoon through the evening several nights a week. She is also not sleeping through the night yet. The pediatrician assures them that colic will resolve itself by 8–9 months. Joe has been experiencing trouble sleeping since his return and when the baby wakes up crying in the middle of the night, Joe often experiences a startle reaction and has trouble getting back to sleep. He often goes for a run to help handle his hyperreaction, which worries Jane and has created a sense that he is not able to be a parenting partner.

In addition, Joe has received notification that he has been accepted into the Infantry Unit Leaders Course, a positive move in his career in the Marine Corps where he can become an Anti-Tank Section Leader. His orders state that he will be temporarily assigned to a station several states away to complete 5 months of advanced training. He leaves in 1 week.

Although this family is new on base, neighbors have welcomed them into the neighborhood and several wives of Joe's colleagues have made a point to contact Jane and give her information on groups and resources available on base.

THE STUDY OF STRESS AND RESILIENCE

One of the first things to keep in mind about this area of study is that the most common terms of stress, coping, and resilience can be used to describe individuals or families. For example, you are likely to read original studies and reports that vary in their focus on (1) individual characteristics (e.g., "I am going to have to find a new job once we relocate to Fort Bragg for my spouse's new PCS"), or (2) family characteristics (e.g., "The medical social worker and physical and occupational therapists are helping us work through issues in our daily caregiving challenges once our son is discharged from Walter Reed Medical Center"). Writers and readers both must be careful to remember the level of focus that is being reported so that we maintain clarity in the state of our knowledge about different level phenomena. Additionally, children, adolescents, and adults have been studied differently (MacDermid et al., 2008), which leads to different emphases on factors involved in resilience. This all means that comparing studies across age groups and from individuals to families can become difficult. So, how are stress, coping, and resilience conceptualized and how are definitions both similar and different when shifting from an individual focus to a family focus?

Individual Stress

The major definitions of **stress** emphasize that it is both a process and a state of being (Hobfoll, 1998; Malia, 2006). Considering stress as a process is useful because it focuses our attention on the interaction of a person with his/her larger environment. The process view highlights a person's cognitive and emotional reactions to a situation and affords us the opportunity to understand what happens when a person's appraisal of a situation or context results in a judgment of a *mismatch* in one's abilities and/or resources to meet the demands of the situation. The state of **being stressed** is due to the tension created by the mismatch. In the discussion on specific theories later in this chapter, you will begin to see some variations in what is included in the researchers' working definitions of stress. Some of these definitions focus solely on psychological aspects of stress (Lazarus & Folkman, 1984), while others include physiological and neurobiological characteristics in their working definitions (Aldwin, 1994; Charney, 2004; Haglund et al., 2007).

Family Stress

Family stress is conceptualized as "an upset in the steady state of the family [system]" (Malia, 2006, p. 143), which requires that the family make adjustments in order to maintain or regain a sense of coherence. Researchers who study the family level of stress look at ways in which the individual members contribute to the family's responses to the stressor and interact with each other and the outcomes they achieve as a family system as a result of these dynamics. Complicating the study of family stress is the reality that families rarely face only one stressor at a time, and it is unlikely that all previous stressors are resolved before a new one presents itself in the family's life. Theorists call the occurrence of overlapping demands **pileup of stressors** (Lavee, McCubbin, & Olsen, 1987; McCubbin & Patterson, 1983b), which itself can increase the sense of stress in the family. Walker (1985) cautions family stress researchers against assuming an idea that a "no stress" standard exists for any family's typical pattern.

Stressors

If individuals and family systems both can experience stress, how are stressors defined and identified? The main elements of a stressor include that it is a life event or occurrence (Boss, 1987) or an environmental context (McCubbin & Patterson, 1983), which either generates or has the potential to generate change as a person or family works to address the identified event or situation. McCubbin and Patterson describe stressors as aligning into two basic categories of normative (expectable) and nonnormative (often not expected or anticipated, sometimes catastrophic) stressors. Boss (as cited in Malia, 2006) expands this classification system to identify whether stressors are "normative or catastrophic, developmental or situational, predictable or unexpected, ambiguous or clear, and volitional or nonvolitional" (p. 145). You will read more about Boss's taxonomy a little later in this chapter and have an opportunity to practice applying it. Researchers also believe that it is important to know other information about the stressor, such as where the stressor originates (internal or external), as well as the duration of exposure to the stressor and whether or not the stressor occurs in tandem with other stressors (Boss, 2001; Lavee et al., 1987; Luthar, 2006; McCubbin & Patterson, 1983a, 1983b).

Chapter 3 identified several stressors that are normative for military families, and MacDermid et al. (2008) name several experiences of life as a military child that are normative, particularly for children in active duty families. But these same stressors may not be normative for Reserve and National Guard families. Military-related stressors include deployment and extended separation of families from their service member, frequent relocations to new stations, spousal employment and education opportunities, risk of injury or death of the service member, and exposure to combat-related activities. Other stressors are similar across both military and civilian families and, depending on their particular characteristics, may be normative or nonnormative. These include family life transitions of marriage, divorce, parenthood, high school graduation, and job advancement/loss/retirement; daily hassles such as a flat tire or sick pet, cranky teenagers who do not want to do their household chores, or surprise visits from family members; and events over which there may be very little control, like an unclear health diagnosis, a natural or human-made disaster, or loss of a family member or close friend.

Resilience

Resilience is studied hand-in-hand with stress and is viewed as a process of positive adaptation and growth after experiencing an adverse event/circumstance. The term "resilience" has been used in much of the literature focused on children and adolescents who are living in or exposed to adverse environments (Luthar, 2006), while the term "hardiness" is used more often in research with adults. **Hardiness** is usually described more as a personality trait and thus more fixed (one is a hardy individual or not), while resilience is conceptualized as more dynamic (one can gain or lose resiliency in the interplay between the person and environment). MacDermid et al. (2008) note that while there is no universally agreed upon definition of resilience, "most definitions include two key elements: 1) exposure to adverse or traumatic circumstances; and 2) successful adaptation following exposure" (p. 1). As such, resilience cannot be assessed in the absence of an undesirable event. These elements apply to studies of individuals in multiple age groups (child, youth, adult) and at individual, family, and community levels.

MacDermid et al. (2008) identify several characteristics that are useful in understanding how resilience can be identified within military families as well as limits and/or threats to attaining successful adaptation after adversity. These characteristics include:

1. Resilience is dynamic and includes both environmental and psychobiological components, similar to the way a child development professional would explain that early brain development is influenced by both genetics and the environments that support or put healthy development at risk.
2. Resilience is a process and develops over time.
3. Resilience is strength-based, and programs that use a strengths-based model build upon identifying existing strengths to support healthy outcomes for individuals and families.
   a. Resilience is situation-specific. Individuals and families have different traits and abilities and develop particular skill sets through their experiences. Not every person or family has identical strengths or abilities.
   b. Resilience can be enhanced through the dynamic interactions of the environmental and psychobiological systems.
4. There are multiple pathways to resilience.
5. When multiple risk factors co-occur, the likelihood of exhibiting resilience decreases.

This all means that resilience can be measured by several different outcome indicators and is influenced by several risk and protective factors. A family's unique mixture of risk and protective factors include the outcome, that is, the family's resilience. So how can we know if an individual or family is exhibiting resilience? Both researchers and human service professionals use psychological health, physical health, quality of life and relationship indicators, a sense of **self-efficacy** (the extent to which persons believe that they can meet a goal or expectation), as well as **family coherence** (satisfaction with interpersonal connections and dynamics among family members), to gain a sense of a person's or family's resiliency (Walsh, 2002).

Coping

Coping is used to describe a variety of efforts to overcome challenges or difficulties. Some researchers (Folkman & Moskowitz, 2007; Lazarus & Folkman, 1984) focus on different individual cognitive and behavioral strategies: (1) to regulate one's distress (**emotion-focused coping**), such as when the evening news reports injuries and casualties of American personnel in the area where a service member is stationed; (2) to address the problem creating the stress event (**problem-solving coping**), such as making alternative caregiving arrangements for children when a single parent is deployed; or (3) to reframe and give different meaning to an event (**meaning-focused coping**), such as when a civilian neighbor tries to give comfort to a National Guard family whose service member just got orders by saying "This is for our country."

Factors including flexibility in family roles and rules, family belief systems, connections to community and other social support, as well as communication and problem-solving strategies are all pieces to understanding family-level resilience (Boss, 2001; Malia, 2006; Walsh, 2003c). Family researchers focus on abilities, behaviors, and strategies available within the family system to meet challenges presented by a stressor. For example, role flexibility (the ability to take on a different role or responsibility when a service member deploys and returns) and family organization and communication patterns are important elements of family-level coping. When studying coping, researchers across disciplines are asking questions such as "How did you think/feel about the stressor event?" (i.e., a cognitive effort), "What did you do?" (i.e., a behavioral effort), and "How well did these thoughts, feelings, and strategies work as you addressed the challenge?".

Context and Resources

As the field of stress and resilience continues to be refined through therapeutic practice, theorists are able to explicate ways in which contextual specifics shape stress, coping, and resilience experiences. Researchers in the fields of psychology and health traditionally have not focused on context beyond immediate conditions, but rather concentrated on learning as much as possible about individual thought processes and coping behaviors (Lazarus & Folkman, 1984) and psychobiological responses and treatments (Ozbay et al., 2007). An exception in the psychological field is Hobfoll and associates, who used an ecological model of **individuals-nested in families-nested in social settings** (e.g., Hobfoll, 1998; Hobfoll, Dunahoo, & Monnier, 1995; Hobfoll et al., 2009). This model centers individuals within their family and larger social settings (neighborhood, religious setting, school/work) and highlights how individuals need meaningful connections with others in order to access and build resources for healthy living. Research using this model centered on interactions between the different levels of their model and how these connections (or lack thereof), particularly to resources, affect an individual's ability to be resilient in the face of stressors.

Access to and utility of resources are part of the overall context of a stressor experience. Most folks could identify a sizable list of potential resources that could be helpful in meeting a challenge: money, doctors, insurance, medical facilities, therapists, and being able to take medical leave from a job are all potential sources of support (i.e., resources) for an individual or family with a health crisis. Being able to access and use these resources can make a huge difference for both the individual directly affected by the health issue and for his/her family members, who are also affected by the challenge. Resources are not just defined by their existence, they are also defined by their utility (usefulness) to the people affected by the stressor event. Other elements of context can shape perceptions of usefulness and the applicability of a given resource.

To illustrate how perceptions of a potential resource of support can be shaped, think about how religious beliefs lead to different assumptions about health, both physical and psychological. A person with a religious belief system that shuns medical intervention in favor of allowing the will of God to prevail will likely not seek out or value resources that are part of the formal medical system. Likewise, a company may have a very good maternity leave policy for female employees when they become mothers, but not have any corollary policies for male employees who become fathers. Thus resources can exist, but not be perceived as useful (as in the case of religious belief) or not be available to a person because of their definition (maternal leave) or status (males). The contextually based work of Hobfoll and associates (Hobfoll, 1998; Hobfoll et al., 1995, 2009) puts the individual at the center of attention while also emphasizing that we need to examine availability and utility of individual, family, and community resources in order to better comprehend individual resiliency. This body of work provides a bridge to contextually based family stress and resilience research.

The disciplines of family science, marriage and family therapy, and social work focus their research on understanding collective coping strategies and resource management utilized by family systems when facing challenges (Boss, 2001; Malia, 2006). One of the central premises in the study of family stress is that context is important (Boss, 1987, 2006, 2007; McCubbin & Patterson, 1983b; Walker, 1985; Walsh, 2003c, 2007). In order to understand the family's responses to a stressor event, one needs to understand the family's condition (strength, health, and resilience) prior to the stressful event. Additionally, helping professionals need to gain an understanding of how the event is stress inducing for a particular family system. Context provides at least a partial glimpse into the effects of a stressor. Context also shapes the stressor event and a person's/family's responses to it. Boss's classification of family stressors (Boss, 2001) mentioned earlier in this chapter, helped define important elements of context that are useful for helping professionals and the people with whom they are working. This taxonomy lends itself well to asking questions that will help both a client and a helping professional gain a clearer sense of the stressor and identify coping strategies and resources for individuals and families. These questions include, but are not limited to

1. *What is the source of the stressor?* Does it originate from within the family system (internal) or outside the family system (external)? Both addiction and tornadoes are stressors, but they have different effects on individuals and families.
2. *What type of stressor is being presented?*
   a. Is this a normative, developmental, or predictable event, such as transitions to parenthood, the "terrible twos" or death of an elderly family member? Or, is it catastrophic, situational, or otherwise unexpected, such as a car accident?
   b. Is the stressor one in which the facts surrounding the event are clear and knowable (clear) or are there limits to knowing what happened and/or what the outcomes might be (**ambiguous**), such as a missing child?
   c. Is the stressor one that was wanted or chosen (**volitional**), such as taking steps to change one's marital status or is this stressor event imposed upon the person/family (**nonvolitional**), such as being laid off of work or having to relocate in order to keep a job?
3. *How long is this stressor expected to last (duration)?* Is the event short-term (**acute**), such as a child having difficulties with a friend, or longer-term (**chronic**), such as an ongoing health issue?
4. *What else is going on that may impact the relative effects of this stressor (density)?* It may be that the event is the only big thing going on at the time and is easily identified (isolated) or there may be a pileup of stressor events, including the identified event (**cumulative**), occurring that contribute to the current situation. For example, deployment may be the stressor of the moment in a family's life where other issues such as caring for young children, spousal health issues, and isolation from other military families are also present.

Thus, it is important for a helping professional to work with clients to identify the nature and context of the stressor event and to facilitate identification of resources that will support resilience in the face of the challenge. In doing so, helping professionals are guided by theory. Tara Saathoff-Wells, one of the coauthors of this textbook, explains and illustrates in Box 5.1 how theory can guide our everyday practices.

BOX 5.1 BEST PRACTICES

USING THEORY TO GUIDE OUR PRACTICE

Theory helps me understand life. I love theory. It uncovers assumptions I make about myself, about other people, and the way things are "supposed to be." It helps me be thoughtful about the way things are and how to improve them.

All my life I've been trying to understand people, their relationships, and how organizations and cultures work. When I was growing up, my family lived in Ethiopia where my dad worked for the United States Agency for International Development (USAID). After high school, I started traveling on my own. I spent a lot of time exploring what I wanted to do with my life (learn about cultures and family life by seeking out international experiences as a young adult) and learning what I did NOT want to do (work in child care at minimum wage). My mom had to buy a new address book every few years. There were so many cross-outs and new addresses, the pages with my contact information were like archaeological digs. Between 1989 and 1994, I spent a lot of time in Africa including working to help reunite children with their families in displacement camps in Mozambique as their civil war was ending and teaching school for American children in Kenya.

I can be easily upset or outraged by things that don't seem "right" or well thought out. In the fall of 2008, I taught my first Military Family Life Class at my former university. Our college football team invited a nearby unit of the National Guard, ROTC students, and staff to come to Military Appreciation Night. A ceremony was planned for halftime. No one from the university came over and visited with families and service members except for me and some of my students.

The weather that night was tough—bone chilling cold with dense, dripping fog. The vapor lights from the stadium created a halo effect, and the tent where service members and their families were gathered was on the backside of the stadium with auxiliary lights. The National Guard had set up examples of their artillery, including a couple of cannons, as well as big inflatables for children to play on during the pregame tailgate, and personnel were stationed around them as dusk and darkness set in. The fog further limited visibility to about 100 yards outside the stadium.

One of the typical pregame activities for football games is the firing of the cannon to get the fans excited for the game. It is also fired when the team scores a touchdown and other points. About a half hour before the game, university staff started firing the cannon for the game, but no one had warned the service members, many of whom had just returned home from a tour in Baghdad.

One of my students who was with me is a Retired First Sergeant and former ROTC instructor. He, his wife, and I were talking with the service members near the inflatables when the first blast from the cannon came. It was startling for all of us, but the service members hit the ground with immediate self-protection behavior—it was a cold, dark, and foggy night in an unfamiliar place with bad lighting and they knew it was not their cannon that had been shot. They automatically used their training for survival in response to an unknown threat, while we (civilians) thought, "Woah—it is getting close to game time!" As the service members realized they were safe, they had to also handle their adrenaline reactions and a couple felt embarrassed about their actions in front of civilians. All three of us responded by reassuring them that their response was normal. The "First Sarge" stayed with them to help them "walk it off" and process their emotional and survival reactions, which was really meaningful to the service members. His wife and I went back to the tent with the families and reassured them about the cannon blast. Later, my student talked with the event coordinators to explain that setting off a cannon at night without warning is not the best way to welcome and honor service members.

At first, I was upset at the lack of preparation, understanding, and connection between the event people and service members. Then, I realized the event planners and staff needed help to make the connections. Good intentions simply are not enough to ensure that a community creates a truly supportive and appropriate event for military families. It is an example of where knowing the theory of stress and coping and individual stress reactions, as well as the basics of deployment experiences, would have been helpful. When planning an event for returning service members and their families, you need to consider the experiences they've had and how they may interpret events differently than the planning committee or general audience.

Another example where application of theory could positively influence how we organize events for military families is on the media and Internet portrayal of surprise reunions between young children and service members who have come home on leave for a holiday or family event. As a child development person who has some understanding of all the feelings and stressors involved around issues of separation, reuniting, and connecting, I think families should be able to reunite in private. It bothers me that it has become acceptable for the public to be there, too. It may feel like I'm crashing the party, but this is something we need to reconsider. How much of a family's life—any family—should be "out there" for everyone to see and take part in? The focus of the video may be on this very emotional reunion, but why should we assume that we should be an audience to this family event? Thinking about the larger ripple effects, when these are recorded in a classroom, are there other children present who also have a deployed parent? What might this mean to them? Military families and children experience enough uncertainty in the deployment cycle. Dates for return are delayed, missions can be dangerous, a service member may opt to stay longer so a buddy can go back. Is there really a good enough reason to promote the public consumption of a family's reunion moment? This is a case where applying theory leads to at least questioning the assumption that this is OK and perhaps modifying our behavior.

Tara Saathoff-Wells
Coauthor of this textbook and Faculty Member in Child, Family, and Community Sciences,
University of Central Florida

THEORIES AND MODELS OF STRESS AND RESILIENCE

Clinicians, therapists, and other human service professionals need to have a strong repertoire of theories and models to use as they work with military families and individual members. Theories that can be applied to real life situations and that can be evaluated for their accuracy and usefulness are extremely important in developing high-quality intervention and prevention programs. Now that you have started building your knowledge regarding concepts in stress and resilience, we present a short review of theories and models that have strong applied components.

Theories and Models of Individual Stress, Coping, and Resilience

General stress and coping theory, as detailed by Lazarus and Folkman (1984), centers on understanding internal aspects of coping, that is, cognitions and emotions. This branch of theory is based in cognitive behaviorism and leads much of the discussion on the different aspects of coping strategies that we defined earlier: emotion-focused, problem-focused, and meaning-focused strategies. Recent theory development has begun to include a study of how specific effects and emotions impact coping strategies and effectiveness, with some support for linking positive effect with healthier adaptations to stress and as an important tool for restoring resources that may be depleted as the result of a stressful event (Folkman & Moskowitz, 2007). This theory also indicates that contextual factors will influence which coping strategies are more or less useful to a person trying to resolve or manage a stressful event.

For example, school-aged children may deal better with a parent's deployment if shown how to use emotion-focused coping actions (e.g., regulating feelings of distress) and meaning-focused coping (e.g., reframing the deployment as the parent helping others live safer lives) rather than a problem-focused perspective (e.g., trying to change deployment orders). In a situation where a service member is returning with a significant injury, members of his extended family system may vary in their individual coping actions. Family members may be similar in their initial attempts to regulate their levels of emotional distress that their son/brother/husband/father has been injured and has survived. As the injury treatment continues over time and family members have different daily life demands and interpersonal connections to their injured family member, coping actions and involvement may vary significantly. Family members who are more distant (physically, psychologically) may turn to more meaning-focused coping to try to make sense of why this happened, while family members who are more immediately connected to and affected by the service member's injury may continue with active emotion-focused coping for the daily distress as well as problem-solving coping. Problem solving may include coordinating child and work schedules around visits to the service member and medical appointments and learning to administer to short-term and/or long-term caregiving needs that may result from the injury. Human service professionals can use the different concepts of stress and coping theory to help clients identify multiple facets of their reactions to a stressing event and process information for addressing their needs.

Psychobiological stress research is useful for clinicians and therapists. This line of research integrates neurobiological research with psychosocial research to include physiological measures of stress, such as cortisol, serotonin, and dopamine levels; autonomic response systems, including respiration and perspiration rates and eye dilation; and magnetic resonance imaging (MRI) brain scans (see Haglund et al., 2007 for a comprehensive overview), as well as self-reports on stressful events and circumstances. Interventions and recommendations focus on teaching a person experiencing stress to recognize physiological messages, such as tensed muscles, shallow breathing, clenched jaws and then to use such coping strategies as deep breathing, muscle relaxation, guided imagery, and exercise to release the physical experience of stress. In addition, a helping professional drawing on this line of applied research would integrate psychosocial bases of distress, coping, and resilience to help the client explore issues such as irrational thoughts about what is/was possible to do during a stressful event. In clinical and therapeutic settings, this research opens up opportunities to prevent and treat stress-related psychopathology by addressing the hormonal and chemical factors involved in stress, coping, and resilience.

Psychobiological research also contributes to our understanding of lifespan development and change with regard to a variety of stressful experiences. Such understanding may be particularly useful for working with children and youth in military families. Research on early brain development shows that there is a high level of **neural plasticity** (flexibility in development of neural connections) that responds to early experiences and deprivations, in effect starting the lifelong process of "tailoring" the brain to the person with all his/her personal, social, and environmental experiences. This process includes early stressful experiences.

Data show that there are hormonal and chemical processes in the human experience of stress. These experiences create pathways in the neural circuitry for response patterns to develop when facing a new potential stressor. Developmentalists often describe two such pathways that early experiences help forge: learned helplessness and strong self-efficacy, both of which are aspects of a sense of self. It is important to note that individuals can and do experience both positive and negative perceptions of self. Research shows that individuals who experience positive outcomes to early stress experiences may be able to incorporate these early experiences to build a foundation for resilient responses to later stress-inducing events (Boyce & Chesterman, 1990), described by Walsh (2003c) as "struggling well." Persons may be more at risk of future negative stress reactions due to development of neurobiological responses if they have early experiences that result in chronic distress or that are not manageable or responsive to coping attempts (Khoshaba & Maddi, 1999). One of the Best Practices segments in Chapter 4 gives insight into how knowing the ways that stress affects both the brain and coping skills in young children can be used to develop programs that support young children who experience parental deployment, injury, or loss.

Conservation of resources (Hobfoll, 1989) is another useful theory in understanding ways that people seek out, invest, and protect resources they find valuable in coping with stressful events. Hobfoll, who was introduced as a researcher who views the person in the context of family and community, posits several assumptions about the roles resources play in facilitating or inhibiting resilience (Hobfoll, 1998; Hobfoll et al., 1995). In general, people invest in resources that they perceive to be valuable and useful, which are in turn shaped by family, community, and culture. When those resources are lost or threatened, stress results and people will try to conserve (maintain) the resources they have. Resource losses are proportionally more powerful than resource gains and some resources, when lost, are always a negative experience. Finally, when resource loss occurs across levels (individual, family, community), successful coping and adaptation may be hindered. To bring this model to a practical level, consider the following two examples.

A school counselor can use Hobfoll's model to work with a child and his family when a mother is called up for active duty in her National Guard unit. The counselor can work with the child to help him identify his resources for support, such as having a sense of humor (individual: enjoying telling and listening to jokes with friends and family, saving a few jokes for video contact with his mom while she is deployed), being able to adjust with his remaining family members by helping with tasks that his mom would normally do (family: adding certain chores such as keeping track of breakfast items for the grocery list, feeding pets), and having friends with whom he can talk and spend time (community: scouts, sports, free time with buddies).

Hobfoll's model could be applied to a very different situation, as well. A medical social worker in a VA hospital can use the model to help map changes in resources and support for a soldier who has returned from theatre with physical and/or psychological trauma. There may be changes in personal resources and abilities (including health issues such as mobility and limb function, traumatic brain injury that can affect a myriad of executive functions), changes in family resources (stresses in a romantic relationship, needing help from parents, not being able to fulfill roles as a parent to his/her children), and changes in community resources (needing to identify specialized therapists, not being able to go back to a job/career due to the injury, strain in friendships, and loss of close connections with fellow unit members). Hobfoll's model facilitates thinking about the ripple effects of a variety of potential events military families and their members face.

The models of individual risk and resilience in this chapter provide a good starting point in building your theoretical map of stress and coping. General stress and coping theory gives insight into how individuals process stressful events, cognitively and emotionally, and different intrapersonal skills and strategies a person may use to try and resolve his or her distress. Psychobiological research contributes to our understanding of the intricate interactions between our physical and psychosocial experiences of stress and the ways in which our physical bodies respond to and try to regulate stress responses of which we may not be consciously aware. The conservation of resources model brings to the forefront how individuals are embedded in a larger social system in which they strive to gain and maintain resources and connections that support continued positive well-being. It also addresses consequences of losing resources for well-being and takes into account how resource loss can have ripple effects beyond a single individual.

Theories and Models of Family Stress, Resilience, and Coping

Family stress theory has generated scholarly and applied interest since just after World War II. One of the earliest scholars was Reuben Hill (1949, 1958) who developed a model of family stress that he called the ABCx Model and is considered to be the father of family stress theory. Hill's work, as mentioned earlier in this chapter, centered on deployment issues faced by World War II veterans and their families. Several scholars have worked to refine and strengthen family stress theory, and several model variations are in use today (see Malia, 2006 for an overview). It would be overwhelming to try to cover each iteration of family stress theory in this chapter, so we have limited it to a group of researchers who proposed one of the more significant expansions of Hill's ABCx Model, called the Double ABCx Model of Family Stress and Adaptation (McCubbin & Patterson, 1983). The value of this refinement is that it tried to account for the passage of time in understanding how stress and adaptation work in a family's life, from precrisis to postcrisis and adaptation.

According to family stress theory, the individual and the family make up the family system, and the family system's adaptation is predicted, in part, from the combination of stressors that occur (A), the resources accessed to address the stressors (B), and the perception (C) of the resulting crisis (x) (McCubbin & Patterson, 1983). Basic assumptions of family stress theory and the Double ABCx Model include a developmental view of the human life cycle. Thus, developmental change (growth, transitions in capabilities and relationships) is seen as a natural and integral part in the family system's growth over time. Stress is part of this developmental process (Figley & McCubbin, 1983). A second key element of family stress theory is that not all stressors are equal. There are important differences between family transitions and experiences that are due to normative and nonnormative stressors. You can review the more detailed definitions of each type in the earlier section of this chapter that defined the major terms, but in general, normative transitions are ones that are expectable and that a person and family may anticipate and look forward to (or at least be aware that it is coming!) while nonnormative transitions are due to experiences that are not expected or typical and may range from being a short-term stressor (such as a health scare) to being a catastrophic event (such as a tornado). Boss's taxonomy (2001), detailed earlier in this chapter, helps us better define the characteristics of stressors and transitions, which can help families understand their circumstances and make choices about resources and coping strategies. You can practice applying Boss's taxonomy of stressor characteristics in one of the exercises at the end of this chapter.

Applying Family Stress and Other Theories to Deployment-Affected Families

Figure 5.1 uses deployment as the initial stressor to illustrate several factors that may influence stress, coping, and resilience in military families. When a service member receives orders for deployment,

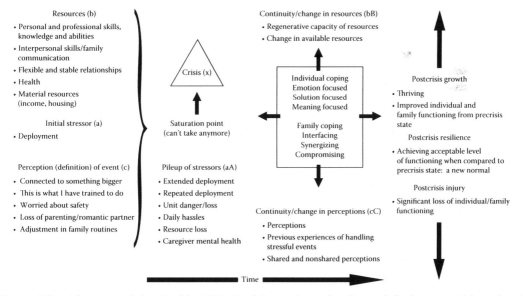

Figure 5.1   Adaptation of the Double ABCx Model to military families and deployment. (Adapted with permission. From McCubbin, H. I., & Patterson, J. M. (1983a). The family stress process: The Double ABCx Model of adjustment and adaptation. In H. L. McCubbin, M. B. Sussman, & J. M. Patterson (Eds.), *Advances and development in family stress theory and research* (pp. 7–37). New York: Haworth.)

several tasks have been identified that both the service member and his/her family must address in order for everyone to meet the needs of both work and family (see the "Deployments" section of Chapter 3). Deployment is just one of the stressors (a) that a family may be experiencing at that point in time. Drawing on the case study presented earlier in this chapter, what other stressors are evident in the family of Joe and Jane Smith when Joe received notice to deploy for the second time?

Individuals and families in the military may have a variety of resources (b) to respond to the demands of military life including a deployment cycle. The service member has been trained to do his/her job under demanding circumstances, is part of a unit with a clear mission, and will have to be cleared with a good bill of health in order to deploy. In addition to a service member's job skills, connections, and health, several skills are useful for all members of the family. These include communication and problem-solving skills, connections to family and community, flexibility and stability, and the ability to maintain family rituals and traditions even when members may be physically separated. Other resources may be more directly instrumental, such as receiving an increase in income due to the special pay linked with hazardous duty or special training. What other interpersonal and community-based resources do you think would be helpful for a family facing deployment? What potential resources are mentioned in the case study?

In the Double ABCx Model, perceptions of the stressor event (c) can influence behaviors and beliefs about an individual's and family's ability to cope with the stressor. Previous chapters have described how a sense of patriotism and participating in something larger than oneself can be an integral part of military service. Service members may look forward to a deployment because they know that they are bringing needed skills and knowledge to address an urgent issue in the field (such as water treatment in Haiti after the earthquake in January 2010) or to give relief to their fellow service members (such as Col. Pereira's work with soldiers under fire in Baghdad). Military spouses and significant others may be simultaneously proud of their partner, yet worried for their safety. If children are involved, there may be sense of loss for both the parenting partner and the children. The ways in which the service member and the family system perceive the deployment event can influence the ways that resources are accessed and the type of coping strategies used to alleviate the distress associated with deployment. In reviewing the case study, what details give insight into the resources Jane drew upon for the first deployment of her husband? Are these resources that you think she could draw upon for the second deployment? Why or why not?

Families do not simply enact their individual and collective coping strategies at just one point in time, but rather over time. Deployment can range from 4 months to more than a year and predeployment preparations may add several additional months to a family's experience of deployment-related tensions. Family stress theorists emphasize that time is an important factor in understanding responses to stressful events. Over time new normative and nonnormative stressors may be introduced into a family system (health issues of a family member, graduation of a high school senior, a tornado hits the local community), and others may dissipate (the baby's colic resolves itself, a sibling is able to care for an aging parent, a reliable and honest mechanic can be counted on when the family car has issues).

Crises (aA) are commonly framed as either a pileup of stressors, such as a family where everyone comes down with the flu and all three children have school projects due in the same week as tryouts for sports teams, or a traumatic event that overshadows other daily needs and schedules, such as natural disasters, loss of a job, or the death/injury of a loved one. Crises give a sense that there is saturation in the amount and/or magnitude of stressors that an individual and family system can accommodate with existing resources. The concept of a spiral of deployment was introduced in Chapter 3 to help describe what families may face with multiple deployments. Framed within family stress theory, what might precipitate a sense of crisis for a deployment-affected family? How might multiple and/or extended deployments tax a family's coping systems and their resilience over time?

In accounting for the possible changes over time in a family system, the second part of the model expands the original list of stressors, resources, and perceptions. Just as there can be change in the number and significance of stressors in a family's life, it is also expectable to see both continuity and change in both resources and perceptions of events. Some resources may have stable or regenerative qualities so that they remain viable over an extended period of time. Examples include interpersonal skills and stable familial and friend relationships. Other resources may not be as stable or have an infinite capacity to serve as a resource. For example, in a family faced with the injury of a service member, a working spouse may use all his/her available sick days in order to be with their injured partner. When those paid sick days (a finite resource) are used, the family member may have to choose other avenues such as going back to work, taking an informal leave of absence, invoking the federal Family and Medical Leave Act, or even leaving his/her job. Similarly, the availability and stability of close friendships and family relationships may change over time due to changes in their lives (children entering different stages of development, changing jobs) or due to a change in their emotional resource capacity to "always be there" for the spouse/children of their deployed service member.

Perceptions of stressors can also change over time. Previous experiences of deployment and other stressful events may change a family's perception of their ability to handle a continued or new crisis. Additionally, not all members of the same family may have shared perceptions of the same event or stressors. What is "no big deal" to one person may be a "very big deal" to another. As you will see below, being able to coordinate differences while being flexible is a set of skills very useful to family systems. This is true for military families facing deployment, families experiencing other normative changes in military life (such as relocation to a new PCS), and families in the civilian population.

The model is useful in describing the context and factors of a deployment-affected family. Yet, family stress theory is not limited to describing a family's stress experience. Practitioners can use this model to help a family find **adaptive coping strategies** for stabilizing and maintaining "balance in the family system which [in turn] facilitates organization and unity and promotes individual growth and development" (Figley & McCubbin, 1983, p. 24). In turn, these adaptive coping strategies influence individual's abilities to meet personal and relational demands. Whereas general stress and coping theory has drawn attention to individual coping strategies, family stress theory focuses on coordination and flexibility of coping skills between family members and their larger community to help meet the challenges presented by the stressor event.

These adaptive strategies, to some extent, involve **restructuring** the family's current operating system and **consolidating** afterward (McCubbin & Patterson, 1983, pp. 22–23). That is, modifications may need to be made within the family system in the areas of roles, family rules, patterns of interaction and communication, and goals. In addition to modifications, the family unit and its individual members are also called upon to consolidate and support individual and group efforts toward implementing these changes. These strategies also include highlighting changes in individual and family needs in areas of support and resources for maintaining or improving quality of life. According to family stress theory, the family's and individual members' efforts at restructuring and consolidation are facilitated by three adaptive coping strategies of interfacing with the larger community, synergizing efforts between family members, and compromising within the family system and between the family system and the larger environment to settle into a satisfying way of life (McCubbin & Patterson, 1983). So what might these coping strategies look like in practice with military families?

Let's take an example of an active duty military family relocating from a large military installation in the Southeastern United States to a university town in the Midwest, where the service member's new assignment is as a military science instructor in the university's ROTC program. This family has one service member parent, a second parent who works as a dental hygienist, and two school-age children. They have been living on a large U.S. military installation for the past 3 years, and the children attend a school on base. Life in the university town will be vastly different. There is no large military installation nearby and no significant group of military families in the area. Several changes are on the horizon for this family.

- **Interfacing**: A family and its individual members operate within the larger social contexts of work, community, and school groups. An active duty military family that receives PCS orders has to interface (i.e., develop relationships) at several levels with a new community that may or may not be similar in culture and sociohistorical contexts. The service member has orders, which specify his/her job duties and place in the ROTC program, while the spouse may be making choices about finding a new job (or not), locating civilian shopping venues because there is no PX or commissary nearby, and finding medical professionals who accept TRICARE (i.e., the military health insurance program). Children will be looking for new playmates, wondering about their new school and teachers, and figuring out a new home and neighborhood. The entire family will be interfacing with a new community across several dimensions.

- **Synergizing**: Synergizing is composed of coordinating all family system and individual members' efforts and is focused on consolidating the various change efforts within the family system. Ideally, the family works in a coordinated fashion addressing issues of change concerning both individual members and the family as a whole. Cooperation and effective communication among family members are key to this coping strategy and families who are able to coordinate their efforts tend to experience lower levels of chaos and anxiety. For the family in the example, the parents work to find effective ways to organize information and tasks about moving requirements, finding housing and schools, keeping track of important family papers (marriage and birth certificates, school and medical records, pet records), and working with their children to help them with transitions in schools and friends and activities, as well as changes in roles they may have as family members.

- **Compromising**: Compromising entails family and individual efforts of achieving balance within the new community. Relocating from a large military installation in the Southeastern United States to a university town in the Midwest may present quite a few cultural challenges for this family. Developing friendships with other children and adjusting to new schools that are not full of military kids and that don't have teachers familiar with military life may take time. There may be a relatively low level of community support for the military, complete with strong ideological stances that are part of the public face of the community. Adjusting to life as a military spouse living far from an installation may mean that the spouse has to expend quite a bit of energy maintaining long-distance social support networks and feel very cautious in developing local friendships and ties outside the other families in the ROTC program. The service member may not be able to help with some key family transitions due to his/her job requirements and expectations. Thus, there are several opportunities for compromising that the family has to negotiate in adjusting to a new community.

Consequently, family stress theory views the family's and individual members' attempts to achieve a good "fit" with the new community as requiring the coping strategies of *interfacing* with the new environment at numerous levels, *synergizing* change efforts within the family system, and addressing family and individual-level issues of *compromise* with differences in community and lifestyle. Family stress theory and the Double ABCx Model provide helping professionals with a practical way to map and identify family stressors, supports, perceptions of events, and coping behaviors that help or hinder the family's adaptation to changes in their lives.

Finding Resilience in the Face of Ambiguity

Other clinical researchers have helped refine elements of family stress theory, such as Boss's (2001) taxonomy of stressor characteristics and Walsh's (2003c, 2007) family resilience framework, in order to strengthen its usefulness in clinical intervention. In particular, Boss contributed to a deeper understanding of when a person experiences unclear losses and unclear shifts in relationships. **Ambiguous loss theory** (Boss, 2002, 2007) represents her work to better help clients experiencing ambiguous loss (a stressor) and boundary ambiguity (a perceptual response), examples of which follow below. This work focuses on stress and resilience when a person or family experiences losses that are not clear in nature and may not be resolvable and a key assumption of this theory is that there are both physical and psychological structures that shape every family system. Walsh's focus on family resilience has shaped clinical work to help families identify and strengthen shared sources of support within their family systems that can help them manage stressors and gain/maintain a sense of well-being in spite of adversity.

The term "ambiguous loss" refers to an unclear loss and the loss may be physical or psychological. For example, a person/family may experience an ambiguous physical loss of a family member, such as when a child goes missing or a parent has migrated for work but his/her whereabouts and safety are unknown. The person may be physically absent but is still psychologically present in the family system. Families may also experience an ambiguous psychological loss when a family elder experiences age-related dementia or when a teenager survives a car wreck with serious brain trauma that permanently alters his abilities and future. These persons are still physically present, but their psychological presence and roles within the family system are changed. In this line of research and clinical application, ambiguous loss is viewed as a relational disorder rather than a psychological disorder as it is a relationship (or series of relationships) that are ruptured (Boss, 2007).

Those military families who have experienced an unclear physical loss of a service member include those listed as Prisoners of War (POWs), Missing in Action (MIA), Killed in Action (KIA), as well as service members who are/were listed as Away Without Leave (AWOL) and have not been in contact with family members. Although the details differ in each of these experiences, families are faced with an unclear loss and one where information may never provide clarity or resolution. The common challenge these families face is to find meaning in their circumstances and to be able to live and grow despite ongoing ambiguity, to be resilient in the face of uncertainty. For helping professionals, it becomes important to work with families so that they can recognize their individual and collective abilities to tolerate ambiguity. Individuals and family systems differ in their abilities to tolerate the unknown and to be able to create meaning when information is not forthcoming (Boss, 2007). Factors that have been identified as influencing tolerance of ambiguity include cultural values and religious belief systems, as well as perceptions of the ambiguous loss experience.

One possible perception of such an experience can be boundary ambiguity or a sense of blurred boundaries as to who is in or out of the family system or relationship. It may not be clear to family members, or there may be disagreement among family members as to whether a person is part of the psychological or physical family system. In military families, examples can stem from deployment issues. For example, when a parent is deployed, is s/he still expected to be an active parent? How do romantic couples maintain a sense of intimacy when they are separated for 13 months and each are experiencing vastly different daily life experiences? What if a service member receives a "Dear John/Jane" e-mail from a spouse while deployed and there are children in the relationship? There can be uncertainties in knowing if a person is still part of the family or not. Both ambiguous loss and boundary ambiguity may result in feeling "stuck" at a particular moment in family development and individual development. The ambiguity of the situation can make decision-making difficult, families may not have access to rituals to help acknowledge changes in relationships, and communities may not know or acknowledge this loss, either due to cultural or religious norms. Human service professionals using information from ambiguous loss research may be able to help families and individuals process their distress that stems from ambiguous circumstances surrounding a loss in relationship so that they find their path(s) to resiliency in spite of challenges, creating meaning out of their experiences and acknowledging their losses and emotions about the experiences.

A third avenue of expansion in family stress theory is a **family resilience framework**. Froma Walsh, a clinical social worker and researcher, expanded our understanding of key processes involved in family resiliency. Walsh identified (2003c, 2007) several different resources that families may draw upon to help manage and reduce stress and cultivate resiliency and positive growth. These resources are categorized in three different domains of family functioning: family belief systems, family organizational patterns, and family communication processes.

Family systems are powerful transmitters of shared values, norms, and interaction patterns to their members and across generations. This characteristic of families does not mean that everyone in the system shares an identical view of the world and how to interact with others, but that there is a semblance of common ground that can be recognized within the family. Family belief systems shape how members make meaning of their world and when faced by a crisis, it is possible that this worldview could be challenged.

Walsh (2003c) identified several ways in which belief systems can provide a foundation for resilience in families. A family's belief system becomes apparent through a number of avenues. One avenue is through a process family members undertake to construct meaning out of a crisis. For example, they see the crisis as a meaningful challenge to unite rather than to divide and resulting distress and other reactions as understandable given the event and circumstances. Infusing a crisis with such meanings can result in less judgment and more compassion being exchanged among family members. In addition, a positive outlook in which family members exhibit perseverance or a "can-do" attitude, tackle what can be changed and acknowledge what cannot, emphasize each other's strengths, and voice hope can overcome debilitating despair. Finally, spirituality and religious expression and supports provide a larger vision beyond the immediate crisis and offer the possibility of transformative growth.

Family organizational patterns is a second domain in which family processes can cultivate resiliency and positive growth. Such processes include family members demonstrating flexibility in their attitudes, thoughts, and behaviors as they respond to the challenges presented by the crisis while also maintaining necessary stability (e.g., being dependable). Additionally, family members grow or maintain strong connections through mutual support coupled with respecting differences and each member's needs. Leadership by one or more family members offers guidance and protection, and members seek to heal distressed relationships among themselves. Finally, family members utilize social and economic resources by having strong community networks, mentors and extended family, and financial security.

The third and final domain of Walsh's (2002) key processes of family resilience is communication. Communication processes include family members presenting and seeking clarity in messages and information; open emotional sharing of a variety of feelings, including empathy, assuming responsibility for one's own feelings and behaviors, tolerating differences, and engaging in positive interactions and using humor when appropriate; and collaborating together to solve the problems that can be solved and to prevent additional ones when possible.

Voices From the Frontline

REFLECTIONS OF A CHAPLAIN

People do recover and gain strength from difficult times. When I'm with an individual or family who is affected by grief and loss, I try to help people find the opportunity that every feeling and experience bring. I don't want to make it sound simple. It isn't. Helping people see possibilities and hope is part and parcel of healing. If I can avoid judgment and stupid questions—if I can "be there"—stories will be told more easily and people will see they are not alone in their grief, shame, guilt, despair, or whatever they are feeling and that there is hope.

Chaplain Charles Purinton
Army National Guard Chaplain

Each of the branches of family stress theory contributes to our overall understanding of how families meet both normative and nonnormative stressors in the course of their development. The Double ABCx Model provides professionals with a way to map multiple aspects of a stressor event and a family system's response(s) to it over time, including family resiliency. Ambiguous loss theory facilitates a deeper understanding of ways individuals and families may experience living with unknown, unclear, and/or irresolvable losses in their family systems and what supports and resources are helpful in those circumstances. The family resilience framework helps families and practitioners identify key resources families need in order to foster resiliency in the face of struggles. Each of the models and branches of theory presented in this chapter, whether individually or family focused, contributes to the larger field of stress and resilience research and practice.

SUMMARY

- Professionals working with military families will see a broad range of normative and non-normative stressors that affect individuals of all ages and in varied family relationships. To reiterate Pauline Boss (2007), "Good theory is useful theory" (p. 110).
- Theories and their models must be useful and testable in both research and practice. It is through the interaction of research and practice that we refine, amend, and strengthen our knowledge of human development, human relationships, and human stress and resilience.

EXERCISES

1. We have identified several key concepts used in studying individual and family stress and resilience and started making connections to how these concepts are important to helping professionals. To better see the connection between theory and practice, divide your group into teams. Each team practices applying at least five concepts to the fictional case study presented in this chapter. When ready, each team presents the description of the case study using the chosen concepts.
2. Continue the theory-to-practice journey by applying one individually focused and one family-focused theoretical model to the case study. What do your models emphasize? Where do you find their greatest utility in providing you with important information? Where do you find their limitations in addressing issues faced by this service member and his family?
3. The Public Broadcasting System (PBS) has two documentaries on its website profiling military men and women available. Choose one of the documentaries and follow the story of at least one of the soldiers profiled. To gain a fuller picture, stay with the same soldier for this practice. By doing so, you can begin to see both the characteristics of their stress and their sources of resilience.

A Soldier's Heart (2005)
http://www.pbs.org/wgbh/pages/frontline/shows/heart/etc/credits.html

Lioness (2008)
http://www.pbs.org/independentlens/lioness/film.html

First, as you watch one of the programs, determine the following dimensions of the stressor experiences by a soldier and her or his family, using the classification of family stress (Boss, 2001):

    Source of stressor: internal or external?

    Type of stressor: normative or catastrophic, developmental/predictable or situational/unexpected, clear or ambiguous, volitional or nonvolitional?

    Duration: acute or chronic?

    Density: isolated or cumulative?

Second, apply the nine key processes of family resilience (Walsh, 2002, 2003c) by finding examples of family members engaging in a key process of family resilience:

    Belief systems: meaning making, positive outlook, transcendence and spirituality

    Organizational structure: flexibility, connectedness, social and economic resources

    Communication processes: clarity, open emotional sharing, collaborative problem solving

Third, what do you wish was included in the storyline of your soldier to give you more insight into her or his challenges and efforts to be resilient?

6

Individual and Family
Development in the Military

In Chapter 6, you will

- Meet Colonel Charles Engel, MPH, MD, Director of the Deployment Clinical Health Center
- Learn about basic institutional sources of support designed to help service members meet job-related milestones in early and middle adulthood and handle challenges inherent in a military career
- Gain insights about typical young adult milestones of marriage and becoming a parent in the military population
- Learn about specific stress and resilience mechanisms in service members and how they relate to personal and family well-being

Meet

Army Colonel Charles Engel, MPH, MD, Director,
Deployment Health Clinical Center

Colonel Engel shares his insights about supporting service members and their families. He leads the RESPECT-Mil (Re-Engineering Systems of Primary Care Treatment in the Military) initiative to train and support primary care physicians to screen for and treat PTSD and depression. (Find more information about this initiative in Chapter 11).

I often refer to the development of RESPECT-Mil as a journey. It began in 1991 when we tried to understand the symptoms experienced by 25%–30% of Gulf War Veterans. After September 11, 2001, our attention turned to a renewed focus on PTSD and broader issues of anxiety and depression after trauma.

We recently piloted an approach that includes the addition of alcohol problems to PTSD and depression. We started in one clinic and are now worldwide in Army primary care facilities. Implementation in the other services is in the planning stages.

Our focus has largely been on the service member. Now we are working with a parallel effort to implement the Patient Center Medical Home [PCMH: A model that gives the patient a "home base" for care. The primary care physician provides care and coordinates care by other health professionals for a more holistic approach to wellness.] that will deal with all medical issues and includes family members.

Research shows that most people prefer to be treated by their primary care doctor. To the extent that we can equip primary care physicians to be able to recognize signs of distress in military members and their family members who may be experiencing PTSD and depression, the greater impact we are likely to have.

This means broadening our sense of what it means to help. In the medical field, we sometimes want to route people through "state-of-the-art" treatments even though it may not be what they want.

We have to be creative and open to options, working with everyone starting where they are. The vast majority of people are looking for something to grab on to—a lifeline. Only if we can provide those lifelines, we will have the opportunity to support people and in some cases, promote treatments that we think may work better.

For example, we have to accept and build upon the fact that though activities like exercise and yoga may not have as large an effect as some medications and therapy, this may be what someone wants and will incorporate into their lives.

We also need to think about how we define success. If someone feels better about who they are by engaging in a leisure time activity, we've had a big impact. If a family moves from not functioning to functioning, we've had a big impact.

We try to let everyone coming through the door know there is a possibility for relief. We are dealing with wounds—seen and unseen—and we need to help. It is a dark mission at times but we swallow hard and keep moving. Sometimes it feels like two steps forward and one back. But as long as you keep taking the two steps forward, it is possible to make a difference.

INTRODUCTION

The previous chapters have drawn your attention to important aspects of military culture, key data about the military family population in both the Active and Reserve Components, common life experiences military families face in times of peace and conflict, and ways that helping professionals frame stress and resilience in their work in order to facilitate healthy coping with military families facing difficult times. By identifying typical and common life course milestones in young and middle adulthood that often co-occur with military service, the goal of the first portion of this chapter is to help you develop a coherent picture of military personnel and their families as they live in our larger society, making comparisons (when possible) to their civilian family counterparts.

Additionally, this chapter focuses on how current research, program, and policy development are being shaped by resilience perspectives both to meet immediate needs of service members and their families and to develop more effective programming that enhances and supports resilience capacities in families. Theory-guided policy and practice help us be more strategic in focusing on important risk and protective factors and developing programs that support individuals and families who may vary greatly in their current stress and resilience processes. However, the amount of research about service members is more extensive than research about their families. The Department of Defense (DoD) initiates a vast array of research about their personnel, tracking, and reporting information to Congress such as the yearly Demographic Profiles. A wide array of information is tracked on installations to assess the utilization of resources and the health and performance of personnel at least in part because personnel (and resources) are funded through the federal government. Military personnel may be expected to participate in surveys and other research by their superiors. Direct information about spouses, children, and other dependents cannot be compelled by unit command, so information about family members relies upon volunteering information and participation in surveys and assessments.

Willerton, MacDermid Wadsworth, and Riggs (2011) note that the scholarship on U.S. military families generally increases during times of military engagement and gradually decreases after actions come to a close. One effect of this cyclical pattern is that researchers draw from current concerns about families in general and can compare and contrast military families with civilian families. This research reveals which issues (e.g., spousal relationships, risk-taking behaviors, trauma/injury, reintegration), organizational factors (e.g., Active or Reserve Component, deployments, combat exposure, unit cohesion), and family characteristics (e.g., marital status, parenting/caregiving responsibilities) are of primary concern during the current military action.

A second potential effect of the rise and fall in research about military families is that most research may be generated when these families are experiencing nonnormative stressors of extended combat deployments. Thus, the body of literature on these families may reflect that we generally know less about everyday resilience and much more when military families face extreme stressors. Researchers and practitioners remind us that it is essential to understand everyday resilience mechanisms in order to better understand how they operate when pileup of stressors occurs (even if stressors are considered typical or short-term) and what happens when the unexpected and/or traumatic events must be addressed while everyday life continues (Davis, Luecken, & Lemery-Chalfant, 2009). A closer examination of the mechanisms of resilience in everyday military life, as well as during times of war, is important in moving beyond crisis management to a focus on resilience and strengths. Such a shift in practice will help us better understand both the daily and extraordinary life events for military families.

Current research trends and program initiatives reflect, in varying degrees, an understanding that stress and resilience are best understood in tandem (Office of the President of the United States, 2011). Since the transition to the all-volunteer force, programs and policies have been implemented that reflect an increased understanding in the importance of strengthening all family systems (not just those identified as high risk), supportive relationships, and community ties (Heubner, Mancini, Bowen, & Orthner, 2009) for enhanced military readiness and family well-being. Yet, there is still a lag in current publications that focus on what we are learning about resilience, particularly with families who may not reach a level of distress that leads to seeking treatment or other interventions designed to help members manage and enhance their resilience strategies.

The next few pages illustrate what we know about common developmental milestones of service members and the material supports that have been developed within the military institution to facilitate these experiences. As you read this chapter and the ones that follow, think about patterns evident in current research about service members and their family systems. Which issues and organizational and familial characteristics have received attention? Which are identified as gaps in our collective knowledge that are important to learn about?

YOUNG ADULTHOOD AND WORK-BASED SUPPORTS IN MILITARY LIFE

As described in Chapter 2, almost half of active duty service members are age 25 or younger and within the Reserve Component one-third are 25 and younger with one-half age 30 and under. Is this also your age group? When you think about the process of becoming an adult in contemporary U.S. society, what are important milestones for young adults in the United States? What are some of the challenges that young adults face today in their efforts to gain expertise for employment, become financially independent, establish a stable residence, form adult friendships and romantic relationships, and make choices about parenthood?

Pursuing work and establishing a career are closely tied to many of these markers of adulthood. When you think about the benefits of employment, what do you list as important or necessary? Perhaps health insurance is a priority, or summers off to spend with children. Maybe the adventures of being highly mobile and traveling to different parts of the United States or other countries is important. Maybe you want to go into a field that has a really good starting salary to help pay off student loans, to help finance your education if you want to go back to school, or to be able to enjoy a certain lifestyle or hobby.

Young adults, whether they are military service members or civilians, face these same questions and challenges both as products of our culture's expectations for this age group and of our current economic, social, and geopolitical circumstances. Take a few moments to reflect on your current financial status. Do you know the average income for full-time employment in your age and education bracket? Does your current (or future) job/career provide a wide array of benefits such as on-the-job training; opportunities for advancement; and help with expenses such as housing, food, child care, and health insurance? Do you know if your chosen field has supportive family policies? The following section reviews many of these material supports for both military and civilian populations in relation to understanding models of stress and resilience.

The military as a major social institution has made significant shifts in both material and social supports for service members since the transition to an all-volunteer force in 1973 (Kelty, Kleykamp, & Segal, 2010). These supports affect many decisions young adults make about entering military service and extending service or transitioning back to civilian life. Under the all-volunteer system, the U.S. military is subject to market forces just as any other business organization and has had to adjust in order to recruit and retain quality personnel. Traditional investment in training and supporting service members expanded after 1973 to include family support in order to provide a viable career pathway that extended beyond the typical 2–4 years' service in the former conscription system.

As Kelty and colleagues (2010) point out, military service functions differently in the transition to adulthood under the all-volunteer system than it did in the earlier conscription era. Conscription led to a force that was primarily young, single, and male with a low likelihood of career service, and these young persons were more likely to delay milestones that are markers of adulthood, such as marriage and parenthood. Additionally, conscripted service was more likely to interrupt progress in education and career development until the advent of the first GI Bill, which specifically funded higher education opportunities for returning service members after World War II. Kelty and colleagues posit that young adults entering military service today are more likely to view this move as either a transformative step to adult roles and responsibilities associated with a career or an investment in gaining knowledge, skills, and abilities to better meet future life goals after military service.

Other than the GI Bill, and the expanded versions that have been implemented since 2001, what types of material and social supports are offered to service members that would be helpful in transitioning into adult roles and responsibilities? Take a moment to review Figure 5.1 and its descriptive text in Chapter 5 that describes sources of support at the individual and family levels. As you make connections between resources of support and well-being, can you identify resources that might be available for one deployment but not always available for multiple deployments? What challenges do military personnel and their families face in finding or accessing resources when there is a combat injury, a move to a new duty station, a child is completing college applications, or a parent has a health crisis? The next few paragraphs highlight ways in which the organizational structure of the military addresses multiple needs of service members and their families, enhancing resources for support and well-being, particularly for the young adult, Active Component population. More detailed information on specific policies and programs that provide support to military families are detailed in Chapters 9 through 11.

Job Training and Unit Cohesion

Each branch within the military provides training for every occupation (MOS) needed to function in its organization and connects individual service members through the hierarchical structures of unit and rank. Entering service members complete both basic and advanced training and continue skill development throughout their time in service by attending both technical and leadership schools. Additionally, each branch utilizes a buddy system that begins in basic training as part of a way to help the new recruit transition from civilian to service member and learn how to work as part of a team with responsibility for the well-being of one's colleagues that extends from work to life (Ramsberger, LeGree, & Mills, 2003). Service members are paired with a colleague who may be at the same level/rank or with a more experienced service member, depending on the overall purpose. This system is called Battle Buddies in the Army, Shipmates in the Navy, and Wingmen in the Air Force. Thus, job skill training, job advancement opportunities, and structured connections to one's work and social community are integrated into military life and culture for the service member.

Compensation, Benefits, and Allowances

All training is "on the job," such that service members are employed (paid with access to benefits) during their training. In terms of pay compensation, there are more than 70 unique types of pay and allowances for which a service member may be eligible in addition to basic monthly pay (http://www.military.com/benefits/military-pay/military-pay-overview). Salary is based on rank, longevity, and annual pay raises or cost of living adjustments (COLA). Service members also receive special pay beyond salary for work such as foreign language learning, hardship or hazardous duty, special duty assignments, combat-related injury and rehabilitation, and overseas extensions, among other work and skill acquisition assignments. Military members are usually paid twice per month and receive a Leave and Earnings Statement (LES; a military "paycheck"). The LES gives monthly information about entitlements (pay, allowances, incentive pay), deductions (e.g., taxes and allotments which are money sent to banks, pay for TRICARE), and status of leave used and available.

Table 6.1 shows the 2009 rates of pay for the general U.S. population by age and education level. This is the latest year for which data about the U.S. civilian population is currently available. A recent report by the Congressional Budget Office (CBO, 2011) specifically compared federal civilian employee salaries with military personnel cash compensation rates. When educational attainment, years on the job, and gender (male federal civilian workers only) are matched, both enlisted and officer rank military personnel earn more than their federal civilian counterparts. The average enlisted person earns more cash compensation than 75% of the average civilian employee; compared to median officer cash compensation, that margin increases after 2 years of service and grows at a greater rate than the enlisted median. Rates for military personnel in 2009 and 2010 are available at the following Secretary of Defense website: http://militarypay.defense.gov/pay/bp/index.html. Table 6.2 shows the average basic pay compensation for service members at the most commonly achieved ranks in their first 4 years in the military. Generally speaking, basic pay comprises about 55% of an active duty service member's total

TABLE 6.1 Civilian Full-Time, Year-Round Mean Earnings by Age and Educational Attainment in FY 2009

	Education Level			
Age	High School Graduate or GED	Bachelor's Degree	Master's Degree	Professional Degree
18–24 years	$25,964	$36,208	–	–
25–29 years	$33,424	$49,354	$64,916	$96,384

Source: Data compiled from the U.S. Census Bureau, Current Population Survey (2010). Annual Social and Economic Supplement. Table PINC-04. Retrieved from http://www.census.gov/hhes/www/cpstables/032010/perinc/new04_001.htm.

TABLE 6.2 Examples of Mean Monthly and Yearly Basic Pay by Rank and Years of Service in FY 2009 (Most Common Young Adult Ranks Shown)

	Basic Pay by Rank					
	E-1 to E-4		E-5 to E-7		O-1 to O-4	
Years of Service	Monthly	Annual	Monthly	Annual	Monthly	Annual
2 or fewer years	$1,604.70	$19,256.40	$2,325.20	$27,902.40	$3,525.45	$42,305.40
3–4 years	$1,726.05	$20,712.60	$2,584.50	$31,014.00	$4,272.56	$51,270.72

Source: Data compiled from Office of the Under Secretary of Defense, Personnel and Readiness (2009b). Monthly basic pay table for 2009. Retrieved from http://militarypay.defense.gov/pay/bp/01_activeduty.html.

compensation package (Hogan & Seifert, 2010) with special pay and allowances constituting the remaining 45%. So what types of allowances are included in the remaining 45% of the compensation?

Basic needs such as housing, medical care, grocery/other shopping, and outlets for recreation are often met through multiple services on a military installation and the costs associated with many of these services are offset by specific **allowances** (a set dollar amount that is designed to at least partially compensate for the costs of items considered necessary for the service member). Active duty service members and their families primarily live on or close to the installation where the service member is stationed. In fact, the majority of single service members are required to live on their installation. Married service members may live on the installation or the neighboring civilian community, and all active duty service members are allotted a Basic Allowance for Housing (BAH). The BAH rate is based on whether the service member has dependents (spouse, children, other dependents) and where the service member is stationed. You can view current and past BAH rates at http://www.military.com/benefits/military-pay/basic-allowance-for-housing-rates. Service members are also provided with a Basic Allowance for Subsistence (BAS), which is intended to offset the monthly cost of meals, but only for the service member. Additionally, all service members and their dependents are covered by the DoD's health-care system, TRICARE. Just as with health insurance in the civilian market, there are different plans and options within TRICARE and these vary in terms of their deductibles, co-pays, and health issues covered. Consequently, military personnel and their families have to research these options to choose what best meets their needs and fits their budget.

Larger installations typically offer several amenities located within their confines where goods can be purchased tax free, including a **commissary** (grocery store), an **exchange** (a series of stores where durable goods and merchandise, as well as restaurants, postal services, and businesses such as hair salons are available), and **shoppettes** (convenience stores). Additional amenities include health-care facilities and various recreation facilities (e.g., bowling alleys, recreational centers, golf courses). Child development centers and schools overseen by the DoDEA are also located on military installations. Large installations within the United States and outside the United States offer these amenities to help meet the needs of daily life for service members, civilian employees, and their families. For both new and established service members and newly activated Reserve Component members, the amenities provided within the installation can help ease the hassles of finding similar facilities in the neighboring civilian community, particularly when new to an installation and community. The establishment of these services on installations indicates a significant commitment by the military to supply a comprehensive infrastructure for community-level material and social supports. These services continue to be available to family members during off-site training and deployments that service members expect as part of their work. By developing this social infrastructure, the military has transitioned to an organization that is both more family and career military oriented than in the conscription era.

FAMILY DEVELOPMENT IN EARLY AND MIDDLE ADULTHOOD AND WORK-BASED SUPPORTS IN MILITARY LIFE

Two significant life milestones often associated with early and middle adulthood are finding a long-term romantic partner and having children and, within the military, each of these milestones can impact recruitment and retention. Both of these milestones are affected by several factors in the U.S. civilian population, including geographic location, age, race/ethnicity, and education level. Research in the active duty military population also indicates that some of these factors influence timing of marriage, such as sex (Lundquist & Smith, 2005) and educational status (Segal & Segal, 2004), while recent research on the links between race, military service, and marriage indicates a significant departure from civilian norms (Lundquist, 2004; Teachman & Tedrow, 2008). How may active duty military status impact the likelihood of marrying in young adulthood? And, are active duty personnel and Reserve Component personnel similar in marital patterns?

Transitions To Marriage

In Chapter 2, you learned the basics of how many service members in the Active and Reserve Components are married as related to their rank and gender and by branch of service. Generally speaking, as personnel progress in rank, they are more likely to be married. This is due, at least in part, to another important factor: age. The marriage rate is one demographic variable where there are some significant differences between the Active and Reserve Component (National Healthy Marriage Resource Center, 2010). Active duty personnel are more likely to be married than both their Reserve Component counterparts and the civilian population. In Fiscal Year (FY) 2009, over half of all active duty personnel were married with just over one-third of active duty personnel married at the lowest enlisted levels (E-1 to E-4) and over one-half of the entry level officer ranks (O-1 to O-3) married across all branches (DUSD, 2010). Percentages of those married increase at each level in both the enlisted and officer groups of the Active Component with married status rates of 84% for those at the highest enlisted ranks of E-7 to E-9 and warrant officers (W-1 to W-5) and 94% of the highest ranking officers (O-7 to O-10) married across all branches in FY 2009. Within the selected reserve, fewer personnel were likely to be married at all enlisted levels as compared to their active duty counterparts (one-quarter in the youngest reserve ranks of E-1 to E-4 versus just over one-third of active duty at similar ranks) and this trend holds true between active duty and selected reserve and in comparing enlisted and officer categories in the two components in all but one group. Junior officers (O-1 to O-3) in the selected reserve were slightly more likely to be married than their active duty colleagues.

There are several factors that may increase the likelihood that active duty members will marry and may influence marrying at an earlier age than in the civilian population (see Box 6.1). The current payout structure of living allowances and other in-kind benefits result in a pay increase for a service member who marries, regardless of rank and time in service (Hogan & Seifert, 2010). Additionally, single service members may want to improve their living quarters by moving out of the single member barracks and into married housing on base or off-base housing in the local community. Both of these options are typically restricted to married service members. Other research has also noted that individuals who choose the military are more likely to adhere to traditional values, one of which is placing a high regard on marriage (Hogan & Seifert, 2010; Karney & Crown, 2007; Lundquist, 2006). The military has also instituted family programming that is focused on strengthening marital relationships, such as *Strong Bonds*, and helping the single and dating population

---

BOX 6.1   VOICES FROM THE FRONTLINE

SUPPORTING MARRIAGE

If you look at students on a college campus, the expectation is that you are single. In the military we bring young, enlisted troops into a campus culture and in subtle and not so subtle ways encourage them to marry young for the benefits.

It's common for a new recruit to think, "If I got married, I'd have a home, kitchen, more space, more income. It beats sharing a room in the barracks."

Wanting to be accepted and loved is a human need, especially when you are on an installation away from your family, your friends are deploying, and some of them may be getting injured or killed. You know you will soon be deploying too and who knows what may happen.

This is a big difference between young people of the same age who have taken different paths in life. It's one that can influence their relationships and families in the years to come.

Evonne Carawan
Director, Personnel Readiness and Community Support, Office of the Deputy Assistant Secretary of the Navy (Military Personnel Policy)

make healthy choices in romantic relationships. *Strong Bonds* and other programs geared toward strengthening family and important social relationships are detailed in Chapters 9 through 11.

Other interesting differences in marriage rates between the Active Component and civilian populations are identified in research that focuses on race/ethnicity and military service. In particular, Lundquist (2004, 2006) and Teachman and Tedrow (2008) have highlighted how military service may act as factor in promoting marriage for African American personnel and sustaining these marriages at significantly higher rates than their civilian counterparts. Lundquist argues that the military offers a structural context that minimizes differences for both racial and economic factors, which are often cited as contributing to significant differences in marriages rates between Black and White populations in the United States (Goldstein & Kenney, 2001; Sampson, 1995). As an integrated, merit-based, and **"total" institution** (one that rewards and promotes based on performance and that has 24/7 influence in an individual's daily experiences on and off the job), Lundquist contends that the military provides an environment in which African American men and women have access to equal employment opportunities and daily living supports that are more difficult to access in the civilian population. Further, as an institution that implemented a highly structured, racial desegregation plan in the mid-twentieth century, military installations and military connected communities that surround installations rank among the least racially segregated communities in the United States (Lundquist, 2004). Racially segregated workplaces and communities are associated with stronger perceptions of racial discrimination and higher reports of minority stress, thus the military context may serve to lessen the effects of both institutional and daily experiences of discrimination based on race for African American service personnel and their families in ways that are supportive of healthier family and relational outcomes.

Transitions to Parenthood

Earlier chapters have highlighted information about military families, such that you already know that in FY 2009 the birth to age 7 group of children constituted over half (53%) of the total number of children in active duty families and 44% of active duty members had children (DUSD, 2010). In the selected reserve the trend of having slightly older personnel translates into a smaller percentage of children in the birth to age 7 group (37%). Table 6.3 gives the average ages at which members across active and selected reserve became parents for the first time in FY 2009. In that year, the average age of the active duty service member at the time of his/her first child's birth ranged from 23.2 years in the Marine Corps to 25.7 in the Air Force, and over half (56.7%) of members were between 20 and 25 years old at the time of their first child's birth. Within the selected reserve the

TABLE 6.3   Average Age at Birth of First Child in FY 2009 by Service Branch and Component

Active Duty		Selected Reserve	
	Average Age		**Average Age**
Marine Corps	23.2	Marine Corps Reserve	24.6
Army	24.6	Army National Guard	25.3
Navy	25.5	Army Reserve	26.4
Air Force	25.7	Air National Guard	28.6
		Navy Reserve	29.1
		Air Force Reserve	29.8
Total DoD	24.8	Total Select Reserve	26.4

Source: Data compiled from Office of the Deputy Under Secretary of Defense (Military Community and Family Policy) (2010). Exhibits 3.21 (p. 60) and 5.19 (p. 124). *2009 demographics: Profile of the military community.* Washington, DC: Author.

age at first birth ranged from 24.6 years in the Marine Corps Reserve to 29.8 years in the Air Force Reserve. Just under half (45%) of all first-time parents in the selected reserve in FY 2009 were between 20 and 25 years of age.

Average age at the onset of parenthood among active duty service members is slightly earlier as compared to the civilian population in the United States, which has seen a gradual rise in age at first birth for women (Mathews & Hamilton, 2009). Additionally, service members are most likely to be in their 20s and less likely to be in their teens or 30s when they become parents, which means that the range of typical ages at first birth is more restricted in the service member population as compared to the civilian population (MacDermid Wadsworth, 2010). Within the civilian population in 2006, age at first birth for women ranged from 22.6 years in Mississippi to 27.7 years in Massachusetts, with an average across the United States of 25 years. According to the 2002 National Survey of Family Growth, for males between ages 14 and 44 years, the average age at first child's birth was 25.1 years (Martinez, Chandra, Abma, Jones, & Mosher, 2002).

The most common age at which active duty males became a parent in FY 2009 was 22 years, while the most common age at birth of their first child for active duty females was 20 years. Within the Reserve Component, the most common age for male service members at birth of their first child was 23 years; it was 20 years for female service members. These average and most common ages at first birth hold steady for Demographics Reports from FY 2003 through FY 2009 (latest available) (DUSD, 2004, 2005, 2006, 2007, 2008, 2009a,2009b, 2010). There is no directly comparable data in overall birthrates between service member and civilian populations although comparisons for first-time births can be made and can give some insight into potential differences between active duty, selected reserve, and civilian populations.

The **first-time birthrate** in the civilian population is calculated as the number of first births per 1000 women, ages 15–44 in a given year. This is different from the **overall birthrate**, which calculates all births per 1000 women, ages 14–44 in a given year. In 2009, the civilian first-time birthrate was 27 per 1000 women or 2.7% (Hamilton, Martin, & Ventura, 2010). Using data from the 2009 Demographics Profile of the Military Community (DUSD, 2010), calculations for first-time births among active duty and selected reserve personnel are achieved by dividing the number of first-time births to female service members (FY 2009 active duty $N = 2343$, ages 17–45 years; FY 2009 selected reserve $N = 2270$, ages 17–44 years) by the total number of women personnel in each component (active duty = 200,888 and selected reserve = 152,220). Thus, the active duty first-time birthrate in FY 2009 was 3.4% (6886/200,888), higher than the civilian rate, while the selected reserve first-time birthrate in FY 2009 was 1.5% (2266/152,220) lower than the civilian rate.

Researchers consistently point to the compensation system of allowances and the economic stability (relative to work in the civilian workforce) of military service, as well as strong support structures for family needs as factors that may lead to higher rates of earlier marriage and childbearing within the active duty service population (Hogan & Seifert, 2010; Kelty et al., 2010; Lundquist, 2004). The additional allowances that cover medical care and child care, in addition to the previously mentioned housing allowance, are part of the material supports to which military families have access.

The DoD has also developed extensive family support programs that extend from spousal hiring initiatives to organized child and youth activities and strong school-community collaborations that may be perceived as family friendly, particularly to a service member who knows that their occupation may demand long and/or frequent separations from family, as well as put them in harm's way. There are also more specialized programs to help families address unique needs that members may have. For example, families who have a special needs family member, such as a child with a developmental delay or a medically fragile parent who is identified as a dependent in the DEERS system, have access to programs including the Exceptional Family Member Program (see Chapter 9 for more details). This combination of allowances and material and social supports creates an institution that encourages family development in young and middle adulthood, in spite of the stressors and dangers that were identified in Chapter 3 as expectable and normative in military life.

Military Connected Communities

The combination of military-based supports may also be viewed as community friendly. In military-affected communities, the local economy and resources are influenced by the presence of a military installation. Families may live off base; spouses may work in the local economy; civilians may work on base; and schools, religious communities, and businesses may provide resources of support and community building for all local persons. One very practical example of the military–community connection is in working with schools. Not all installations, particularly within the United States, have schools on base, and those that do are most likely to have elementary level only, with secondary students attending schools in the community.

School districts are funded by a variety of sources and often receive some funding on a *per student* basis. Thus, it is important to have a very close approximation of the number of students in a school district in order to have an accurate budget for operating costs and be ready to hire or release instructors and other personnel based on these changes. In a community that is connected to a military installation, the student count can vary based on restructuring, deployments, periodic turnover of personnel, and the addition or deletion of services (and thus personnel) at an installation. The DoD is required to coordinate with Local Educational Agencies (LEAs) to identify specific installations that are scheduled to experience population shifts that will affect the local school systems (*Update to the Report on Assistance to Local Educational Agencies for Defense Dependents' Education* [DoD, 2010c]). This coordination is viewed as an important aspect of both family and operational readiness and is designed to meet several needs: school districts can plan ahead for changes in student population and prepare staff for changes that students may experience while in attendance (such as relocation and parental deployment/reunification) and families can rely on the coordination of the military and community to help accomplish the multiple tasks of helping children change school systems.

One initiative of this mandate is the Interstate Compact on Educational Opportunity for Military Children. In Chapter 4, you learned that this initiative is designed to help streamline multiple aspects of paperwork involved in enrolling a child into a new school system. Children in active duty families attend an average of eight different schools between kindergarten and high school graduation. Each change is an exercise in tracking paperwork and learning a new school district's requirements. Families receive a direct benefit from the military–local community connection through the establishment of the Interstate Compact. By working with local communities and school systems, this Compact simplifies the school transition process and supports children who experience high mobility in their school age years.

Connections between the military and the local community can come in other forms, too. As you read below about Chaplin Purinton's experiences and his perspective on his role in the military and the community, what other connections do you think would be useful and promote healthy relationships and interactions in military connected communities? Do you know of any connections in your communities that try to improve connections between military families and the larger community?

<hr/>

Voices From the Frontline

ON BRIDGING THE INFORMATION GAP BETWEEN MILITARY AND CIVILIAN COMMUNITIES

One of the chaplain's roles is that of pastor, to provide religious leadership. We are also trained to various degrees in counseling. As clergy in uniform, our job is supporting people as they experience the cycle of life while moving through the cycle of deployment.

Some states have developed initiatives such as the Military, Family and Community Network (MFCNetwork) of Vermont. Its mission is, "To develop and maintain a multi-group network among community, military, government and private sectors that creates awareness of challenges, identifies resources and provides services to all service members and their families throughout the deployment cycle" (http://www.vtmfen.org). I am a member of this group and I spoke to the state Chiefs of Police organization as a member of the network. Weeks after a 15-minute presentation, I began to hear from law enforcement professionals and members of our community that something had changed. When stopped for speeding, people were being asked: "Are you a member of a military family?" and if yes, "Have you recently returned home from deployment?" There are many small things all of us can do that when added together make a difference for military families.

Chaplain Charles Purinton
Army National Guard Chaplain

Several sources of military-based support have been developed since the transition to the all-volunteer force that supports significant developmental milestones expected in early and middle adulthood, namely marriage and parenthood. In order for these support systems to flourish and improve, reviews of their effectiveness and value to both the service member and his/her family are conducted. As you learned in Chapter 5, most theories on stress and resilience acknowledge that individuals and families may perceive potential resources very differently and, based on their perceptions of need, they may or may not choose to access or rely on particular resources. Additionally, some resources may only be useful in the short-term, and the family may have to make adjustments as to which resources are tapped when confronted with a stressor or a series of stressors. The next section focuses on what we have learned about resilience and capacity building in military families and, when possible, makes connections to the supports that have been identified in the first part of this chapter.

UNDERSTANDING RESEARCH ABOUT RISK AND RESILIENCE

This section presents a growing body of research that has focused on identifying protective and risk factors in relation to resilience in service members and military families. Chapters 7 and 8 review current research specifically focused on how service members and their families are affected by war. For those of you who may not have taken a research class recently, some basic elements that define who/what is studied, how the group/topic is studied, and the strengths and limitations of different kinds of research are briefly reviewed.

Both the DoD and military family scholars have adopted **longitudinal** approaches to research on service members and their families. Longitudinal studies allow us *to follow people over time*, gathering data at multiple points, noting changes, and identifying factors that predict both vulnerability and resilience. For example, Karney and Crown (2011) report on the likelihood that deployment (deployed status, multiple or extended deployments) increases or decreases the risk of marital dissolution over time. Their dataset included all personnel (active duty and selected reserve) who were active between FY 2002 and FY 2005.

Perhaps the most significant undertaking in longitudinal research with service members is the Millennium Cohort Study. In 2001, the DoD began a 22-year longitudinal cohort study on the effects of military service, including deployments, on service member health and well-being while serving and after separation from military service. This study is the most comprehensive ever undertaken in U.S. military history to study the long-term effects of military service (http://www.millenniumcohort.org/index.php), and data are being collected every 3 years until 2022. The intent is to follow respondents even if they separate from service in order to learn about the development of any patterns related to their service experiences and physical and psychological health outcomes. The data collection process identifies each new set of respondents as **cohorts**. A cohort consists of new enrollees who join the study at the same time and the research design calls for multiple points of new enrollments. In 2011 the study was expanded to include a fourth cohort. The 2011 cohort will be the first to include both service members ($n = 50,000$) and spouses ($n = 10,000$), which will create opportunities for learning about couple dynamics and family level health.

Cross-sectional studies are also useful in learning about service members and their families. This type of study can provide us rich information about events, incidents, and perceptions by *collecting data from a group at a single point in time*. Flake, Davis, Johnson, and Middleton (2009) offer an example of a cross-sectional study that relied on self-reports of Army spouses to report about their school age children's well-being during a deployment that affected a large Army base community. Cross-sectional studies often are referred to as "snapshots" that capture information at a specific point in time. Cross-sectional research can be helpful in assessing current moods, conditions, and needs of a population or community and provide information that can be used for longer-term planning and research.

Both types of studies are useful in their application to military personnel and families, although there are differences in **scope** (how broad the research question is and how widely it can be generalized) and application. Helping professionals can use findings from Karney and Crown (2011) to develop marital support programs for groups that are at higher risk of marital dissolution, such as women service members in the Active Component and in the Army National Guard and Navy Reservists who do not have children. This study also disputes the conventional wisdom that families who experience deployment are automatically or commonly at risk for divorce, particularly if they have children. Programs for marriage enrichment can identify positive aspects of deployment for both the service member and his/her family while offering skills and resources to help families attain positive growth despite the stressors of deployment.

Professionals working on particular installations can use the findings from Flake et al. (2009) to identify and address current issues deployed families are facing at a particular installation or in a community and tailor support programs to better meet the specific needs that those family members are facing. For example, if a unit has experienced a high injury rate, there are likely several families who now need to navigate the health-care system; make decisions about travel to medical facilities, care of children and time off of work; and face the possibilities of death or long-term injury care of their service member. Although there are multiple resources to address these demands, the ways that family support professionals help families navigate these demands may differ in what it "looks like" at an active duty installation versus a four-county National Guard community affected by the same events. Critical skills for helping professionals include being able to take into consideration details about the unique experiences in the family system, their local military and civilian communities, as well as the in-theatre experiences of deployed service members.

Other aspects of research that scholars must address include defining how in-depth the study will be, how broadly one can **generalize** what is learned from the study (Does it apply to everyone all the time? Or to specific groups at a specific point in time?), and the best ways to communicate the findings to different **constituents** (people and organizations that can benefit from the knowledge gained, as well as any sponsors of the research). As you read the next section, keep these questions in mind to help you understand how much each study can tell us about service members and family life and where gaps in our knowledge still exist.

RECENT RESEARCH ON RISK AND RESILIENCE IN SERVICE MEMBERS

There is no shortage of research within the military community. In fact, research informs almost every facet of military life and organization. As an organization, the DoD relies on healthy and highly trained individuals who will remain in service for time spans ranging from a few years to a lifelong career. Thus, organizational research primarily focuses on issues that create risks to maintaining a physically and psychologically healthy unit ready to answer the call of service. Overarching questions include what experiences/issues pose threats to or promote strength and health in service members, what kinds of prevention and intervention policies and programs address these threats or strengths effectively, and what improvements in services (physical, psychological, medical, familial) are needed. Although most of the research about service members reviewed here has been since 2001, a large body of research on service members predating 2001 exists and some of it will be included.

Several behaviors and experiences have been identified, many in the years prior to OIE/OIF, as contributing to either heightened risks for or protection against negative effects of trauma. **Risky behaviors** include, but are not limited to alcohol and other drug misuse, disordered eating, increased risk-taking, and both sexual and nonsexual aggression. Life experiences that may put a service member at increased risk for negative physical, emotional, and/or relational well-being include combat and trauma exposure, traumatic injury, family history of violence and previous experiences as a victim of personal violence (familial, interpersonal, sexual), and family history of mental health risks (e.g. depression, anxiety, PTSD) (Solomon, Zur-Noah, Horesh, Zerach, & Keinan, 2008). **Protective factors** are those skills and resources that individuals and families can draw upon to help them cope with adversity. Protective factors can include staying connected with family and friends, being part of a unit with high trust and cohesion and strong leadership, maintaining or implementing behaviors such as getting enough rest and eating healthy, and having a positive sense of one's ability to persevere in tough times.

Interestingly, many of these risky behaviors, experiences, and protective factors are also a focus for screening within adolescent medicine (Hutchinson, Greene, & Hansen, 2008), which refers to health care for persons between the ages of 10 and 25 years. Hutchinson and colleagues advocate using and/or modifying two psychosocial evaluation tools common to this branch of medicine with service members, as 45% of the active duty and 33% of the selected reserve are ages 25 and under. The HEADSSS (Home, Education, Activity, Drugs, Sex, Suicide, and Safety) interview, with a few modifications to address military life, is designed to screen both for risky behaviors and contexts, as well as potential protective factors while framing the assessment in a strengths model that helps the adolescent become more aware of their behaviors and motivations, as well as sources of stress and support (Duncan et al., 2007; Goldenring & Cohen, 1988). Hutchinson and colleagues also recommend the CRAFFT (Car, Relax, Alone, Forget, Family, and Trouble) screening instrument, which focuses specifically on behaviors associated with substance abuse (Werner, Walker, & Greene, 1994). Both tools can augment other behavioral screenings and have validity in nonmilitary populations. Screening instruments such as these can give insight into the health and safety of a young military population, both of which may impact readiness.

Baseline Data from the Millennium Cohort Study

As mentioned earlier, the Millennium Cohort Study is longitudinal and is expected to have a wide variety of implications on the physical and psychological effects of military service for both service members and their families, across Active and Reserve Components, extending to life after service (veteran status). Data from the first cohort ($n = 77,000$ participants from 2001 to 2003) provided a baseline of information about rates of mental disorders and health issues found in this representative sample. **Baseline data** is the first data gathered in a longitudinal study, and it provides a comparison point for all future data. An important aspect of baseline data of the Millennium Cohort Study is that it was collected *prior to* our current involvement in OIE/OIF. Thus, the data reflect information about service member's health and wellness during peacetime and will allow researchers to assess the effects of multiple military service experiences, such as deployments and types of deployment exposures on both physical and mental health outcomes.

Physical and psychological health. What has the Millennium Cohort Study Team learned so far? Baseline data from the first cohort indicates that this cohort was as healthy or healthier when compared to the civilian population with the exception of alcohol use. This baseline data also established the prevalence rates of key mental disorders and risk-taking behaviors that can be followed over time for specific subgroups within the military population. These preconflict data allowed the study team to design **prospective** studies or studies that start in the present and continue into the future to see what experiences are linked to physical and psychological health outcomes late in life.

To date, the publications generated from the early waves of data collection have begun to identify prevalence of risk factors and threats to both physical and psychological well-being for service members.

Health risk factors, including changes in risky behaviors and the development of health problems, are being tracked with this data set in relation to deployment experiences. Recent reports about these data find that negative behavioral changes include disrupted sleep patterns (Seelig et al., 2010), disordered eating patterns (Jacobson et al., 2009), cigarette smoking (Smith, Ryan, et al., 2008), and alcohol use (Jacobson et al., 2008). Health problems diagnosed since deployment include the development of diabetes (Boyko et al., 2010), high blood pressure (Granado et al., 2009), and respiratory problems (Smith, Wong, et al., 2009).

Psychological risk factors are also under consideration by the study team, and links between protective and risk factors to PTSD, depression, and anxiety are beginning to come into focus. Recent research from the Millennium Cohort research team indicates that predeployment experiences of both physical injury and psychological distress (Sandweiss et al., 2011) and prior trauma exposure (Smith, Wingard, et al., 2008) are linked with higher risk for postdeployment PTSD. As the study progresses through to 2022, researchers will be able to identify patterns that contribute to well-being and resilience when service members face adverse events, repeated or multiple types of military-based stressors, and the roles that spouses and other social relationships play in affecting overall resilience.

There are several other studies, not tied to the Millennium data set, currently underway and recently completed that augment our knowledge about risk and protective factors for service members. Each study helps fill in gaps in our knowledge, improve measurement of risk and resilience, and gives better direction for program and policy development in supporting healthy outcomes for service members. A closer examination of three specific risk-taking behaviors follows below. From a helping professional's perspective, engaging in risk-taking behaviors may be important indicators of psychological distress and may be the ways in which the service member is trying to manage his/her distress.

Problem drinking. Alcohol misuse is a significant area of concern within the Armed Forces and is a topic also widely studied in the general U.S. population. Several recent studies have examined alcohol use in different military populations: women (Wallace, Sheehan, & Young-Zu, 2009), junior personnel (Williams, et al., 2010), active duty personnel (Stahre, Brewer, Fonseca, & Naimi, 2009), and National Guard (Ferrier-Aurbach et al., 2009). Additional research has also focused on alcohol use in relation to combat deployment experiences (Jacobson, et al., 2008).

Gender and age are consistently associated with increased risk of alcohol misuse in the military context. Women, representing approximately 15% of the military (DUSD, 2010), and junior enlisted personnel, those between the ages of 18 and 25, are considered to be at higher risk for problem drinking, similar to their same age civilian counterparts. Previous research indicates that women in traditionally male occupations (Wilsnack & Wilsnack, 1995) and women in the military (Ames & Cunradi, 2004) have higher rates of problem drinking than women in traditionally female occupations and men in the military, respectively. Junior personnel in both the Navy and Air Force have also been found to be at higher risk for problem drinking, such as binge drinking, than their older counterparts, both when compared to their respective branch and to other service branches in the recent baseline report from the Millennium Cohort Study (Riddle et al., 2007).

Binge drinking rates in the Active component, across all branches and ranks, were very common in anonymously reported behaviors on the 2005 Department of Defense Survey of Health Related Behaviors ($n = 12,197$ reported at least one episode out of 16,037 total respondents). Two-thirds reported at least one binge-drinking episode occurring between the ages of 17 and 25 (Stahre et al., 2009). Marines reported the greatest prevalence of binge drinking within 30 days of completing the survey (51.4%) and over the past year (28.2%). Men, across all branches, averaged just under 42 episodes per year, while women (again across all branches) averaged just under 19 episodes of binge drinking per year. As a point of comparison, binge-drinking rates in the civilian population gradually increased from 1995 to 2001 (Naimi et al., 2003), and the 2001 rates of binge drinking were estimated at 12.5 episodes per year for men and 2.7 episodes per for women.

Binge drinkers were more likely to experience negative health and social and job outcomes than their peers who consumed alcohol without bingeing (Stahre et al., 2009). These negative outcomes included job performance issues, alcohol-induced injury/risky behaviors, interpersonal relationship issues (although no domestic violence data was gathered as part of this study), and both civilian and military legal issues. Although the highest risk group was composed of younger (17–25 years), less educated (high school or less), and single persons living on base or stationed onboard ships, there were also substantial numbers of older, higher ranking, married service members reporting binge drinking patterns as well. Thus, interventions for alcohol misuse need to be tailored to the local unit, and Naimi and colleagues recommend that programming go beyond common screening/treatment for alcoholism, include local community partnerships, and address the role of alcohol within the military culture.

Current alcohol research is also focused on understanding the relationship between deployment and changes in drinking behaviors (Jacobson et al., 2008) and in identifying alcohol usage patterns of National Guard and Reserve service members (Ferrier-Auerbach et al, 2009). Jacobsen and colleagues, using data from the first and second panel of the Millennium Cohort Study, were able to identify predeployment and postdeployment data on drinking behaviors for active duty, Reserve, and National Guard participants, as well as identify those who experienced combat exposure during deployment and those who did not and compare information with a group of participants who did not deploy between the two data collection periods. Overall, they found that combat-experience deployment for Reserve/Guard personnel increased the likelihood of new onset drinking, of continued heavy weekly drinking as well as binge drinking, and the number alcohol-related problems. Combat experience was linked to new onset binge drinking for active duty personnel across all branches. Personnel across both components, who also reported mental health symptoms including PTSD and depression in addition to combat exposure, were at significantly increased odds for escalation in problem drinking behaviors.

Ferrier-Auerbach and colleagues, in a cross-sectional study, tested predictors of *predeployment drinking behaviors* in a National Guard Brigade Combat Team (National Guard, 2009) and found, similar to other studies, that age (being younger) and marital status (being single) were linked with greater risk of various problematic drinking behaviors. Additionally, personality traits of negative internalizing and externalizing behaviors, such as high negative emotionality and disinhibition, respectively, were significantly predictive of problem drinking.

Problem drinking patterns that are identified predeployment are of significant concern to unit leaders, as the negative effects can compromise not just the individual but also the entire unit and the mission. Further research is recommended to learn if these patterns were temporary, typical, or a result of learning about their upcoming deployment. Within the Reserve Component context, changing status from civilian to active military status and all the significant life changes and stressors that entails may put these service members at higher risk than their active duty counterparts. They may also have less access to useful resources to lower this risk, such as base and unit tailored programs and proximity to a community of Guard/Reserve colleagues.

Other drug usage (both legal [i.e., energy drinks] and illegal [i.e., barbiturates, methamphetamines]), with the exception of tobacco, is not as well studied in the military population. Tobacco reduction education efforts within the active duty population and changes in smoking policies at installations have significantly decreased overall tobacco use (Klesges, Haddock, Lando, & Talcott, 1999; Woodruff, Conway, & Edwards, 2000). Jacobson and colleagues (2008) found links between increased risk in negative outcomes for new onset drinking and increased heavy drinking after deployment when both alcohol and tobacco use were co-occurring.

Alcohol use and misuse are of primary concern to the military community. Its links to individual negative personal, social, and career outcomes pose a threat to health, well-being, and readiness for both the individual and the unit they serve. Additionally, problem drinking is linked with negative interpersonal relationship outcomes, including relationships with family members and work colleagues. Interventions and policies are recommended by researchers to address a wider spectrum of maladaptive drinking behaviors and tailor programs to better meet the needs of military personnel at different ages and stages in both their life and career development.

Disordered eating. Weight control is one aspect of maintaining physical fitness to serve, and both active duty and selected reserve personnel must routinely go though fitness testing, including weighing-in. Military weight and percentage of body fat (%BF) standards are part of the physical fitness criteria and play a role in assessing job performance and consideration for promotion. Personnel who exceed established %BF standards are required to participate in a weight control program and may face disciplinary action if they fail to meet standards (Bathalon et al., 2006). Interestingly, one study found that being mandated to enter a prescribed weight loss program increased the risk of engaging in disordered eating patterns for military women (McNulty, 2008). Military standards for ideal weight and %BF are lower than standards set for the general population (Garber, Boyer, Pollack, Chang, & Shafer, 2008), thus personnel may meet criteria for the general population, yet still be considered overweight by the military. This conflict may increase body image dissatisfaction and the risk for disordered eating. Changes in assessing %BF are underway to try to minimize this conflict while increasing the effectiveness in identifying personnel at increased risk for weight-related health issues (Bathalon et al., 2006).

Disordered eating patterns have been identified in multiple military personnel surveys (Beekley et al., 2009; Carlton, Manos, & Van Slyke, 2005; Garber et al., 2008; Lauder & Campbell, 2001; McNulty, 2008) and in the baseline data of the Millennium Cohort Study (Riddle et al., 2007). Data from these studies indicate that disordered eating practices, including clinical diagnoses of anorexia nervosa and bulimia nervosa, occur more frequently in female personnel than male personnel and are more prevalent in the 17–25 age group, for those who have 14 or more years of service in their military career, and for those serving in the Navy.

Prevalence rates of disordered eating in a sample of military academy cadets were comparable to civilian college reports (Beekley et al., 2009), indicating that there is no identified significant difference between military and civilian populations in young adult populations. Although most studies have focused on the overweight aspect of physical fitness in the military, Beekley and colleagues also identify risks associated with severely underweight individuals. They noted that an eating disorder multidisciplinary team, including clinical psychologists, a registered dietitian, and a physician, had been established for intervention efforts with cadets. One treatment avenue available for cadets who were severely underweight was involuntary treatment in a clinical program, which showed at least short-term success.

Other research noted that temporary or "situational" disordered eating patterns spiked within the 2 months immediately prior to fitness testing and weigh-in (Lauder et al., 1999), as personnel felt the pressure to "make weight" —a bit like cramming for an exam. The behaviors identified in situational patterns included crash dieting, binging, purging, using laxatives and other pills, and fasting. Recommendations to reduce both situational and pervasive disordered eating included creation of preventative programming to instill healthier behaviors for new recruits and expansion of supportive interventions year round for all personnel. Interventions included individual nutritional education/counseling and healthier menu options on base (Garber et al., 2008) to mitigate both risky behaviors focused on passing the fitness tests and the development of lifelong patterns of disordered eating. Recent research with female veterans has also linked specific disordered eating behaviors with exposure to trauma and seeking treatment for mental health (Rowe, Gradus, Pineles, Batten, & Davison, 2009). Specifically, women veterans who indicated that they were survivors of **military sexual trauma** (MST: sexual trauma experienced while in active service) were at increased risk of both bingeing and starving behaviors. Women veterans who did not indicate MST, but did indicate exposure to other traumatic events also were at increased risk of bingeing behaviors.

Increased risk-taking. The current study of other types of risk-taking behaviors focuses almost exclusively on postdeployment behaviors. Although some research has employed a longitudinal, pretest/posttest design, many studies have relied on cross-sectional studies, which limits the ability to clarify the predictive connections between deployment and increased risk-taking. Additionally, this topic is overshadowed by a very strong research presence on PTSD and other mental health problems that may have more "clinical presence" (Killgore et al., 2008). Killgore and colleagues view increased risk-taking behaviors as an unaddressed public health concern and one that may be able to be linked to combat exposure and prolonged deployment. Although not explicitly tested in their study, they raise the possibility of being able to measure combat and deployment stressor changes in the limbic system (neurochemical and functional adaptive responses to stress in the human body) as an indicator that adjustment postdeployment is not simply a matter of setting aside service and survival skills once home, but requires a reorganizing of the stress response system.

Within the military population, the most commonly studied postdeployment risky behavior beside alcohol use is that of aggressive driving (Bell, Amoroso, Yore, Smith, & Jones, 2000; Hooper et al., 2006). Motor vehicle accidents are a major cause of death for both nondeployed (Bell et al., 2006) and recently returned soldiers (Hooper et al., 2006). The majority of these service member deaths occur within the youngest age group, 17–25 years. Fatal motor vehicle accidents are a leading cause of death within the civilian population in this age group as well (National Highway Traffic Safety Association [NHTSA], 2010). Earlier in this chapter, Chaplin Purinton described how communicating this known fact of aggressive driving with the Vermont State Police made a difference in how traffic stops were handled. Can you think of other ways information about risk-taking behaviors in military service members could have a practical impact for human service and public servant professionals in a community?

Killgore and colleagues expanded our understanding of other risky behaviors in their 2008 study of postcombat invincibility and risk-taking practices. One of the unique contributions of this study was the ability to identify specific combat experiences that confer either increased risk for or protective factors against engaging in risky behaviors after deployment. The risky behaviors in this study were alcohol use and aggressive behavior toward others and property. Three of the combat experiences were significantly and uniquely associated with increased use of alcohol, drinking in greater quantities, and drinking more than they meant to, respectively. Five of the combat experience categories were significantly associated with an increased risk of a variety of aggressive behaviors and with different levels of aggressive actions:

1. Violent combat exposure—more likely to get angry with unit member and yell/shout
2. Human trauma exposure—increased angry verbal outbursts, likelihood of destroying property, and threaten unit member with physical violence
3. Surviving a close call—increased destruction of property and threatening of others
4. Killed enemy—more yelling/shouting, destruction of property, threats of physical violence, and actual physical violence against someone
5. Killed friendly/nonhostiles—same increased risks as category 4

This study also highlighted a few protective factors. Specifically, the combat experience of surviving a close call reduced alcohol consumption on a typical day of drinking, and experience with the death/injury of a buddy reduced the likelihood of driving while under the influence of alcohol or riding with a person who had been drinking. The authors caution that the magnitude (strength) of the associations for both risks and protection were modest, but that they were statistically reliable (not a fluke or accident). Killgore and colleagues recommend that the Veteran's Administration and civilian health-care systems need to be informed of increased risk-taking behaviors as service members return from deployments and transition out of the service. The VA and civilian health-care systems become the frontline primary care settings for veterans once they separate from military service, but their service experiences, particularly combat experiences, may have a profound effect on their later health and risk-taking behaviors.

Work-Based Supports and Risk and Resilience

At the beginning of this chapter, job training and unit cohesion were identified as important material supports for service members. Recent research has identified limitations and opportunities of these material supports to enhance resilience in service members and their families.

Job training. Each service member trains for a particular MOS in order to gain specialized technical and operational skills, in addition to maintaining good physical health. Although developing a high level of technical proficiency and the ability to perform one's work under pressure are primary goals of job training, there has been a recent increase in attention to enhancing psychological resilience that is tied to MOS training (Adler & Dolan, 2006; Maddi, Kahn, & Maddi, 1998; Thomas, Adler, Wittels, Enne, & Johannes, 2004). Previous research has shown that service members report faster physiological recovery than psychological recovery from intense mission training (Thomas et al., 2004) and that occupational stressors unique to particular jobs create specific types of occupational stress (Dobreva-Martinova, Villeneuve, Strickland, & Matheson, 2002; Pflanz & Sonnek, 2002).

An increased focus on psychological resilience in concert with physiological health and training in technical skills may be particularly relevant for specializations with a higher likelihood of exposure to danger (such as combat arms, combat support, and medical care) and the need to manage distressing situations for others (such as casualty assistance notification, unit leadership, and combat stress prevention). In one study of personnel completing combat medic training (Robinson et al., 2009), several mental health symptoms worsened from the beginning to the completion of the training, including increases in depression, anxiety, and suicidal ideation. The majority of personnel in this study had been enlisted for less than 1 year (84%) another 9% enlisted for 1–3 years, and just over half (53%) had attained college or more education. Additionally, over half of the sample participants were active duty personnel (59%), while the remaining personnel were serving in the Reserve Component.

The prevalence rates for all three mental health concerns were indistinguishable from the general entry level enlisted population at the time of entry into the program but increased by the end of training. Risk factors for this increase were associated with gender (women at much higher risk), age (younger at higher risk than older personnel), education (those with lower education at higher risk), status (active duty at higher risk than Reserve Component), and previous service history (those with no experience at higher risk). The general increase in symptoms from the beginning to completion of training argues against the idea that technical training offers protection against psychological distress within this particular study and indicates that service members may benefit from a training approach that incorporates both the technical and psychological aspects of an occupational specialization as part of a mission.

Unit Leadership and Cohesion

A growing body of research has linked leadership behaviors and organizational climate to the morale and well-being of service members. In a highly structured organization such as the military, leadership style and attitudes are linked to psychological outcomes for personnel (Hardy et al., 2010) and perceptions of stigma in needing and accessing mental health services (Wright et al., 2009). In the field of public health, targeted interventions that address both the public stigma (cultural attitudes about characteristics of persons with mental health needs that lead to biased assessments) and self-stigma (internalization of cultural attitudes and biases) have been created to reduce stigma as a potential barrier to treatment (Corrigan, 2004; Rosen, Walter, Casey, & Hocking, 2000). Positive ratings of unit leadership and unit cohesion, both as independent factors and in concert with one another, are related to lower perceptions of stigma about and help-seeking behaviors related to depression (Britt, Davison, Bliese, & Castro, 2004; Pietrzak et al., 2010), PTSD (Pietrzak et al., 2010), and general mental health (Wright et al., 2009). Recommendations from this line of research include targeting military leaders as change agents for their units, relaying more positive organizational attitudes toward mental health issues, and stressing the role of buddy care as part of military leadership training. One program that implemented this approach is Resilience Training (U.S. Army Medical Department, 2010b). This and other programs are detailed in Chapters 9 and 11.

Social Support

Several studies have noted that positive social support plays a key role as a protective factor for service members. Social support is broadly conceptualized to include relationships with family, friends, coworkers, employers, and community members and the extent to which these relationships are characterized by helpfulness and emotional care. Pietrzak and colleagues included measures of social support in their recent resilience studies, which indicated that higher levels of social support were linked with better mental health outcomes for Reserve Component personnel after deployment (Pietrzak et al., 2010) and OIF/OEF veterans up to 2 years after service (Pietrzak, Johnson, Goldstein, Malley, & Southwick, 2009).

A longitudinal study with a small National Guard population found that prior life stressors, perceptions of readiness for the mission, and concern about life/family disruption were important predeployment risk factors for experiencing postdeployment PTSD while both social support and experiencing fewer life stressors after deployment served as protective factors against the development of PTSD (Polusny et al., 2011). This builds on a body of research that acknowledges that the transition of Reserve Component personnel from citizen to service member and back to citizen is comprised of both events that are similar to their active duty counterparts (deployment experiences, training) and life events that are potentially very different from Active Component personnel (disruption in education, work, unfamiliar and extended separations from friends and family, lack of community support resources tailored to military experiences). More research on the ways that social support contributes to service member resilience is needed in both the Reserve and Active Components. In particular, learning more about the types of connections (family, friends, community members/organizations) and the use of both informal (personally chosen) and formal (program/organizational based) connections would facilitate our understanding of service member resilience in different contexts and access to support systems that are valued. Additional research should also consider how connections may result in negative effects. For example, if a unit develops a strong connection that establishes that risky behaviors are part of its "identity" and leadership develops in such a way that seeking help is discouraged, these social connections with coworkers and employers may have serious negative consequences for members of the unit.

SUMMARY

- Scholarship on military families generally increases during times of military engagement and gradually decreases after actions come to a close.
- Due to the cyclical nature of research on military families, everyday mechanisms of resilience may be better understood within the service member population due to the extensive monitoring of information on their demographics, health, and performance than in the military family population.
- More knowledge about everyday resilience in military families would enhance our understanding of how families remain resilient or struggle with resilience when under the extreme stressors of military engagement.
- Young adults, whether in the civilian or military population, face similar developmental tasks related to gaining job skills and financial independence, establishing a household, forming adult friendships and romantic relationships, and making choices about parenthood.
- The military, as an organization, has made significant investments in material supports that foster positive personal and relational development, as well as support daily living needs, in spite of the typical risks inherent in military service.
- New service members complete both basic and advanced training and are expected to continue their skill development throughout their careers by attending technical and/or leadership schools.
- Basic pay comprises about 55% of an active duty member's total compensation package with special pay (such as foreign language learning, hardship or hazardous pay, special duty assignments, combat-related injury and rehabilitation, and overseas extensions) and allowances constituting the remaining 45%.
- Differences in living allowances and other in-kind benefits between single and married active duty service members and relative job stability may foster an environment conducive to earlier marriage and parenthood, on average, than the civilian population.
- The Millennium Cohort Study is the most comprehensive research project ever undertaken by the DoD. This longitudinal study is already generating new knowledge of characteristics

and experiences of military life predict vulnerability and resilience in both active duty and selected reserve personnel. This study has recently included spouses to begin collecting data about couple dynamics and family resilience.

- Risk factors including problem drinking and other substance misuse, risk-taking and aggressive behaviors, disordered eating, and increased life/family stressors compromise individual health and readiness, as well as unit readiness. Many of these risk factors are thought to be common to late adolescence and young adulthood, which includes 45% of the Active Component and 33% of the Reserve Component personnel.
- High unit trust and cohesion, job training that includes psychological skill building in addition to technical skill building, positive perceptions of unit leaders, and positive emotional connections with others act as protective factors for service members and foster resilience.
- Meaningful connections between military and civilian communities can facilitate better understandings of military stressors that affect behaviors, health, and relationships of all family members.

EXERCISES

1. This chapter highlighted several ways in which the developmental task of pursuing work and establishing a career are shaped by military service. What resources do persons who choose to work in the civilian sector rely upon to develop their professional lives?
2. Generally speaking, how important do you think financial and residential independence are in forming long-term romantic relationships and becoming a parent? What research literature would help you find out more about these choices in the civilian population?

3. Go to the Millennium Cohort Study website, at http://www.millenniumcohort.org/index .php, and select a few research publications to review. What are your chosen studies trying to learn more about? How do these studies add to useful knowledge about service members?

7

The Effects of War on Service Members

In Chapter 7, you will

- Meet Rick L. Campise, Colonel, U.S. Air Force, BSC Commander, 559th Medical Group
- Learn about the physical and psychological impact of combat on service members
- Develop an appreciation for the risks that service men and women take when they agree to defend the United States
- Acquire information that you, as a helping professional working with military families, can apply to help family members deal with the effects of deployments on their loved ones

Meet

Rick L. Campise, Colonel, U.S. Air Force, BSC, Commander, 559th Medical Group

This excerpt is from a letter Colonel Campise wrote to his family on July 12, 2009 while in Iraq.

You may wonder, "Exactly what does a psychologist do in a deployed environment?" The duties vary depending upon the location and the number of other mental health staff present. I am the only mental health provider for 1200 Airmen and Soldiers, but there are also 30,000 Soldiers in the local area that might come see me rather than their own mental health providers. In addition, the military airport is a ten-minute walk away so sometimes one of the 100,000 people who pass through the airport each month finds their way to my office.

Throughout the week I visit units, sometimes just two and sometimes up to ten a week. The average person is afraid to visit mental health and wouldn't come see me if their hair was on fire and I had the only water in camp. So I try to visit units and walk around, giving them a chance to see that I don't have horns, am relatively sane, and let them ask any questions about "their friend." I've done more counseling in units than in my office.

There is of course the obvious trauma associated with the real and potential loss of life and limb in a war environment. Perhaps on a previous deployment you were exposed to some horror that you successfully defended against but for some reason a recent event has brought it all out of the closet and the nightmares or flashbacks are weighing you down. Or during this deployment you might have watched the occupants of the vehicle in front of you die when an IED exploded and except for luck that could have been your vehicle. You feel frightened you almost died and guilty that you lived. You may have even been flying an aircraft that almost crashed.

But a lot of what I see is a product of the sacrifices America's men and women make being deployed. You might see me because someone you trusted to take care of your affairs while you are fighting a war instead emptied your bank account; you have been deployed three and a half of the last five years and no longer know your children; your all consuming stateside work schedule made you oblivious to the state of your marriage and you and your spouse are reflecting on things that need to change; your romantic partner wants to break-up; your romantic partner tells you if you don't come home right now they will break up; your romantic partner or a neighbor tells you your romantic partner is sleeping around; your grandmother or favorite aunt is dying but since they are not immediate family members you can't go home; your wife is having a baby and since it's a normal birth you can't go home. (The Army would let you go; but for the Air Force, it would have to be a problematic birth to go home.)

You might see me because you are in charge of people and really aren't very good at it. Or, you are a good leader that worries about their people and you are the person responsible for placing them in harm's way.

Maybe you suffer from "toxic leadership syndrome" and need some tips on how to survive a bad boss. Or perhaps you are on a new shift and want help resetting your biological clock by 10 hours so that you can sleep.

I lead tobacco cessation groups, a monthly workshop on how to study and a parenting forum. Every Tuesday morning and Wednesday afternoon I team up with the chaplain and give the "reunion briefing." Last week I started participating in "Right Start" briefings designed to prepare newly deployed people for their time in the sand. My role: give a 10-minute briefing on suicide prevention and how to take care of themselves and others. Also volunteer to work issues that affect all the mental health providers who are deployed and love doing that work.

INTRODUCTION

By the end of 2010, more than 2 million service members had been deployed to Afghanistan and Iraq in support of OEF, OIF, and OND since the terrorist attacks on the United States on September 11, 2001 (Office of the President of the United States, 2011). By the end of 2009, more than 793,000 of those service members had been deployed more than once with longer deployments and shorter breaks between deployments than in prior wars (Tan, 2009). The wars in Iraq and Afghanistan have exposed U.S. military personnel to life-threatening combat, hazardous duty, and dangerous environmental conditions. Many have returned home and have had to deal with severe physical injuries and permanent physical and/or neurological changes and limitations, psychological health problems, homelessness, and joblessness.

Environmental conditions and individual experiences such as poor or restricted diet, weather (e.g., extreme heat and arid conditions), poor or unfamiliar sleeping and living quarters, prolonged separations from family members, and the disruption of careers or educational goals (particularly for National Guard and Reserve service members) can add stress to the already challenging deployment experience (Litz, 2005) and can have negative implications for service members' psychological and physical well-being. Even the stress of not being able to deploy, when one is expected to, can be a stressor.

PHYSICAL EFFECTS OF WAR ON SERVICE MEMBERS

Although shrapnel from artillery bombs, mortars, and grenades were responsible for approximately 60% of the 9.7 million military deaths during World War I (Alexander, 2010), advanced battlefield medicine and improved protective combat gear have resulted in service members surviving severe wounds that would have been fatal in past wars. Many are alive because of these advances in battlefield medicine and protective equipment but are coming home with extensive physical injuries, such as missing limbs and head injuries.

By the end of May 2011, 6,034 service members had died and 43,822 had been wounded serving in Operations Enduring Freedom, Iraqi Freedom, and New Dawn. Of those wounded, 12,751 or 29% sustained injuries so severe as a result of direct combat action that they required medical air transportation to move them to a location where they could receive the appropriate level of medical treatment for their injuries. Medical air transports can also occur for nonhostile reasons (e.g., illness, disease, injuries). By the end of May 2011, in addition to the wounded transports, there were 55,243 nonhostile medical air transports (DMDC, 2011a, 2011b, 2011c, 2011d).

The most frequent injuries and reasons for evacuation of service members from the OIF/OEF combat theaters from the beginning of 2004 to the end of 2007 were musculoskeletal and connective tissue injuries (24%), combat injuries (14%, some of which incurred during combat missions but were not caused by enemy fire; e.g., back pain and overuse injuries), neurological disorders (10%), psychiatric diagnoses (9%), and spinal pain (7%) (Cohen et al., 2010). However, the two "signature injuries" from these conflicts are TBI and PTSD (Department of Defense Task Force on Mental Health, 2007). Because of the prevalence of these conditions—up to 22% of returning veterans reported having experienced a TBI (Okie, 2005) and approximately 14% suffer from PTSD (Tanielian & Jaycox, 2008)—and the potentially chronic character of their symptoms, they have the potential for being long-term, challenging concerns for those working with military members, veterans, and their families.

Voices From the Frontline

STORY OF A WOUNDED WARRIOR

If you see that a person you know and love has a problem, say something. I was in the Marines and served in Fallujah and Ramadi, Iraq. On April 17, 2006, I was shot in both legs. A bullet went right through the right leg. Another blew out the knee and femoral artery in my left leg. I've had 16 operations and am now looking at a semi-constrained knee replacement.

I got addicted to painkillers, but I was never depressed enough that I thought about killing myself. That wasn't me. I was depressed knowing I couldn't be a police officer or play soccer ever again.

It took me 4 years to realize I needed help. I just completed the PTSD program at the Lyons VA in New Jersey where we had group therapy two times a week and individual therapy as well. Now I am participating in outpatient therapy at a VA clinic and at a Vet Center.

The most important thing for friends and families is to be supportive. There will be times we do not want to talk or be around anybody. Know it and respect it. Then there will be times we want to talk. So just be there and listen. Don't force it.

But don't walk on eggshells either. Be yourself around me. My friends never said anything like, "You have a problem with pain killers," but my family did. They said, "You are going to detox because we want our son back."

I got clear for a little bit. Then I fell and hurt myself. I started taking painkillers that a doctor prescribed. It wasn't as bad as before. This time I went in, got clean, and have stayed clean. I'm doing well now even though I'm in pain all the time.

I want to be me again. I know I'll never be that person, but I'll get as close as I possibly can. I want to get back to what made me happy before—helping people.

Michael Sarbu
Veteran

Traumatic Brain Injury

Approximately 1.7 million Americans suffer from traumatic brain injuries (TBIs; a strike or jolt to the head or penetration of the head by an object, disrupting brain function) annually, making brain injuries a significant health concern in the United States (Centers for Disease Control and Prevention, 2010). A TBI can affect language, emotions, behavior, and the ability to think and learn. It can also cause epilepsy and seizures and can increase the risk for Alzheimer's disease, Parkinson's disease (a disorder of the nervous system that affects movement), and other brain disorders that usually occur later in life. Falls (35%) and motor-vehicle traffic accidents (17%) are the leading causes of TBI in the general public. However, military service members deployed to combat zones are at high risk for experiencing TBIs as a result of bullets and blasts from IEDs, bombs, land mines, mortar rounds, and rocket-propelled grenades (Defense and Veterans Brain Injury Center, 2009). Improved protective equipment is one major reason for the increased numbers of service members who survive TBIs in combat. Enhanced body armor and helmets protect service members from bullets, shrapnel, and flying debris; the injuries from these objects would have been fatal in prior wars. However, this new equipment cannot protect service members from the closed brain injuries and TBIs caused by the blasts of IED explosions (Okie, 2005; Warden, 2006).

Brain injuries are more common in the wars in Iraq and Afghanistan than in other recent wars involving U.S. forces (Okie, 2005). Approximately 19% of service members returning from deployments reported that they had suffered a probable TBI during their deployment (Tanielian & Jaycox, 2008). However, the prevalence of brain injuries among service members injured in Iraq and Afghanistan may be greater than 22%, since some injuries are not recognized and counted as TBIs until later in the diagnosis and treatment process (Okie, 2005).

Many of these injuries are mild TBIs, concussions, or injuries in which there is "loss of consciousness or altered mental status (e.g., dazed or confused)" (Hoge et al., 2008, p. 453). The severity of TBIs can range from "mild" (i.e., a change in mental status or consciousness for a brief period) to "severe" (i.e., an extended period of unconsciousness or amnesia for an extended period after the injury) (Centers for Disease Control and Prevention, 2010). There are five types of TBIs (Johnson, 2010):

- Contusions (bruises of the brain)
- Hematomas (bleeding in the brain)
- Skull fractures (breaks—penetrations, cracks, or dents—in the skull)
- Diffuse axonal injuries (tears in the small nerve fibers of the brain)
- Concussions (temporary brain injuries involving confusion, loss of memory, or loss of consciousness)

When a service member suffers a TBI, there are often accompanying physical/neurological, cognitive, psychological, and behavioral changes that can be long-lasting (Kushner, 1998; Vaishnavi, Rao, & Fann, 2009). Cognitive problems often include short-term memory problems or attention problems; difficulties planning, organizing, and strategizing; difficulties processing information; and language problems. Physical/neurological changes can include headaches, dizziness, balance and coordination problems, pain, low energy and fatigue, and problems sleeping. Psychological problems often include anxiety, depression, irritability, emotional volatility, blunted emotions (lack of range of emotion), and lack of empathy. Behavioral issues can include increased impulsivity, decreased inhibition, a lack of spontaneity, and apathy. The severity of these symptoms in mild TBI can range "from transient mild symptoms to ongoing disabling problems" (Kushner, 1998, p. 1617).

One of the primary medical and research challenges of the current war on terrorism is the overlap of TBI and psychological stress in terms of what kinds of trauma cause these conditions and their resulting symptoms. Many of the same kinds of traumatic combat events (e.g., blasts and impacts) can cause TBI and psychological problems, or both. In addition, many of the symptoms are common to both of these conditions. In an examination of current research on the chronic multi-symptom illness observed in many service members who deployed in the first Persian Gulf War, Friedl, Grate, and Proctor (2009) state that two pressing challenges facing the medical and research communities are the ability to distinguish between them and an understanding of the impact of their interaction on causing later psychiatric or neurological problems.

Return to Duty

Approximately 5%–6% of service members deployed in support of OIF/OEF are medically evacuated; of these, about one-third to one-fifth return to duty (Cohen et al., 2010). The conditions that most frequently prevent service members from returning to duty are combat injuries, psychiatric disorders, musculoskeletal or connective tissue (e.g., cartilage) disorders, and spinal pain. Service members with chest or abdominal pain, urinary and genital organ disorders, gastrointestinal disorders, and neoplasms (tumors or other abnormal tissue growths) are more likely to be returned to military duty.

Injured or ill service members receive medical and psychosocial screening; then appropriate treatment for their recovery is arranged (Department of Defense [DoD], 2008b). Those who are unlikely to recover sufficiently to return to duty within 180 days are likely to be separated or retired from the service. The Military Department Wounded Warrior Programs, which are managed by each of the military services, track recovering service members as they undergo treatment, recovery, rehabilitation, and return to duty or separation or retirement and reintegration into the civilian community (DoD, 2008a). In December 2004, the DoD instituted a policy that allows active duty and reserve troops wounded on active duty to stay on active duty and work within their capabilities (Smith, 2006). Thus, if service members opt to remain on active or reserve duty, they are able to do so—provided that they can still complete their jobs or are approved for retraining into another job specialty. Growing numbers of wounded service members, including those severely wounded are choosing to continue their military service. Even severely wounded service members, with 30% or higher disability ratings, have applied to stay on active duty and have been approved (Miles, 2007). The DoD recognizes that these service members have specialized skills and leadership experience that they can continue to contribute to the military.

PSYCHOLOGICAL EFFECTS OF WAR ON SERVICE MEMBERS

Voices From the Frontline

PROVIDING MENTAL HEALTH SUPPORT IN THE FIELD

I was a combat stress prevention officer. Small teams of two to four of us would drive out with convoys to provide mental health support. Everyone has a breaking point and will need some help. Who knows what it is for any one person? How many IEDs?

We'd say something like, "We're just here to get you through this stressful time. Combat is stressful." We might talk about "loose ends at home," instead of saying, "You have a problem with your marriage." Or maybe we'd say, "This is a time to talk about losing someone. For the next hour or two we can talk about this, and it's OK. Then it's over. We'll use no names." Soldiers felt it was helpful. When you frame it as having short-term stressors, people are more receptive.

A service member might lose a buddy in the Humvee next to them and need a few days to recover. That person would come to our Restoration Clinic. Hopefully in 72 hours they could go back to whatever they were doing, which might mean being up on turret of Humvee the next day and maybe experiencing more loss. If someone was being transported to a restoration program they did it with a battle buddy. We did the combat stress clinic with a buddy. When it comes to the military, there aren't any loners out there.

Mostly people relied on each other for resilience, though we weren't using that word in 2005. You are in a shared, similar experience with other Soldiers, Airmen, Navy guys, Marines, civilian contractors. We're all in the same boat. We understood each other. As for my support, I looked to the chaplain and my fellow team members. The whole thing is that you take care of your fellow Soldiers.

Chris Sullins
Former Army Reserve Combat Stress Prevention Officer

The Continuum of Stress Reactions

Since the American Civil War, **combat stress reactions**—"expected, predictable, emotional, intellectual, physical, and/or behavioral reactions of service members who have been exposed to stressful events in combat" (Department of the Army, 2006b, p. Glossary-5)—have been observed and named. During the Civil War, they were called "soldier's heart" and "nostalgia." Since World War I, the U.S. military has been aware that these reactions were the psychological effects of combat on its members, and extreme reactions to combat stress were then called "shell shock" (Jones & Wessely, 2003). Initially, during World War II the same phenomenon was called a "nervous" reaction or "exhaustion." These terms were later changed to "battle fatigue," a term that only very recently was changed to "combat stress reaction," or CSR, the term currently accepted and used by all U.S. military branches (Department of the Army, 2006b).

The DoD recognizes that there is a continuum of CSRs, from adaptive (positive) stress reactions to maladaptive (negative) stress reactions (Department of the Army, 2006b). Combat stress includes all of the physical and psychological stresses that can result from exposure to all of the dangers and demands of combat—both positive and negative. "Focused stress is vital to survival and mission accomplishment" (p. 1–2). However, prolonged or extremely intense stress impairs the ability of service members to function effectively and can progress into disabling CSRs, which can include behavioral problems or psychological distress.

The DoD attempts to control the impact of combat stress on military members by "minimizing maladaptive stress reactions while promoting adaptive stress reactions, such as loyalty, selflessness, and acts of bravery" (Department of the Army, 2006b, p. viii). The DoD also attempts to prepare service members mentally and physically, through intense and frequent training, to endure the stressors of military life and combat. In some cases however, extreme stress can tax service members beyond their ability to cope with the stress. Examples include exposure to extremely traumatic events during combat, interpersonal conflicts with unit members that compromise the service member's support network, and concern about the welfare of family members and relationships back home. If not addressed, these reactions can lead to long-term psychological problems or to maladaptive behaviors that can threaten the well-being of service members.

Perceived Invincibility and Risk-Taking

Sometimes, one of the consequences of exposure to the violence and trauma of high-intensity combat is engaging in unsafe behavior and taking potentially dangerous risks. A study sponsored by the Walter Reed Army Institute of Research (Killgore et al., 2008) revealed that many of the soldiers who served in Iraq were engaging in risky behaviors after their return home. The specific risky behaviors examined in the study were related to alcohol use and to aggressive behaviors. These included increased frequency and amount of alcohol consumed, driving under the influence of alcohol, riding with someone who was under the influence of alcohol, yelling or shouting, threatening someone with physical violence, and destroying property. However, the researchers noted that high-risk behaviors among returning service members might include many other health-threatening or life-threatening activities. Thrill-seeking by engaging in dangerous recreational activities, driving too fast or recklessly, using illegal drugs or abusing prescription drugs, engaging in unsafe sexual practices, gambling, and smoking are behaviors that can adversely impact on the health and well-being of service members returning from combat. Although the findings were not specific to soldiers who had deployed, the U.S. Army reported a total of 146 deaths of active duty members related to high-risk behaviors in 2009, including 74 drug overdoses (Department of the Army, 2010). In fact, in 2009 more soldiers died as a result of high-risk behavior than died in combat. Killgore et al. (2008) suggest that one of the contributors to the phenomenon of increased risky behavior after deployment might be that "an individual's perceived threshold of invincibility" (p. 1112) is elevated after having witnessed and survived extremely dangerous and violent combat experiences.

HOME AGAIN

It takes a while to adapt back into civilian life. Life at home felt kind of dull. It took awhile for that feeling to diminish. I talked with other soldiers. They felt the same way.

Sometimes I'd stop and hesitate for a second on my way to work. I'd think, "I forgot my weapon" and then laugh at myself because I don't have a weapon. It's startling, and then you use humor to push it away.

Once walking down the street in the middle of Chicago, a garbage truck was letting down a dumpster and there was a big crashing sound. I stopped in my tracks. Another time, I saw a beat up car without a license. My heart started beating fast. My first thought: "It's an IED, a car bomb." My second thought: "In the middle of Chicago?"

There were many times I was scared in Iraq, but I never thought I'd die. A lot of other people have a much harder transition back than I did.

Ted Cravens
Army Reserve Combat Stress Prevention Officer

Psychological Health Problems

Combat deployments have exposed troops to extreme psychological stress and trauma that increase the risk for developing psychological health problems. The exposure to trauma can result in **post-traumatic stress**—a spectrum of reactions to a trauma (The Management of Post-traumatic Stress Working Group, 2010). Those who survive a trauma may only experience some of the reactions, while others may experience the entire spectrum. The first two reactions listed below are not diagnoses as defined by the ***Diagnostic and Statistical Manual IV*** (DSM IV) (American Psychiatric Association, 2000), the American Psychiatric Association's publication that lists mental health disorders).

Acute stress reaction is used to describe temporary symptoms (e.g., disorientation, agitation, anxiety, confusion) in response to a traumatic event. These symptoms usually disappear in hours or days.

Combat and operation stress refers to the physical, mental, and emotional symptoms (e.g., anxiety, hyperarousal, fatigue, depression, concentration problems) that extend beyond 4 days after a traumatic event.

Acute stress disorder indicates symptoms that begin within 4 weeks of the traumatic event and last up to 1 month. The person exhibits anxiety and has impaired functioning in one area of life (e.g., work, family). Symptoms may include reexperiencing the trauma (through dreams, flashbacks, reoccurring thoughts), avoiding stimuli (e.g., locations, smells, sounds, people) that may be reminders of the event, detachment from others, and emotional numbing.

PTSD is an anxiety disorder resulting from experiencing a traumatic event (e.g., threat of death, threat of death of another, or threat of physical, sexual, or psychological integrity) with symptoms that persist more than 1 month after the traumatic event resulting in impairment in functioning in one or more areas of life. Symptoms include reexperiencing the traumatic event, avoiding trauma-associated stimuli, numbing, and increased arousal. Symptoms can begin soon after the trauma or months later. Acute PTSD is defined as symptoms lasting between 1 and 3 months after the trauma, and chronic PTSD is defined as symptoms lasting more than 3 months.

PTSD is one of the most common psychological consequences of combat (Dedert et al., 2009; Hoge et al., 2004). Other common psychological health problems resulting from combat include major depression, alcohol abuse or dependence, and other anxiety disorders. The lifetime prevalence of PTSD is 6.8%, and the lifetime prevalence of depression is 16.6% in the general public (Kessler, Bergland, Demler, Jin, & Walters, 2005). About 14% of OEF and OIF veterans suffer from PTSD and 14% experience major depression (Tanielian & Jaycox, 2008). In fact, Hoge et al. (2004) found that approximately 17% of service members returning from combat duty in Iraq and Afghanistan screened positive for these psychological health disorders. Several years later, in a study of Army and Marine service members who completed a routine health screening form after returning from deployments in Iraq or Afghanistan, Hoge, Auchterloine, and Milliken (2006) found that 19% of service members who served in Iraq and 11% who served in Afghanistan reported having a psychological health problem. They reported problems with PTSD, depression, or other psychological health problems. The same study revealed that 35% of those who had served in Iraq sought psychological health services in the year after returning from the war. A recent study of the prevalence rates among returning veterans of PTSD or depression with serious functional impairment (Thomas et al., 2010) suggests that PTSD and depression cause a significant impairment in level of functioning for over 8%–14% of returning veterans and some impairment for 23%–31%.

The rate of PTSD and other psychological health disorders among returning service members may be underdiagnosed. For example, the first participants in the Millennium Cohort Study were enrolled between 2001 and 2003. Of the 75,000 military members enrolled in the study, 2% of those who had deployed to combat zones reported symptoms of PTSD without reporting a diagnosis—over four times more than those who reported both symptoms and a diagnosis of PTSD (Smith, Wingard et al., 2009).

In studying data from the 2008 DoD Survey of Health Related Behaviors, researchers (Bray, Spira, Williams, & Lane, 2010) found that the prevalence of psychological health problems was greater for those service members who had experienced higher levels of combat exposure (e.g., exposure to more traumatic types of combat experiences or more instances of engaging in direct combat with the enemy; being exposed to mines, IEDs, or other explosions; seeing bodies or human remains; or having unit members who were casualties). Service members who had experienced higher levels of combat exposure reported higher levels of work and family stress, anxiety, symptoms of depression and PTSD, and more frequent thoughts of suicide. Other types of combat exposure have also been associated with PTSD symptoms. Exposure or perceived threats of exposure to biological/chemical agents, including having to don protective clothing and a mask when hearing alarms warning of the presence of biological/chemical agents increases the likelihood of developing PTSD symptoms (Smith, Wingard et al., 2009). Depression has also been found to develop more frequently in service members with high levels of combat exposure than for service members who have not deployed or those with less combat exposure during deployment (Wells et al., 2010).

Psychological health problems may also be more prevalent in Reserve Component service members following deployment. In a study of soldiers from four Active Components and two National Guard infantry brigade combat teams, active duty and National Guard soldiers reported similar rates of combat exposure during deployment and similar prevalence rates of PTSD and depression 3 months following deployment (Thomas et al., 2010). However, 12 months after returning from a deployment the prevalence rate of PTSD and depression, accompanied by an increase in aggressive behaviors and the misuse of alcohol, was significantly greater among National Guard soldiers. DoD and Army researchers believed the difference in prevalence rates at this point in the deployment cycle relates to readjustment to civilian life, lack of health care, or both. National Guard members return from deployment to their civilian lives, while active duty members continue to work with one another daily, perhaps providing needed social support. Also, National Guard members are entitled to free military medical coverage, including psychological health care, for 6 months after returning from a deployment. They must purchase the medical coverage after that time, which may not be financially feasible, or seek services at Veterans Affairs facilities whose locations may be at great distances.

Greenberg, Langston, and Jones (2008) identify the following additional indicators of current psychological problems or possible risk factors for service members developing PTSD or other psychological problems:

- Perception that they were out of control during the event
- Perception that their life was threatened during the event
- Blaming others for what happened
- Shame/guilt about their behavior during the event
- Experiencing acute stress following the event
- Exposure to substantial stress since the event
- Problems with day-to-day activities since the event
- Involvement in previous traumatic events
- Poor social support (family, friends, unit support)
- Drinking alcohol excessively to cope with stress

Friedman (2004) is concerned that the reported prevalence of PTSD among service members returning from combat deployments will increase in the coming years. He believes that the rate of PTSD may increase significantly among service members within 2 years after their return from war. Friedman's assertion is supported by a study of Gulf War veterans (Wolfe, Erickson, Sharkansky, King, & King, 1999), which concluded that rates of PTSD increased over time. Friedman (2004) further states his belief that psychological problems will continue to increase over time despite the changing nature of the U.S. Armed Forces missions in Iraq and Afghanistan from a "campaign for liberation to an ongoing armed conflict with dissident combatants" (p. 76). Again, Friedman draws on evidence from research on past conflicts; this time from a study of the psychological impact of deployments to Somalia (Litz, Orsillo, Friedman, Ehlich, & Batres, 1997). The Somalia study suggests that service members who are involved in peacekeeping-type deployments in life-threatening conditions are at increased risk for PTSD.

In a 2010 survey of 911 soldiers and marines assigned to combat forces in Afghanistan, the rates of psychological problems among the participants was compared to similar groups of service members who had been surveyed while serving in support of OIF and OEF in 2005 and 2009. The results of the study indicated that the rates of acute stress were significantly higher in 2010 than in both 2005 and 2009 and that the overall rates of psychological problems (i.e., acute stress, depression, and anxiety) were significantly higher in 2010 than in 2005. Possible reasons suggested for the increase are that more service members had experienced multiple deployments and more had been exposed to higher levels of combat over the years. Thus, as long as the current deployments for U.S. service members remain dangerous and the number of service members who are deployed and exposed to traumatic events continues to rise, we can expect the prevalence of PTSD and other psychological problems to continue to increase. Friedman (2004) suggests that it may "be too early to assess the eventual magnitude of the mental health problems related to deployment to Operation Iraqi Freedom or Operation Enduring Freedom" (p. 76).

Some of the common psychological disorders associated with combat deployments and the associated symptoms are listed in Table 7.1.

Overlap of TBI and PTSD

Although TBI is a neurological condition, not a psychiatric disorder, most individuals who have had a TBI also were exposed to an event that could also lead to PTSD—an event in which the person felt in danger of his/her life, helpless, and powerless. Many of these individuals will display symptoms of a stress reaction and may have a TBI and PTSD resulting from the same event(s). Some individuals with TBI may have had exposure to events leading to PTSD prior to or subsequent to the TBI. Psychological health problems may also result from the experience of living with the results of a TBI (e.g., losses in function, changed career prospects, changed family roles and goals). In addition, PTSD and TBI share many of the same symptoms; and other mental health problems, such as substance abuse problems, may be present in individuals with PTSD or TBI. The overlap of symptoms between TBI and PTSD can be seen in Table 7.2.

TABLE 7.1   Symptoms of Common Psychological Disorders Associated with Combat Deployment

Depression	Anxiety	Stress Reactions	Substance Abuse
• Depressed mood (sadness or emptiness) • Reduced interest in activities • Sleep disturbances • Loss of energy or reduction in energy level • Difficulty concentrating, holding a conversation, paying attention, or making decisions • Suicidal thoughts or intentions	• General feelings of anxiety • Mild heart palpitations • Dizziness • Excessive worry	• Dissociative symptoms (numbing, detachment) • Reduction in awareness of surroundings • Reexperiencing of the trauma • Avoidance of trauma-associated stimuli • Significant anxiety • Irritability • Poor concentration • Difficulty sleeping • Restlessness	• Impairment in functioning • Recurrent use resulting in failure to fulfill major obligations at work, school, or home • Recurrent use in situations that are physically hazardous (e.g., driving while intoxicated) • Legal problems resulting from recurrent use • Continued use despite significant social or interpersonal problems

Source: Information from the American Psychiatric Association (2000). *Diagnostic and statistical manual of mental disorders* (4th ed., text revision) (DSM-IV-TR). Arlington, VA: American Psychiatric Association.

TABLE 7.2   TBI and PTSD Symptom Similarities

Mild TBI	PTSD
Anxiety	Anxiety
Depressed mood	Depressed mood
Memory problem	Memory problems
Poor concentration	Poor concentration
Irritability	Irritability
Insomnia	Insomnia
Fatigue	Fatigue
Headaches	Intrusive thoughts
Dizziness	Avoidance behaviors
Noise & light intolerance	Emotional numbing

Source: Information from Kennedy, J. E., Jaffee, M. S., Leskin, G. A., Stokes, J. W., Leal, F. O., & Fitzpatrick, P. J. (2007). Posttraumatic stress disorder and posttraumatic stress disorder-like symptoms and mild traumatic brain injury. *Journal of Rehabilitation Research & Development, 44,* 895–920.

Suicide

One of the tragic consequences of psychological health problems among returning service members is that more and more service members are committing suicide. The suicide rate among U.S. military has historically been significantly lower than among civilians, which is approximately 19 per 100,000 people (Department of the Army, 2010). However, a larger number of service members than ever before are dying by suicide (Kuehn, 2009). Suicide rates began increasing in the military in 2004 (Department of the Army, 2010). Between 2001 and 2007, suicide rates in the Army and Marine Corps, "which have borne the majority of ground combat operations increased steadily," while the Navy and Air Force rates increased only slightly (p. 16). In 2008, the Army suicide rate surpassed the national average, reaching 20 per 100,000; and for the first time in 28 years, the suicide rate among military personnel is higher than that of a comparable civilian population (Kuehn, 2009). The DoD estimates that 2% of the Army attempted suicide in 2008 (DoD, 2008a). In 2009, 160 active duty soldiers committed suicide, making it the third highest cause of death among soldiers (Department of the Army, 2010). Of the suicides completed by active duty Army personnel in 2009, 96.9% were committed by male service members. A total of at least 334 service members (all services and active duty and reserve members combined) committed suicide in 2009 (Donnelly, 2010).

Psychological health disorders can increase the risk of suicide among those who suffer from these conditions (Kuehn, 2009). In addition, the 2007 Army Suicide Event Report found that "there was a significant relationship between suicide attempts and number of days deployed to OIF/OEF" (Suicide Risk Management & Surveillance Office, 2008, p. 2).

The Department of the Army (2010) report on suicide identified the following principal risk factors and stressors associated with suicidal behavior among soldiers:

- Relationship problems
- Military or work stress (e.g., voluntary or involuntary separation from the Army, combat/dangerous work environment, and increased optempo)
- Legal problems, encounters with law enforcement personnel/systems, and military disciplinary or administrative actions
- High-risk behaviors and medical conditions

Stigma and Other Barriers to Care

Often, service members who need help with psychological problems after returning from a deployment do not seek help. One of the reasons that service members do not report psychological health problems upon their return from deployments is that they may not experience symptoms immediately. Even if they do experience symptoms, they may not be willing to report them. One reason is that they do not want the psychological health assessment and treatment process to delay the start of their postdeployment leave (vacation) and reunion with their families. Barriers to care can also include not understanding what kinds of treatment are available, not knowing how to access them, and not having adequate time to invest in obtaining treatment (Britt et al., 2008). Hoge et al. (2004) found that service members cited not knowing where to get treatment and not being able to get time off for treatment as barriers preventing them from accessing care for psychological health problems they were experiencing.

The continuing stigma of psychological health within the military is a larger deterrent to reporting problems and seeking assistance with psychological health problems; it is the most frequently cited barrier to care (Hoge et al., 2004). Of those service members who screened positive for psychological health disorders, "only 23 to 40 percent sought mental health care" (p. 13); they were twice as likely as those returning service members who screened negative for psychological problems to cite stigmatization as a main deterrent to seeking help. The Department of the Army (2010) has stated that stigma continues to be the leading deterrent to seeking help. However, based on a comparison between National Guard and active duty soldiers on the rate of use of psychological health services and the impact of stigma (Kim, Thomas, Wilk, Castro, & Hoge, 2010), Reserve Component service members appear to have fewer concerns about stigma and seek psychological health care more readily than active duty service members.

The impact of the stigma of psychological disorders takes several forms. Corrigan (2004) cites two types of stigma that can impede individuals from seeking psychological health care—public stigma (prejudice and discrimination against those with psychological disorders) and self-stigma (internalization of the public's biases against those with psychological illnesses).

Since military personnel are expected to function at a high level of performance at all times and to be dependable and steadfast, the impact of stigma may be more pronounced for military personnel than for civilians. Many service members are embarrassed or ashamed of having psychological problems, which they may view as a weakness. They may also be reluctant to admit that they need help for fear that they will be viewed as inferior, inadequate, and unable to complete their mission by their leaders, since this information is not kept confidential from their superiors.

Voices From the Frontline

MILITARY CULTURE AND MENTAL HEALTH

The military culture has always been that you don't stick your head up and ask for things. In the military you are dealing with a portion of the population that is the strongest and best adapted. They don't want to feel like they are draining the resources. They want to feel they are the resource.

Military culture wants support to be like a checklist. "Help me figure out what I need to do for myself. Give me the tools and let me move on with things."

In most cases, it is effective. If you run into a serious mental health issue, extra assistance is needed. It can be hard to ask for help when the checklist approach/culture doesn't work. At those times, we hope that a buddy intervenes and helps them ask for help.

Chris Sullins
Former Army Reserve Combat Stress Prevention Officer

In an exploration of the impact of officer leadership and unit cohesion (togetherness and bonding) on military personnel's propensity to seek psychological health care, Wright et al. (2009) found that lower stigma and barriers to care were associated with high officer leadership qualities and cohesion within their units. The researchers also noted that recently implemented training programs for military personnel and leaders have begun to address stigma and the importance of military leadership in changing attitudes about psychological health.

Alcohol and Substance Use/Abuse

Data from the 2008 DoD Survey of Health Related Behaviors suggest that service members who had greater levels of exposure to combat-related experiences were more likely to engage in health threatening behaviors (Bray, Spira, Williams, & Lane, 2010). They tended to smoke more, to increase the use of or become dependent on alcohol, or to use illicit substances. The National Survey on Drug Use and Health (Office of Applied Studies, 2005) compared the use of alcohol, the rate of driving under the influence of alcohol, and daily cigarette smoking among veterans and nonveterans in 2003. The results indicated a greater incidence of these behaviors among veterans than nonveterans. Approximately 57% of veterans used alcohol within the past month, 13% reported driving under the influence, and almost 19% reported smoking daily; nonveterans reported rates of approximately 51%, 12%, and 14%, respectively. Alcohol use, alcohol misuse, and alcohol-related high-risk behaviors are associated with increased rates of injury, automobile accidents, and psychological health problems. Both cigarette use and alcohol misuse are associated with numerous physical health problems.

Women and Combat-Related Psychological Disorders

Women comprise approximately 15% of the military. The wars in Afghanistan and Iraq are the first combat operations in which a large number of women have had repeated exposures to direct combat and multiple deployments. Women are still prohibited from serving in direct combat specialties or assignment to ground combat units. For example, they are not allowed to serve in the infantry or as special operations personnel (e.g., Army Special Forces, Navy SEALS). However, women are serving in all specialties but those that traditionally would have exposed them to direct engagement with the enemy through enemy fire, direct physical contact, or capture. They are in combat support specialties and units as truck drivers, pilots, medics, mechanics, military police, intelligence and civil affairs personnel, and numerous other specialties.

Now women are serving in, around, and near hostile territory. They have a substantial role in supporting direct combat activities (Smith, Jacobson, Smith, Hooper, & Ryan, 2007), which means they are often co-located with military personnel directly engaged in combat. Additionally, the locations and directions of attacks are unpredictable in the current wars, and there is no clear distinction between the "front" line and "rear" areas—those areas which were relatively "dangerous" areas and "safe" areas in traditional wars. Women are now frequently exposed to direct fire, engagement with the enemy, and traumatic events. Like male service members, they have been subjected to firefights, ambushes, security operations, mortar and grenade attacks, and IEDs. They have also handled corpses and body parts and witnessed and/or experienced severe injury or death.

In an overview of current research on the effects of combat-related stressors and deployment experiences on the physical and psychological health of military service women, Pierce (2010) states that we do not fully understand the effects of multiple deployments and stressors not related to deployment on women in the military. There are few studies of how women are affected psychologically by these experiences. The findings of the studies that do exist are mixed. Studies on American veterans who served in prior wars (e.g., Perconte, Wilson, Pontius, Deitrick, & Spiro, 1993) suggest that women may develop higher levels of psychological health problems as a result of combat exposure. Although not specifically limited to women veterans who have deployed, research comparing suicide rates of female nonveterans and veterans (McFarland, Kaplan, & Huguet, 2010) suggests that female veterans are more likely than female nonveterans to complete suicide.

To examine a possible gender difference, Hoge, Clark, and Castro (2007) reviewed the existing research to identify possible differences among men and women Iraq war veterans and the development of PTSD and other psychological health disorders. They concluded that, at that time, there was no evidence of a significant difference in the likelihood of men and women developing PTSD or depression after serving in Iraq and that further research was warranted.

The impact of deployments on the psychological health of military women may correlate to the types of jobs they have. In a study on the effects of serving in combat-related occupations on the psychological health of women Navy and Marine Corps service members, researchers found that women in combat support occupations were less likely to be hospitalized for reasons related to psychological health than women in non-combat-related jobs (Lindstrom et al., 2006). The researchers offered two possible explanations for their results. First, women serving in nontraditional combat-support occupations may be more afraid of stigma related to seeking help for psychological issues. Second, women working in nontraditional career fields may have developed more effective coping skills and, therefore, experience less stress in combat-related occupations.

Pierce (2010) asserted that research is needed to distinguish between the impact of stress of work–family conflict (when the needs of a job or career interfere with family life and the responsibility of raising children) and the impact of combat stressors on women in the military, in order to better assist women service members in preparing for deployment, returning home after deployment, and continuing their military careers. Although the levels of work–life conflict have not been determined for the military population, 42% of employees in the general U.S. population have reported that their work and family life interfere with each other (Tang & MacDermid Wadsworth, 2010). In an initial study to determine the impact of work–family conflict and combat stress on the psychological well-being of military women, Pierce (2010) studied the relationship between work–family conflict and psychological well-being in Air Force women who had deployed to Iraq. She found that both higher work–family conflict and greater combat exposure were predictive of higher levels of depression, PTSD, and poorer emotional functioning. She suggests that while exposure to combat stressors is difficult to control for women who choose military jobs or careers, the stress of work–family conflict may be a target area for offering assistance to military women in an effort to reduce their overall stress.

In another attempt to differentiate the impact of different stressors on service members (Vogt, Pless, King, & King, 2005), researchers examined the impact of mission-related stress and interpersonal stress on men and women deployed in support of the 1990–1991 Gulf War. The results of the study suggest that both men and women were affected by both mission-related stress—"stressors that are specific to the deployment mission"—and interpersonal stress—"stress associated with social interactions and relationships during deployment" (p. 282), including family relationships. However, women reported that they had experienced more interpersonal stress than men, and interpersonal stress had a stronger impact on the psychological well-being of female veterans than on that of male veterans. Thus, the research suggests that women service members may benefit from help in coping with the stressors of work–family conflict and with interpersonal stress.

OTHER CONSEQUENCES OF COMBAT DEPLOYMENTS ON SERVICE MEMBERS

Sexual Assault and Sexual Harassment

Both men and women service members are at higher risk for sexual assault and sexual harassment in combat environments (Litz, 2005). However, during the 1990–1991 Gulf War, women were over 16 times more likely to be the victim of sexual assault and 25 times more likely to experience sexual harassment than men (Kang, Dalager, Mahan, & Ishii, 2005). Women serving in job categories that have recently been opened to women may have a less developed social and peer support network and may be at increased risk for sexual assault and harassment when working in jobs dominated by male service members (Vogt et al., 2005).

Estimates from studies on female service personnel during the Gulf War suggest 3% to over 7% of women experienced sexual assault and 24%–66% experienced sexual harassment (Committee on Gulf War and Health, 2008). For men, the corresponding estimates were 0.2% for sexual assault and 0.6%–8% for sexual harassment.

The results of the Armed Forces 2002 Sexual Harassment Survey (Lipari & Lancaster, 2003), which also included questions on sexual assault, revealed that the rates of sexual assault for women in the military were 6% in 1995 and 3% in 2002; for men, the rate for both years was 1%. The rates of reported sexual harassment for women were 46% and 24% in 1995 and 2002, respectively; while the corresponding rates for men were 8% and 3%. The DoD reports that the rates of reported sexual assault were 69.1 and 70.0 per 100,000 service members in 2002 and 2003, respectively (DoD, 2004). These rates suggest that the incidence of sexual assault and sexual harassment in the military is much lower during times when the United States is not engaged in large-scale combat operations. In addition, data from OIF and OEF indicate that the instance of sexual assault during deployments is significantly greater than when not deployed. The Department of Defense Fiscal Year 2009 Annual Report on Sexual Assault in the Military (Office of the Secretary of Defense Sexual Assault Prevention and Response Office, 2010) stated that the number of sexual assaults among service members deployed in Iraq and Afghanistan was 26% higher in 2009 than in 2008, while the overall increase for active duty service members (deployed or not deployed) was 8%.

Although women are more likely to experience sexual assault and sexual harassment while deployed, sexual assault and harassment impact negatively on the psychological well-being of both female and male service members (Kang, Dalager, Mahan, & Ishii, 2005; Vogt et al., 2005).

Living Conditions and Environmental Stressors

One of the consequences of engaging in combat in overseas locations is the challenging change in living conditions and environments, which often creates additional stressors in an already stressful combat environment. In the case of recent U.S. military deployments to OIF and OEF, both the living conditions and the environment have added significant stress for service members. Poor living conditions can include crowding in camps or in sleeping quarters (e.g., tents); uncomfortable cots (portable folding beds); lack of privacy and personal space; constant noise from small-arms weapons (guns, rifles, and machine guns), larger artillery, and explosions; and lack of adequate shelter from bad weather. Means for good hygiene and sanitation can also be insufficient: latrines may be primitive, unavailable, or inadequately maintained; washing facilities may be communal and lack privacy; showers are often infrequent, not available, or cold; and clothes washing facilities or services may not be available. Harsh environmental conditions can include hot dry summers, with temperatures often reaching over 140°F, and relatively cold winters, with night temperatures that can drop below freezing; wind, blowing sand, and severe sandstorms; scorpions, snakes, camel spiders (solifugae, which are large, quick spiders that can bite if disturbed); and packs of feral dogs.

Voices From the Frontline

A NOTE HOME FROM IRAQ

We are getting dust storm after dust storm and temperatures between 110°F and 130°F every day now. The dust gets so thick that it looks like thick fog. The ground is so dry now that when a vehicle passes by, it leaves a huge cloud of dust that takes minutes to settle and leaves one tasting the dust and feeling it stick to sweat and lips, and burn one's eyes. The intense heat saps our energy quickly. It's easy to get dehydrated, and we have to work at getting enough water to drink. If find myself getting headaches, feeling light-headed, feeling worn-out, and getting muscle aches, I get an extra bottle of water (1.5 L) and keep drinking until I have finished the bottle.

Angela Pereira
Colonel, U.S. Army, Retired

Environmental threats can include exposure to numerous chemicals and other substances. Exposure to these environmental stressors during the Gulf War included kerosene, diesel, and gasoline used in tent heaters, stoves, and generators (Committee on Gulf War and Health, 2008). These substances are still used in OEF and OIF. Other environmental stressors can include exposure to pesticides, depleted uranium, and numerous other substances that may not yet have been identified as environmental threats.

Many of these harsh living conditions and environmental stressors clearly pose a threat to the physical health of military service members who are deployed. Some are currently being studied to assess their impact on health. The Committee on Gulf War and Health (2008) has acknowledged, however, that these exposures are "psychologically stressful and physiologically challenging" (p. 39).

Joblessness and Homelessness

Although these are not problems common among active duty service members, joblessness and homelessness can be very real issues facing Reserve Component service members and veterans who have separated from the military who do not have the consistent pay that active duty members earn. Reserve Component service members often have difficulties maintaining a civilian career because of the requirement to go on active duty status whenever called upon by their reserve units. Reservists must be prepared to leave jobs, sometimes suddenly, and their employers must be prepared to let them go. This can severely disrupt the business for the employer and the career for the reservist.

The U.S. Department of Labor (2011) reported that the 2010 unemployment rate for veterans who served in the Armed Forces since September 2001 was over 11%. However, for young male veterans, ages 18–24, the unemployment rate was over 21%.

By analyzing data from the Department of Veterans Affairs and the Census Bureau, the Homelessness Research Institute at the National Alliance to End Homelessness (Cunningham, Henry, & Lyons, 2007) learned that, "Homeless veterans can be found in every state across the country and live in rural, suburban, and urban communities" (p. 3). This report suggests that, in part, the high rate of homelessness among veterans stems from a lack of affordable housing causing veterans to have to pay too much for rent and from the large numbers of veterans returning from combat with PTSD and TBI.

The Good News

Most research to date focuses on the negative consequences of deployment and exposure to combat-related trauma and the impact of those experiences on service members. However, recent interests in the role of resilience in overcoming hardship and trauma and in the contribution of exposure to trauma in the development of resilience in military members have led to greater attention to the potential for positive outcomes from exposure to combat-related trauma and hardship. Exposure to stress and involvement in traumatic events can lead to positive adaptation and growth. It can help one develop new perspectives on life and living and wisdom. Growth as a result of stress and trauma can include new perspectives on vulnerability and strength; positive changes in relationships; and philosophical, physical, and spiritual growth.

In a study on the possible beneficial effects of exposure to combat and combat-related trauma on Gulf War veterans (Maguen, Vogt, King, King, & Litz, 2006), researchers found that several factors contributed to positive postdeployment growth. They found that being in the National Guard or Reserves (versus active duty) and having experienced "perceived threat" (fear for safety and well-being) while deployed were associated with an increased appreciation of life. Adequate postdeployment social support (emotional and tangible help) was associated with an enhanced ability to relate to others, personal strength (the ability to handle difficulties), and posttraumatic growth (overall personal growth after experiencing a traumatic event). The results of the study also suggest that some ethnic minority service members might experience greater hope in "new possibilities" (establishing a new path for their lives) after a combat deployment.

Voices From the Frontline

A MESSAGE TO FAMILY AND FRIENDS AFTER AN INSURGENT ATTACK IN IRAQ

When the attack was over, 59 people, including 44 U.S. troops, had been wounded, some seriously, but none killed—by some miracle. Thirty-three of the wounded were the Marines who guard our perimeter. We are all grateful that they were here since four vehicle-borne IEDs came from various sides with Iraqi insurgents attempting to breach our perimeter. Even as other insurgents came through the holes they created, the Marines were there to shoot them.

I did a series of critical event debriefings with the Marine unit after the attack. It was the third time I had done intensive work with this group and they treated me like "part of the circle." I'll never forget or repeat some of the gruesome things they told me. They were very stoic about their experiences during the attack and used a lot of humor when describing what they saw and did. But they were also able to express their thoughts and feelings and listened carefully when I described possible responses to what they had experienced and warned them that they might have some difficulty dealing with what they lived through once they got home.

At the end, they left a signed book for me—*Being Happy*—a motivational book by Andrew Matthews.[*] In it they each wrote some messages: "We are well adjusted, despite the killing," "I'm OK ... really," and "I will not hurt anyone when I get home, I promise." I feel extremely proud that I was able to help them cope with what they experienced.

Angela Pereira
Colonel, U.S. Army, Retired

SUMMARY

- Combat deployment exposes U.S. military personnel to life-threatening combat, hazardous duty, and dangerous environmental conditions.
- Veterans often return with severe physical injuries and permanent physical and/or neurological changes and limitations, and psychological health problems.

---

[*] Mathews, A. (1988). *Being Happy*. New York: Price Stern Sloan.

- TBI and PTSD—the two "signature injuries" from the current conflicts—are prevalent among returning veterans; they present unique, long-term challenges to the military and civilian communities and are often missed or confused because of the sometimes hidden and overlapping symptoms characterized by these conditions.
- Both men and women service members are at increased risk for sexual assault and sexual harassment while deployed.
- Other potential consequences of exposure to combat are engaging in unsafe behavior and taking potentially dangerous risks that threaten veterans' health or lives.
- Reserve Component service members and veterans who have separated from the military are increasingly facing joblessness and homelessness.
- Positive outcomes from exposure to combat-related trauma and hardship contribution of exposure to trauma include the development of resilience to positive adaptation and growth.

EXERCISES

To further explore the physical and psychological effects of war on service members, answer the following questions:

1. What knowledge, skills, and sensitivities do you need to talk to someone who has been in combat about the physical and psychological effects of war on them?
2. Go to the Library of Congress Veterans History Project website at http://www.loc.gov/vets/about.html. Go to the digitalized collection and listen to two or three firsthand accounts of veterans' experiences during two different wars. Compare and contrast the impact of war on their lives.
3. Locate a copy of the Kessler et al. (2005) article on the prevalence of mental health disorders based on the results of a national survey. The article is listed in the references. Find the lifetime prevalence of PTSD in the general public according to the survey. How does this differ from the rate of PTSD in the military? What do you think will be the long-term societal consequences of combat-related PTSD?
4. Change your physical appearance in some way (e.g., use crutches or a wheelchair, wear a blindfold) for 2–3 hours of your normal daily routine to get a small glimpse of what it might be like to return home from war with a disfiguring scar or a physical injury. Write a short essay on your experience. What did you learn about yourself and others? What insights into wounded warriors daily lives did this experience provide?

8

The Effects of War on Families

In Chapter 8, you will

- Meet Benjamin Karney, PhD, a leading researcher at the University of California, Los Angeles, in the field of family science who studies change and stability in intimate relationships
- Learn about recent and cutting edge research that helps us understand the ways in which war affects family systems and familial relationships
- Learn how everyday assumptions about the role of stress in military families can be empirically tested
- Be able to identify current gaps in our knowledge about military families and war

Meet

Benjamin Karney, PhD, Social Psychologist

I have been studying marriage for 20 years. The research is pretty clear—the effect of stress on marriage is negative. When I had an opportunity to study military marriage, I thought, "This is going to be easy. We know military families are under stress, especially during wartime."

I am not in the military and I didn't have any friends in the military when I started this work. That didn't stop me from assuming divorce rates should be higher during wartime. Not only because of stressful deployments but because many people who join the military are young and I know young people have higher divorce rates.

All of this together, suggested to me, a scholar of marriage, that all I had to do was to document what was happening. As it turned out, I was in for a big surprise: In 2005, divorce rates were about where they had been in 1996. The data looked at divorce in all services starting 5 years before and after the start of the current conflicts. Though the stress and demand on families had increased greatly, the divorce rate hadn't.

I wondered, "What if we look only at people who were deployed—those people who were more likely to divorce?" We did another analysis comparing them to married civilians in the years from 2002 to 2005. We matched both groups by age, ethnicity, race, employment status, and education level. They were very similar except one group was in the military and one wasn't. The divorce rate among the civilians was higher.

I realized that I knew about marriage, but I didn't know military families. I had to step back and ask, "What did I miss?"

- *First, the military does a lot of things to take care of military families. It offers the best health care and child care in the United States. It provides a housing allowance. Separation pay. These benefits and others are protection against stress.*
- *Second, the stress of military families has a higher meaning that changes the way it is experienced. I met a young woman whose new husband signed up to redeploy. When I asked how she felt about that, she said, "I'm proud of him for serving our country." She told me that when he gets home they will have enough money to buy a house.*

Looking at the impact of war on marriage is complex. We don't know about how husbands and wives are communicating, how children are doing, and if people are feeling sad and lonely even when they are together. Just because we aren't seeing the negative effects now, doesn't mean they won't occur. The way families are reacting to stress may be changing over time. We're starting to see some of this with a rising suicide rate over the last few years.

The big lesson from my experience is to check your assumptions at the door. Keep listening to families and be open to what you might see and learn.

INTRODUCTION

Approximately 1 million children and their families have experienced at least one military deployment since 2001 (McFarlane, 2009). The decade since 9/11 has created unique opportunities to examine how family life is impacted by a myriad of events within military service. Researchers are identifying particular kinds of wartime experiences in order to better understand differential connections to family, spousal, and children's stress and resiliency. Some of these experiences include distinguishing types of deployment experiences (e.g., combat and noncombat deployments, repeated deployments and extended deployments), deployment-related trauma and injury, extended use of Reserve Component service members, and separation from service into the civilian world.

Our understanding of the effects of war on families continues to evolve, with researchers from multiple disciplines adding to our knowledge. Researchers vary in their backgrounds; some are career military service members, some are career civilian employees within the military, some are faculty at universities and colleges throughout the United States, and some are consultants for independent research corporations.

This chapter discusses research focused on risk and resilience experienced in family systems and familial roles in relation to war and deployment experiences. Common family system relationships include those of the family of creation: spousal and parent-child. However, these are not the only family relationships. Service members often negotiate relationships with their own parents and siblings, as well as with extended family members; and parents of service members may also be involved in caregiving for their service member's children. Each of these relationships offer opportunities to better understand strengths and concerns for military family well-being. In turn, these findings also inform policies that are directed toward these families.

You may recall from Chapter 2 that our knowledge about military family relationships is guided, in part, by the definition of family member (dependent) used to identify those members who are enrolled in DEERS and have access to military-based services and supports. This definition influences which relationships are of primary importance to the military research community and also helps us identify the limits of our knowledge.

THE DEPLOYMENT–REINTEGRATION CYCLE AND FAMILY WELL-BEING

With the continuing increased optempo of service member deployments and activation of Reserve Component personnel to active war zones, research has identified stressful transitions families negotiate, as well as positive and negative effects of deployment for families, spousal relationships, and children. Several studies highlight deployment and pre-deployment related stressors (see, for example, Di Nola, 2008; Warner, Appenseller, Warner, & Greiger, 2009) while others focus more on changes and challenges in relational processes as the deployment cycle moves from one phase to the next (Faber et al., 2008). Research in the field of communication examines spousal patterns of communication with their deployed partner and use of community supports in coping with stressors and in relation to marital satisfaction (Joseph & Afifi, 2010). McNulty (2008) focuses on concerns and assumptions about family reintegration after deployment, and work by Sayers, Farrow, Ross, and Olsin (2009) highlights the role of family distress in service members who have been referred for a mental health evaluation upon return from deployed status. Several researchers have focused specifically on alcohol misuse of the service member and the risk of interpersonal violence with romantic partners (McCarroll, Fan, & Bell, 2009; Newby, Ursano, et al., 2005) and whether or not there is an increased risk for child abuse and neglect while a service member parent is deployed (Gibbs et al., 2007; Lincoln et al., 2008). Each of these areas of research helps us learn more about resilience processes and challenges for families and highlights areas that need further investigation.

Marital Stability

There is a common perception, as Benjamin Karney mentioned in his interview, that the stresses of the ongoing engagement in Iraq and Afghanistan must be linked with higher rates of marital distress and divorce in military marriages. Researchers at the RAND Corporation conducted a study of military marriages for the Office of the Secretary of Defense in 2007 (Karney & Crown, 2007). This detailed study of 10 years of military personnel records from FY 1996 to FY 2005 led researchers to note the following.

First, marital dissolution rates were similar in 1996 during a time when fewer demands were placed on the military and in 2005 during a time when the military was experiencing greater demands. Marital dissolution (including divorces, annulments, legal separations, and cases in the process of legal divorce) among active duty branches peaked in FY 1999 and hit a 5-year low in FY 2000. From 2000 to 2005, the rate of marital dissolution gradually increased in the Army, Air Force, and Marine Corps, to the point of being similar to the dissolution rate of 1996. The Navy showed a slightly different pattern. Marital dissolution increased after FY 2001 but then declined in FY 2004 and 2005 to a rate similar to 1996. Marital dissolution among the selected reserve showed similar patterns during this decade.

Second, enlisted personnel were at greater risk of divorce than officers. This difference was likely due to the older age of officers when marrying, as marriage at a younger age is related to an increased risk of divorce (Karney & Crown, 2007).

Third, female service members displayed a much higher risk of divorce than their male counterparts. Their greater likelihood of being married to another service member (48% of female active duty service personnel were in dual-military marriages compared with 12% of male service members) does not explain this increased risk of marital dissolution (Karney & Crown, 2007).

Fourth, deployment did not seem to increase the risk of divorce for those service members married after OEF or OIF began through FY 2005. Only for active Air Force enlisted personnel and officers did the risk of divorce increase with more days deployed during this time. This lack of influence on marital stability seems contrary to popular beliefs that separations, particularly separations in which the service member is at risk of injury or death, can stress a marriage so much that the couple divorces. This study was unable to analyze the relationship between marital dissolution and level of combat experienced during deployment. Also, this study could track only those who remained in the military during the study and tracked service personnel for only 4 years or less (those who married after OEF or OIF began, through FY 2005).

Other research suggests that military combat increases the risk of marital dissolution. A recent **Mental Health Advisory Team** (MHAT-VI, 2009; a team established by the Office of the U.S. Army Surgeon General to examine behavioral health of service members and behavioral health care in OIF and OEF) reported that there has been a steady increase in the percent of junior enlisted soldiers (E-1 to E-4) in maneuver units (an Army or Marine Corps unit deployed in OIF) who indicated their intention to seek a separation or divorce, from 12.4% in 2003 to 21.9% in 2009. A similar trend was seen in their response to "I have a good marriage." In 2003, 79.2% agreed or strongly agreed with this statement but by 2009 only 57.8% did so. However, there has been no statistical change to indicate that the soldiers who reported these intentions actually followed through with separations or filing for divorce.

Additional research with veterans and with service personnel who remain in the military will be necessary to determine whether deployment, the number of days deployed, and combat experiences increase the risk of divorce in those who served in OEF and OIF (Karney & Crown, 2007).

Other researchers have noted that active duty personnel, who tend to marry earlier than their civilian counterparts, also divorce and remarry earlier than the civilian population (Adler-Baeder, Pittman, & Taylor, 2005). When coupled with the greater likelihood of becoming parents in their early 20s as compared to the civilian population, the trends of earlier divorce and remarriage indicate that many young military families may be comprised of single parents, blended families with stepparent and stepchild relations, and divorced service members with children who are nonresidential and with whom they may or may not have partial custody. You learned in Chapter 2 that military women are more likely to divorce than both their male counterparts and civilian women. Additionally, of children who live in single parent households in the United States, about 85% live with their biological mothers (U.S. Census Bureau, 2008) and military service women are almost three times as likely to be single parents as compared to male service members (DUSD, 2010). Thus, one area of research identified as a current priority focuses on single parent families, particularly custodial mothers who are service members and the ways in which deployment affects both their well-being and that of their children (Kelley, Doane, & Pearson, 2011).

Marital Satisfaction and Distress

A second, related research interest is that of marital satisfaction and distress for both service members and their spouses and how the quality of the relationship is connected to retention, readiness, and deployment experiences. Previous research has linked spousal commitment to military life with a service member's intention to remain in the service (Gade, Tiggle, & Schumm, 2003; Hosek et al., 2006), and the military has realized that family conflict and stress can have a negative impact on service member readiness and intention to remain in the service.

An emerging body of research is examining change and continuity in marital satisfaction through the deployment cycle in general and when the service member reports combat experiences, trauma, or injury during deployment (McCleland, Sutton, & Schumm, 2005; Renshaw, Rodrigues, & Jones, 2008). Both compromised physical and/or psychological health have been shown to increase the complexity in maintaining resilience at the individual and family levels. In Chapter 7, you learned about the prevalence of PTSD and depression in service members returning from deployment. You also learned that TBI has significant overlap of behavioral symptoms with PTSD.

Service members and veterans who are identified with any one or a combination of these health issues have been found to be at increased risk of marital distress (Fear et al., 2010; Hoge et al., 2004). Spouses of service members with PTSD, depression, or TBI are also at higher risk of developing psychological and marital distress themselves (Dekel, Solomon, & Bleich, 2005; Goff, Crow, Reisbig, Hamilton, 2007; Sayer et al., 2010) and may exhibit aspects of **caregiver burden** or **secondary traumatization** (Calhoun, Beckham, & Bosworth, 2002; Dekel et al., 2005; Dirkzwager, Bramsen, Ader, & van der Ploeg, 2005). Caregiver burden refers to the increased sense of responsibility and stress that a caregiver experiences in attending to the needs and welfare of another person. In the context of military families, service members who return with physical or psychological injuries may need increased assistance in completing daily activities and may have injuries that compromise their ability to resume a variety of familial roles, such as romantic partner, parent, son/daughter, or aunt/uncle. Secondary traumatization refers to the indirect exposure to trauma because of interactions with the traumatized person, which begins to affect the well-being of the persons around the individual. This indirect exposure to trauma can include spouses who are likely to be engaging with their service member partner in daily family life activities and renegotiating family roles, and children who are stepping back into parent–child roles after an extended absence and may be at different developmental levels than when the parent deployed. The transmission of secondary trauma to children has been described in World War II and Vietnam era research as **intergenerational trauma** as it indicates that the well-being of the parent can have a profound effect on the well-being of the child.

One area of this research has focused on spousal mental and physical health risks that can be linked to the deployment cycle experience of the at-home spouse (Warner et al., 2009). Army Combat Brigade Team (CBT) spouses participated in a cross-sectional study at the time that their service member spouses were deploying for a 15-month tour in Iraq. They were asked to identify deployment stressors and potential barriers to seeking care for themselves. Of the 295 spouses who participated, 43% met or exceeded the threshold level for moderate depression and about 20% reported that they had sought mental health care within the past year (including currently) or during their spouse's last deployment (Warner et al., 2009). The spouse sample was comprised of mostly females (96%), who had been married 5 or fewer years (49%), had one or more children (70%), and had at least some college education (74%). Their military spouses were mostly enlisted personnel (E-1 to E-4: 41%; E-5 to E-9: 45%).

The most frequently cited stressors for this group of spouses included safety of the deployed spouse (96%), feeling lonely (89%), raising a young child without spouse present (63%), having problems communicating with spouse (61%), and caring/raising/disciplining children with spouse absent (56%). Further, over half cited trying to balance work/family obligations as a stressor (Warner et al., 2009). These stressors link back to the family roles and relationships that are functionally altered with deployment: increased danger in the service member's daily work environment, less family member support in maintaining daily schedules, maintaining a spousal relationship, and having a partner to share caregiving responsibilities for children.

Warner et al. (2009) assessed the ranking of potential barriers to seeking mental health care after dividing the sample into two groups: nondepressed ($n = 177$) and depressed ($n = 128$). Overall, 85% of the sample agreed that they would be willing to seek mental health care if they or others thought they were having problems. However, those in the depressed group differed from the nondepressed group on several items indicating that there were several barriers to seeking that care: being seen as weak or feeling embarrassed, belief that their mental health could have an adverse effect on their spouse's career, belief that the military spouse would view them differently, worry that it could possibly hurt their own career, and depressed spouses were less likely to endorse taking medication to help than their nondepressed counterparts. The timing of this study must be taken into consideration. It was beneficial to gather the data at the time spouses were experiencing predeployment activities. These responses represented their current feelings and worries as their spouses readied for an extended combat deployment. However, the ability to complete at least one follow-up with the spouses could assess if either the stressors or perceived barriers to care changed once the deployment was underway and if there were changes in depressed status for the group. As this study was published very recently, it is possible that future reports are forthcoming that will note changes over time.

A current limitation to a broad understanding of marital satisfaction and distress in military families is that studies often only elicit information from one person, either the service member or the spouse. **Dyadic research**, where data is gathered from both members of a couple, is the typical method of studying shared and nonshared perceptions the couple has about their life and marriage although it can be more challenging—particularly with couples who are geographically separated for an extended period of time and who likely have unequal access to technology used for data collection (e.g., imagine being asked to use your weekly 30-minute window of technology access time in the chaplain's tent to complete an online survey about marital satisfaction while deployed with a combat support team instead of talking with your wife and children). Thus while this type of data collection can inform us as to the degree to which couples share common and have unique concerns about their lives together and stressors that their family system faces with military life, the increased burden on a service member during the deployment cycle may make this type of research difficult to accomplish. Lastly, research on marital satisfaction and distress would also benefit from longitudinal study so that we can learn more about the process of building and maintaining marital satisfaction in the military context (Willerton, MacDermid Wadsworth, & Riggs, 2011).

Voices From the Frontline

A DUAL-MILITARY COUPLE: TRYING TO BE TOGETHER

Colonel Angela Pereira (retired) and her husband, Major Tony Vargas (retired), knew it would be difficult to be together because of their high ranks in different specialties: Angela is a social worker and Tony is a physician assistant (PA). They shared this time line of a family trying to be together.

1993–Summer 1994: Angela is assigned at Fort Jackson in Columbia, South Carolina, and Tony at Fort Stewart in Hinesville, Georgia. It is a 200-mile drive to be together on weekends.

Summer, 1994: Tony is assigned to Fort Jackson after they marry. He packs up and moves to South Carolina.

Before he completes a 3-week orientation, unpacks, or sees a single patient: Tony is sent to support a reserve unit for 6 months in Guantanamo Bay, Cuba.

Spring, 1995: Tony returns from Cuba.

Fall, 1995: Tony hears that he might be sent to Korea on a 1-year unaccompanied tour. Tony explains he wants to stay in Columbia to support Angela who is working on her doctorate. He is given no choice—or guarantee—that he would be assigned back to Fort Jackson after the year in Korea. After the time and effort of getting into the joint domicile program for married spouses, it could be 4 years before their assignments match up again.

1996: Tony retires with 20 years in the military. It is the only way he and Angela can be together. He returns to the same job as a civilian.

1998: Angela finishes her PhD and is assigned to Aberdeen Proving Ground, Maryland. Tony moves to Maryland with Angela and applies for PA positions in Maryland. They buy a house nearby, deciding they would eventually retire in Maryland.

2001: Angela is assigned to Germany. Tony applies for PA positions in Germany and, 3 months later, follows Angela to Germany.

2004: Angela returns from Germany and is sent to Fort Belvoir, Virginia. Tony follows in 5 months and moves back into their home in Maryland.

90 days later: Just after she signs a lease for an apartment in Virginia and before her car arrives from Germany, Angela is deployed to Iraq.

2005: Angela returns from Iraq and works at Fort Belvoir, VA. Tony works in Maryland. There are 2 more years of weekend commuting.

2007: Angela is assigned to Germany. Tony stays in their home in Maryland and keeps his job as a PA at a VA Medical Center.

2009: Angela retires and returns to Maryland. They can now be together.

Spousal Communication and Role Negotiation

Two small research studies have focused on relational processes couples use to share information during deployment (Joseph & Afifi, 2010) and negotiate family role expectations due to the deployment cycle (Gambardella, 2008). Both of these studies have the potential to be easily translated into practice. Two of the practical decisions at-home families have to make, often more than once, are if and when to disclose stressful information with their deployed family member and how to be flexible in adjusting expected family member roles and ways in which those roles are met after a return from deployment.

One consideration the at-home spouse or other family member may take into consideration is if sharing information about a stressful event would add to the stress of the deployed person (Hagedoorn, Kuijer, Buunk, DeJong, & Wobbes, 2000). For instance, stressful events at home could range from an adolescent being suspended from school to a natural disaster that damages the family home or a medical crisis of a close relative. Yet, the at-home family member may be hesitant to add to the burden of the deployed family member.

Joseph & Afifi (2010) specifically studied communication decisions wives made in regard to sharing stressful family information with their deployed husbands. They hypothesized that the wife's perceptions of her husband's danger/stress and expectations for how her husband would respond to the disclosure, as well as the wife's level of military community support, would predict whether to disclose or not. Using the concept of **communal coping**, the authors framed spousal disclosures of stressful events as consequences of two types of coping processes: appraisal of the situation (is an individual or group responsible for the problem) and action taken to solve the problem (is an individual or group responsible for taking action) (Joseph & Afifi, 2010). Communal coping acknowledges that individuals are nested within groups, such as marital dyads and family systems, and that the other members of the group are likely to be affected when one or more members are distressed (Lyons, Mickelson, Sullivan, & Coyne, 1998). A decision to **buffer** the deployed family member from stressful events would be a result of appraising a situation as being a group problem (such as a teenager's truancy from school affects the whole family) but deciding to take responsibility for solving individually ("I will meet with the school and decide the discipline for the youth and not worry my husband"). The authors caution that protective buffering is actually associated with decreases in marital satisfaction (Coyne & Smith, 1994) for both partners and increases in distress (Suls, Green, Rose, Loundsbury, & Gordon, 1997) for the bufferer, indicating that it is not a good long-term communication strategy for marital couples.

The results of this study indicated that wives did indeed buffer stressful events from home if they thought sharing would increase risks for their husbands' safety. However, if wives thought that their husbands would be supportive of the disclosure, wives were more likely to disclose, and having community support networks did not influence their decisions to disclose or buffer stressful information. The authors speculate that disclosure to one's deployed spouse served the function of keeping the deployed partner engaged with family life, even if the news was not positive and created stress for the service member (Joseph & Afifi, 2010).

The second study examined dyadic processes in military couples focused on helping military couples to identify role changes and challenges after deployment (Gambardella, 2008) with an aim to lower marital discord. This was a small clinical study with ten couples who ranged in age from 21 to 47 years and who each sought out counseling to address concerns about couple conflict. Nine couples were active duty and one couple was in the Reserve Component. Six of the couples had been married 7 years or less, while the remaining four couples had been married between 14 and 21 years. Six of the service members had been in the military for more than 10 years and all had experienced at least one deployment, with the reservist reporting a high of six deployments.

The couples attended between 10 and 15 therapeutic sessions lasting 90 minutes each and, as part of the therapeutic work, each person identified their respective family roles predeployment, during deployment, and postdeployment and compared their perspectives for areas of agreement and disagreement (Gambardella, 2008). The therapist worked with the couples to renegotiate roles that each person identified as important, but in conflict. Each person kept a journal between counseling sessions to keep notes on instances when role change processes worked and when the couple needed to continue working on a particular stress point.

Six of the ten couples reported an improvement in their relationships at the end of the therapeutic intervention. Gambardella (2008) noted that three of the four couples who did not show improvement had a deployment history of either a very long deployment (18 months) or multiple deployments for extended periods of time, indicating that the couples who spent the most time apart had the most difficulty in reentering existing roles or renegotiating those roles upon reunion. It may be that these three couples were challenged to maintain a close relationship that consistently built a shared perspective for important couple and familial goals. Flexibility to adapt to changes in the family system while maintaining a sense of stability has previously been identified as a common challenge military families face. Another group of clinicians refers to this process as the need to find a "new normal" for spousal roles and expectations (Lapp, Taft, Tollefson, Hoepner, Moore, & Divyak, 2010).

Voices From the Frontline

ANGELA'S HUSBAND TALKS ABOUT THE YEAR SHE WAS IN IRAQ

When Angela was in Iraq, the specialness of life was gone.

Angela left for Iraq with 3 weeks notice. What was most difficult for me was providing general emotional support. Even though I'd been in Iraq under combat, I was never in a situation like she was.

I could e-mail her but I couldn't call. So there were limits to how often we talked. To her credit, she called me as much as she could. I had to listen to very few words and try to understand what was really going on. I understand—you don't want to retell things because that means experiencing them again. Even years later, we haven't discussed things Angela might want to talk about but not relive.

Some of the roughest times were when it looked like she was coming home, then didn't because they wanted to keep someone there that they could count on. It wasn't just that I wanted to be with her. I wanted her to be out of there. I would have been happy knowing she was sent somewhere not so bad.

It was a pretty solitary life for me—and a long year. My mission was to make it through the year. We have a big house, in a fairly rural area. There weren't lots of people stopping by. I didn't receive any support from her new unit. So I stayed very busy doing things at work and with the house. I focused on tasks rather than the bigger picture. Angela helped out in that regard. Even from Iraq, she would call with honey-do lists.

It felt like it was backward to have my wife at war. I would have been more comfortable with me there knowing Angela was safe at home. Angela and I first met in Iraq. In a way it helped me–I saw that Angela could handle herself. She had soldier skills and could take care of herself.

On the other hand, I also knew that she would go out to places that others wouldn't because she thought it was the right thing to do. She would be careful but she'd take risks. That got her into trouble more than once—during the Gulf War and in OIF. Once during the Gulf War, she got caught outside the camp perimeter gates in a dust storm on her way back from helping a unit. Then, during OIF, she was walking around the Abu Ghraib prison compound, checking to see how soldiers were doing, and was trapped in the cross fire of an insurgent ambush.

I liked to add things to the boxes I sent to Angela. She'd put the basics together before she left. So I added some fun and frivolous stuff. I found these cotton pajamas with little monkeys and bananas. Then I saw some fuzzy cow slippers. I thought it would make her—and other people smile. I sent some dark chocolate made by Bomboys, a local candy maker. When I explained I was sending it to my wife in Iraq, they gave me a 10-pound block for half price. Those were just little touches. There wasn't a whole lot I could do, but I tried to do whatever I could for her.

Tony Vargas
Major, U.S. Army, Retired, Physician Assistant and Gulf War Veteran

---

Intimate Partner Violence

Acts of sexual aggression, including intimate partner violence and military sexual trauma, have serious legal, psychological, and relational ramifications for both the aggressor and the survivor.

Research in this area does not fit easily into one level (individual/family) of analysis and discussion. One the one hand, we implicitly frame these topics at the individual level: aggressor, victim/survivor, and then focus therapeutic and preventive programs on individual behaviors with a one-on-one focus. On the other hand, these are experiences that are inherently relational, whether between two people who are intimate partners and family members, colleagues, or members of the larger community.

Voices From the Frontline

TURNING RESEARCH INTO POLICY

We started looking at how deployment affects family violence in 2003, early in the conflicts in Iraq and Afghanistan. The Army documents every incident of family violence worldwide. They provided us with data files, with no identifying information, on active duty families that experienced child maltreatment or partner abuse.

It is common sense that in times of enormous change and stress, some families doing fine will rise to the challenge and thrive. Others may crumble. Some already-fragile families may become even more so.

Our bottom-line conclusion was that the rate of child maltreatment increases when soldiers are deployed. At the same time that we did our study, Danielle Rentz, a doctoral student working with our team, did a study using different data and came up with similar findings.

Putting good numbers on what people out there working with families already know from their own experience is helpful. Our studies raised awareness of the issue for the Army and in the public.

One of the striking things about the military is that even though it is a big, complicated system, findings can become the operating policy of the system all over the world. Our findings were used to get more support to families during deployment, such as respite child care. As another example, The Army's Surgeon General directed all physicians in Army facilities to ask parents seeking primary care for themselves or their child(ren), "How are you doing?" Physicians were also instructed to screen for depression, which is related to child maltreatment, and, if it seemed indicated, to refer parents for support.

There are a lot of ways in which people can make a difference in the world. Some people have the skills, temperament, and training to work directly with military families. My training and temperament is to be a researcher. You hope to do good quality research but you don't have final say as to if your research changes policy and practice.

I've been fortunate to collaborate with people in the military who are learners. People who want to take what they can learn from the research and use it to improve the lives of families. They have the mechanisms in place to create and implement new programs and policies, although not always easily. Having no personal ties to military, I'm constantly struck by the commitment and hard work of the people I've collaborated with.

In trying to support the families we studied, it is important to keep in mind that the larger body of data suggests that military families have many strengths and are highly resilient. Every military family has at least one adult who is employed in a structured environment. They have access to health insurance and social services that our many civilian families do not have.

You might assume repeated deployment adds to the issue, but that research hasn't been done yet. Now families are into their third, fourth, and fifth deployments. We'll see what the numbers have to tell us.

Deborah Gibbs, MSPH
Senior Health Analyst at RTI International

The subject of intimate partner violence has been the focus of several different types of studies within the military community. Some researchers have approached this topic from the perspective of identifying individual level psychological disorders that have higher co-occurring rates with family problems, including domestic violence (DV) (Sayers et al., 2009). Other researchers have documented unique trends in rates of nonmutual and mutual DV incidents within military couples and the role alcohol plays in the prevalence of these incidents (McCarroll et al., 2009). Recent studies of service members who have experienced deployment for OIF and OEF have helped clarify our understanding of links between deployment to and traumatic experiences in a combat zone and incidence rates of intimate partner violence (Newby, Ursano, et al., 2005).

Sayers et al. (2009) found several interesting links between specific clinical conditions and prevalence of certain family problems in their sample of recently returned veterans who had been referred for a mental health evaluation by their primary care providers. The sample was comprised of 199 veterans from all branches of the armed forces and from the Active and Reserve Components. Each respondent had returned from deployment and then separated from service within 2 years of their referral, experiencing two major life transitions in a very short period of time. The most common clinical conditions and provisional diagnoses reported in the study included any depression, PTSD, generalized anxiety disorder, major depression, and at-risk alcohol use.

Sayers et al. found that over 75% of the married/partnered respondents reported at least one family readjustment issue with many of these same respondents stating that these concerns were ongoing, rather than one-time issues. Significant and somewhat surprising to the researchers was the high rate of self-reported mild to moderate levels of DV in the sample (53%), as self-reports of DV tend to be underreported by as much as 10% compared to reports made by both partners. The most commonly reported specific item within the domestic abuse questions was that the service member's partner was afraid of them (27.6%) with 4.4% reporting injury due to a DV incident. Higher rates of family reintegration struggles were associated with other co-occurring risks of depression and PTSD in this clinical sample, indicating that as the number of individual stressors and risks increases, there is a corresponding increase in the likelihood of poorer family functioning and relationship satisfaction.

McCarroll et al. (2009) reviewed data from 1998 to 2004 collected through the Army Central Registry for verified DV incidents (physical or emotional) that occurred within enlisted Army personnel spousal systems. These researchers were interested in identifying characteristics of the DV event, including whether an event was nonmutual (one aggressor, one victim) or mutual (each member of the couple listed as both aggressor and victim) and if alcohol was included as a factor in the event. Analyses indicated that overall incidence rates for both nonmutual and mutual incidents decreased significantly over this 6-year period (by 23% and 57%, respectively), that men and women were represented equally as victims in the mutual DV episodes but that women were significantly overrepresented as targets of DV in nonmutual episodes (72%), and that alcohol contributed to both aggressor and victim experiences. More severe violence in both types of incidents was associated with offender drinking and, while the overall incidence rates for both types of DV incidents decreased over the study period, that decrease did not hold true for rates where the offender was drinking. McCarroll et al. recommend that programs focusing on DV and alcohol misuse include material on the increased risk of interpersonal violence when alcohol is a factor.

With the ongoing military actions related to OIF/OEF/OND, as well as peacekeeping efforts and episodic disaster intervention both in the United States (such as the flooding in Memphis, Tennessee, in May 2010) and abroad (including the Haitian Earthquake in January 2010), deployment is a common aspect of present-day military life. Experiences during deployment with violence, loss, and threats to life and health have been shown to impact service member health and risk-taking behaviors. Previous research (McCarroll et al., 2000) found that risk of severe DV by Army soldiers was linked to length of deployment but that the overall *unique* contribution of deployment to DV rates was quite small. The most consistent risk factors for postdeployment DV in this study were prior history of DV, being young, and living off base. Another study of soldier reports of DV rates between 3 and 5 months after deployment found no support to indicate that deployment was related to DV (McCarroll et al., 2003). Newby and colleagues (2005) further contributed to our knowledge of how deployment may contribute to understanding rates of DV within the Army by examining spouse reported DV rates at 10 months past a specific deployment.

The emotional cycle of deployment is often described as having a "honeymoon" phase shortly after return, even though research has not shown this characterization to be common or consistent across families. However, family support professionals use the description of the emotional cycle of deployment to help families identify when the honeymoon phase recedes and the challenges of reintegrating into everyday family routines may begin.

One possible indicator of this change is a potential increase in spousal conflict and violence. Thus, studies examining postdeployment rates are usually very specific in defining the window of time postdeployment that was investigated. In their 2005 study, Newby and colleagues found that deployment was not a significant risk factor at 10 months past deployment. Instead, the significant risk factors for postdeployment DV were being younger and having a history of DV prior to deployment. This research group cautions that while the specific deployment in their studies (Bosnia, 6 months) did not have a unique or significant contribution to postdeployment DV rates, other aspects of military life not included in their studies, such as longer and repeated deployments, may have an effect on both spousal conflict and DV rates.

Different approaches to the study of interpersonal violence in military and veteran couples lead to different findings, which limits the ability to make any broad-sweeping summary statements. Sayers et al. (2009) found that DV was a common element in a clinical sample of veterans with deployment experiences and noted that mental health issues including depression and PTSD were likely to be present when DV was present. Newby and colleagues (2000, 2003, 2005) found little (2000) to no support (2003, 2005) for the hypothesis that a specific deployment was a significant factor in later DV rates at a large Army post. Through their study of substantiated DV incidents over a 6-year span, McCarroll et al. (2009) were able to show significant decreases in both nonmutual and mutual DV rates in the Army, unless alcohol was used by the aggressor. These varied findings contribute to our overall understanding of interpersonal violence and give support to prevention and intervention programs that are multifaceted (attending to more than one issue) and targeted to higher-risk groups.

The study of couple violence in the military is ripe for cross-disciplinary research. Current concepts used in family research with heterosexual couples distinguish between **situational couple violence**, **coercive controlling violence**, and **violent resistance** and posit that these different forms of intimate partner violence produce different consequences within family systems and need tailored prevention and intervention strategies (Johnson, 2009; Kelly & Johnson, 2008). Situational couple violence tends to be much more gender symmetrical (both men and women engage in violent action) and is linked with particular couple conflicts unique in the relationship of the couple while coercive controlling is primarily perpetrated by men and is based upon a motivation to dominate a spousal relationship through violent force and control. The term violent resistance describes the partner's actions (usually female) to resist against an attempt by a spousal partner to control her actions and opportunities. While the research cited in this section has included studies on mutual and nonmutual DV, connecting research in this area with the larger body of interpersonal violence research may help shape interventions and prevention programming to better address the needs of couples who experience different kinds of violence in their family system.

COMBAT-INJURED FAMILIES

Working with and learning from **combat-injured families** is yet another area of research linked with the current conflict and is still in its infancy. There is very little research published on these families at this time although there are ongoing studies. Combat-injured families are comprised of the spouses, children and stepchildren, parents, ex-spouses, siblings, and other extended relations of an injured service member. As you learned in Chapter 7, the most common type of physical injury in OIF/OEF/OND is musculoskeletal/connective tissue injury (Cohen et al., 2010), while the most common sources of injury are blasts and IEDs (Owens et al., 2008). Concussive blasts are also responsible for one of the signature injuries of this conflict: traumatic brain injury. Due to advances in both protective gear and medical treatment from emergency care to rehabilitation, service members in the current conflict are surviving devastating injuries yet face extensive recovery and rehabilitation needs (Gawande, 2004).

The **recovery trajectory**, or the process of recovery over time from illness or injury with expected advances, setbacks, and potential changes in abilities, is a concept used in the medical and rehabilitative fields. Cozza and Guimond (2011) outline the complexity that service members and their families face when a deployment-related injury occurs. The complexity of deployment-related injury and recovery is derived from extensive variability in several factors: Injuries vary widely in their severity and ability to heal to the satisfaction of the service member; the service member's family composition is likely complex with parents of the service member, spouses/significant others or ex-spouses, children who may range in developmental age and ability, family history and patterns, and siblings; and the medical treatment required can range from a few interventions to many months and years of rehabilitative and reconstructive work.

Family members face additional stressors once injury occurs, including logistical concerns (families are likely not located near the medical facility), negotiating complex health-care decisions, meeting the needs of children to help them understand what has happened to their parent while trying to maintain a stable caregiving environment, negotiating potential conflicts between members of the family (such as parents of the service member and spouse/significant other) over care decisions, and working through ambiguous loss and grief due to facing the unknown as family and relational roles are challenged.

Service Members and Spouses in Combat-Injured Families

Earlier in this chapter, the term *caregiver burden* was defined with a list of examples describing how it might operate in combat-injured military families. When a combat injury occurs, not only is there the immediate crisis of the injury, there is an ongoing need for couples to make adjustments related to injury-induced changes in physical and emotional health as well as to negotiate reintegration (Badr, Barker, & Milbury, 2011). Earlier research indicates that wives of wounded veterans report more distress than wives of noninjured veterans (Calhoun et al., 2002), which is congruent with the research described earlier in the chapter that wives of service members who are diagnosed with psychological trauma such as PTSD and depression also report higher distress than wives whose husbands do not have these additional psychological challenges (Dekel et al., 2005; Goff et al., 2007; Sayer et al., 2010).

What challenges are likely for the service member? Badr et al. (2011) caution that the type and severity of the injury will create different consequences and challenges for the service member and the spousal/romantic partner (see their chapter for a detailed overview of different injuries and their unique recovery challenges). Briefly, the service member may incur physical disfigurement such as burns and other injury scarring; partial or complete amputation of an injured limb; and limitations in mobility (ability to move in one's environment: e.g., stairs, depth perception, balance) and in dexterity (fine motor skills: e.g., writing, tying shoes, buttoning shirts, opening jars). As well, there may be hidden injury due to TBI that impacts sensory systems (vision, hearing, taste, smell, and touch), emotional regulation, short- and long-term memory, and body control. The service member is challenged with a potentially significant change in his or her capabilities, both physically and psychologically. These changes may, in turn, affect the service member's sense of identity and ability to fulfill family roles (Cozza & Guimond, 2011) such as being a provider, identifying with a career, being a romantic partner, being an adult son or daughter, and being a parent, uncle, or aunt.

Spousal partners are also faced with a significant amount of ambiguity as they wait, watch, and support their injured spouse. Again, depending on the injury and the expected level of recovery, spouses face pressure to keep the family going, often with increased stressors and conflict in being present for their spouse and being present for their children and other family members. Spouses and romantic partners also face the possibility that their injured spouse may be significantly changed because of the injury and may not be able to relate with them and other families members in the same ways as before an injury (e.g., not being able to practice soccer dribbles with a daughter, forgetting names or important family memories). If the injured spouse cannot resume or reshape expected spousal and familial roles, there is potential for increased marital conflict or distress.

Children in Combat-Injured Families

Parental emotional distress of the at-home parent and the injury of the deployed parent create a challenging caregiving environment for children that is linked to poor child outcomes (Beardslee & Wheelock, 1994), and stressful family environments have differential effects on children depending on their developmental age (Cozza & Guimond, 2011). The onset of a family crisis can trigger behaviors that are not usually experienced by individuals and families, some of which are categorized as **developmental regression**, particularly in very early childhood. Developmental regression describes an individual's inability to maintain developmental gains and revert back to earlier behaviors. For children experiencing crisis, this is often framed as the child seeking a safe and stable level of operating in the world that does not add to the stress of learning and making developmental gains. Examples of developmental regression triggered by increased stress or crisis in a family system include toddlers going back to self-soothing techniques (thumb sucking, needing a nightlight or comfort object like a blanket or stuffed animal) and regressing in toilet training. Older children may seek more reassurance about family life and decisions to participate in activities that take away from being with family (sports, scouting, special religious or school events).

Infants and toddlers look to their primary caregivers to gauge what is safe, to implement predicable routines that help them learn about the social and physical world around them, and to foster their ability to cope when distressing events occur (Fogel, 2010). When parents are not able to mirror effective coping or offer comfort, stability, and a sense of security, very young children pick up on the distress but have limited skills and experience in meeting extreme coping demands.

As children enter the preschool and early elementary years, the developmental phenomena of **magical thinking** (making incorrect assumptions about cause and effect: e.g., "If I wish hard enough my Daddy will be OK") paired with a limited **theory of mind** (a limit in the ability to understand things from another person's point of view: e.g., "Why is grandma happy that Daddy is going into surgery? Isn't surgery bad?") can shape their perceptions of their role(s) as a family member. Cozza and Guimond (2011) posit that normative developmental processes can lead a child to mistakenly assume responsibility for the stress in the family system (e.g., "Mommy left me with Grammy and Papa because she is mad at me") or for the injury to their parent (e.g., "I forgot to pray for Daddy's safety and that's why he got hurt").

School-age children and adolescents have more mature cognitive, emotional, and coping capabilities than younger children but still have anxiety over what they "should" do when a parent is injured and the family system is experiencing crisis. Older children and adolescents also look to the adults around them to assess the seriousness of the crisis and injury to the parent, as well as rely on their familial relationships to help mediate distress and keep their **sense of self** (how one views one's self and abilities; a self-definition of who one is) intact in the face of the crisis.

Factors that offer protection to children and parents in combat-injured families include previously established patterns of family routines and care and availability of extended support relationships of family and friends (Cozza & Guimond, 2011). Additionally, standard practices developed by the Child Life Council (the professional organization for child life specialists who have completed training and certification in working with medically fragile children and children in medical environments) focus on ways to foster effective coping for children facing medical crises and chronic illness. Child life specialists are skilled in parent education and serve as a liaison in helping families cope with the challenges of an injured or ill child. The professional organization has recently begun to expand areas of service to include traditional physician's offices, hospice facilities, child and youth camps for fragile children, and funeral homes (Child Life Council, 2010).

A logical extension would be to include Child Life Services in military and VA hospitals and rehabilitation centers.

UNDERSTUDIED RELATIONSHIPS AND DIRECTIONS FOR FUTURE RESEARCH

Military family research has primarily focused on spouses and children of the service member and understandably so. These relationships are directly affected by daily military life and cultural context because of the service member's work. Yet, not all spousal and parent–child relationships are equally represented in the literature, and there are other familial relationships that are not well understood. Little is known about sibling relationships of military children and the role they play in individual and family adjustment. Remarriages and blended families are not differentiated in the data that are reported by the individual branches or by the DoD. Marital stability and satisfaction in the Reserve Component have not been as well studied as those in the Active Component (Renshaw et. al., 2008). The transitions Reserve Component families negotiate as they move between civilian and active duty status may offer new insights into our understanding of military family resiliency. In particular, marital satisfaction, parent–child relations, and the strengths and challenges that their social networks and communities face in providing effective supports and resources are all topics that would benefit from further inquiry. Knowledge about other aspects of Reserve Component family life also lags behind research with Active Component families. For example, very little is known about divorce and remarriage rates, interpersonal violence, or child maltreatment that occurs when the service member is not activated.

Other romantic relationships are also understudied (MacDermid Wadsworth, 2010). Dating relationships and processes of couple formation are two areas with very little research although programs to enhance dating and mate selection skills and prepare for marriage (e.g., PREPARE/ENRICH) are offered to service members. Additionally, the DADT policy that had prohibited gay and lesbian service members from serving openly, in concert with the federal **Defense of Marriage Act** (DOMA: a federal act passed in 1996 that explicitly states that marriage at the federal level is only recognized if it occurs between one man and one woman and reaffirms that individual states are not compelled to recognize same-sex marriages that occurred in a different state), has also limited our understanding of romantic partnerships within this particular service member population (Defense of Marriage Act, 2011). Same-sex marriage is legal only in six states and the District of Columbia with an additional four states allowing civil unions. Given the broader U.S. context, romantic and long-term partnerships in this population are extremely difficult to study systematically and without adding to the potential risks of exposure for these service members (National Conference of State Legislatures, 2011). With the recent repeal of DADT and the evolving status of legal marriage and civil union within the United States, research that describes and identifies stress and resilience processes for same-sex military couples and families may not be too far off into the future.

Parents and siblings of service members are also not well represented in the family literature. Considering that just under half of the Active Component and just over half of the Reserve Component are single and that 68% of active duty personnel and 36% of the selected reserve are 30 years or younger (DUSD, 2010), it is reasonable to assume that connections to parents and siblings are important in service members' lives as well as their children. Parents may also contribute to caregiving for grandchildren while their service member parent is deployed, and similarly aunts and uncles can be important family supports including acting as temporary parents. Prevalence of extended familial and **extrafamilial** (caregivers outside the family system) caregiving and the challenges and strengths of these caregiving environments are not known.

In addition, a small proportion of family members identified in DEERS is classified as a group of **adult dependents**. These are family members who are a parent, grandparent, former spouse, sibling, disabled older child, or any other individual who is claimed by the service member as a dependent (DUSD, 2010). Among active duty families, in 2009, there were just more than 8,800 individuals in this category in addition to more then 1.2 million children and more than 700,000 spouses. Among families of the selected reserve, there were almost 2,000 recognized adult dependents, more than 730,000 children, and more than 400,000 spouses enrolled in DEERS in 2009. The majority of individuals in the adult dependent category across both groups were older women: 50% of adult dependents of active duty were between 51 and 62 years with another 39% at age 63 years or more, and 51% of adult dependents of selected reserve members were 63 years and older. While the numbers are much smaller for the adult dependent category in both Active and Reserve Components, we do not know much about military service members and families who are caring for adults in their daily lives.

Two small studies are beginning to expand our understanding of parents and their adult service member children: one from the perspective of male senior officers' concerns about their aging parents (Parker, Call, Dunkle, & Vaitkus, 2002) and one from the perspective of parents' emotional processes, stressors, and supports when their adult child deployed to a combat zone (Crow & Myers-Bowman, 2011). These studies provide a beginning point for researchers and practitioners to think more systemically about extended family relationships in military families.

Parker et al. (2002) conducted their research with 277 senior-ranking male officers who attended the U.S. Army War College (USAWC) over the course of two summers. The vast majority of these participants were between 40 and 49 years (95%), were married (98%), and had at least one child still at home (93%), while relatively few (16%) reported that they have responsibility for caring for an elderly person. At the time of data collection, 40% had experienced at least one combat deployment and about 75% had experienced a deployment that lasted 12 months or longer.

Within this sample, aspects of military life created opportunities for stress in maintaining connections with their parents: high mobility with assignments far from their parents, potential limits in being able to communicate with one another on a regular basis, and lack of military housing suitable for bringing a frail parent into the family home. Some of the factors that were linked with increased worry about parents included previous illnesses of the parent(s), parental age, and if the service member had an angry temperament (Parker et. al., 2002). Factors that helped ease officers' worry included having siblings (presumably to help share the care and concern for parents) and having a "parent care plan" so that if a medical crisis were to occur, the adult child(ren) would know the wishes of the parent in regard to medical decisions and care.

This study was not able to access the role of the military spouse in the parental caregiving process or address potential worry about parents-in-law. However, it does give some insight into family processes that are commonly identified as part of midlife and being in the "sandwich" generation of an extended family system.

The second study focused on parents of service members and their sources of concern and support as their adult child deployed to a combat zone (Crow & Myers-Bowman, 2011). This small, qualitative study elicited in-depth, written responses from 42 parents to a series of ten open-ended questions. These questions were framed to let the parents "describe their feelings and experiences with their child's first deployment … [those] whose children had deployed more than once were presented the same ten questions again with the focus on the most recent deployment rather than the first " (p. 170). Both mothers ($n = 33$) and fathers ($n = 9$) participated and had both sons ($n = 38$) and daughters ($n = 4$) who had deployed.

The most commonly reported responses to learning about their adult child's deployment included fear and worry, closely followed by anxiety and concern. While most of their emotional responses were focused on their adult child—fear for safety, concern for the types of danger he/she might be facing—some parents also indicated that their response extended to their adult child's spouse and children. Thus parents worried about their child and the family their child had created. Many parents reported these concerns with other, more positive responses. For example, parents also felt proud knowing what their children were about to do in service to their country and that they would be putting their skills to use, and confident that their children were capable of doing what they were being called to do.

Some of the functional stressors that parents reported included difficulties or inconsistency in being able to communicate with their deployed son or daughter and worry when planned communications were delayed. Additional communication difficulties were reported in trying to gain information from unit command, and one parent noted that she realized that her son's first priority for communication was going to be with his wife, not his mom. Along with difficulties in communication, parents often noted that both knowing what was happening and not knowing what was happening could be stressful. Some parents had either been service members themselves or been military spouses, and they noted that the experience of seeing their adult child deployed was a qualitatively different experience than being the service member or the spouse. One parent reported that since her son was single at the time, he came to her to complete his predeployment paperwork, including going over his funeral arrangements. Her feeling of helplessness and awareness that she could not protect her child highlighted a significant change in their parent–child relationship.

Many parents also identified that finding both informal and formal support was difficult (Crow & Myers-Bowman, 2011). When asked about coping techniques parents used to help with the stress of the deployment experience, the authors found that parents described far fewer details about their coping strategies than about their reactions and struggles. The most number of strategies reported was four, but the average was just under two strategies. Having friends who were against the war and living in a community that hosted events protesting military involvement increased feelings of isolation; not living near a military installation or having strong ties to other parents who also had children in the service were also difficult. The two most common sources of support were a sense of spirituality or having religious faith and having supportive friends and family members. Nearly a third reported that they used media outlets to try and stay updated, while a few stated that they actively avoided media reports as a way to lower their distress. One-fifth joined formal support groups and less than one-fifth stated that they actively sought out ways to maintain connection with their deployed child. Three of the parents responded that they had not found any useful coping strategies, which prolonged feelings of distress.

Parents reported a range of possible effects that their adult child's deployment had had in their own marital relationships. For about 40% of parents, the deployment had very little effect on the quality of their marital relationship. Another 40% reported that they thought this experience had brought them closer with their spouse. The remaining parents indicated that the experience increased emotional distance between themselves and their partners or had a mixed effect, both positive and negative. The parents who reported greater emotional distance often commented that their partner was not a source of support in coping with the stress of their child's deployment.

This study is one of the first to systematically draw in information about how parents of service members experience deployment. Though small, it has the potential to be very useful in guiding human service professionals to develop empathetic and supportive environments in a wide variety of communities and organizations. Many parents do not live in or near military communities and may not have easy access to military friendly support programs. Lay leaders in religious communities can identify ways of providing support to parents and extended family members; community counselors and family life educators can create programming that specifically meets needs of parents of service members and make connections with existing support programs.

A last area of research and writing that is missing from the military family literature is that of understanding the ways families grieve the loss of a military family member. While there are publications on families and children experiencing military death that are directed to the professional human service community (Cohen et al., 2006; Scott, 2010), studies that give voice to grieving experiences across familial relationships (parent of service member, sibling, spousal/romantic partner, and children) are not yet available. Listening to and representing the experiences of families who have lost a service member are important, however, and can contribute to a better understanding of how to support grieving families. We end this chapter with one mother's voice.

Voices From the Frontline

A MOTHER TALKS ABOUT LOSING HER SON

My mission is to be sure people remember that Daniel was here and made the ultimate sacrifice.

Daniel arrived in Ramadi, Iraq, early in July, 2005, and passed away September 28, 2005. He was killed with four other soldiers from the 109th Infantry Unit out of New Milford, Pennsylvania, when their vehicle was attacked.

Losing a child is the most devastating experience any parent could ever have. It's been 6 years, and the pain never goes away. At first grief overtakes you. But now there's a lot of pride too as I learn to appreciate who Daniel was, where he was, and what he did.

Daniel left two boys, and they were his world. Devin who was 3½ when Daniel died didn't smile for 6 months. He and Daniel had a special relationship. It's like he was attached to Dan's leg. If Dan went downstairs, Devin did, too. It amazes me how much he can remember. He's always saying, "Grandma, do you remember when Daddy and I…." I'm so glad he had time with Daniel even though it was cut short.

Kody was 17 months old. As he got older, he'd say: "Okay, Grandma, the next time I come, can we go to Heaven and get my dad? He's been gone long enough." I didn't know what to say to him. He doesn't say that any more. I think he knows his dad isn't coming back.

We are fortunate the boys live nearby and their mother, Kim, shares them with us. We share holidays and vacations. Every year we go to Washington, DC, together for Family United's celebration for Fallen Soldiers.

Right before Daniel left for Iraq, he wrote letters to Kim, the boys, and to my husband and me. Kim hung on to them and gave us our letter after he died. He told us how proud he was to serve whether or not we understood. He asked us to be sure his sons always remember him and to make them a part of the Arnold family.

Daniel was my son. I knew what kind of person he was. But I didn't understand his commitment to serving our country until I read his letter. It can be hard to understand, and I'm part of a military family. My husband served. So did my two sons. My son-in-law just got back from Kuwait. Whether they believe in war or not, each of them performed their duties. Without them we wouldn't have the freedoms we have. A lot of people don't think about that.

Did Daniel want to make the ultimate sacrifice? No. But he would if it would make someone's life better and our country safer for his boys. I don't know if I could make so deep a commitment, but I am glad there are people like Daniel who will.

Everyone handles grief in their own way. We've been offered counseling anytime we need it for the rest of our lives. For now, I told a counselor, "I lost my son. Unless you can take away my pain, this is something I have to learn how to deal with myself."

Even though it is painful, it helps to talk and for people to remember Daniel. Because Daniel was part of the National Guard and we are from a small community, our experience may have been different than in bigger places. Daniel's unit still considers us part of the family. We've been visited by everyone from the Adjutant General all the way down. I can see now why my son wanted to be part of this unit.

That September after Daniel died, we met personally with President Bush. We have received letters from the Governor, Senators, and people all around the world. A lady in Iowa made us a personalized quilt with photos and stories of Daniel. Two artists each painted a portrait of him. We even received a plaque from the Iraqi government thanking Daniel for his service. All these will be treasured and passed along to his sons one day.

Janet Arnold
Mother of Staff Sgt. Daniel L. Arnold (1977–2005)

SUMMARY

- Marital dissolution rates were similar in 1996 during a time of fewer demands placed on the military and in 2005 during a time when the military was experiencing greater demands. There is a worrisome trend of an increase in the number of junior enlisted from 2003 to 2009 who report their intention to seek a separation or a divorce and a decrease during the same time of the number who report being in a good marriage.
- Active Component personnel tend to marry earlier than their civilian counterparts and also divorce and remarry earlier than the civilian population.
- When coupled with the greater likelihood of becoming parents in their early 20s, the trends of earlier divorce and remarriage indicate that many young military families may be comprised of single parents, blended families with stepparent and stepchild relations, and divorced service members with children who are nonresidential and with whom they may or may not have partial custody.
- Military service women are almost three times as likely to be single parents as compared to male service members.
- Service members and veterans who are identified with any one or a combination of TBI, PTSD, or depression are at increased risk of marital distress. Spouses of service members with PTSD, depression, or TBI are also at higher risk of developing psychological and marital distress themselves and may exhibit aspects of caregiver burden or secondary traumatization.
- A current limitation in understanding marital satisfaction and distress in military families is that studies often only elicit information from one person, either the service member or the spouse because of difficulties in the data collection process.
- Two of the practical decisions military families have to make, often more than once, are if and when to disclose stressful information with their deployed family member and how to be flexible in adjusting expected family member roles and ways in which those roles are met after a family member returns from deployment.
- Frequent and extended deployments may pose a significant challenge for couples to maintain a close relationship that consistently builds a shared perspective for important couple and familial goals.
- Research into the connections between DV and deployment shows limited and inconsistent links. More consistent risk factors for DV in military families are young age and having a history of DV prior to deployment.
- Combat-injured families are comprised of the spouses, children and stepchildren, parents, ex-spouses, siblings, and other extended relations of an injured service member.
- The complexity of deployment-related injury and recovery is dependent upon the extensive variability in several factors: injury severity and ability to heal; the service member's family composition, family history and patterns; and the medical treatment required.
- The type and severity of the injury will create different consequences and challenges for the service member and the roles they have within their family system (parent, adult child, romantic partner, sibling).
- Factors that offer protection to children and parents in combat-injured families include previously established patterns of family routines and care and availability of extended support relationships of family and friends.
- There are several areas of military family research that need attention: blended and same-sex families, National Guard and Reserve families, extended family relations in service members' lives, parents and siblings of service members, and the ways in which service member injury and death affect their family members.

EXERCISES

1. You have been asked to develop a community interest group for families who are caring for adult dependents at your installation. What would you need to know about your population before beginning the interest group? What resources do you think would be helpful as you build this interest group?

2. Examine the materials produced by the Zero to Three organization for caring for very young children in military families who experience deployment, combat injury, and death (http://www.zerotothree.org/about-us/funded-projects/military-families/).
   a. What guidelines do these materials recommend to help young children process these stressors at a level that is developmentally appropriate for their age and cognitive and emotional abilities?
   b. How would you adapt and/or develop similar programs for elementary school age children or adolescents?

3. The research on DV in military families does not yet frame violence between couples using current terms of situational couple violence, coercive controlling, and violent resistance. Choose and read one of the studies on DV discussed in this chapter and then read Michael Johnson's work in describing the current terms (Johnson 2009; Kelly & Johnson, 2008 among other publications).
   a. How would the study you chose be changed if it were framed using these terms?
   b. What differences in conclusions and recommendations could you envision if the study were reframed to include these terms?

4. Combat-injured service members often face months of hospitalization and rehabilitation, and these facilities are not necessarily family or child friendly.
   a. What practical challenges do these facilities face in accommodating spouses, parents, and children?
   b. What practical recommendations would you offer to help minimize the stress of visits for children and other family members?
   c. Children's hospitals offer a different model of providing care and creating environments that lower stress levels for patients and families. What aspects of this model could be transferred to military and VA hospitals and rehabilitation centers?

5. Chapter 4 offers detailed information about children's experiences with deployment and the stressors their families and at-home parents face. What new connections can you make between the research on academic performance, well-being, and risks for maltreatment now that you have a better understanding of how war affects the important adults in their lives?

6. There are several areas of research with family members that need more attention. If you had the opportunity to design a study that gave voice to National Guard and Reserve families, siblings, parents, or same-sex partners, what would you include in your study and what method(s) and design(s) do you think would be most useful for your research and friendly to the families?

9

Military Support for Military Families
Military Policies and Programs

In Chapter 9, you will

- Meet Jonathan Douglas, Major, U.S. Marine Corps, Retired; a prior Branch Head at Personal and Family Readiness Division, Headquarters, Marine Corps
- Learn about the different ways that the Department of Defense (DoD) ensures that Active and Reserve Component families from all branches of the military are supported as they respond to the challenges associated with being military families
- Be introduced to the various policies and programs that the DoD has established to assist military families
- Learn how you, as a helping professional working with military families, can assist those families in accessing the appropriate help for their issues

Meet

Lieutenant Colonel Jonathan Douglas, U.S. Marine Corps (Retired) and a prior Branch Head at Personal and Family Readiness Division, Headquarters, Marine Corps

I joined the Marines in 1983. Back then, your family was not considered part of the military. The attitude was, "that's your baggage." There were limited programs available and no focus on children of different ages.

I was a helicopter pilot. That's all I wanted to do. Eighteen years later, I found myself running all of these programs for families. In part, I chose this assignment because of location. It was this or a 2-hour commute. I ended up loving the work. Everything we did day-by-day supported Marines and/or their families including spouses, children, parents, extended family, and others that our marines and sailors designated.

I had a staff of 14. All but two were civilian. Their professions included counselor, recreation directors, health educator, physical education teacher, and nurse.

I oversaw many programs, including suicide prevention, recreation departments, and aquatics programs in 54 swimming pools across the world.

We ran a Single Marines Program. We aligned with sororities and fraternities so we could get ideas and learn how to serve 18–26 year olds. Think about college kids going off to school, not knowing how to do their laundry. Some of the new recruits were in the same position but unlike their peers in college, they had to be neatly dressed and at work at 6:30 AM. I never thought about anyone in the Marines trying to arrange for a concert tour to play close to an installation, but that's the kind of thing we did.

Our work could have immediate impact on someone's life. Say we had money on hand to start a new program. Within 30 days it would be up and running. Thirty days later we'd know if it was working and if there were changes to make, we could make them.

We worked with the civilian community when we could. For example, say we were underfunded for youth football at an installation. We'd build a connection with a team and tell families, "This team outside the gate will give you a good rate and be glad to see your child."

The military is a great way of life if done right. We're not perfect at it but now we see how important family programs are. People just don't join the military. They come with a family or often get one soon after they join. Families are part of the infrastructure. If doing something is possible, you are happy to try to figure out how. Something as simple as turning two racquetball courts into child care so moms can exercise and get a little time for themselves, can make someone's life better.

INTRODUCTION

As discussed in Chapter 1, the DoD understands that the welfare and success of military families is vitally important to its overall success. DoD leaders realize that in order for its military members to be able to carry out their responsibilities, there must be an extensive infrastructure with the sole purpose of taking care of military families. Therefore, the DoD has created and maintains a wide variety of policies and programs that are in place to assist families with all aspects of their lives—from military-specific issues like moving to a new installation or having a loved one go off to war to managing a wide variety of problems that can occur in any family. Some of the programs are voluntary programs for the military family; others are mandated by the service member's chain of command. Some programs provide information or are intended to make life more convenient for the military family; others are there to provide basic necessities for the military family.

Most of the programs described in this chapter were developed and are more useful for families of Active than Reserve Component military members especially installation-based programs. However, over the past decade, as the role of the Reserve Component has become more prominent and the needs of their families have become more salient, programs have been developed specifically for the National Guard and Reserves and others have been expanded to better reach these families. Those programs will be discussed in Chapter 11.

You are reading this book because you are interested in helping military families. One of the ways that you can assist military families is by acquiring a basic understanding of programs and policies in place to help them. Although the specific policies and programs may change from time to time, the infrastructure that directs the policies and oversees the programs is always in place. A program may be renamed or modified to meet current demands, but most of the programs described in this chapter will remain in place in one form or another. However, a large percentage of military families do not know or have accurate knowledge of available benefits and services, due in part to "the plethora of resources that are offered by a complicated patchwork comprising DoD, the services, civilian support agencies, and state government" (MacDermid et al., 2008, p. 19). Understanding the kinds of programs that are available to military families will help you assist military families in accessing the appropriate programs to meet their needs.

INFRASTRUCTURE

Among the active duty, National Guard, and Reserves, there are approximately 3 million military family members who are part of the United States Armed Forces community (DUSD, 2008). The DoD is responsible for programs and policies that support these family members. The Active and Reserve Components each have a senior civil service assistant and advisor to the Secretary of Defense who is responsible for creating and managing these programs and policies. For active duty families, it is the Deputy Under Secretary of Defense for Military Community and Family Policy (DUSD/MCFP). For Reserve Component families, it is the Assistant Secretary of Defense for Reserve Affairs. The

DoD family support infrastructure includes a mixture of service members, civil service employees, and contractors who work together but often have very different roles in developing and managing the programs and policies that support military families.

Deputy Under Secretary of Defense for Military Community and Family Policy

The DUSD/MCFP is responsible for establishing and maintaining all military community programs and policies for active duty service members and their families (Office of the Under Secretary of Defense for Personnel and Readiness, 2010). It is responsible for policy, advocacy, and oversight of all quality of life issues; family and casualty assistance; morale, welfare, and recreation (MWR) programs; the Military OneSource (MOS) and MilitaryHOMEFRONT websites; the DoD Education Activity; and the DoD's commissary (similar to a grocery store) and exchange (similar to a department store) services. You will learn more about all of these programs in this chapter.

Assistant Secretary of Defense for Reserve Affairs

The Assistant Secretary of Defense for Reserve Affairs is the principal staff assistant and advisor to the Secretary of Defense on all matters involving members of the Reserve Components of the United States Armed Forces, including the Army and Air National Guards and all Reserve Components of the Army, Navy, Marine Corps, Air Force, and Coast Guard (Office of the Assistant Secretary of Defense for Reserve Affairs, 2010b). To ensure that all Reserve Component members and families receive the support they need through appropriate policies and programs, the Office of the Assistant Secretary of Defense for Reserve Affairs and the DoD Office of Family Policy formed a strategic partnership (Office of the Assistant Secretary of Defense for Reserve Affairs, 2010a). This partnership and commitment to provide exceptional quality of life programs for the Reserve Component is part of the DoD's commitment to make sure reservists and their families are not left behind in the effort to provide quality family support programs across the entire military force.

COMPREHENSIVE RESOURCES FOR MILITARY FAMILIES

The following resources are the results of DoD's attempts to provide easy access to information and referral sources for programs and policies available to military members and their families. They are excellent starting points for finding information that can help military families you may be working with. First, military family assistance centers are one-stop service and support centers for military members and families. Second, MilitaryHOMEFRONT is a good source for service providers working with military families. The third, Military OneSource, is intended to help service members and family members locate resources that can help them.

Military Family Assistance Centers

The Active Components of each branch of the military service have family assistance centers that house many of the family programs you will learn about later in this chapter. Each branch has its own name for its family support centers: Army Community Service (ACS) Centers; Marine Corps Marine and Family Service Centers; Navy Fleet and Family Support Centers; Air Force Airmen and Family Readiness Centers; and Coast Guard Work-Life Centers (*Air Force Times*, 2010). For all services, these are one-stop centers for military members and their families to go to find information, get assistance, enroll in programs, and become volunteers in their communities. Family centers usually provide outreach services for families in remote or isolated areas. The centers also serve mobilized National Guard and reserve members, DoD civilians, and military retirees. In addition, the National Guard sets up family assistance centers during times of deployment or mobilization and has permanent family assistance coordinators to perform information and referral functions when units are not mobilized. Typical family center programs include the following:

- Counseling and crisis assistance
- Deployment and mobilization support services
- Family advocacy programs
- Financial management
- Employment assistance
- Information and referrals
- Outreach programs
- Parenting, stress management, and life skills education
- Relocation assistance
- New parent-support programs
- Special-needs family member assistance programs

MilitaryHOMEFRONT

MilitaryHOMEFRONT (http://www.militaryhomefront.dod.mil/) is the DoD's official website for Military Community and Family Policy (MC&FP) information (DoD, 2010j). It is designed to provide information and guidance on all aspects of military life to military members, family members, military leaders, and those who provide services to military members and families. The web page has extensive information on all DoD program and policies designed to improve the quality of life for military members and their families and has numerous links to state and civilian programs for military members and families.

Military OneSource

MOS provides information and resources on a large variety of topics that impact on military life (DoD, 2010k). Trained MOS consultants are available 24 hours a day, 7 days a week by phone, online, or via e-mail to provide information and referrals and to offer personalized support to active duty, Guard, and Reserve members and their families at no charge. MOS programs include the following:

- Individual, marital, and family counseling
- Strategies and resources on dealing with stress
- Financial counseling
- Child care planning and referrals
- Parenting issues
- Deployment and reintegration support
- Spouse employment assistance
- Education and relocation assistance
- Information on local resources and recreational opportunities
- Assistance in using the online, virtual DoD morale, welfare, and recreation library to download books, write a resume, or take practice college entrance exams
- Wounded warrior information and referrals on Veterans Affairs (VA) benefits, health-care services, and military facilities

Short-term, problem-focused counseling sessions on life issues are also available through MOS (DoD, 2010k). These sessions can be provided in person, via telephone, or online. This service is designed to address a variety of issues, such as improving relationships at home and at work, marital issues, normal grief and loss issues, and adjusting to life changes and challenges. Military members who are more comfortable going outside the military community for counseling services can choose this option for issues that do not require more extensive mental health care from the military medical care system. They can receive up to 12 free counseling sessions through MOS.

Additionally, MOS offers personal health coaching to help military members and their families improve their health through healthy eating, exercise, and stress management. Participants work one-on-one with a trained personal health coach to develop and implement goals and a program for change. The coach supports the participant throughout the program.

MILITARY AID AND CHARITY ORGANIZATIONS

There are several types of emergency and charitable associations and organizations that serve military members and their families. Although they are not DoD-sponsored programs, they are heavily supported by military members and are considered extremely important "safety nets" for military members and families. Military members are strongly encouraged to contribute to these organizations and willingly do so, as they provide a mechanism for military members to "care for their own." Each branch of the service relies on a charitable organization to assist its members. These organizations are private, nonprofit organizations, however, they have close ties to the DoD, are largely funded through service-specific fund drives, and rely on command or installation personnel to distribute funds to military members in need. They provide emergency assistance, emergency grants and loans, advocacy services, counseling services, and other emergency and support services for Active and Reserve Component members and their families. The service branches' emergency relief organizations have a cross-servicing agreement so that personnel who are not located near an installation of their own branch can request help through the emergency relief offices of the other organizations.

Because each military branch's emergency and charitable organization was created differently and in response to varied needs, emphasizes diverse needs, and provides slightly different types of assistance, they will be discussed separately below.

Army Emergency Relief

Army Emergency Relief (AER) was created in 1942 by the Secretary of War and the Army Chief of Staff to help soldiers and their family members (AER, 2002). Although AER is a private, nonprofit organization, it is the Army's own emergency financial assistance organization dedicated to "Helping the Army Take Care of Its Own." AER is supported by voluntary contributions from active, reserve, and retired soldiers during the Army's annual AER fund-raising campaign; repayment of AER loans; AER fund investment income; unsolicited contributions from Army or civilian individuals or organizations; and contributions in the form of memorials honoring deceased soldiers or family members or bequests from individuals or estates. Active duty soldiers and their families, members of the Army National Guard and the U.S. Army Reserve on active duty for more than 30 days and their family members, retired soldiers and their families, and spouses and children of soldiers who died while on active duty or after they retired are eligible for AER assistance.

AER funds are available to unit commanders to provide emergency financial assistance to soldiers and their family members when there is a valid need (AER, 2002). Assistance can be accessed through an installation AER Section or a unit AER Officer and is provided in the form of an interest-free loan, a grant if repayment of a loan would cause hardship for the service member, or a partial loan and a partial grant. AER provides emergency funds for the following needs:

- Food
- Rent and utilities
- Emergency transportation and vehicle repair
- Funeral expenses
- Medical and dental expenses
- Personal needs when the military member's pay is delayed or stolen
- Undergraduate-level college scholarships for children of soldiers, when there is a financial need

Air Force Aid Society

The official charity of the U.S. Air Force is the Air Force Aid Society (AFAS, 2010). Founded in 1942 as a private, nonprofit organization, AFAS provides emergency assistance, sponsors education assistance programs that finance higher education, and provides base community enhancement programs for airmen and their families. The AFAS obtains much of its funding from individual contributions generated primarily during the annual Air Force Assistance Fund Campaign and the annual Air Force Charity Ball, paybacks of existing loans, and income earned through the AFAS investment fund. Active duty and retired Air Force members and their families, family members of airmen who died on active duty or in retired status, and Air National Guard and Air Force Reservists who are on active duty for more than 15 days are eligible for AFAS assistance. AFAS programs can usually be accessed through AFAS Sections located in Airman and Family Readiness Centers (the Air Force family assistance centers, discussed earlier in this chapter) or within military personnel offices (personnel administrative or management offices).

Like the Army's AER, the AFAS provides interest-free loans and grants for emergency needs such as food, rent, utilities, and emergency car repair and travel (AFAS, 2010). In addition, the AFAS Respite Care Program provides financial assistance to pay for child or adult care to provide a break for Air Force active duty personnel who have family members with special needs and ongoing care requirements. On many Air Force bases the AFAS now offers the "Give Parents a Break" program that funds periodic child care during some evenings and weekends.

Navy-Marine Corps Relief Society

Both the Navy and Marine Corps receive emergency assistance through the private, nonprofit Navy-Marine Corps Relief Society (NMCRS), which was founded in 1904 and is sponsored by the Navy (NMCRS, 2010). The NMCRS is funded through the Secretary of the Navy's annual fund drive and through contributions from the Navy and Marine Corps retired community. Recipients of assistance can include active duty and retired Active and Reserve Component sailors and marines and their families, family members of active duty and retired Active and Reserve Component sailors and marines who died, and reservists on extended active duty greater than 30 days and their families. Assistance is also provided to widows and mothers (65 years or older) of deceased service members who are impoverished and have no family to provide for them, and ex-spouses of sailors and marines who have not remarried and who were married to the service member for at least 20 years while the service member was on active duty. Assistance can be requested from one of the nearly 250 NMCRS also offices, which are located at Navy and Marine Corps installations and on naval ships.

Like the Army and the Air Force relief organizations, the NMCRS provides financial assistance in the form of interest-free loans and grants and scholarships and interest-free loans for education (NMCRS, 2010). In addition to providing emergency funds to pay for basic requirements—food, rent, utilities, emergency transportation, vehicle repair, medical and dental expenses, and funeral expenses—the NMCRS provides interest-free loans or grants to help with disaster relief assistance, child care expenses, and other unforeseen family emergencies. The NMCRS also offers financial counseling, budgeting workshops, thrift shops, and visiting nurse services.

SPECIAL PROGRAMS FOR IDENTIFIED OR POTENTIAL PROBLEMS

Two of the following programs are mandated programs designed to identify and assist families requiring special services. The third program, the New Parent Support Program (NPSP), is intended to strengthen families so that they are less likely to be at risk for child abuse or neglect.

Exceptional Family Member Program

The DoD's Exceptional Family Member Program (EFMP), called Special Needs Identification and Assignment Coordination in the Air Force, requires service members to identify family members with special medical or educational needs and helps those families obtain required services (DoD, 2010p). The family members are enrolled in the program and the services they require are documented. The documentation includes requirements for special educational needs and specialty medical services. In decisions about the military member's future assignments, special family needs are heavily considered and attempts are made to match the family needs with military assignments and communities that can support those needs. This process ensures those families have access to necessary services, wherever they are assigned. The EFMP helps families connect with medical and educational programs with the goals of increasing family self-sufficiency and improving family self-advocacy skills.

The DoD's EFMP website, a part of the Defense Department's MilitaryHOMEFRONT site, (http://militaryhomefront.dod.mil) has resources and information on various programs available to special needs families. The website includes a downloadable tool kit for parents with children of 3 years and under and a social networking feature so that families whose children have special needs can network and share information. In addition, a "Plan My Move" website, also available through the MilitaryHOMEFRONT, offers tips for families with special needs who are preparing to move to a new duty station. Indicating that there is a family member with special needs will generate a calendar with advice about when to accomplish specific tasks and where to obtain help.

Family Advocacy Program

Changing to an all-volunteer force has resulted in higher numbers of service members who are married and have children. Since the number of military families has grown, so has the awareness of potential spouse and child abuse and neglect in the military services. The stressors of military life, including deployments, separations, frequent moves, and distance from extended family and friends, have also been associated with an increased risk and incidence of abuse. A study at the University of North Carolina at Chapel Hill (Rentz et al., 2007) showed that prior to October 2002, the rate of abuse and neglect was slightly higher among nonmilitary families when compared to military families. However, between October 2002 and June 2003, after the United States started sending larger numbers of troops to Afghanistan and Iraq, the rates of abuse and neglect in military families increased substantially; while the rates for nonmilitary families remained stable. The average number of incidents of child abuse in military families doubled. In fact, the rate of child abuse in military families increased by about 30% for each percent increase in the number of military members leaving for or returning from deployments.

The DoD Family Advocacy Program (FAP) is a coordinated effort to prevent, identify, report, and treat all aspects of domestic abuse and violence. The FAP provides policy and program guidance to assist each military branch FAP, which has staff at each installation where families are assigned. These Army, Air Force, and Navy FAPs (the Marine Corps families receive services from the Navy FAP) provide local outreach, prevention, and intervention. They provide a wide range of services and programs in order to address the specific needs of families.

The FAP is a command support program for identifying and helping military families who are at risk for or impacted by issues of domestic abuse or violence, such as child abuse or neglect and spouse or partner abuse (DoD, 2010f). The FAP tries to prevent or stop domestic abuse by educating service members and families about domestic abuse; identifying and assisting families experiencing domestic abuse; providing support and counseling services to victims of abuse; and providing treatment and discipline for abusers.

The FAP staff members work with military commander and leaders, law enforcement personnel, the medical community, family support personnel, victim advocates, and military chaplains to assist families involved in domestic abuse (DoD, 2010f). The FAP staff coordinates with civilian organizations and agencies in communities where service members and their families live to provide a community response to family and intimate partner abuse and to ensure that military families get the help they need to recover from and prevent further domestic abuse. Intervention includes safety planning, counseling, educational programs, advocacy, and other services.

Two important additional services available to family members who are victims of domestic abuse are transitional compensation and shipment of household goods (DoD, 2010g). Transitional compensation is a congressionally authorized program that allows the DoD to provide temporary (12 to 36 months) financial assistance and limited military benefits to the family members of service members who are separated from the military due to domestic abuse. This program helps victims of domestic abuse establish a new life apart from the abusive service member. The limited benefits include military shopping privileges and medical and dental services. When the FAP staff has determined that an abused spouse's safety is at risk and that relocation is advisable, abused spouses can request shipment of their household goods and car.

New Parent Support Program

The NPSP offers primary prevention for young families as well as intensive services for those at risk for abuse or neglect. Focused on expectant and new parents, services include information on child development and positive parenting skills, parent/infant groups and sibling groups, and a lending program (DoD, 2010m).

In an evaluation study, surveys from 821 program users, both active duty and family members, from 22 NPSP locations across the Navy were analyzed (Kelley, Schwerin, Farrar, & Lane, 2007). A majority of users reported the program was much better or better than expected. Over 75% of program users reported that the program helped them quite a bit or a great deal with coping with parenting stress appropriately, improving their parenting skills, and feeling a greater sense of community. Over 90% of users who attended the parenting classes or received home visits agreed or strongly agreed that the program demonstrated concern for and contributed to the health and safety of sailors and families and that it contributed to their quality of life; 62% of those who attended parenting classes and 72% who received home visits indicated that the program helped them to concentrate at work; and over 70% of users agreed or strongly agreed that it contributed to readiness. However, a majority neither agreed nor disagreed that it contributed to their decision to remain in the Navy.

PROGRAMS AND POLICIES DESIGNED TO HELP FAMILIES DEAL WITH DEPLOYMENTS

The following programs are vital to family members during times when their service member is preparing to deploy, while he or she is gone, and when he or she returns from a deployment.

Voices From the Frontline

BUILDING CONNECTIONS

It's common for people today to think, or say, "Just give me a pill and I can get better." It's true for civilians and for people in the military. But it doesn't work that way. People need other people to support them but today everyone is so busy it is hard to find the time to get together. Having a one-on-one support network is hard. Life moves fast. Sometimes the technology that is supposed to be enhancing communication between us gets in the way. Many people don't know how to connect. But that doesn't change the need. Some of our best family support programs today come from what naturally emerged among families. For example, Key Wives and ombudsmen volunteer spouses who support other spouses.

Evonne Carawan
Director, Personnel Readiness and Community Support, Office of the Deputy Assistant Secretary of the Navy (Military Personnel Policy)

Family Readiness Groups

The Family Readiness Group (FRG), also called the Key Volunteer Network in the Marine Corps, is one of the most important programs for supporting family members while individual service members or units deploy. Providing support for family members allows deployed service members to focus on their mission without unnecessary worry about their families. The FRG is a command-sponsored organization made up of service members, civilian employees, and family member volunteers (Office of the Assistant Secretary of Defense for Reserve Affairs, 2007). Its purpose is to provide a structure and forum for service members and their families to provide social and emotional support and outreach services and to distribute information to each other. The FRG is a vital organization for helping maintain family member morale and for helping families resolve problems.

Family Readiness Group activities might include voluntary telephone rosters, or "trees" with family member contact information, in case of emergencies or to relate important information; deployment-related (before, during, or after a unit goes to a combat zone) or mobilization-related (Reserve Component units called to active duty for deployment or training) information briefings/meetings; newsletters with information on unit missions, self-help programs and services, benefits and entitlements, and events; free or low-cost social activities for spouses and/or families (Department of the Army, 2000). The following are some of the FRG's goals:

- Foster resilient families
- Provide official and accurate information about the unit
- Provide mutual support
- Provide a link between the unit command and each military family
- Build unit morale and cohesion
- Provide feedback to the command about family needs and status
- Directly support **rear detachments** (unit members staying behind when the unit deploys)
- Educate family members about their benefits and entitlements

The Navy Family Ombudsman Program

In addition to the FRG program, the Navy also has a Family Ombudsman program as part of its family support system (San Diego Fleet & Family Support Center, 2010). The Navy Family Ombudsman program provides support to Navy families during times of deployment and when units are home. Like FRG volunteers, Navy ombudsmen are volunteers and spouses who wear no uniform and hold no rank but are vital members of the command support team (DoD, 2010d). All Navy commands, including Navy Reserve commands, have a command-appointed ombudsman. Navy Reserve Ombudsmen are fully trained to assist both activated and nonactivated Navy Reserve families.

Navy Family Ombudsmen serve as information links between command leadership and Navy families. They are official command representatives and points of contact for all family members associated with the command, including spouses, parents, and extended family members (San Diego Fleet & Family Support Center, 2010). They provide information, referrals, and advocacy for spouses, parents, and extended family members within the command. Ombudsmen are an important resource for family members, especially before, during, and after deployments. In addition to providing referral information on military and civilian agencies that can help families with countless issues they may face while their family member is deployed, ombudsmen act as liaisons between unit leaders and family members during the deployment.

Navy Ombudsmen roles and responsibilities go well beyond services provided during the deployment cycle and can include the following (Chief of Naval Operations, n.d.):

- Serve as a liaison between families and the unit at all times
- Keep the commander informed about the general morale, health, and well-being of families in the unit

- Provide information on services available to families through the Fleet and Family Support Centers and other agencies and how to contact them
- Provide emergency and crisis information and assistance
- Coordinate services for families during deployments and other separations or geographic separation

The Rear Detachment

Whenever there is a deployment of a military unit to combat or to another military operation, a group of military members of that unit is selected to remain at the home installation. This group is called the "rear detachment." In the past the rear detachment was often made up of individuals who had medical conditions, family issues, or other reasons that prevented them from deploying. However, senior military leaders learned that the rear detachment personnel played a vital part in the success of a deployed unit's mission. More and more unit commanders are selecting their most competent and dedicated personnel to make up the rear detachment.

The rear detachment is responsible for all of the personnel and equipment that remain at the unit's home installation (Office of the Assistant Secretary of Defense for Reserve Affairs, 2010b). One of the main responsibilities of the rear detachment is to coordinate closely with family readiness staff (paid staff members who work directly for the unit commander) and volunteers (usually military spouses who act as leaders and advocates for the collective families of the unit) to ensure that the families of military members who deploy are well-informed and well cared for. The rear detachment is the liaison between the family members and the deployed unit. The rear detachment, the deployed portion of the unit, and the family readiness staff and volunteers must have a good working relationship and an open exchange of information in order to have a good family readiness program (i.e., a means to disseminate information to families, address their concerns, and involve them in the unit). A good family readiness program keeps the morale and well-being of its families high during the deployment in spite of the fact that their military member is absent.

The rear detachment's family readiness program often uses one or more of the following means to engage families (Office of the Assistant Secretary of Defense for Reserve Affairs, 2007):

- Social activities
- The Internet (a unit website and e-mail)
- A newsletter
- Teleconferences
- Telephone trees
- Toll-free family readiness phone numbers that family members can use to call the rear detachment personnel or family readiness staff and volunteers

HEALTH CARE

The following programs are the DoD's ways to ensure that military members and their family members are able to access health care that is at least as high in quality and availability as those afforded to civilian families.

The Military Health System

The DoD Military Health System (MHS) is an enormous organization that includes the Office of the Assistant Secretary of Defense for Health Affairs and the medical departments of the Army, Navy, Marine Corps, Air Force, and Coast Guard (MHS, 2010b). It provides the oversight for all military medical programs, including medical education, research, and the provision of medical care for all beneficiaries (i.e., military members and their families, retirees, and eligible DoD civilians and their families). The MHS is responsible for medical care during all military operations, natural disasters, and humanitarian missions with which the U.S. military is involved.

The MHS works together to ensure that medical care is available to service members world-wide. The Army, Air Force, and Navy (also responsible for medical care to the Marine Corps) each have medical departments that operate hospitals, health clinics, and dental clinics on installations throughout the world. They also have mobile hospitals and clinics that are set up where military operations are taking place and are responsible for ensuring that every beneficiary receives the best possible care—either through local MHS facilities, through an MHS facility in another location or in a civilian facility.

TRICARE

TRICARE is the DoD's regionally managed health-care program that provides medical and dental care services for active duty service members, activated Reserve Component members, retired members of the uniformed services, their families, survivors, and other DoD beneficiaries of military benefits (MHS, 2010a).

Although the military services have their own health-care systems, the primary mission of those organizations is to support military operations, which sometimes reduces the ability of the military health-care system to provide all of the medical and dental care that military members and their families require. To provide better access and high-quality service to all beneficiaries, TRICARE brings together the health-care resources of the military branches with medical facilities—the Army, Navy, and Air Force—and supplements them with civilian health-care networks and professionals, including civilian health-care providers, hospitals, and pharmacies (TRICARE Management Activity, 2010c). The Marine Corps has no separate medical facilities; it obtains its medical support from the Navy and from the civilian networks that participate in TRICARE.

Members of the Reserve Component and their family members are eligible for different TRICARE benefits depending on their status (TRICARE Management Activity, 2010a). Generally, Reserve Component family members are eligible for medical and dental care through TRICARE when certain qualifying conditions exist: The reserve military member is a member of the selected reserve; is serving on active duty for a period of more than 30 consecutive days; is medically retired due to a service-connected injury, illness, or disease that occurred in the line of duty; completes 20 years of qualifying active duty service, reaches age 60, and starts receiving retired pay; or dies on active duty or due to a medical condition incurred or aggravated while on active duty. Family members are covered under TRICARE for additional periods—up to 90 days before the member reports to active duty and up to 180 days following release from active duty—if the RC member is on active duty for more than 30 days.

Psychological Health

As the United States' involvement in military operations continues in frequency and intensity, psychological health is a growing issue among the military and military family members. The DoD has responded by encouraging military members and their families to seek psychological health care promptly (DoD, 2010c). The DoD is actively attempting to reduce stigma against psychological health treatment, to encourage military leaders to be aware of and support military and family members who might need psychological health care, and to improve the quality of and access to psychological health care.

Psychological health care is available through most health clinics and is provided by highly trained and licensed military and civilian providers. Often, however, the availability of psychological health care is limited, so family members are often referred to civilian providers in the local communities through TRICARE. TRICARE covers outpatient and inpatient psychological health care for military members or family members when it is medically or psychologically necessary as determined by a health-care referral (TRICARE Management Activity, 2010b). A consultation is written by the health-care provider for therapy or for hospitalization. The local military health-care facility can approve and renew the authorization to go to a civilian provider for a limited number of therapy sessions.

EDUCATION, CHILD CARE, AND YOUTH PROGRAMS

One of the most challenging issues facing military members is providing consistency and quality in child care, a quality education for their children, and regular after-school and summer activities in spite of the frequency with which they are required to move to new communities. The following programs can be found on U.S. military installations throughout the world; they ensure that the children in military families can enroll in a school and be at approximately the same educational level as his or her new classmates, quickly join children the same age in extracurricular or after-school activities, or be started in a safe, affordable child care program.

Department of Defense Education Activity

Most of the 1.2 million children of military service members attend civilian—private or public—schools in the communities where they live or are home-schooled (Department of Defense Education Activity [DoDEA], 2010a). However, just under 7%—approximately 80,000—attend schools established specifically for DoD family members and located on military installations. These schools are managed by the DoDEA, a DoD organization that falls under the direction of the Under Secretary of Defense for Personnel and Readiness and the DUSD/MCFP. The DoDEA consists of two separate school systems: the DoD Dependents Schools (DoDDS) overseas (located in Europe, Guam, and the Pacific) and the DoD Domestic Dependent Elementary and Secondary Schools (DDESS) in the United States. The DoDEA manages the education programs for family members of U.S. military personnel and civilian DoD employees.

Family members of military personnel face unique challenges during the course of their education (DoDEA, 2010a). For example, they usually move more frequently than students whose parents are civilian. They are also subjected to the additional stress of having parents who could be or have been deployed to combat or are absent for long periods for other military requirements. Students also frequently are in countries where they do not speak the language and/or are unfamiliar with the local customs and culture. The DoDEA schools provide students with a standardized curriculum that makes it easier for students of military families to move from school to school, particularly from a domestic school to an overseas school or vice versa. They also provide resources and support to help students deal with the stress of frequent moves and other stressors that come with being a military family member.

The DoD also provides resources to civilian schools attended by military family members so that even those students who are not in a location with a DoD school can get help dealing with the challenges of being a student in a military family (DoDEA, 2010a). In October 2009, the DoDEA granted $56 million dollars to public schools throughout the nation that serve military children for improving the education for military students and for providing professional development for educators in schools that serve military students.

Voices From the Frontline

A DoDEA TEACHER TELLS ABOUT HER WORK

I'm an art teacher in Sicily working with children from kindergarten through the fifth grade. I also teach fourth grade social studies, science, and health. We have 373 children in our elementary school. They score above national standards on Terra Nova, the standardized tests that the military gives. They always score above stateside education standards. Our children are world travelers. I think this is one of the reasons we don't have bigotry in our schools.

In some ways, stress is lower for our children than for many in the United States. Each has one family member employed, all have a home, and all have food.

In other ways, stress is higher, especially with today's repeated deployments. I find children often imagine the worst when their parents are deployed. Added to that, they have no control over when their parents come home and leave again.

In the school, we have a deployment support group for kids. We teach children how to deal with stress. We do breathing exercises and counting. We all learn to take time-outs when we need a little break from the group. We visit parents at work so children can see all the equipment parents have to keep themselves safe. We use humor and try to put as much joy in our lives as possible.

Every time a child comes to art class, I greet them at the door. I look them in the eye and they have to smile before they come into the classroom. For that one moment of the day, they can get beyond the hard things in their lives.

Lately there have been leaking pipes in my classroom. I'm using them to show children that I'm not superhuman, that things get to me but I can handle them. Military children living overseas don't have the chance to see how Grandma or other close family members and friends respond when things happen. Here, I'm one of their models.

Outside of school, our base is a community. We all shop at the same store and go to the same movie theatre. I meet parents at the commissary who ask me questions they would ask their mother or sister if they were home. Though it's sometimes hard when everyone knows everything about you, the closeness we have is supportive.

The average age of DoDEA teachers is mid-50s. We're an educated workforce. Over three-quarters of our staff have master's degrees. A few are teaching overseas as a second career. Some of us are at a time of big change in life such as a divorce. Some, like me, chose this work because we love to travel. It's not for everyone. You aren't with your family. To work for DoDEA, you have to be the kind of person who can take initiative and take care of yourself out in the middle of nowhere.

Francie Hammond
Teacher with DoDEA

Child Care and Youth Activity Programs

Military service entails many deployments and separations, frequent moves, long work hours, and changing schedules. These hardships often create a need for child care for the military family. Another factor increasing the need for child care is the fact that military spouses often work outside the home or attend educational programs to attain higher degrees. Additionally, the number of families where both parents are military members and the number of single-parent military members have increased (Military Advantage, 2010). For many military families, child care plays a vital role in their being able to continue to contribute to the military service. In fact, service members are required to have family care plans in place as they are expected to put their military mission ahead of all personal needs. In order for military members to contribute to the military to this extent, they must be assured that their children are safe and thriving while they are being cared for by people outside the family. Yet, finding child care can be very challenging in many of the areas where military families are assigned.

The DoD mandates, reviews, and creates programs for child care and youth activities in order to provide the best possible programs for military families. The DoD programs include the Child Development Program, Youth Activities, Family Child Care (FCC), School-Age Care (SAC), and child care resource and referral (DoD, 2010a). The DoD provides subsidy funding to most military Child Development Centers and FCC providers (certified child care providers who care for children in their own homes). Those centers and individuals can, thereby, charge lower fees to the families. The FCC providers may receive subsidies in monetary form or through other means, such as by receiving training required in order for them to be certified as an FCC provider. The DoD subsidies often makes child care costs for the military family lower than in the civilian community. In addition, because of the high standards for child care center accreditation and for individual provider certification, the quality of child care often exceeds that received by nonmilitary families.

The DoD operates approximately 800 Child Development Centers in 300 locations throughout the world (DoD, 2010a). These centers care for approximately 200,000 military and DoD civilian children each day. Most centers provide full-day, part-day, and hourly care for children from the age of 6 weeks to 12 years old. The centers are usually open during the normal work week, but commanders may decide to extend center hours to meet the work and deployment needs and schedules of their installation population.

The FCC program meets the needs of those families who want their children to be cared for in a home environment or whose schedules are not conducive to using child care centers (DoD, 2010a). The FCC program provides lists of installation-certified providers who provide in-home child care. These providers often provide overnight or longer child care, when needed.

The DoD child care and youth program also includes the SAC program (DoD, 2010a). The SAC program provides structured before and after-school and summer and holiday child care for children 6–12 years old. Social and recreational programs for children over 12 years are provided by youth and teen programs sponsored by military youth services and community centers found on larger military installations.

OTHER QUALITY OF LIFE PROGRAMS AND SERVICES

The following programs and services are overseen by the Under Secretary of Defense for Personnel and Readiness. They are designed to improve quality of life for military members and their families.

Commissaries and Exchanges

The Defense Commissary Agency (DeCA) operates tax-free grocery stores on military installations throughout the world. These military grocery stores, called "commissaries," are reserved for use by military beneficiaries only. Military families and other beneficiaries are able to purchase the same kinds of items they can at civilian grocery stores, but at significant savings. Groceries are sold to patrons at the same cost that DeCA pays for them, plus only a 5% surcharge; and patrons pay no taxes on the groceries (DeCA, 2010). By using this military benefit, military families can purchase their groceries at an average of 30% less money than they would spend for the same groceries in civilian grocery stores.

Exchange services—the Army and Air Force Exchange Service (AAFES), Navy Exchange (NEX), and the Marine Corps Exchange (MCX)—are similar to civilian department stores (DoD, 2010b). They provide merchandise and services to active duty, guard and reserve members, military retirees, and their families at competitively low prices. Exchanges save military families approximately 20% compared to civilian low-cost department stores. When military members and families deploy to combat, overseas, or remote locations around the world, exchanges quickly set up shopping and service facilities to bring them products, making it easier and more affordable to obtain items that they require or that will make their lives more comfortable. Exchange services are also designed to give money back to military communities by generating money that helps support MWR programs.

Morale, Welfare, and Recreation Programs

The DoD knows that in order to attract and keep quality service members, it must provide a quality of life at least as full and satisfying as that of civilians. A large part of that is the opportunity to participate in recreation programs. Military recreational programs and services are managed very similarly by each service, but are known by different names: Army Morale, Welfare, and Recreation; Marine Corps Community Services; Navy Morale, Welfare, and Recreation; U.S. Air Force Services; and Coast Guard Morale, Well-Being, and Recreation (DoD, 2010l).

The MWR programs in each of the military branches provide a large variety of recreational programs both on and off the installation to service members and their families. Most MWR programs fit into several major categories: fitness and sports centers and activities, library and information services, recreational/art skill development programs, travel and vacations, and programs specifically designed for single service members (Office of the Under Secretary of Defense for Personnel and Readiness, 2009a). These programs are operated by civilians with military oversight. They provide service members with the opportunity to relax, promote fitness and esprit de corps, promote a strong sense of military community, and result in a higher quality of life for all members of the military community. About 45 different programs fall under MWR; however, not all installations offer every MWR program or service. These programs are essential for keeping up the morale of military personnel and their families. See Table 9.1 to learn more about what programs MWRs typically offer.

TABLE 9.1   Morale, Welfare, and Recreation Programs

Fitness and Sports Centers and Activities	Library and Information Services	Recreational/Art Development Programs	Travel and Vacations	Single Service Member Programs
Swimming Individual, unit, or intramural sports and athletics Sports competitions	Professional military and technical materials Education and training materials Personal and technical skill development information Education, transition, and career assistance Relocation assistance Leisure planning information	Free movies, parks, & picnic areas Recreation equipment checkout Camping, horseback riding, fishing, rappelling, hiking, bicycling, swimming, and water and snow skiing Video games and board games Special interest recreational programs (flying/aero clubs, parachute/sky diving, fishing and hunting, scuba diving) Individual recreation skill programs (amateur radio, performing arts, arts & crafts, and automotive skills)	Economical opportunities for service members and their families to travel and enjoy vacations at premier locations Packaged or group tours Economical recreational lodging (cabins, trailers, chalets, cabanas, beach houses/cottages hook-ups in trailer/recreational vehicle parks) Free or discounted museums and attractions Affordable movies, concerts, plays, and sports events	Identify well-being issues and concerns of single service members Help single service members plan recreational and leisure activities Opportunities to participate in and contribute to communities

Source: Information compiled from Office of the Under Secretary of Defense for Personnel and Readiness (2009a). *Military morale, welfare, and recreation (MWR) programs (DoD instruction 1015.10).* Washington, DC: Author.

SUMMARY

- A highly developed array of military policies and programs serve military personnel, veterans, and their families.
- The DoD family support infrastructure is made up of service members, civil service employees, and contractors who develop and manage the programs and policies that support military families; for active duty families, the DUSD/MCFP and for Reserve Component families, the Assistant Secretary of Defense for Reserve Affairs are responsible for creating and managing these programs and policies.
- Military family assistance centers house many of the family programs that provide key support to military families.
- Military programs and organizations that provide key support to military families include MilitaryHOMEFRONT, MOS, military aid and charity organizations, the EFMP, the FAP, and the NPSP.
- FRGs, the Navy Family Ombudsman Program, and the "rear detachment" help families deal with deployments.
- Health care, including psychological care, is provided by the MHS and TRICARE.
- Education and care for children of military members are provided by the DoDEA, the Child Development Centers, FCC providers, and youth activities and after-school programs.
- Quality of life services are provided by the DeCA (groceries), military exchanges (retail stores), and MWR programs.

EXERCISES

To further explore the types of policies and programs available to military families through the DoD, answer the following questions:

1. What do you think are the most important programs that the DoD offers military families? Why?
2. Can you think of any problem you may have personally encountered in your life that might have been easier to deal with if you would have had the resources described in this chapter available to you? Which resources would have been particularly helpful?
3. What policies or programs described in this chapter would you refer a military family member to for each of the following problems or issues? (Some issues may be addressed by more than one program or policy.)
   a. A child who is having problems reading in school.
   b. A military member and his or her spouse are arguing a lot and think they need help with their marriage.
   c. A spouse who is new to the military and doesn't know where to go to learn about the resources on his or her installation.
   d. A teenage family member who wants to get involved in some sports and recreational activities.
   e. The wife of a military member who is afraid of her husband because he has hit her on several occasions.
   f. Parents of an active duty service member who returned from deployment are worried about their son's adjustment.

4. How would you approach a military family member you think could be helped by one of the DoD programs or policies, knowing they have not asked for your support. What would you say to them? What program contact information (phone numbers, web addresses) do you think you should memorize in order to be prepared such situations?

10

Civilian Supports for Military Families

In Chapter 10, you will

- Meet Dr. Shelley MacDermid Wadsworth, Director of the Military Family Research Institute at Purdue University
- Learn about laws and policies that respond to unique situations faced by military members, veterans, and their families
- Discover how civilian organizations advocate for and assist military families
- Gain insight into how institutions of higher education can make their campuses friendly to service members and veterans

Meet

Shelley MacDermid Wadsworth, PhD, Director of the Military Family Research Institute at Purdue University

Work-family issues have been a focus of my work for a long time. One day in 1999, a colleague at Purdue called to tell me about a request for a proposal to study military families with a work-family bent. We applied and were awarded the grant. That was the start of my education about the military and the Military Family Research Institute (MFRI). We were given a crash course about the military from people who live it and also a rare opportunity to think about all the branches of service at once.

Learning about military families, I learned about myself, my assumptions, and stereotypes. I had always thought that people who join the military instead of going to college didn't care about education. The reality is people in the military go to extraordinary efforts to deepen their education.

I thought military people were attracted to violence. Instead, I discovered that military life is about discipline, judgment, and staying calm. It is not seen as acceptable to lose control and inflict unnecessary damage whether on a mission or at home. While service members are expected to never leave someone behind and to pursue the mission using their last drop of energy, it is always under this umbrella of discipline.

In my office I have a photo of a marketplace in Baghdad right after a bomb went off. Everyone is running away except for a U.S. service member who is running towards the spot where the explosion took place. If someone walked into my office with a gun, I would hide behind my desk. A service member would be prepared to go toward the gun if necessary. It's humbling to work with and on behalf of people who would literally die for me.

For our first 5 years, we were solely a research organization. In 2007, we received funding from another source to expand our mission to make Indiana a better place for service members, families, and veterans. So we're now also working to figure out what our state is like and what resources we can leverage to create positive change.

Our research projects are varied. For example, a few years ago, we were asked by DoD to prepare a literature review about risk and resilience. We posted it on our website, and it has turned out to be influential. A highly placed military official told me that it changed her thinking about how families should be supported.

When the Family Medical Leave Act (FMLA) was recently revised, we were asked for input about how to structure the law. MFRI is quoted twice. We made a difference—maybe a small difference but one that influenced many families.

We have been bringing researchers together from around the United States and the world to share their work about military families. Their work has led to a book that was recently published. This book too will add to our efforts to help people learn about military families and to create a future workforce to support military families.

At MFRI, we consider ourselves engaged scholars. It is our responsibility as researchers to do work that practitioners will find useful, just as practitioners have a responsibility to continue learning about and applying research to their practice. Together we can ensure that the state of our knowledge and our programs and policies are as responsive to families as possible.

INTRODUCTION

As discussed in Chapter 9, the DoD's infrastructure offers many services and programs for military families, and these services have been more plentiful and accessible for active duty families. While service members who are part of the Active Component usually live near or on a military installation, members of the National Guard, Reservists, and veterans and their families live across the United States in communities that may have limited access to DoD programs and services.

Military families, civilians, and civilian organizations can advocate locally and nationally for improvements in DoD's support of military families and the Department of Veterans Affairs' services to veterans and their families. As citizens, they can advocate and voice appreciation for public policies that recognize unique situations facing families, such as long-term care of injured veterans who were severely injured while carrying out their military duties. Supporting these service members, veterans, and their families can be considered a societal responsibility (Tick, 2005).

One way to carry out this responsibility is by building community capacity to support families of military members and veterans. Civilian organizations and partnerships reviewed here are sharing the responsibility for the welfare of the military community and enhancing the competence of practitioners who serve military families.

Community capacity includes assuming a *"shared responsibility* for the general welfare of the community and its members and *collective competence,* demonstrating an ability to take advantage of opportunities for addressing community needs and for confronting situations that threaten the safety and well-being of community members" (Huebner, Mancini, Bowen, & Orthner, 2009, p. 219, emphasis in original). The community capacity approach suggests formal and informal networks generate social capital that leads to families positively adapting to a stressor (Mancini, Bowen, & Martin, 2005).

When applied to the military, formal networks include military leadership and military and civilian organizations and agencies. Informal networks include those personal relationships formed voluntarily, such as relationships with neighbors, friends, and work colleagues. Huebner et al. (2009) argue that one function of formal supports is to grow informal networks. For example, two spouses may meet at a predeployment briefing and develop a friendship that includes sharing emotional support and practical help such as providing child care for one another during the deployment.

This chapter reviews formal civilian networks of support in the form of policies and organizations available to service personnel, veterans, and their families. Such civilian networks, programs, and services in local communities are important to extended family members and to Reserve Component families. As you read about these policies, organizations, and initiatives, imagine how they also assist families in growing their informal networks of support.

POLICIES

Strengthening Our Military Families

In January 2011, President Barack Obama announced a presidential initiative, **Strengthening Our Military Families**, to support military families through a coordinated federal approach that directs cabinet secretaries and heads of agencies to focus on four priorities central to the lives of military families [*Strengthening Our Military Families* (Office of the President of the United States, 2011)]. The goals of this unified approach are to

- "enhance the well-being and psychological health of the military family, …
- ensure excellence in military children's education and their development, …
- develop career and educational opportunities for military spouses, … [and]
- increase child care availability and quality for the Armed Forces" [*Strengthening Our Military Families* (Office of the President of the United States, 2011, p. 2–3)].

The goals of this presidential initiative reflect the research on and feedback from military families and service members about the challenges that most affect them. Efforts noted in the initiative, some of which are already in progress, include improving and expanding mental health preventive services and treatment at the community level, training school staff on the educational needs of military children, increasing employment opportunities in careers in federal government and the public workforce for military spouses, and increasing access to child care.

National Defense Authorization Act

The **National Defense Authorization Act** is a federal law that is passed by Congress every year to grant the DoD, including Active and Reserve Components, funds to operate and specific guidance on how to spend those funds. The law is a way for Congress and the U.S. President to ensure that the DoD is accomplishing goals that are set by Congress and to closely control how American tax dollars are spent on national defense. The law specifies the number of military personnel and equipment types that each branch of the service should have as well as other activities that the services should be engaged in (e.g., the types of aircraft that the Air Force should have, the requirement to purchase new body armor for service members to wear when deployed, how much and what types of research and testing will occur).

The National Defense Authorization Act also ensures the well-being of military members and their families. For example, the National Defense Authorization Act for Fiscal Year 2010 includes a pilot program that allows the DoD to reimburse federal agencies for the costs of hiring a military spouse as an intern; a revised plan for implementing the services' sexual assault prevention and response policies; a requirement that the services report to Congress on the effects of domestic violence on military families; and a mandate to assess the impact of deployment on children of military members (National Defense Authorization Act for Fiscal Year 2010, Pub. L. No. 111-84, 123 Stat. 2190, 2009).

The Family and Medical Leave Act

The **Family and Medical Leave Act** of 1993 offers eligible employees of covered employers job-protected, unpaid leave of up to 12 workweeks for care of seriously ill family members, to attend to their own serious health condition, or upon the birth or adoption of a child. FMLA applies to all public agencies (i.e., state, local, and federal employers), schools, and private-sector employers with 50 or more employees. Employees are eligible for FMLA once they have worked for the employer for 12 months, worked at least 1250 hours the previous year, and work in an location where at least 50 employees are employed in a 75-mile radius. Family members are defined as parent, spouse, daughter, or son. Employers are required to maintain preexisting group healthcare coverage for employees on FMLA leave and to "reinstate [them] to the same or an equivalent job with equivalent employment benefits, pay, and other terms and conditions of employment" (Family Medical Leave Act Regulations, 2007, p. 35550).

The National Defense Authorization Act for Fiscal Year 2008 (Public Law 110-181; 2009) amended the FMLA to include military family leave entitlements, and the National Defense Authorization Act for Fiscal Year 2010 (Public Law 111-84) expanded these entitlements. The first entitlement allows employees up to 12 weeks of leave for a "qualifying exigency" due to the active duty or call to active duty of a spouse, parent, daughter, or son. Qualifying exigencies include situations related to notification of deployment on short notice (7 days or fewer); military service-related activities such as family support programs and informational sessions child-related responsibilities such as arranging child care or schooling financial and legal arrangements related to the military member's absence; counseling sessions; up to 5 days of leave to be with a military member on short-term leave during deployment; postdeployment activities (e.g., arrival ceremonies, reintegration briefings) and other official military programs for a period of 90 days after completion of active duty status; issues related to the death of the service member; and any other employer-employee agreed upon event (U.S. Department of Labor, 2010).

The second military family leave entitlement is the military caregiver leave. This entitlement allows an eligible employee up to 26 weeks of unpaid leave within a single 12-month period to care for a service member with a serious illness or injury. The employee must be the spouse, parent, daughter, son, or next of kin of the service member. A covered service member is a veteran within five years of seeking medical help or a current member of the Armed Forces, including the National Guard and Reserves, who is in outpatient status undergoing medical treatment, recuperation, or therapy or is on the temporary retired list because of a serious illness or injury incurred or aggravated while on active duty, or a veteran (U.S. Department of Labor, 2010).

FMLA leave can be taken as a block or intermittently. Employees should try to schedule medical treatments to cause the least disruption to the employer's operation (U.S. Department of Labor, 2010). The Wage and Hour Division of the Department of Labor investigates complaints (see http://www.dol.gov/whd).

Uniformed Services Employment and Reemployment Rights Act

The **Uniformed Services Employment and Reemployment Rights Act** (USERRA) prohibits employers from discriminating on the basis of an employee's consideration of joining the military or an employee's current or past military service. It applies to all employers in the United States regardless of size, including foreign companies with locations in the United States, its territories, or its possessions. USERRA also protects reemployment rights for service members returning from deployment. They must be reemployed in their original or an equivalent position (i.e., similar seniority, status, and pay) and are entitled to increases in benefits or seniority that would have occurred if they had not done military service. Once back from military service, an employer cannot fire a service member without cause within 180 days of reemployment if the military service was between 31 and 180 days or within 1 year of reemployment if the military service was over 180 days (U.S. Department of Labor, 2009).

A service member returning to work after 30 days or fewer of military service must report back for the next regularly scheduled work period, allowing for travel. If the service period was 31–180 days, the service member submits an application of reemployment with the employer no later than

14 days after completing their military duties. If the service period was 181 days or more, the service member submits an application of reemployment with the employer no later than 90 days after completing their military duties. Service members hospitalized for or convalescing from injury or illness incurred or aggravated during service have 2 years to report to the preservice employer. Reasonable efforts to accommodate disabled veterans are expected of employers (U.S. Department of Labor, 2009).

Service members are to provide written or oral advance warning of the absence and that it is due to military service. As noted above, service members must follow the timeline for application for reemployment, and if discharged from the military, it must be under honorable conditions. In general, the cumulative time in service cannot exceed 5 years while employed by the employer (U.S. Department of Labor, 2009).

USERRA is administered by Veterans Employment and Training Services (VETS), which is part of the U.S Department of Labor. Individuals who believe their USERRA rights are being violated have three levels of assistance. The first level, the most informal, is use of Employer Support of the Guard and Reserve (ESGR; see http://www.esgr.org and Chapter 11 for more information on ESGR). The ombudsman program informs employers and employees about USERRA, offers informal conflict resolution services, and provides referrals. If a conflict is not resolved or the individual would like formal resolution services, then VETS will attempt to resolve complaints filed. If not satisfied with the outcome, the individual can ask that the case be referred to legal representation at no cost. Cases that involve a private employer or a state or a local government are referred to the Department of Justice. Cases involving a federal employer are sent to the Office of Special Counsel (U.S. Department of Labor, 2009).

Interstate Compact on Educational Opportunities for Military Children

The **Interstate Compact on Educational Opportunities for Military Children** is an agreement among states on how to handle educational issues that often vary across states, such as enrollment, placement, eligibility, and graduation requirements (Council of State Governments, 2008). The compact was drafted by the **Council of State Governments** (a nonprofit, nonpartisan organization for state governments) in response to guidance provided by an advisory group convened in 2006 and in cooperation with the DoD to examine the educational needs of military children resulting from parental deployment and relocation. The advisory group consisted of members from the DoD's Military Community and Family Policy office, the Military Child Education Coalition (MCEC), the National Military Family Association, USA4 Military Families, the Sloan Work and Family Research Center, selected schools, and state and national educational associations.

The compact was developed to avoid educational inconsistencies across states. For example, a child who begins kindergarten in one state may be denied enrollment in kindergarten in another state 4 months later when the family relocates. Or a child in a gifted and talented program may be barred from placement in an equivalent program in a new school. At times, military children who transfer schools find themselves repeating or missing courses (e.g., Algebra I, U.S. History) or coursework, or barred from participating in extracurricular activities because of missing deadlines for tryouts. For example, a military officer was transferred 4 times in 4 years, resulting in his son changing schools each time. In each school the son was required to study *Romeo and Juliet* (Council of State Governments, 2008). The Interstate Compact on Educational Opportunities for Military Children provides guidance to school personnel to recognize and appropriately address these unfortunate situations.

Both sending schools (i.e., a school the military child is leaving) and receiving schools (i.e., a school the military child will be attending) in member states have responsibilities. The sending school must prepare educational records for parents to take to the new (i.e., receiving) school and provide and verify information sought by a receiving school. The receiving school must enroll a student based on the unofficial records pending validation by official records and must request official records; allow students 30 days to obtain the required immunizations; and allow students, regardless of age, to continue in kindergarten or first grade or enroll a student at the next highest grade if the prerequisite grade was completed. The receiving school is also to place students in courses (e.g., honors, technical, advanced placement) and programs (e.g., gifted and talented, English as a Second Language) based on those at the sending school, and recognize the current Individualized Education Program (IEP) and make reasonable accommodations and modifications to address needs of students with disabilities. Receiving schools should approach prerequisites or preconditions to courses or programs with flexibility and facilitate a student's participation in extracurricular activities regardless of deadlines. If course requirements completed satisfactorily at another school are not waived, then the receiving school is to provide coursework so graduation may occur on time. If students transferring at the beginning or during their senior year are ineligible to graduate from the receiving school, they are to receive a diploma from the sending school if the met the sending school's graduation requirements. In addition, the receiving school is to accept the sending school's graduation requirements or exams, national achievement tests, or alternative testing. Schools are to allow students additional excused absences to visit a parent or legal guardian who will be deploying, or is on leave or returning from combat deployment (Council of State Governments, 2008).

Finally, receiving schools are to recognize a special power of attorney or guardianship for actions requiring parental consent; not charge tuition for a military child placed with a noncustodial parent or other person acting in loco parentis who lives in the school jurisdiction other than the custodial parent; and allow a child residing with a noncustodial parent or other in loco parentis to continue to attend the school enrolled in while residing with the custodial parent. If parents encounter difficulty in transferring their children from one school to another, they can contact the National Military Family Association or the MCEC for guidance about the compact and ideas for advocating on behalf of their children (Council of State Governments, 2008).

As of fall 2011, 39 states had joined this interstate compact to facilitate a smoother transition for military children as they transfer schools and experience a parent's combat-related deployment. Legislation is pending in other states (Military Interstate Children's Compact Commission, 2011).

Caregivers and Veterans Omnibus Health Services Act of 2010 (S. 1963)

The **Caregivers and Veterans Omnibus Health Services Act** was signed into law in May 2010. This law provides assistance to caregivers of veterans injured in the line of duty training on or after September 11, 2001 and in need of personal care services. It also improves provision of health care to veterans, including women veterans and veterans living in rural areas. Under this law, family caregivers will have access to training in order to provide care, respite care, mental health services, medical care, and a monthly personal caregiver stipend. The law also requires training and certification of mental health care providers of the Department of Veterans Affairs to deliver services for sexual trauma and posttraumatic stress disorder. Another provision of the law is establishment of peer outreach and support services and readjustment counseling and services for veterans who served in OEF and OIF, particularly those from the National Guard and Reserves. In addition, for 3 years following return of the veterans from OEF and OIF, their immediate family members will have access to services (e.g., education, counseling) pertaining to veterans' readjustment to civilian life, recovery of veterans from injuries or illness incurred during the deployment, and family readjustment to the return of veterans. Among additional provisions, the law also authorizes the Department of Veterans Affairs to carry out demonstration projects to examine ways to expand care of veterans in rural areas (Caregivers and Veterans Omnibus Health Services Act of 2010, Pub. L. No. 111-163, 124 Stat. 1130, 2010).

ORGANIZATIONS

Describing all of the civilian organizations and programs available for military families and veterans is not possible in a textbook of this size. Rather than offering an exhaustive list, we want to introduce some of the key organizations and examples of programs at national and state levels. Many program and organizational websites contain links you can use to discover other services and resources.

The following section begins with an overview of the Department of Veterans Affairs, a department of the U.S. federal government. We then look at examples of civilian organizations that serve military families exclusively and those that serve military families among other constituents. We highlight a few examples of collaborations that have occurred at the state level and examples of associations and organizations for service members and veterans. This chapter ends with a review of services on college and university campuses for veterans and military service members.

The Department of Veterans Affairs

Beginning with the Continental Congress of 1776 that provided pensions for soldiers who were disabled, benefits for veterans and their families have grown. Following the Revolutionary War, states and local communities provided some medical and hospital care to veterans. Domiciliaries and medical facilities were open in the first half of the 1800s, and in subsequent years, benefits and pensions were expanded and included widows and dependents. Following the Civil War, states established veterans' homes to provide medical and hospital treatment. As the United States entered World War I in 1917, Congress enacted programs for disability compensation, insurance for military members and veterans, and rehabilitation services. These programs were administered by three federal agencies: the Veterans Bureau, the Bureau of Pensions of the Interior Department, and the National Home for Disabled Volunteer Soldiers. In 1930, these programs were combined and assigned to the newly created the Veterans Administration. The National Cemetery System, minus Arlington National Cemetery, was placed under the Veterans Administration in 1973. Finally, in 1989, the **Department of Veterans Affairs**, commonly referred to as "the VA," was made a cabinet-level position and has three units: the Veterans Benefits Administration (VBA), the Veterans Health Administration (VHA), and the National Cemetery Administration (U.S. Department of Veterans Affairs, n.d.).

Most VA benefits require that the military member receives a discharge from active service under other than dishonorable conditions. Reservists and National Guard members may qualify for VA benefits if they called to active duty by federal order and served the full time ordered. Prior to separating from active duty or postdeployment for Reservists and National Guard, military members apply for enrollment (U.S. Department of Veterans Affairs, 2010a).

The Veterans Health Administration   The **Veterans Health Administration** (VHA) operates more than 1400 facilities where health services are provided. Facilities include hospitals, community-based outpatient clinics, community living centers (i.e., nursing homes), domiciliaries, and readjustment counseling centers. As the largest integrated healthcare system in the U.S., it provides care to 5.5 million veterans annually (U.S. Department of Veterans Affairs, 2011a).

The VHA is responsible for providing care and support for disabled veterans. When applying for enrollment for VA health care, each veteran is assigned to a priority group. The highest priority goes to veterans with disabilities rating of 50% or more and/or veterans determined to be unemployable because of service-connected conditions. The lowest priority goes to those veterans with no service-connected disabilities. Veterans discharged on or after January 28, 2003, are eligible for enhanced priority for 5 years under a "combat veteran" designation (U.S. Department of Veterans Affairs, 2010a).

Medical Centers, Domiciliaries, and Outpatient Clinics The 153 medical centers provide a range of services, including surgery, critical care, mental health services, pharmacies, physical therapy, and specialty areas (e.g., neurology, oncology, dental, prosthetics). Each medical center has an OEF/OIF Care Management Team that coordinates a patient's care. The VHA domiciliaries provide residential care for veterans with medical, psychiatric, educational, vocational, or social challenges. Over 800 community-based outpatient clinics provide outpatient medical and health and wellness services (U.S. Department of Veterans Affairs, 2011a).

Vet Centers Unlike other VHA benefits, **Vet Centers** are open to all veterans who serve or have served in military operations or expeditions during times of armed hostilities and to their family members (see http://www.vetcenter.va.gov). Congress established Vet Centers in 1979 to serve Vietnam veterans with readjustment challenges. Since then services have been added and extended. The nearly 300 community-based Vet Centers, including mobile units, offer individual and group counseling, family therapy related to military issues, sexual trauma counseling, employment and substance abuse assessment and referral, screening and referral for medical issues (e.g., TBI, PTSD, depression), and outreach and education. Bereavement counseling is available to parents, spouses, and children of service members, including Reservists and National Guard, who die while on duty. Services at the Vet Centers are free. (U.S. Department of Veterans Affairs, 2011b).

The Veterans Benefits Administration

The **Veterans Benefits Administration** is responsible for managing education benefits (e.g., the Post-9/11 GI Bill, the Montgomery Bill), disability compensation, pensions, burial allowances, vocational rehabilitation, home loans, life insurance, and survivors' benefits. The Post-9/11 GI Bill will be discussed in Chapter 11 (U.S. Department of Veterans Affairs, 2010a).

The National Cemetery Administration

The **National Cemetery Administration** is responsible for national and state veterans' cemeteries, as well as headstones, markers, and presidential memorial certificates. Burial in a national cemetery is available for service members on active duty who die; veterans discharged under conditions other than dishonorable and who served for 24 continuous months or for the full time called for active duty; and members of the Reserve Component eligible for retirement pay or who die while training, hospitalized, or undergoing treatment for medical conditions incurred during service (U.S. Department of Veterans Affairs, 2010a).

Organizations for Military Families and Service Members

American Red Cross

One of the primary missions of the **American Red Cross** (2011) is to provide assistance to victims of wars and natural disasters. The Red Cross will send emergency communications to military members stationed anywhere. Messages are delivered 24 hours a day, 7 days a week throughout the year. The Red Cross sends factual and verified descriptions of the emergency through the military chain of command, and unit commanders rely on such verification of emergencies when deciding whether emergency leave is possible. Families will need to provide details about the emergency situation (e.g., the name of the individual who is ill or who has died, the family relationship, and the contact information for the hospital or funeral home) and information about their service member (http://www.redcross.org). To facilitate timely contact, families must be prepared to give the service member's full name and military address, social security number or date of birth, rank and rating, branch of service, unit name, and if deployed, the name of the home unit.

Along with military aid societies, the Red Cross provides financial assistance to eligible active duty and retired military personnel, their dependents, and widows of retired military personnel. Through the Red Cross Casualty Travel Assistance Program, two immediate family members may receive transportation attend a memorial or funeral service for a military member killed in a combat zone or to go to the bedside of a service member wounded in a combat zone. As in other conflicts, the Red Cross maintains canteens in Iraq and Afghanistan where service members can relax, make phone calls, use e-mail, watch a video, or chat with one of the workers or other service members (http://www.redcross.org).

Armed Services YMCA   The **Armed Services YMCA** is an affiliate of Young Men's Christian Associations (YMCA) of the United States with locations near many military installations. In addition to recreation and fitness, it offers numerous family and children programs (e.g., parenting workshops, spouse support, after-school enrichment), including Operation Hero for children 6–12 who could benefit academically and socially from after-school tutoring and mentoring. In 2007, Operation Outdoors began offering day and residential camp for military children of junior enlisted personnel and family camps. DoD has contracted with the Armed Services YMCA to provide Y memberships and respite child care of up to 16 hours per month for families of deployed Reservists and National Guard; membership is also available for relocated spouses of deployed service members (http://www.asymca.org).

Blue Star and Gold Star Organizations   Beginning in World War I, small "service flags" were hung in front of windows of homes of service members. The home's service flag had a blue star for each member of the family who was in military service. The blue star was changed to a gold star if the military member died. From this practice emerged the terms *blue star mother* and *gold star mother* and the formation of organizations recognizing those families.

American Gold Star Mothers, Inc., (http://www.goldstarmoms.com) was incorporated as a non-profit in 1929. Members provide comfort to one another, volunteer at hospitals for veterans, and offer support to veterans and their families. They participate in national holidays that recognize veterans and service in the military.

Gold Star Wives, Inc., (http://www.goldstarwives.org) was formed after World War II, and today is open to widows and widowers of service members who die on active duty or due to a military-related cause. Members provide support to one another, participate in national memorial services, and volunteer at VA medical centers and in their local communities.

The beginnings of Blue Star Mothers of America, Inc., trace back to World War II (http://www.bluestarmothers.org). Members volunteer at VA hospitals or clinics, send care packages to service members, assist other veteran organization, and promote patriotism.

Blue Star Families (http://bluestarfam.org) was started in 2008 to advocate for military families with policy makers and connect citizens and military families. Programs include distributing books to libraries on military installations; offering an online survey for military families to indicate their concerns; and assisting civilians through Operation Appreciation to communicate their gratitude to military families.

Founded in 2005, Military Families United is a coalition of Gold Star and Blue Star families (http://www.militaryfamiliesunited.org). It hosts Gold Star Family luncheons where families who have lost a service member may meet one another, a database of service members who died since World War II, and other projects.

Fisher House Foundation   The not-for-profit Fisher House Foundation constructs houses with 8–21 suites where military family members may stay while their service member is hospitalized for injury, illness, or disease. The 54 Fisher Houses are located on military installations with a major medical center and VA medical centers. The Foundation donates the houses to the U.S. Government, and secretaries of the military departments and the VA operate and maintain the houses. Stays at a Fisher House are free to military families.

Between 1990 and 2010, over 142,000 military families stayed at a Fisher House. In 2010 the average length of stay for a family whose service member had experienced a combat-related injury was 45–60 days. The Fisher House Foundation also supports three other programs: Hero Miles, Newman's Own Award, and Scholarships for Military Children (*Fisher House Facts*, n.d.).

Military Child Education Coalition

The MCEC is a nonprofit organization that promotes quality education for military children who may experience multiple transitions as they change schools during a parent's military career. MCEC works with military installations and schools that serve military children to provide information for families with school-age children. It offers access to school requirements for each state and the DoDEA. MCEC offers workshops for parents, so they can advocate for quality education for their children, and materials that address how deploying parents can remain involved in their children's schooling, how parents can encourage development of literacy skills, and how parents and other family members can support learning prior to a child entering school. It also sponsors military student peer-to-peer programs to help students transitioning to and from schools. It offers educational materials for communities and schools to raise awareness of the military culture and ideas on how they can support military children (http://www.militarychild.org).

MFRI at Purdue University

Celebrating its 10th year in 2010, the MFRI at Purdue University conducts research on military families, designs and implements outreach activities, and builds partnerships within civilian and military communities. The idea for this textbook emerged from the leadership of MFRI and is an example of MFRI's mission to "extend and strengthen" the ability of people and organizations to understand and support military families.

MFRI's research projects have focused on children and youth; military families, particularly National Guard and Reserve families; and public health and family support. Outreach activities include Operation Diploma, an initiative to educate colleges and universities in Indiana about student service members and veterans transitioning to higher education; encourage higher education institutions to enhance services and support to student service members and veterans by providing competitive grants; support student veterans' organizations; and generate new knowledge about student service members and veterans.

In addition, MFRI administers a small grant program for military-sponsored family readiness or support groups in Indiana. It also creates resource listings for military support group leaders and professionals who work in civilian organizations who serve military families. Through MFRI's Community Mobilization Grant Program, Indiana communities can access monetary grants to expand and improve services to military families at a local level (http://www.cfs.purdue.edu/mfri/public/default.aspx).

National Military Family Association

The National Military Family Association, formed in 1969 as the Military Wives Association, advocates for benefits and programs that support military families and educates military family members on how to advocate for their families (see Box 10.1). The association is often called to speak before Congress on behalf of military families. It has three prominent programs: Military Family of the Year, educational scholarships for military spouses, and Operation Purple camps (http://www.militaryfamily.org).

Each year, the association chooses one family from each of the uniformed branches (i.e., Army, Navy, Marine Corps, Air Force, Coast Guard, National Oceanic and Atmospheric Administration, and U.S. Public Health Service) to represent that branch. From these seven families, one family is named the Military Family of the Year. The association also offers educational scholarships for military spouses to apply to tuition, fees, room, and board.

In 2004, National Military Family Association began **Operation Purple camps** for military children from all branches of the uniformed services, including National Guard and Reserve. **Purple** indicates an activity that includes all services. Children who have a parent in the cycle of deployment are given priority. Camps are offered every summer in multiple locations throughout the United States, including national parks. Additional camps include leadership camps for 15–17 year olds, family retreats, and wounded active duty or medically retired service members and their families.

BOX 10.1   BEST PRACTICES

NATIONAL MILITARY FAMILY ASSOCIATION

We know we can make a difference.

The National Military Family Association is more than 40 years old. We don't take government funding. Instead we have a lot of backing from concerned citizens, foundations, and corporations. This backing has allowed us to expand as the need for services grow. Grounded in our knowledge of, research about, and commitment to military families, we develop services in different ways:

- *We listen and respond to families.* For instance, we developed our *Operation Purple®* program from asking families what they needed. Early in the war, spouses told us: "We're fine. Help us help our kids." The first summer 1000 kids came to one of our overnight camps and connected with other kids from military families and experienced activities that helped them deal with their parents' deployment. In the program's 8 years, we have sent almost 45,000 kids for free to camp. We've also started family retreats in National Parks to help families come back together after the service member's return from deployment. We also hold special family retreats for wounded warriors and their families.
- *We educate members of Congress.* Because of the massive call ups of Guard and Reserve, every member of Congress now has military families in their district and is concerned about military personnel and family issues we had always been working on. Members call us asking, "What can I do to help?"
- *We build on existing community initiatives.* Most military families live in civilian communities and not on military installations. Their children attend community schools, military spouses work for civilian employers, they attend places of worship in the community, and they may seek medical care from civilian health-care providers. Military families need the support of their communities. We work with many organizations, such as camping programs or community groups, to enhance support for military families.
- *We guide people who want to support military families but don't know how.* We created resources on our website (http://www.militaryfamily.org) and publications to help people who want to help military families. Our *10 Things Military Kids and Military Teens Want You to Know* toolkits and our *Finding Common Ground* community toolkit give people concrete ideas about how to help military families and their children. Some ways are really simple. If your kid is on a soccer team with a kid from a military family, offer to car pool. Organize members of your place of worship to send care packages.

Because so many organizations and individuals are developing ways to help military families, we emphasize the need to evaluate and collaborate more to be more effective and to sustain support over the long term. We have to work smart. When troops start coming home, will people think "The war is over" and turn their attention to something else? We need to build a sustainable support structure, so we can continue to be flexible and meet needs of military families.

Joyce Wessel Raezer
Executive Director, National Military Family Association

National Resource Directory for Military and Veteran Communities   The **National Resource Directory** is a web-based gateway to military and civilian resources and services for ill, injured, or wounded service members, veterans, family members, and those who offer support. The directory lists national, state, and local programs that assist with the recovery, rehabilitation, and

reintegration processes. Included are veteran service and benefit organizations, nonprofit and community agencies, universities, and professional organizations. Glossaries provide definitions of terms used by the DoD, the VA, the Department of Labor, TRICARE, and mental health and long-term care settings (http://www.nationalresourcedirectory.gov).

Operation: Military Kids

Operation: Military Kids (OMK) is a partnership of Army Child, Youth, and School Services (CYS) and the 4-H National Headquarters of the U.S. Department of Agriculture to support National Guard and Army Reserve children. OMK has six goals: to create local networks that support for military children during deployment; to provide military children educational, social, and recreational programs through local community organizations. To support military children as they cope with stress related to combat deployments; to collaborate with schools so teachers and staff are prepared to support military children; to educate the public on the deployment cycle and its implications for families; and to connect Guard and Reserve families with OMK's partner programs offered by 4-H Clubs, the American Legion, Boys and Girls Clubs of America, and other organizations (Oram, n.d.).

OMK includes four main programs (http://www.operationmilitarykids.org). First, the *Ready, Set, Go!* program provides community members and groups training about the experiences and military children, military culture, and deployment so that they can be better prepared to work effectively with military children. Second, the *Hero Packs* project allows community groups, including nonmilitary children and youth, to prepare backpacks for children whose parent will soon deploy. Each Hero Pack contains items of support (e.g., information about OMK partners), appreciation (e.g., a letter expressing thanks) and connection (e.g., an item that encourages communication such as a disposable camera to take photos to send to the deployed parent or a scrapbook to record what happens while separated from the parent, and a fun item such as stickers or a stuffed toy).

Third, *Speak Out for Military Kids* (SOMK) is a means by which military and nonmilitary youth educate their communities about deployment and encourage support of military youth in local communities. The youth decide how they will accomplish these goals. Projects have included a public broadcast of a panel of military youth discussing deployment, development of a deployment board game, and a theatre production. Fourth, the Mobile Technology Lab travels to community locations so military children can have access to digital cameras, scanners, video and photo editing and other software. In addition to enhancing their technology skills, military children create banners, podcasts, photos, and videos to share with their deployed parents. Service members also use the lab to prepare video messages for their children.

Sesame Workshop

In 2006, Sesame Workshop began addressing military family issues with its English and Spanish versions of **Talk, Listen, Connect** programs for children and adults (see Box 10.2). Separate programs address deployment, homecoming, changes brought about by injuries to a service member, and grieving the death of a service member. Each of these programs includes video segments for adults and children, materials for download, activities for children and families, and links to other organizations. In the Family Connections section of the Sesame Street website, families can create their own online family network where members can post messages, artwork, and photos and record video messages. Sesame Street, in collaboration with the USO (United Service Organizations), also tours a Muppet show as part of the *Talk, Listen, Connect* initiative. The latest project related to military families is Sesame Rooms in which more than 30 military installations will receive a Sesame Street makeover of a space into an inviting room that welcomes young children and their parents.

Studies conducted on the *Talk, Listen, Connect* programs (i.e., deployment, multiple deployments and homecoming, and changes due to injuries) indicated program materials were widely appealing, understandable, and relevant. Military parents and those caring for military children reported the materials changed the way they helped children cope with deployment and parental injury and increased their level of comfort in doing so. They cited increased communication with children and encouraging children to ask more questions. A majority of parents and caregivers reported the information presented was "very" or "extremely" helpful (Burton & MacDermid Wadsworth, 2011; Chawla & MacDermid Wadsworth, 2011).

BOX 10.2   BEST PRACTICES

SESAME WORKSHOP SUPPORTS MILITARY FAMILIES

Our goal is to give parents words they can use to help children share their feelings during these difficult times.

One morning in 2005, on his train ride to work, Gary Knell, President and CEO of Sesame Workshop, saw a newspaper article about challenges facing military families. He called me saying, "There's a problem here. We need to understand military families and their children."

We know about the Muppets and media. So we brought together experts about military children to help us understand what they were experiencing and how we could help. We learned there were 800,000 preschoolers in active duty and National Guard and Reserve families. Support materials for them existed but they were antiquated and not in "kid-speak."

It was the start of an amazing journey for all of us as we began developing resources to help children and their adults talk about changes in their lives when a parent goes away, comes back changed visibly or invisibly, and when a parent dies. You can find many of them at http://www.sesameworkshop.org/initiatives/emotion/tlc.

It is comforting to children—and their parents—to hear Elmo speaking about what they are experiencing as the 3½ year old he is. When people can talk together, they are not alone and life feels more manageable. When children in military families are doing well, their parents can focus on their work.

We've been received well at all levels up to Admiral Mullen. I think it is important to see that an organization like ours, outside the military, cares about military families. We are continuing to assess what the needs are, with the goal of reaching out to other members of children's support community including extended family members, doctors, and teachers. Military families are going to need support for a long time as service members return home changed to families that have changed.

When we started this work, I did not know one person in the military. It has changed my perspective on life. Learning about military families' bravery, loyalty, and dedication to our country has made me a better mother, wife, and friend. I feel blessed to have had the opportunity to oversee this work.

Lynn Chwatsky
Assistant Vice President, Outreach Initiative and Partners, Sesame Workshop

Tragedy Assistance Program for Survivors   Started by the wife of an Army officer after her husband died in a military plane crash, **Tragedy Assistance Program for Survivors** (TAPS) is a nonprofit organization for families whose service member has died. The organization's cornerstone program is the peer support network staffed by volunteers who are at least 1 year beyond the death of their military member and who have attended TAPS peer-mentor training. TAPS also offers crisis response professionals by phone 24 hours a day, assistance with understanding military benefits, a quarterly magazine, a guide for survivors, and online chats and webinars. Its Survivor Seminars provide social support and education about grief and traumatic loss, and its Good Grief Camps offer children social support and coping skills (http://www.taps.org).

U.S. Department of Agriculture and Land-Grant Universities   The DoD has partnered with the U.S. Department of Agriculture (USDA), land-grant universities, and the Extension Service to conduct research and offer education and extension programs for military personnel and their families (U.S. Department of Agriculture & Department of Defense Partnership, 2010). In the nineteenth century, states were granted land by the federal government to establish **land-grant universities** to make education more accessible to it citizens and to teach agriculture, engineering, sciences, and military tactics; to conduct research; and to provide extension services (Washington State University Extension, 2009). The Extension Service, also referred to as the Cooperative Extension Service, is part of the USDA. Extension services are offered in each state through the state's land-grant university. The goal of extension services is to "reach out" and "extend" research-based information and education to the state's citizens (USDA, 2011).

The partnerships among the DoD, USDA, the Extension Service, and land-grant universities are many; we will focus on a few here. To learn about others, go to the partnership webpage (http://militaryfamilies.extension.org/mission).

The **Clearinghouse on Military Family Readiness** is housed at Pennsylvania State University. Its purpose is to disseminate scientifically based information about military family readiness, including evidence-based programs; to offer guidance to professionals who work with military families, youth, and children; and to create a virtual library of research on Exceptional Family Member Program Support and practices to enhance the effectiveness of professionals working with families.

The **Military Extension Internship Program** is housed at Purdue University. Interested college students apply for internships at child and youth development programs on military installations.

BOX 10.3   BEST PRACTICES

INTERNSHIP OPPORTUNITIES FOR COLLEGE STUDENTS

There are many benefits for students.

I coordinate the Military Extension Internship Program at Purdue Extension Service for college students and recent graduates who want to learn about hands-on work with youth and child care programs and program management. We recruit nationwide and look for people with a commitment to the field. The program is a collaboration between the Department of Defense and the Cooperative Extension Service.

Our interns typically have an academic background in family studies, education, sports and recreation, or management. Some of them are members of military families or soon-to-become members. Others know nothing about the military when they first apply. They live and work on military installations around the world for 10 weeks to 6 months. They are compensated with a stipend or an hourly wage, depending on the military branch.

There are many benefits for students. The military's child care programs are accredited and people working in them know what they are doing. Students have amazing opportunities such as planning a curriculum or a big event for a program. They develop a sense of self as a professional. Being an intern is a tremendous opportunity to network, not within a single center but with other interns and education and recreation programs around the world.

To get everyone off to a solid start, we have a 5-day orientation where we bring together interns, supervisors, points of contact with the Armed Services, and experts on military families. Interns learn about our program guidelines, military culture, and military children, youth, and families. We take them to an installation for the day. It is comforting for people with no experience with military. I think what surprises people the most is that even though the military has a clear hierarchy, they can be creative, have fun with children they work with, and have the opportunity to grow as a professional.

Anyone who is interested in being an intern must be ready to work hard. These are challenging positions. The people who work with the interns are very busy, so interns need to be able to take the initiative at times; however, there is also lots of support. People at these programs love their jobs. I tell our interns, "You are walking into a supportive community of people who are committed to each other and to the children and families they serve."

Amy Schott
Internship Coordinator, Cooperative Extension Service, Purdue University

Program staff conduct initial training in military culture and family life prior to the interns leaving for their placements. Amy Schott, Internship Coordinator, describes the program in more detail in Box 10.3.

In Voices From the Frontline, Laura Peterson describes her experience in the Military Extension Internship Program.

Voices From the Frontline

A FORMER INTERN SHARES HER EXPERIENCE

Thinking about doing an internship? Do it. During my internship I worked with the Navy Child and Youth Programs (CYP). I gained personal friendships and professional colleagues. I applied what I learned from classes and textbooks about children and families to the program.

Thanks to my internship I am now the Training and Curriculum Specialist at Naval Support Activity, Annapolis. I provide annual required training for staff in our child development center, youth center, and child development homes. The military is a strong community. I'm big on creating community in our programs, too. I believe in collaborating with families and invite them into our programs.

Children in military families do face stressors. How the stressors impact them depends on the child, the family, and the supports available. Civilian children experience stress as well; however, they may not have access to the supports they need. If we give children support, they can be resilient whether they are part of a military or civilian family.

Laura Peterson

Training and Curriculum Specialist at Naval Support Activity, Annapolis

---

Zero to Three   **Zero to Three**, a nonprofit organization, provides information, support, and training to parents, professionals, and policy makers on health and development of infants and toddlers. Through the organization's web page (http://www.zerotothree.org), parents and professionals can access brochures on how to support infants and toddlers during deployment, relocation, and times of stress. Coming Together Around Military Families® (CTAMF) is a joint project with the DoD to train professionals from multiple disciplines to learn ways to support and foster resilience in families with young children who are facing the trauma of complicated deployments or a service member's injury or death and to collaborate with other professionals. A second training addresses the needs of early childhood professionals to manage stress, including compassion fatigue. A CTAMF quarterly online newsletter spotlights practical ideas to assist young military children during stressful times (ZERO TO THREE, 2011).

Examples of State-Level Collaborations

The past decade has seen the formation of partnerships between the Reserve Component and universities within states. Four examples are given here to illustrate how such collaborations are resulting in services to Active and Reserve Component families.

The Buddy-to-Buddy program is a result of a collaboration between teams from the University of Michigan and Michigan State University and the Michigan Army National Guard leaders. This peer-to-peer program trains soldiers selected by the command to be a buddy who initiates regular contact with an assigned group of Michigan Army National Guard (MI ARNG) soldiers returning from deployment. During "check in" calls, a buddy normalizes getting help when necessary, conveys knowledge of resources and referrals, and maintains contact when a soldier seeks help. Second level buddies are trained more extensively in motivational interviewing and civilian and military resources; they staff the National Guard Armories during drill weekends (Greden et al., 2010).

Deployment programming for the MI ARNG resulted from a partnership that developed between the MI ARNG and faculty from Michigan State University and the University of Michigan

Medical School. Programming at predeployment and reintegration 2-day events include educational presentations about stress reactions, TBI, and military and civilian community resources; and sessions in which service members and family members speak about their deployment experiences. Lessons learned from this partnership include the importance of integrating two cultures, military and university, that differ in management structure and expectations about research and program development (Dalack et al., 2010).

Essential Life Skills for Military Families is a program designed specifically for Reserve Component members to strengthen relationship and practical skills. Supported by funding from the U.S. Department of Health and Human Services and the Administration for Children and Families, the program is housed at East Carolina University and is offered through county Cooperative Extension agents. University faculty, North Carolina National Guard family support leaders, and Cooperative Extension agents worked together to design the curriculum (Carroll, Robinson, Orthner, Matthews, & Smith-Rotabi, 2008). A key feature of this program is that it creates a community-level partnership between a civilian support organization and the National Guard and Military Reserves (Huebner et al., 2009). The 8-hour, evidence-based curriculum addresses unexpected challenges, financial matters, legal issues, and family resilience. A parenting together and apart session can be added to the core curriculum (see http://www.militaryfamilylifeskills.org/).

Passport Toward Success is a reintegration program for military children and youth ages 5–17, offered at Indiana National Guard Yellow Ribbon events 60 days after a unit returns from deployment (Wilson, Wilkum, Chernichky, MacDermid Wadswoth, & Broniarczyk, 2011). Staff from the MFRI at Purdue University developed the program, which is delivered by trained facilitators and community volunteers, thereby building the local community's understanding of military children (Huebner et al., 2009). Informed by models of family resilience (e.g., Walsh, 2003c), the program promotes skill development and family processes in such areas as sharing emotions, perceiving and receiving social support, and communication. Grouped by ages, children visit three "islands" (i.e., feelings, relaxation, and communication). Evaluation of the program in its initial 2 years showed, among other findings, that a majority of youth who participated in the program reported acquiring new ideas about resiliency skills. Youth who reported more stress related to deployment and reunion evaluated the program as especially beneficial (Wilson et al., 2011).

Associations for Service Members and Veterans

Military service members may choose to belong to a professional association just as helping professionals may belong to an association (e.g., the American Association for Marriage and Family Therapy, the American Counseling Association, the American Psychological Association, the National Association of Social Workers, the National Council on Family Relations). Many professional associations for military members exist. Examples include:

- Military Officers Association: http://www.moaa.org
- National Guard Association of the United States: http://www.ngaus.org
- Non-Commissioned Officers Association: http://www.ncoausa.org
- Society of American Military Engineers: http://www.same.org
- Special Forces Association: http://www.specialforcesassociation.org

Likewise, many organizations exist for veterans. Those organizations noted here were chosen to illustrate some of the most visible or some of the newest veterans groups. They advocate for veterans and their families at a national level and often provide local community services. Membership in these groups is restricted to veterans although most offer a way for nonveterans to be affiliated.

American Legion: http://www.legion.org
Iraq and Afghanistan Veterans of America (IAVA): http://iava.org

Service Women's Action Network (SWAN): http://servicewomen.org
Veterans of Foreign Wars (VFW): http://www.vfw.org
Veterans for Peace: http://www.veteransforpeace.org

COLLEGE AND UNIVERSITIES

Military veterans and students serving in the Reserve Component (i.e., National Guard, Reserves, and ROTC) have been present on many college and university campuses for decades as have their spouses, children, and parents. Active duty personnel have been pursuing degrees with universities that offer degree programs on military installations and now online. With the passage in 2008 of the Post-9/11 GI Bill, the number of veterans on college campuses, either the brick and mortar campus or the virtual campus, is expected to continue to increase in the coming years. With the transferability of the Post-9/11 GI Bill, the number of family members of veterans on campuses may also increase. This section notes the administrative services that can facilitate the transition to college or university life. It also highlights the experience of transitioning from being a service member to being a student, whether as a veteran or as a "military student" who is still serving in the Active or Reserve Component. Finally, it offers recommendations for creating welcoming classrooms and campuses.

On-Campus Services

Military-friendly institutions of higher learning typically are members of the **Servicemembers Opportunity Colleges** (SOC). To join SOC, the institution of higher learning must be listed in the Council for Higher Education Accreditation (CHEA) database as accredited; grant degrees and be accredited by an agency recognized by the U.S. Department of Education (DoE) or by CHEA; meet appropriate provisions of DoD Directives 1322.8 (*Voluntary Educational Programs for Military Personnel*) and 1322.25 (*Voluntary Education Programs*), and related service regulations if offering courses on military installations; be approved by the state's approving agency for veterans' benefits; agree to submit relevant data for the SOC Consortium Guide; not have an excessive student loan default rate as determined by the DoE; have an administrator who commits the institution or a subdivision of it to comply with and support SOC principles and criteria; and be approved as meeting the SOC principles and criteria (SOC, n.d.).

Likewise, many institutions of higher education adhere to the American Council on Education guidelines for credit evaluation recommendations. *ACE Military Guide to the Evaluation of Educational Experiences in the Armed Services* is the reference book for evaluating learning acquired in the military for college credit. The first guide was published in 1946. Institutions, service members, and veterans can explore the guide by military training course to see the recommended number of credits (the guide is accessible online at http://militaryguides.acenet.edu).

More colleges and universities are establishing an office dedicated to serving military students and veterans and encouraging the development of military student and veteran organizations (Cook & Kim, 2009). The **Student Veterans of America** (SVA; a national organization for veterans on college and university campuses, see http://www.studentveterans.org) suggests that establishing a center for military students centralizes services and programs and provides easier access to information and assistance that would otherwise be spread among various campus offices. A physical center provides a location for camaraderie with peers, so they can support one another as they become more comfortable with campus life. Office staff who understand the potential physical and psychological health issues faced by some veterans and military students, academic preparation, military experience and training, drill requirements, and activation facilitate the transition from military life to campus life. Such policies, space, and understanding encourage retention (Garcia, 2009).

A center ideally would be staffed by a liaison or coordinator serving as the point of contact to coordinate services, make referrals, develop programs, address students' financial and enrollment processes and concerns, and advocate for military students. In addition, a veteran benefits certifying official would serve as the campus liaison with the VA and state education agency and assist veterans, military, and family members with required paperwork to access VA, state, and other benefits. Some institutions may be eligible for a VA work–study position for a student veteran, and a veteran in this position could assist staff members and provide support services and referrals for students (Garcia, 2009). The following Voices From the Frontline describes how one university established an office to serve military students and veterans.

Voices From the Frontline

THE FOUNDING OF AN OFFICE OF MILITARY AND VETERANS AFFAIRS

Veterans are a special population and a valuable population to bring back into the education world.

As an advisor of nontraditional students and 6 years ago, I recognized I had service members among my students. When I looked over their transcripts, I noticed incompletes, low grades, and Xs showing they had disappeared from a course due to deployments. I wondered what was going on. I started looking into it with the support of the university president. I sent out a survey but received few responses. I started learning when I started talking with veterans about their experiences. Then they knew we cared and meant business.

I met a veteran who had walked out of a class when a book dropped on the floor. Another veteran had passed out in class and then was too embarrassed to return. More than one had trouble concentrating because of PTSD. These and other issues impacted their academic success.

We started learning that vets are not only transitioning to school but back to civilian life. They may feel they are different—even strange. Their experiences and sense of the world and themselves are different from those of a typical student. They have been part of a very different culture. Vets bring a focus and a sense of priority. They know what is important in life. They want to apply the skills they have developed in the military to their lives today.

To make our university a good place for veterans it would take everyone. We started having meetings. Presenters included people who worked with veterans and veterans themselves. Other veterans attended. Faculty and staff came. So did university officials and administrators. We created an oversight committee of faculty, staff, and students to keep track of how we were doing and provide their input and talents.

As we worked to create a caring community, we opened the Advocacy Office for Military Affairs, now known as the Office of Military and Veterans Affairs. My role as director was to support students. I listened. I explained about deployment and PTSD to professors. We made policy changes. Now at the university any veteran returning from deployment has priority registration for a year. If GI Bill money doesn't arrive on time, and it rarely does, a veteran can still enroll. We made a link with a nearby veterans' hospital, so we could get priority status for a student to see someone if it was necessary. Making our university a good place for veterans is a gift we give for their service. They have enriched our community in return.

Gerry Schma
Founder of Western Michigan University's Office of Military and Veterans Affairs

What Military Students and Veterans Bring to Campus

For some, joining the military is, to a small or large degree, a means to a college education. For others, transitioning out of the military prompts them to consider earning a college degree for the first time. Military undergraduates (i.e., student service members and veterans) as a group are older than traditional undergraduates, yet younger and more diverse than the larger group of veterans. In the 2007–2008 academic year, 85% of military undergraduates were age 24 and older, and they were more likely to be non-White. In the same year, 27% of military undergraduates were women (Radford, 2009).

Voices From the Frontline

GOING TO SCHOOL: LIVING A DREAM

I appreciate school. Education is my goal.

I often hear people say they are going back to school when they get out of the military. But life doesn't always happen that way. By the time you retire, you might have a family, a house, and bills to pay.

After 17 years in the military, I was medically discharged. I'm a wood carver and aspiring artist and always wanted to go to art school. My wife Jackie encouraged me to "live my dream." Thanks to her encouragement and support, I am. I am forever grateful.

At 40, I'm older than three of my teachers. I've been told I look like I'm 24–26, so I don't think my fellow students see me as an icon of days gone by. They know I've been working. I think as we get to know each other and they realize I'm older and have been in the military that they will have some questions.

I think I appreciate school in a different way than many of my younger classmates. Some see education as a means to the end. For me, education is my goal. I know I text more slowly. The other day some of them texted me and didn't think I was answering because I was so slow typing out my response.

I entered school this year as a sophomore. I received credit for five classes based on my military equivalency paperwork. I've received a lot of support from the Military and Veterans Affairs Office. I was surprised at the length they go to. For example, at my university, if you are coming off active duty, tuition is covered for the first semester. That saves a lot of money and will make my GI Bill money go further. I'd like to get my master's degree so I can teach art history and that will take a lot of schooling.

I know my wife is behind me, and my kids are, too. While they don't come up to me and say, "I'm proud of you," they don't get mad when I have to do my homework and they want to play Pictionary. The other day I heard my daughter tell a friend, "My dad is in art school." I hope living in a family where parents are living their dreams teaches our kids that doing so is doable. I certainly hope the path to turning their dreams into reality is shorter and easier than mine.

Patrick Chandler
SFC (Retired)

Military students come to campus likely having lived in or been deployed to other countries. Students will have a variety of cross-cultural experiences—some positive, some negative, and some life-changing. In addition to first-hand experiences in other countries, most service personnel have been introduced to basic tenets of cultural sensitivity through training to develop skills about how to interact with others of differing values, religion, and language, which are critical to mission success (McFarland, 2005).

The perspectives they share in the classroom reflect their often wide-ranging life experiences and training. Those stationed at one of the permanent U.S. military installations outside of the United States for one or more tours may have acquired basic or advanced language skills in a second or third language. Many will have traveled extensively throughout Europe or Asia, visiting major cultural, religious, and national locations that they then study in history, geography, art appreciation, language, anthropology, design, music, engineering, and business courses.

Military students may seen Renaissance masterpieces in the Louvre, gazed at the dome of the Pantheon, worshipped in Trier Cathedral, been groundlings at the reconstructed Globe Theatre, strolled through Hiroshima Peace Memorial Park, felt the cramped rooms of the Secret Annex, or viewed the modern architecture of Hong Kong. The Pyramids, the Great Barrier Reef, the Alps, the Greek Isles, Istanbul, Lisbon, or Mount Fuji could have been their weekend get-away destinations.

As veterans and service members transition to college or university, they bring these and many more experiences and dreams with them (see Box 10.4). A study of 25 veterans and National Guard and Reserve force members in college noted the self-awareness, maturity, and determination brought to campus by those who have experienced combat. They can also bring experiences of great loss, fear, and visible and invisible injury (Ackerman, DiRamio, & Garza Mitchell, 2009). Preliminary analyses of the first wave of data from a longitudinal study of 354 college students (i.e., 195 student veterans/active duty, 68 enrolled in a ROTC program, and 91 civilian students with no prior military service) indicated that veterans reported less stress, fewer psychological and somatic symptoms, and no differences in PTSD symptoms than the ROTC and civilian students (Whiteman & Barry, 2010). However, they did perceive less social support from university friends and greater role overload than the other two groups. Implications of this study include acknowledging that veteran and student service members form a unique subgroup among the college population. These students could potentially benefit from facilitation of formal and informal social support; encouragement to connect with faculty, advisors, and peers; and support as they balance multiple roles (Whiteman & Barry, 2010). Included below are additional ideas for student service members, veterans, military family members, faculty, and staff to ease the transition to campus.

BOX 10.4   TIPS FROM THE FRONTLINE

TRANSITIONING TO SCHOOL: SERVICE MEMBERS, VETERANS, AND FAMILY MEMBERS

- *Acknowledge that going back to school is a balancing act, particularly for those with families.* Pat Chandler notes, "It's different being in school when you have a family and bills. On Wednesday I have a class and have to leave right afterward to make sure my son gets to Cub Scouts on time. When my fellow students stay up until 2 AM finishing their paper, I've long ago gone to bed. I'm older. I get tired. And I have to get my kids up and off to school in the morning."
- *Find support from family and friends.* Encouragement or a few hours of uninterrupted time to study make a difference.
- *Allow time to get back into the education groove.* The rules and culture of higher education are different from the military and take time to learn until they feel comfortable. Talk with faculty. Structure time so readings, papers, and projects are done on time.
- *Investigate programs and benefits for veterans.* Use the services of the military/veteran advocacy office, and talk with other veterans. If the institution does not have an office, seek out an administrator, faculty member, or advisor who listens and cares.
- *Look into and fill out military equivalency paperwork.* As Pat reflects, "Why should you need to pay for and take a physical education class if you've been in the military?"
- *Recognize possible stressors.* Transitioning to school may occur while still carrying out military duties if a member of the Reserve Component and/or while attending to visible or invisible injuries. These realities may add a layer of stress as self-perceptions change. Pat explains, "For me, it was an injury and evaluation leading to a medical discharge that has changed how I see myself."
- *If stressed, take action early.* Use assistance available to facilitate the transition to school. Seek guidance on study tips, managing stress, or dealing with an injury.

FACILITATING THE TRANSITION TO SCHOOL: WHAT STAFF AND FACULTY CAN DO

- *Listen and learn.* When talking with staff and faculty, Gerry Schma suggests, "Let veterans and families know you care and are committed. Do not judge. Do not feel you have to have the answers. When vets know you care and are supportive, they, like all of us, are more likely to share their stories, concerns, and ideas."

- *Empower veterans and service members to seek support in achieving their success.* "Veterans don't expect you to solve their problems, but sometimes they need guidance and support as they do." Gerry concludes, "It boils down to respecting their experience and dignity."
- *Avoid letting the fact that you have not shared similar experiences interfere.* Gerry Schma explains, "When vets or families tell me, 'You can't understand,' I acknowledge, 'You're right, but I can listen.'"
- *Learning basic information about military life can help faculty facilitate completion of courses.* A professor may insist a student never miss a class session until learning about the demands of training and preparing for deployment. Be flexible in terms of due dates if they or loved ones are mobilized in the middle of a semester or term. Be aware that not every deployed service member has easy access to the Internet.
- *If veterans, student service members, or military family members stop by to talk, do so if possible.* If it is time for class or a meeting, still take a moment or two to check in to determine if there is a crisis. If so, use campus resources. If not, agree on a time to talk in the next day or so.
- *If veterans or student service members have difficulty with the course material or do not come to class, e-mail and offer to meet with them.* Let them know you have noticed their absence and offer to talk with them.
- *Involve the entire college or university community, including veterans and families.* A single office or advocate on campus cannot do it alone.
- *Provide guidance on maneuvering through military education benefits, particularly the New GI Bill.*
- *Publicize student services and local community services that support veterans and student service members.* Ensure staff and faculty are familiar with the range of support services and how to refer students to them.
- *Provide professional development to staff and faculty on relevant issues.* For example, train staff to meet the needs of students with brain injuries and physical disabilities.

Cook and Kim (2009), Patrick Chandler SFC (Retired), Gerry Schma

SUMMARY

- Key policies for military families include the recent presidential initiative, Strengthening Our Military Families; the annual National Defense Authorization Act by which key services are funded and new programs are mandated; the amended FMLA that includes military family leave entitlements; the Interstate Compact on Educational Opportunities for Military Children that is facilitating educational practices for military students across states; and the Caregivers and Veterans Omnibus Health Services Act of 2010 that directs assistance to caregivers of military members injured while serving.
- Many civilian organizations provide key support to and advocate on behalf of military families.
- Organizations are partnering with the DoD to develop and offer programs, services, and resources to military families. Local units of the Reserve Component and civilian institutions and communities are also collaborating in the development of new initiatives.
- Professional associations and organizations exist for service members, veterans, and family members. They provide support and guidance to their members and encourage service to the local and greater military community.
- Increasing numbers of student service members and veterans are enrolling in colleges and universities. These institutions of higher education are making their campuses more veteran friendly.

EXERCISES

1. Edward Tick, a psychotherapist who has worked with hundreds of veterans with post-traumatic stress disorder, stated, "[t]he moral responsibility for a war must ultimately fall not upon the common soldiers who fought it but upon the nation and its leaders who created it …. The social group must not only witness the stories of its warriors; it must also accept responsibility for their deeds during war and their condition afterward" (Tick, 2005, p. 236). Consider the following questions:
   - To what degree are citizens of a nation responsible for the actions of its political leaders? For its military?
   - To what degree do you agree with Tick's view that the members of society that send someone to war must accept responsibility for the deeds committed during that war and for the well-being of military members upon return from that war?
   - To what degree do public policies and programs such as the ones reviewed in this chapter demonstrate our society taking responsibility for the well-being of its service members, veterans, and their families? What else, if anything, needs to be done to fulfill a responsibility?
2. Read more about one of the policies described in this chapter. If possible, talk with someone who benefitted from the policy.
3. Explore the origin and purpose of Memorial Day and Veterans Day and then identify what your community does in recognition of these federal holidays. How do they play a part of building the capacity of a community to attend to the welfare of its members?
4. If possible, visit one of the 131 Department of Veterans Affairs National Cemeteries or Arlington National Cemetery. If visiting a cemetery is not possible, view a video about one of the 24 U.S. military cemeteries found in other countries. A link to them can be found on the website of the American Battles Monuments Commission (http://www.abmc.gov/cemeteries/cemeteries.php). Read information about the cemetery that is available, either at the cemetery or online, and consider the role of cemeteries and monuments in demonstrating a community's capacity to care for its members.
5. Go online and learn more about the history of a group for veterans and a group for military families. If possible, interview a member from a local chapter about why she or he joined the group.
6. Interview two college students who are veterans or are serving in the National Guard or Reserves. Ask what recommendations they have for other veterans or service personnel who are transitioning to college. Ask what observations they have of college students with no military background and recommendations for working with classmates who do.

11

Supporting Military Families
Recent and New Programs

In Chapter 11, you will

- Meet Barbara Purinton, Vermont National Guard Family Readiness Support Assistant, and the wife of a soldier and mother of a soldier, both serving in Afghanistan
- Learn about the programs that the DoD has developed in response to the increased challenges and stress that military families experience as a result of the sustained U.S. military involvement in numerous military operations around the world
- Learn how the DoD is attempting to change the military view of psychological health and to encourage military members and their families to seek psychological health care when they need it

Meet

Barbara Purinton, Vermont National Guard Family Readiness Support Assistant; Wife and Mother of Soldiers Serving in Afghanistan

Family Readiness Support helps people know that they are connected to the resources and support. They are not alone. Our goal is to build a social and emotional support network that happens more naturally on military installations. We provide deployment and reunion briefings, help family members understand the Unit's mission, and provide information and referrals.

My work takes me all over the state working with 11 Family Readiness Groups, one for each armory that has soldiers serving in the 86th Infantry Brigade Combat Team. We also reach out to the other states that are part of the Brigade (seven plus small groups from other states who have sought to join the mission).

The chain of concern is supposed to work like this:

- *We have developed telephone trees headed by volunteer trained callers who check in with families once a month. If families have questions or the furnace breaks, this person is their first point of contact. Families know they are not alone.*
- *Callers then report back to the Telephone Tree Coordinator, who is supervised by the Family Readiness Group Leader. To maintain confidentiality, info passed up the chain may describe a situation but not name a person unless permission is given or if it is an emergency.*
- *The telephone tree callers let the coordinator know of any issues that need to be addressed. Sometimes those come to me but more often go directly to the Family Assistance*

Center, the "one-stop shop" for issues: TRICARE, finances, legal, whatever it may be. We also remind families of the other services available to them: a Military Family Life Consultant who works with families and children and visits school and educates the educators about the unique challenges of military children; the youth coordinator who oversees programs and camps for military children; a psychologist; Military OneSource; and outreach specialists who work with veterans and their families.

- *Every family receives a From the Home Front newsletter that continues to list the resources available as well as upcoming support groups and other events.*

Being military family members helps my coworker and me reach other military families. We understand what they are experiencing and can respond to some of their needs. For example, the Family Readiness Program has offered programs called Beyond the Yellow Ribbon. These are offered premobilization for soldiers and families, during mobilization for the families, and postmobilization at 30 and 60 days for the soldier and family. The mid-deployment event was aimed at supporting the families (this we planned and a Yellow Ribbon Brief that lasted a whole day). We wanted to give people time to relax a little, to talk with each other, and to ask questions. It's hard to take in information when so much is changing in your life. When my family members were deployed the first time, the brief lasted only 3 hours. I'm smart, but it took me a year after the briefing to realize that I was covered by TRICARE, the military health insurance. I don't want that to happen to other family members.

INTRODUCTION

In Chapter 1, you learned that the DoD has recognized that families are vital to the success of the U.S. military forces. The DoD understands that service members whose families are well cared for and doing well in the military community are more likely to stay in the military, civilians who know that their families will be taken care of are more likely to join the military, and service members who do not need to worry about the welfare of their families while they are deployed or otherwise away from their families are more likely to concentrate on their jobs when necessary.

You learned in the last two chapters that there are numerous DoD and civilian programs and policies designed to ensure that military families get what they need to thrive. However, the needs of military families change constantly. The DoD understands this and is committed to continuing to meet the changing demands of military life caused by the increase in the past decade in deployments to war zones and in other military operations, such as humanitarian missions. The Army has declared its gratitude and commitment to Army families though "The Army Family Covenant" (U.S. Army Installation Management Command, 2010), a unique contract and promise to provide Army families with accessible and high-quality support programs and services (see Box 11.1).

BOX 11.1   BEST PRACTICES

THE ARMY FAMILY COVENANT: KEEPING THE PROMISE

- We recognize the commitment and increasing sacrifices that our Families are making every day.
- We recognize the strength of our Soldiers comes from the strength of their Families.
- We are committed to providing Soldiers and Families a Quality of Life that is commensurate with their service.
- We are committed to providing our Families a strong, supportive environment where they can thrive.
- We are committed to building a partnership with Army Families that enhances their strength and resilience.

- We are committed to improving Family readiness by:
  - Standardizing and funding existing Family programs and services
  - Increasing accessibility and quality of health care
  - Improving Soldier and Family housing
  - Ensuring excellence in schools, youth services, and child care
  - Expanding education and employment opportunities for Family members

(U.S. Army Installation Management Command, 2010)

Each individual branch of the military service and the DoD have demonstrated their flexibility and responsiveness to the increased demands on military families. The DoD is constantly revising programs and creating new ones to help reduce the impact of increased stress on military families. The DoD's work in devising and implementing programs to care for military families will never be complete. However, this chapter will introduce you to some of the new programs, policies, and attitudes adopted by the DoD in its attempt to honor its commitment to military families.

In addition, many civilian agencies are concerned about military families experiencing a particularly long period of additional stress to their normally challenging lives as military families due to the ongoing conflicts and humanitarian missions that the U.S. military forces have been engaged in for the past decade. Numerous organizations across the United States that are concerned about the well-being and the psychological health of families in America have developed programs that include or were specifically developed to address the needs of military families. Some of those programs will be introduced in this chapter as well.

Voices From the Frontline

CREATING NEW SERVICES

The military is very responsive given its size. In my appointed role as Deputy Assistant Secretary of the Navy for Force Support and Families in the first Bush Administration, I had oversight of all quality of life issues for the Navy and Marine Corps for the Secretary of the Navy. My job was to develop and implement policy for Navy and Marine Corps quality of life programs including medical care, military housing, family support, and child development centers.

It's not a mystery as to how new services are created. To create family support programs I went out to commands and listened to families. It takes listening to understand what people in different places need. What works for Naval Air Station Jacksonville is not necessarily the right thing for Naval Air Station San Diego.

We used to meet regularly with family support groups like the National Military Family Association, a private nonprofit organization that works to improve the quality of life for military families, that let us know what supports they saw were needed. I'd share what I saw. Sometimes the military could provide a needed service. Sometimes military support civilian organizations could provide services we couldn't.

It helps you reach more families any time you can sit at the table, tell people what you need, see what they can provide using their personnel and, in return, give them visibility.

Marianne "Mimi" Blackburn Drew
Rear Admiral, U.S. Navy (Retired)

FAMILY RESILIENCE PROGRAMS

This section features examples of family resilience programs. They include deployment programming for active duty personnel, reservists, and their families; Families OverComing Under Stress (FOCUS); and Strong Bonds. These programs are characterized by a focus on strengths, resilience, and on how things go "right" instead of on problems and on what is going "wrong." A commitment to this focus is reflected in the following programs, as well as in many newly developed programs designed to assist military families.

Deployment Cycle Programs

Predeployment programs are common across the services. In fact, deployment programming was common in some services prior to September 11, 2001, especially in the Navy, where sailors have always been away from families for long periods of time. Now in all of the services, families are invited to presentations on financial, legal, emotional, and relationship preparation for separation. The family support centers typically offer a presentation for couples and another for parents and children. These presentations may occur in the evening or over a weekend and at the family support center or through a command (i.e., the families are invited to a deployment readiness briefing at the unit's location, e.g., onboard the ship). Some of the Navy's Fleet and Family Support Centers may also conduct command-requested Return and Reunion programs for service members aboard ships as they transit back to the homeport (Blaisure & Arnold-Mann, 1992).

The DoD's Yellow Ribbon Reintegration program offers assistance to service personnel in the Reserve and National Guard and their families throughout the cycle of deployment, from mobilization to reintegration. You will learn more about the Yellow Ribbon Program later in this chapter.

The Navy offers a Returning Warrior Workshop (RWW) for individual augmentees (i.e., service members who are temporarily assigned to another command, deploy with the new command, and return to their parent command upon completion of the deployment) and their guest. The guest may include a spouse, a significant other (e.g., boyfriend or girlfriend), or a family member (e.g., sister, brother). The RWW is offered so sailors and their loved one can reconnect and learn how best to support one another during the reintegration phase.

FAMILIES OVERCOMING UNDER STRESS

The FOCUS project is a multiservices resiliency-building program for military families with children (Saltzman, 2010). FOCUS includes structured parent–children sessions designed to strengthen family resiliency skills such as goal setting, problem solving, regulating emotions, managing reminders of combat and deployment, communication, and mutual support (Saltzman, Lester, Beardslee, & Pynoos, 2008). The core components of FOCUS include family-level education on child development, the combat operational stress continuum, and trauma; an individualized family deployment timeline used to bridge misunderstandings, promote co-parenting, and connect skills to family members' experiences; and links to additional services and resources. FOCUS also provides workshops and community outreach; consultations with families and providers; and family checkups (Saltzman, 2010).

Evaluation of FOCUS has been ongoing. An analysis of 821 families who had used FOCUS revealed that 42% were self-referred. Other sources of referral included schools, military organizations, health and mental health providers, and chaplains. Children who attended reported significant positive increases in problem solving and emotional regulation. Parents reported significant improvement in children's prosocial behavior and reductions in children's problematic conduct and symptoms of anxiety and depression. In addition, parents reported significant decreases in their own symptoms of anxiety and depression. Families improved in the areas of problem solving, communication, affective responsiveness, behavior control, and roles (Saltzman, 2010).

Initiated by the Navy's Bureau of Medicine and Surgery (BUMED), in 2009 FOCUS was expanded to designated Air Force and Army installations. In addition, FOCUS is being adapted for couples

(FOCUS C); wounded, injured, or ill service members and their families (FOCUS WW); and families with young children (FOCUS EC). These adaptations are undergoing pilot testing (Leskin, 2010).

Strong Bonds

The Strong Bonds program began as an Army marriage-enhancement program for couples in 1997 (see Box 11.2). Because of the current frequency of deployments, the use of the Strong Bonds program has become more widespread and is used to assist couples and families in the process of reuniting after a deployment. It now also includes a series of new training modules: single soldiers, couples, families, predeployment, and redeployment. Chaplains facilitate Strong Bonds workshops, which take place in a weekend retreat format. Strong Bonds for couples is based on the Prevention and Relationship Enhancement Program (PREP) originally developed for civilian couples (Stanley, Blumberg, & Markman, 1999). Researchers are conducting a longitudinal study in which couples were assigned to either PREP for Strong Bonds or a control group (Allen & Markman, 2010). Initial results indicate that recent deployment was related to husbands' posttraumatic symptoms which, in turn, were related to marital functioning (Allen, Rhoades, Stanley, & Markman, 2010). Results also indicate that marital functioning may be improved by marriage education (Allen & Markman, 2010). At one year post intervention, approximately 6% of the control couples had divorced compared with approximately 2% of the Strong Bonds couples. Soldiers interested in participating in one of the Strong Bonds workshops can locate events at https://www.strongbonds.org.

BOX 11.2   BEST PRACTICES

A RESEARCHER TALKS ABOUT HIS WORK

PREP is a research-based divorce-prevention/marriage-strengthening program that Scott Stanley and I developed. We know from research that training about communication skills, intimacy, and conflict management has a positive impact on marriage satisfaction and reduces rates of violence and divorce. In PREP, we teach couples skills to strengthen and enhance their relationship before and during marriage.

We've worked with the military since 1989. Our work started with Navy chaplains who took our PREP training and now provide it for their service members. The word spread and today I'm proud to say that PREP has been adapted for the Army's Strong Bonds program. As you can imagine, battling inside the home is not good for people coping with battle outside the home. In the words of the Army, "Stronger relationships mean a stronger Army."

We have also developed Got Your Back, a curriculum designed to help single service members with skills for communication, conflict resolution, and making good choices in terms of partners. These are skills that soldiers can use in current and future relationships in their personal and professional lives.

Working with the military has been a highlight of my career. I am grateful to have the privilege to do my small part to help our country by supporting our soldiers and their families.

Our entry to collaborating with the military was our research and wanting to learn from the people working with soldiers and their families. Research can open many career paths. At our university, we have undergraduate and graduate students analyzing our data and publishing their findings. For example, one student is focusing on how relationships can impact soldiers' PTSD symptoms. If you enjoy trying to understand the story that data tell and know how to ask good questions, I suggest looking into teaming up with a researcher working in an area that interests you.

Howard Markman, PhD
Codirector, Center for Marital and Family Studies, University of Denver

ASSISTING MILITARY MEMBERS AND THEIR FAMILIES REINTEGRATE AND REUNITE

The following programs are designed to help military members with issues related to continuing their lives successfully after deploying and to help military families reunite after a long and difficult separation.

Operation Healthy Reunions

Operation Healthy Reunions is sponsored by Mental Health America (formerly known as the National Mental Health Association), a community-based nonprofit agency committed to improving the psychological health of everyone who lives in the United States (Mental Health America, 2010b). Operation Healthy Reunions was developed to improve the psychological health of military members and families after their return from deployments (Mental Health America, 2010a). Its goal is to facilitate a healthy reunion among military couples and families. The program provides education on reuniting with spouses and children after a deployment, coping with war, and the psychological health problems that can result from the war experience (i.e., depression and PTSD). Often, Operation Healthy Reunions staff members and volunteers provide psychological health services in military families' local communities free or at low cost to the family. Many of Mental Health America's over 320 nationwide affiliates provide some or all of the following additional services to military families:

- Confidential evaluations and treatment by professional mental health providers
- Case management (coordination of treatment)
- Support groups
- Symptom recognition and management classes
- Couples and family counseling
- Advocacy

Voices From the Frontline

NEW SUPPORTS FOR FAMILIES

Today families are getting more support with homecoming.

In late 2005, there were no family reintegration programs. My return home was quick. My family had some idea I was coming back in November. They didn't know exactly when until 48 hours before I came back. Our unit came into Fort Benning. We did our out-processing, and each of us got a plane ticket and scattered in all different directions.

The system is so large it is difficult to navigate. I got that airplane ticket home and there I was—the little guy in the big system … on my own. Today families are getting more support with homecoming. They don't have to navigate this complex time totally alone.

Chris Sullins
Former Army Reserve Combat Stress Prevention Officer

Post-9/11 GI Bill

Since 1944, the Department of Veterans Affairs has sponsored an educational benefit package for veterans who have successfully completed an enlistment in the military service (DoD, 2010h). However, no educational benefit has been as comprehensive as the Post-9/11 GI Bill, which became available to veterans in 2009. The new GI Bill is authorized for qualified Active and Reserve Component service members who served in the U.S. military after September 10, 2001. Eligible service members can receive up to 36 months of educational benefits—tuition and fees, a monthly living allowance, and a stipend for books and supplies. Costs for tutorial assistance and reimbursement for any tests required for licensing and certification are also provided by the Post-9/11 GI Bill. All educational programs must be offered by an institution of higher learning approved by the VA. Approved training includes graduate and undergraduate degree programs and vocational or technical training.

An unprecedented feature of the new GI Bill is that qualified career service members can transfer their unused benefits to family members (Department of Veterans Affairs, 2009). A service member can transfer the entire 36 months of benefits—if the member has used none—or up to the total remaining months of unused Post-9/11 GI Bill benefits. The service members can transfer the benefits to a spouse, to one or more children, or to any combination thereof.

Voices From the Frontline

ADVOCATING FOR FAMILIES

I'm an advocate for military families. My job is to support their overall readiness and well-being so that they can be constantly ready for a deployment. We're a purple service—meaning that I support any military family. We currently have 998 Air Guardsman on base and about 1000 families. I'm on call 24 hours a day. If a family has a deployment-related need, I will provide direct service. For other issues, I am like a resource and referral agency and help guide people to services they need.

Part of my job is to bring awareness of family needs to senior leaders on base. I go to all the major meetings so I can be aware of what is happening and see how families might be affected. I also reach out to the broader community. I educate people about the military as I build relationships with organizations and agencies so that I can help our families connect with resources.

Guard and Reserve families don't always identify themselves as military families until deployment is upon them. They are trying to adjust and get to know the military culture as they deal with deployment without the same support network that active duty families get. National Guard and Reserve children and families often feel alone. They are flooded with media and may hear frightening or negative things about the war on the news, from teachers, classmates, and even from people in the grocery store. When you are active duty and live on an installation, most people are careful about what they say and your community buffers you from negativity.

My role as family advocate was not created until 2001. Prior to that we did not have a full-time position for family support in the Air National Guard. There was no funding for family programs. Services were provided by family members and volunteers.

The shift toward supporting families started before 9/11 but it increased in speed afterwards. Leaders learned that the members of the Guard were not so quick to respond if they felt their families were in peril. Since then, families have become a priority of command and leadership—it's good to see. The military culture now is "Mission first, but family always."

Robin Berry
Airman & Family Readiness Manager, 110th Air Wing,
Michigan Air National Guard

PROGRAMS DESIGNED TO SUPPORT NATIONAL GUARD AND RESERVE MEMBERS AND THEIR FAMILIES

In 2010, the DoD aligned several programs designed specifically to provide support to National Guard and Reserve military members and their families under a new directorate. The newly created Family and Employer Programs & Policy directorate falls under the Office of the Assistant Secretary of Defense for Reserve Affairs and includes the Yellow Ribbon Program, ESGR program, and Individual and Family Support (IFS) Policy. While not a Family and Employer Programs & Policy program, the Joint Family Support Assistance Program (JFSAP) also exists to provide services to National Guard and Reserve members and their families. Through these programs, the DoD hopes to better meet the needs of Reserve Component service members and their families and to provide them with more information and greater access to resources.

DoD Yellow Ribbon Reintegration Program

The Yellow Ribbon Program was developed by the DoD specifically to provide assistance and support to National Guard and Reserve military members and their families (DoD, 2010p). The program provides services, information, and referrals to Reserve Component members and families before, during, and after they are called to active duty and eases the process of transitioning to active duty during mobilization and back to civilian life during demobilization. It also helps Reserve Component members and their families connect with local resources before, during, and after deployments.

The program uses comprehensive outreach methods to reach Reserve Component members and families in even the most isolated locations. Yellow Ribbon activities can include informational presentations (e.g., coping with deployment), family social activities, and reunion events. Events usually occur on one or two weekend days during which presentations on topics such as health care, education and training, and financial and legal benefits are given. Staff from DoD and civilian organizations (e.g., Military OneSource, Military Family Life Consultants, the Red Cross) provide information about their services and answer questions.

The Yellow Ribbon Program also provides referrals to DoD and other government agencies (e.g., VA) and civilian programs.

Employer Support of the Guard and Reserve

ESGR was established by the DoD in 1972 because the DoD recognizes that civilian employers are crucial in supporting the large numbers of reservists who defend the nation (ESGR, 2009). Employers must comply with existing employment laws that protect the rights of those who hold civilian jobs while also serving in the Reserve Component. ESGR's mission is to enhance cooperation and understanding between Reserve Component members and their civilian employers, to encourage employer support for reserve members, and to help resolve conflicts arising as a result of an employee/military member's military commitment. ESGR accomplishes this by increasing civilian employers' awareness of applicable laws governing reservists called to active duty and their civilian job status, recognizing exceptional support by civilian employers, and resolving conflicts between employers and service members when they arise. Through an extensive network of volunteers, ESGR provides services throughout the United States and its territories.

Individual and Family Support Policy

The Office of the Assistant Secretary of Defense for Reserve Affairs' IFS Policy program is designed to strengthen family support programs, policies, and partnerships with civilian agencies (DoD, 2010e). The IFS guides DoD policies and partnerships in support of Reserve Component members and their families.

Joint Family Support Assistance Program

In 2007 Congress authorized the DoD to develop a JFSAP for National Guard and Reserve members and their families (DoD, 2010i). While the newly created Family and Employer Programs & Policy directorate does not include the JFSAP, the JFSAP also exists to provide services solely to National Guard and Reserve members and their families. The primary goal of the program is to provide high-quality services to those families who are located in areas where there are no military installations from which they could receive support and services. The JFSAP reaches out to isolated military families.

The JFSAP has been available in all states and U.S. territories since September 2008 and provides ongoing support to Reserve Component families during the full deployment cycle—before, during, and after deployments (DoD, 2010i). It also provides mobile and community-based support services, including information and referral, financial assistance, child care, outreach by the military grocery and department stores, transition assistance, recreational programs, and counseling services. The services are delivered by federal, state, and local government organizations and by nonprofit agencies, with the JFSAP coordinating the provision of these services. The following are the DoD's goals for the JFSAP (Managed Health Network Government Services, 2010a):

- Create a "high-tech, high touch" web-enabled community to connect military families with each other and with supportive resources 24/7
- Increase availability of resources for family members
- Increase awareness of active/Guard/Reserve members and families of existing services
- Inform leadership and service providers about the range of available programs and services, and how they may be accessed
- Provide child development resources and referral services
- Sponsor volunteers and family support professionals
- Assess the need for enhanced support
- Integrate services and programs into a comprehensive delivery system that responds to members and families at all stages of the deployment cycle

Voices From the Frontline

THE JOINT FAMILY SUPPORT ASSISTANCE PROGRAM

The JFSAP was launched in 2008 by the DoD Military Community & Family Policy (MC&FP) program. Its creation was in response to a congressional mandate to provide mobile family support and services for Guard, Reserve, and active duty families whose access to support was challenging because they live away from installations.

JFSAP was visionary. Congress said to augment, not replace services. We took this to mean build community capacity. Rather than creating separate programs, we went to State Family Program Directors and said, "We are here to augment your needs." Every state now has a JFASP team of four people: one Military and Family Life Counselor (MFLC), one Child and Youth Behavioral MFLC, one Military OneSource Consultant, and one additional position chosen by the state (most chose a Personal Financial Counselor).

This partnership approach has been invaluable. Every state is unique. Family Program Directors have been out there for years. They know their community, their service members, the geography, and local culture. Because they didn't have many resources for so long, they became creative problem solvers and thinkers. We went out to offer them support but it didn't take long before we were asking, "What can we learn from them?"

There's a shift occurring from thinking about Family Centers as bricks and mortar and a collection of programs to seeing them as service delivery systems. This is vital. Over the last 10 years, money has been flowing for the creation of services. Now commanders, families, and professionals are saying there is too much out there and it's confusing.

We have to look at the connections between programs always being grounded in who families are and what they need. We need to think carefully about the services we provide and why, then assess our effectiveness.

Families will be in communities for their whole lives. Communities are going to be left supporting service members and their families with challenges due to multiple deployments to combat theatres long after funding is diverted elsewhere. It is going to take coordination and collaboration between health and human services agencies, nonprofit and for-profit organizations, and state and local agencies to integrate services to promote military family readiness and resiliency in a sustained and ongoing way.

Gerry Carlon
LCSW, Senior Policy Analyst, Office of the Deputy Assistant Secretary, Defense

CARING FOR MILITARY MEMBERS WHO HAVE BEEN INJURED AND HELPING THEIR FAMILIES

As the length of time that the United States has been involved in violent conflict increases, so does the number of military service men and women who have been injured in combat or who have been impacted by serious illnesses. These injuries and illnesses significantly change their lives and the lives of their loved ones. Many DoD and civilian programs have been developed to reach out to these families and help care for them.

Wounded Warrior Programs

Each branch of the military has programs for wounded, injured, and ill service members and their families: the U.S. Army Wounded Warrior Program (AW2), the Air Force Wounded Warrior Program (AFW2), the Marine Corps Wounded Warrior Regiment (WWR), and the Navy Safe Harbor (which also provides assistance to wounded, injured, or ill Coast Guard members and their families).

These wounded warrior programs provide assistance and advocacy for severely wounded, ill, and injured service members and their families (Navy Personnel Command, 2010; U.S. Air Force, 2010; U.S. Army Medical Department, 2010a; U.S. Marine Corps, 2010). Services include providing support and advice about medical treatment and rehabilitation and help during the transition back into the military service or into the civilian community. The programs help military and family members access federal, state, and civilian programs that often require beneficiaries to negotiate difficult systems to access. These include medical, financial, educational, employment, and legal programs; assistance with retirement or transition to civilian life; individual and family counseling; and information about benefits to which they are entitled.

Heroes to Hometowns

The American Legion—a nonprofit veterans' mutual help organization—sponsors Heroes to Hometowns (H2H), the only nationwide transition-assistance program for severely wounded veterans injured in the Global War on Terror (The American Legion, 2010). The focus of H2H is to provide prompt and easily accessed services and benefits to service members who cannot remain in the military because of their injuries. In order to facilitate services and avoid duplicating services, H2H has established networks at the national, state, and local community levels that can coordinate government and civilian resources. The H2H program offers a support network and coordinated resources for individual service members and their families.

The H2H helps transitional service members and their families deal with every aspect of leaving the military service. Services range from psychological support to practical assistance and can include such services as help with paying bills, adapting vehicles and homes to accommodate physical limitations, transportation to medical care, and a referral to the U.S. Paralympics Military Division (a division of the U.S. Olympic Committee that promotes an international sporting event for athletes with physical disabilities every 4 years).

Homes for Our Troops

Homes for Our Troops is a national nonprofit organization founded in 2004 to provide homes for service members who have come home from combat deployments since September 11, 2001, with serious disabilities and injuries (Homes for Our Troops, 2009). Homes for Our Troops raises money, building materials, and professional labor through donations. They also coordinate the building of homes that provide disabled service members with greater independence and the maximum freedom of movement allowed by their injuries. Homes for Our Troops works with the VA to ensure that the homes are provided at no cost to all veterans, including military members still serving. Veterans and service members who are eligible can receive a grant from the VA for specially adapted housing. If the grant is insufficient for the building of a home for the veteran's needs, Homes for Our Troops will cover all costs not covered by the grant.

Intrepid Fallen Heroes Fund and National Intrepid Center of Excellence

In June 2010, the Intrepid Fallen Heroes Fund opened the new, state-of-the-art National Intrepid Center of Excellence (NICoE) as a research, diagnosis, and treatment center for service members and veterans with TBI and psychological health conditions (Defense Centers of Excellence [DCoE], 2010c). The NICoE is located on a Navy installation in Bethesda, Maryland, next to the new Walter Reed National Military Medical Center. It has close access to the Uniformed Services University, the National Institutes of Health, and the Veterans Health Administration.

The Intrepid Fallen Heroes Fund was originally established in 2000 to provide financial support for family members of military personnel killed in the line of duty (Intrepid Fallen Heroes Fund, 2010). It receives its funds through fundraising and contributions. After September 11, 2001, and the beginning of the war on terrorism, the fund was expanded to help meet the growing numbers of families with financial hardships as a result of losing their military family member. In 2003, the fund officially became an independent nonprofit organization and continued to provide monetary gifts to military families needing financial assistance. In 2005, the U.S. government substantially increased the benefits to families who lost a loved due to military duty, and the fund turned its efforts to helping service members who have been critically injured in the performance of their duty.

The NICoE is equipped with the most advanced diagnosis and treatment equipment and facilities (Intrepid Sea, Air & Space Museum, 2008). It will share state-of-the-art screening, diagnosis, and treatment methods with the military and VA hospitals and with medical facilities throughout the United States. Long-term follow-up care will be part of each client's care plan, ensuring that when service members separate from the military, they continue to receive the treatment they need. The NICoE is also colocated with two 21-room Fisher Houses to accommodate the families of service members and veterans receiving services at the NICoE (Fisher Houses provide accommodations to families of military patients at no charge, similar to civilian Ronald McDonald Houses, which provide a temporary home for families with a hospitalized child).

PROGRAMS THAT REFLECT A NEW VIEW OF PSYCHOLOGICAL HEALTH

Traditionally, the U.S. Armed Forces trained its troops by focusing on physical strength and endurance along with skill development. This physical and job-skill training, along with a strong spiritual belief, were seen as the attributes that would keep service men and women strong in combat and while carrying out other military operations. In recent years, however, the DoD has begun to develop a new attitude about the importance of psychological health as part of military fitness and readiness. It now uses a comprehensive mind–body–spirit model of strength and fitness. This new incorporation of psychological health in the DoD and its focus on the holistic—psychological, physical, social, and spiritual—health of military members and their families is the basis of the following programs:

Defense Centers of Excellence for Psychological Health and Traumatic Brain Injury

The DCoE for Psychological Health and Traumatic Brain Injury was created in 2007 to address the needs of the growing numbers of service members and families who are challenged with psychological health issues and TBI (DCoE, 2010a). The DCoE develops standards for preventing, identifying, and treating psychological health and TBI in the U.S. military forces. The DCoE works closely with the DoD medical and research communities and senior leaders, the Department of Veterans Affairs, civilian and military clinical experts and researchers, and academic institutions. The DCoE takes the best practice models from this collaborative network and helps service members and families deal with psychological health and TBI issues through the most advanced treatment methods, education, and outreach programs. It also evaluates and monitors programs that prevent, identify, and treat psychological health and TBI.

The DCoE also works to reduce the stigma that prevents many service members and families from getting treatment for psychological health (DCoE 2010a). Through its Real Warriors Campaign, the DCoE promotes resilience, recovery, and the reintegration of returning service members and their families. The campaign includes printed educational materials, an interactive Internet site, and media outreach featuring stories of real service members who have successfully been treated for psychological health issues.

Post-Deployment Health Reassessment

Every service member who deploys is given a health screening before and after every deployment. Any health issues identified at that time are then further assessed and treated. However, because many service members do not want any identified problems or treatment to delay their deployment or their return home after the deployment, the DoD developed an additional screening —the Post-Deployment Health Reassessment (PDHRA)—which is administered 90–180 days after returning from deployment (Force Health Protection & Readiness Policy & Programs, 2007).

The first priority for many service members after deployment is to get home to their families and to return to a more normal life. It is common and normal for them to think that their health and emotions will return to what is normal for them after they have spend some time in a more stable, home environment. But many deployment-related health and psychological problems may not be apparent until 3–6 months after a deployment, when service members have had time to readjust and recognize how deployment affected their health and emotional well-being (Force Health Protection & Readiness Policy & Programs, 2007). The goal of the PDHRA is to identify and begin treating any health and emotional issues before they become chronic problems. Psychological issues are especially critical to identify and treat early; therefore, the PDHRA includes specific questions on emotional well-being and on any traumatic experiences that might have occurred during the deployment.

It is every commander's responsibility to ensure that all service members, active duty and reserve, complete the PDHRA (Force Health Protection & Readiness Policy & Programs, 2007). The assessment includes a medical screening questionnaire, education, and follow-up health assessment and treatment for any identified health and psychological health issues. After completing the questionnaire, service members speak with a healthcare provider individually to review their responses. Together the service member and the healthcare provider determine if follow-up evaluation and treatment are necessary. Often, a mental health provider is available at the screening site as well. Depending on how the process is set up, every service member might be screened by a mental health provider or this might take place only for service members with a psychological health concern.

Since families often worry that deployments affect their loved one's health, completing the PDHRA can reduce their concern by assuring them that any health concerns the service member might have will be addressed. To ensure that this occurs, family members can encourage their loved one to disclose any emotional or physical problems they are having.

Resilience Training

The Army's Resilience Training program—also called "Battlemind Training," the original name for the program—is the Army's mental health resilience training system (U.S. Army Medical Department, 2010b). As you learned in Chapter 5, resilience is the ability to cope with and recover quickly and effectively from difficult experiences or situations. The Army's resiliency program stems from a new attitude about the importance of psychological health as part of a comprehensive mind–body–spirit view of strength and fitness. Resilience Training supports the new DoD focus on the physical, spiritual, emotional, family, and social health of military members and their families by encouraging self-awareness, a strong mind, and psychological well-being. The program is comprised of an integrated series of modules specifically designed to correspond with the potential stressors that service members and their families might encounter at various points in their lives and military careers.

The Army's Resilience Training program provides education about psychological health and self-awareness presentations and discussions to soldiers and their family members throughout their careers (beginning with entry-level training, during continuing military education, and at other key points during their careers) and throughout the deployment cycle (before, during, and after deployments). The training provides a developmental approach to mental health skill building timed to the specific phases of a solider's career and deployment cycle. The program also provides specific resiliency training to leaders and medical and psychological healthcare providers so that they can encourage resiliency and identify soldiers and family members who may need additional assistance to deal with difficult issues in their lives.

Training for soldiers is intended to help soldiers recognize evidence of stress in themselves and in their fellow soldiers, develop healthy ways to reduce the effects of stress, deal with hardship effectively, reduce stigma about seeking help for psychological issues, and increase their ability to face the psychological impact of combat and other military operations (U.S. Army Medical Department, 2010b). The U.S. Army's Mental Health Advisory Team (MHAT) (MHAT V, 2008) found that soldiers who received resiliency training prior to deploying reported fewer mental health problems than those who did not. Training for family members is available for spouses, children, siblings, and parents of soldiers. Family resilience training addresses how to deal with family issues that are common during a deployment—such as coping personally, helping children cope, staying connected, and normal reactions that can occur during separation and reunion.

RESPECT-Mil

In an effort to reduce stigma-related barriers to seeking psychological health care in the military, the DoD Deployment Health Clinical Center designed RESPECT-Mil. RESPECT-Mil stands for Re-Engineering Systems of Primary Care Treatment in the Military; however, it is known simply as RESPECT-Mil (Deployment Health Clinical Center, 2010b). It is a program based in the military health-care system that takes advantage of the fact that service members are seen frequently by general practice or family physicians. Often, psychological health concerns are first discussed by service members in health-care clinics, where they are less afraid of stigma and where physical complaints seen often have a psychological component. RESPECT-Mil teaches these physicians and other medical staff members who support the program to screen, assess, and treat active duty soldiers with PTSD and depression.

The program encourages routine and consistent screening for these psychological problems through the use of questionnaires that are filled out by the soldier and assessment tools that are filled out by the health-care provider (Deployment Health Clinical Center, 2010b). These screening tools help to identify when a soldier may be suffering from depression or PTSD. Soldiers who have symptoms of depression or PTSD are also screened to determine if they are at risk for suicide. Other elements of the program include educating patients about depression/PTSD and treatment options and encouraging patients to be more involved in their care. Treatment could include medication, counseling with a RESPECT-Mil psychological health-care provider, or a combination of the two.

The U.S. Army Medical Command has implemented RESPECT-Mil—for active duty soldiers or National Guard and Reserve soldiers while they are on active duty status—in many of the Army's primary care facilities. A study of the program (Engel et al., 2008) concluded that RESPECT-Mil is a feasible program that is safe and accepted by military health practitioners and patients and that the psychological health of participants often improved. The DoD is planning to implement the program for the other branches of the military as well.

Military Family Life Consultants

In 2004, the DoD established the MFLC program to provide short-term, situational, problem-solving counseling services for issues that do not require more extensive psychological health care (Managed Health Network Government Services, 2010b). MFLC counselors are masters or PhD level, licensed, and credentialed counselors, usually psychologists, social workers, or other mental health professionals. They provide up to 12 sessions of counseling per person, per issue for issues such as anger management, stress and coping skills, parenting, communication, couple and family relationships, deployment, separation and reunion, loss and grief, work-related issues, and other military-life-related topics. The MFLCs can provide crisis intervention and can help identify appropriate resources and services for issues requiring psychological health services through the military health-care system. They can also provide group psycho-educational presentations on deployment, mobilization (for Reserve Component units or individuals being called to active duty), communication, stress management, and grief and loss to units and family member groups.

The MFLC program is a good option for service members and their families who are uncomfortable going to their medical treatment facilities for counseling services, since MFLCs provide confidential services, unless there is any indication of child or domestic abuse or threat of harm to self or others. Since MFLC counselors can travel to remote and distant locations to provide services to military families, this program is also extremely important for Reserve and National Guard families who often live hundreds of miles from a military installation. The MFLC program is available to all military services within the continental United States, Alaska, Hawaii, Europe, and the Pacific.

Military Pathways®

Military Pathways®—formerly called the Mental Health Self-Assessment Program—is a DoD mental health and alcohol screening program for service members and military families (Deployment Health Clinical Center, 2010a). Individuals can complete a screening questionnaire anonymously online, by phone, or in person at education and awareness events held on military installations and at National Guard and Reserve units. Separate screening questionnaires are available for depression, alcohol use, anxiety, PTSD, and **bipolar disorder** (characterized by mood swings that range from depression to feeling euphoric and energetic). Results are provided at the completion of the assessment, with a list of resources and respective contact information.

SUMMARY

- The DoD understands that the needs of military families change constantly and is committed to continuing to meet the changing demands of military life caused by the increase in the past decade in deployments to war zones and in other military operations.
- Many civilian agencies are also concerned about long periods of additional stress on military families due to the increase in military missions.
- DoD and civilian organizations working in conjunction with the DoD have developed new programs to address the needs of military families.
- Programs and organizations that were recently developed to assist military members and their families reintegrate and reunite include Operation Healthy Reunions and the Post-9/11 GI Bill.
- The DoD Yellow Ribbon Reintegration, ESGR, the IFS, and the JFSAP are new policies and programs designed to support National Guard and Reserve members and their families.
- Programs designed to provide care for military members who have been injured and to help their families include Wounded Warrior Programs, H2H, Homes for Our Troops, the Intrepid Fallen Heroes Fund, and the NICoE.

- The DoD now uses a comprehensive mind–body–spirit model of strength and fitness and is encouraging a new attitude about the importance of psychological health as part of military fitness and readiness.
- DCoE for Psychological Health and Traumatic Brain Injury, Post-Deployment Health Reassessment, Resilience Training, RESPECT-Mil, Military Family Life Consultants, and Military Pathways® are programs that provide military members and their families with alternative methods to learn about psychological health needs and to obtain assistance when they need it.

EXERCISES

To further explore the types of new and recent programs available to military families, answer the following questions:

1. How important is it that the DoD and other organizations continue to develop new programs for military members and their families? Why?
2. Why do you think it would be particularly difficult for service members and their families to seek help with psychological problems? Can you think of any time in your life when you could have used help dealing with an emotional or psychological problem? Did you seek help? Why or why not?
3. To which programs described in this chapter would you refer a military family member for each of the following problems or issues? (Some issues may be addressed by more than one program.)
   a. A child who is having problems adjusting to the deployment of a parent.
   b. A military member and his or her spouse who are having problems understanding each other since he or she returned from combat.
   c. A teenage family member whose father or mother is deployed is having problems relating to his or her peers.
   d. Parents of an active duty service member who returned from deployment are worried about their son's angry outbursts and withdrawn behavior.
4. What programs that could assist wounded warriors transition to civilian life are available in your community?
5. What are the benefits of online services and programs for military families? In what situations would military families want assistance beyond what is available online?

12

Supporting Military Families
Applying Theory and Research to Practice

In Chapter 12, you will

- Meet Kathleen Marin, Director of Installation Services, U.S. Army Office of the Assistant Chief of Staff for Installation Management, and Dee Geise, Chief, Soldier & Family Readiness, U.S. Army Office of the Assistant Chief of Staff for Installation Management
- Gain insights into how the military is using a focus on resilience to guide prevention and treatment of combat and operational stress in service members and families
- Consider principles of care to use when working with injured service members and their families
- Review treatment approaches to TBI and PTSD
- Learn about supporting military families who are engaged in caregiving or are grieving the death of their service member

Meet

Kathleen Marin, Director of Installation Services, U.S. Army Office of the Assistant Chief of Staff for Installation Management, and Dee Geise, Chief, Soldier & Family Readiness, U.S. Army Office of the Assistant Chief of Staff for Installation Management

Ms. Geise begins: *Prior to 9/11, we had done a lot of work with family support providing programs to help address needs of soldiers and their families such as providing child care and assistance with handling finances. It wasn't always that way. The Wickham white paper, "The Army Family," published in 1983 by Army Chief of Staff General John A. Wickham Jr., changed how the Army provided for soldiers and their families. "The Army Family" recognized the integral support role of soldiers' families and the initiative marked the first systemic effort to design programs and policies comprehensive enough to address Army family concerns as a whole.*

The last 10 years with multiple deployments has been a game changer. A service member may be unmarried on a first deployment, married on the second, and a parent by the third. Families are experiencing stresses we never imagined, and these stresses reverberate within a family, affecting everyone.

In 2007, General Casey (36th Chief of Staff of the Army) and Mrs. Casey went out to talk with and, most importantly, listen to families. The Caseys found that service members and families felt they were being left to handle extraordinary demands on their own. We were not focusing on the important things like what happens when a service member returns home.

The Army Family Covenant signed by General Casey in 2007 recognizes the link between readiness and the well-being of families and a new level of commitment from Army leaders to families. It was saying to families, "The Army is behind you."

Ms. Marin continues: *Today we have a more holistic view of family support and building resilience. We want to go beyond just reacting and helping families when they are hurting to help them not hurt as much when bad things happen. We want to help build on the strengths they develop in the military and mitigate experiences of combat.*

The composite life cycle model has pinpointed stress points so that we can all see and talk about them. The resiliency continuum shows how resilience is built in the individual, family, and society. It is a visual representation of a spectrum of care that says everyone has a responsibility for promoting resilience. These research-based models are helpful at both a content and conceptual level.

We can deconstruct them to be sure we are providing needed services. For example, we can develop a memorandum of agreement (MOA) so that a child of a military family entering her senior year in a new high school doesn't have to take a course in the history of that state to graduate when she already did so in the state where she used to live.

The models add to our understanding of stress and resilience. They are wonderful training tools and have led us to develop our Comprehensive Soldier Fitness and Family Members Program. This path of lifelong learning begins by providing individuals a chance to assess their strengths and weaknesses in four dimensions: emotional, social, spiritual, and family. It then links them to tailored self-development training around thinking skills and coping strategies. They can track their growth over time to enhance performance and build resilience skills.

They can work at a holistic level allowing everyone to see how they can contribute to creating a culture of resiliency. Service providers can see themselves as part of the bigger effort to build resiliency as they realize that any and every contact with a family can make a difference. Think, for example, about clerks at the lending closet who give out pots and pans to new families on an installation. If clerks are schooled as to stress points and ways to promote resilience, they might take an extra minute to smile or ask an open-ended question that could lead a family member to a resource on the base and help them feel welcome.

INTRODUCTION

This chapter explores recent innovations in promoting a culture of resilience within the military and families; provides direction for working with those who have experienced traumatic events and injuries, such as TBI and PTSD, and their families; and gives information pertaining to families who have experienced the death of their service member. The overarching theme to this chapter is the application of what has been learned about the process of resilience and the responsibility of individuals, families, military units, and military and civilian health care and social services to build and sustain a culture that recognizes the centrality of psychological health and supports resilience-related practices that are family-focused.

INNOVATIONS IN RESILIENCE MODELS

As Kathleen Marin and Dee Geise emphasized earlier, the military is moving beyond a medical treatment model to prevention by enhancing psychosocial strengths of service members and their families (Casey, 2011). Such an approach recognizes the strengths of individuals and families while also acknowledging the challenges of the military life. The Stress Continuum, the Comprehensive Soldier Fitness (CSF) program, and the Composite Life Cycle Model direct attention to early signs of stress reactions, emphasize ways to recognize and respond to stress in order build and nurture resilience, and acknowledge the possibility of a pileup of stressors in the lives of service members and their families. As a result, the models offer guidance about the timing of support services and programs to those who work with military families.

Stress Reactions and the Stress Continuum

Combat operational stress reactions refer to the physical, cognitive, emotional, and/or behavioral stress symptoms as a result of combat or as a result of other operations such as humanitarian assistance missions or peace support operations (Moore & Reger, 2007). Individuals may experience stress reactions because of a life threat (experiencing an event or events that provoke horror, terror, helplessness), wear and tear (result of accumulated stress, the daily grind of a job, or unpredictable events that do not provide time to adjust), loss (grieving loss of people, relationships, dreams), and inner conflict (doing something inconsistent with personal moral code, loss of faith in leaders, guilt about what one did or did not do to try to change a bad circumstance or event). (Nash, Westphal, Watson, & Litz, 2011). Stress reactions are common in humans, whether military or civilian. For example, imagine seeing a car accident, losing a close friend or family member, or carrying a full load of college courses while working full time. Exposure to these stressors is likely to result in stress reactions. While reactions may be experienced for just a few hours or days, or persist for weeks, months, or longer, they do not disrupt functioning. However, while also beginning with exposure to one or more stressors, a stress injury does disrupt functioning; and the more stressors experienced, the greater the risk of a stress injury. Stress injuries include traumatic, fatigue, grief, and moral injuries (Nash et al., 2011).

Combat Operational Stress Control (COSC) is a **core concept** (a principle that guides military leaders as they develop regulations and policies and that sets standards and expectations that leaders are to support) initiated by DoD for implementation by each of the services and coordinated by the DCoE for Psychological Health and Traumatic Brain Injury. According to the Army's *COSC Field Manual,* "the word control is used with combat and operational stress, rather than the word management, to emphasize the active steps that leaders, supporting BH [Behavioral Health] personnel, and individual Soldiers must take to keep stress within an acceptable range" (Headquarters, Department of the Army, 2006, p. 1-1).

COSC policies and programs emphasize enhancing resilience and performance through prevention and early interventions with individuals and families who experience psychological injury. COSC policies guide leaders' responses to and treatment of injuries and illnesses that are often called "invisible" when compared to "visible" physical injuries and illness (Nash et al., 2011).

In the past decade, each branch of the service has developed models and programs to improve, protect, and conserve the emotional health and resilience of their service members in order for them to perform their mission (Vythilingam, 2010). Toward the goal of early intervention, services are training their members to recognize the signs and symptoms of impaired psychological health that are often visible in behaviors, cognitive functioning, and affect; learn that seeking help for such an injury is as wise as seeking help for a physical wound; and know how to seek help for themselves, a buddy, or someone in their command when signs and symptoms are present. To augment the efforts at command levels to reduce the stigma of seeking help for combat and operational stress reactions and injury, the Real Warriors Campaign, launched in 2009 by the DCoE for Psychological Health and Traumatic Brain Injury, provides educational information about and video examples of service members seeking care for psychological health issues and continuing successful military and civilian careers.

The Navy and Marine Corps developed the Stress Continuum, an evidence-based model, for their COSC doctrine. The model was then adopted by DCoE for Psychological Health and Traumatic Brain Injury (n.d.) and other services. The Stress Continuum replaces a medical-illness model in which a service member was considered either ready for duty and not, that is, considered "a go" or a "no go" (Bureau of Medicine & Surgery and Deployment Health Directorate, 2008). Table 12.1 is an adapted an adapted version of the Stress Continuum that includes examples of indicators of stress reactions, injury, and illness for individuals and families (Department of the Navy, 2010; U.S. Marine Corps, n.d.-a; Westphal & Woodward, 2010).

In the prior medical-illness culture, a service member not ready for duty was turned over to medical caregivers for "fixing" and turned back to the unit when command leadership would again take

TABLE 12.1 An Adapted Version of the Stress Continuum

Ready	Reacting	Injured	Ill
Individuals	Individuals	Individuals	Individuals
• Optimal performance • Prepared for deployment • Functioning well emotionally, socially, academically, vocationally • Optimistic outlook	• Feeling overwhelmed • Irritable, anxious • Mild or temporary distress or impairment • Sleep disturbances • Problems with concentration	• Guilt, anxiety • Decreased energy • Social isolation • Panic attacks • Addictive behaviors	• Severe stress injuries impacting daily life • Anger, rage • Depression, anxiety, addictive disorders, PTSD • Danger to self/others
Families	Families	Families	Families
• Communicate productively • Children secure, well-adjusted • Positive routines • Emotionally close	• Communication difficulties • Children insecure, acting out • Loss of routines • Reduced emotional closeness	• Silence/fighting • Behavioral problems • Chaotic • Loss of emotional closeness • Verbal/physical abuse	• Persistent problems • Trouble functioning

Self-help useful ⬅━━━━➡ *Professional help needed*

Source: Adapted from Department of the Navy. (2010). *Combat and operational stress control (NTTP 1-15M, MCRP 6-11C).* Washington, DC: Author.; U.S. Marine Corps (n.d.-a). *Combat operational stress continuum for families.* Retrieved from http://www.usmc-mccs.org/cosc/coscContMatrixFamily.cfm?sid=ml&smid=6&ssmid=2.

over responsibility. Reflecting a major change in approach, the Stress Continuum describes indicators of psychological health for individuals, families, and commands and refocuses responsibility for promoting psychosocial health on everyone in the system. Therefore, the common goal becomes building a culture that promotes resilience for service members and for families (Westphal & Woodward, 2010).

Recognized in the continuum is the knowledge that stress and trauma may be so overwhelming that individuals, families, or units experience stress reactions, injury, and illness. Prevention of stress reactions occurs through training and education of service members, noncommissioned and commissioned officers, and families about developing and maintaining resilience, including seeking help early when experiencing stress responses as a means to prevent injury and illness. For service members who are injured or ill, treatment is assumed to lead to reintegration with their units. The goal of reintegration is for service members to incorporate their traumatic experiences to establish a productive "new normal" in which they attain or exceed pretrauma levels of functioning (DCoE, 2010b).

The Department of the Navy Stress Continuum information includes guidance about actions individuals and families can take to maintain or regain adaptive coping and positive functioning while stress is present. The Continuum includes a "decision matrix" for determining when to intervene and what to do (U.S. Marine Corps, n.d.-a). Such information educates individuals and families about what signs warrant concern and intervention both for themselves and for others. Applying this guidance, individuals and families are considered "ready" when they are taking good care of themselves, engaging in productive family processes (e.g., clear communication about a stressor, productive conflict resolution, stressors seen as meaningful challenges), and using appropriate community and social resources (e.g., using the free YMCA membership available to families experiencing deployment in order to exercise when feeling tense, seeking out other military families for social and emotional support). The ongoing goal is to continue these positive coping strategies regardless of stressors.

An important expectation in the Stress Continuum model is the responsibility of family, friends, and colleagues and leaders in the the military community for promoting and supporting positive coping and for intervening early. When an individual shows initial signs of distress (e.g., sleep disturbances, excessive worry, or anger), family, friends, or colleagues and supervisors at work can encourage the person under stress to engage in healthy behaviors (e.g., adequate sleep, good nutrition, exercise), obtain social support, and seek assistance if distress worsens. Of course, individuals and families can also identify that they need to begin or return to these positive coping strategies. If distress worsens and individuals have loss of functioning (e.g., isolation, outbursts, panic attacks) or a family experiences major disruptions in communication or verbal or physical abuse, families, friends, and others are to provide social support, remain calm, and encourage the person to seek help. If distress or diminished functioning persists (e.g. problems persist and worsen, the person becomes suicidal, they are to obtain medical help for the person, support resulting treatment, and provide social support (COSC, 2007). Coping effectively with challenges includes being aware of one's own stress reactions and personal stressors and using strategies, including seeking assistance, that promote and maintain physical, psychological, social (e.g., family relationships, friendships, work relationships), and spiritual health (Nash et al., 2011; Westphal & Woodward, 2010). In doing so, an individual or family is more likely to be resilient, that is, adapt successfully to exposure to an adverse or traumatic circumstance (MacDermid et al., 2008).

The Army's CSF Program

Comprehensive Soldier Fitness is a strength-based program rooted in positive psychology and designed to enhance soldier, family, and civilian worker resilience and performance. It combines a confidential personal assessment, online training, and unit training (Casey, 2011; Cornum, Matthews, & Seligman, 2011). Individuals assess themselves periodically in four psychosocial domains by taking the Global Assessment Tool (GAT), an online and confidential self-report questionnaire. The results of the GAT in turn direct individuals to relevant training tailored to their individual profile of strengths and assets. The four psychosocial dimensions of fitness are social (e.g, trust in others, feeling respected and valued), emotional (e.g., positive mood, life satisfaction, optimism, active coping style), spiritual (e.g., sustaining beliefs and values), and family (e.g., close relationships, safe and loving home life) (Peterson, Park, & Castro, 2011). In addition to the GAT and tailored training, master resilience trainers conduct unit-level trainings in these psychosocial areas (Reivich, Seligman, & McBride, 2011). Family members can take the GAT and access resilience materials for managing deployment and reintegration by going to the CSF website (http://csf.army.mil).

The Army's Composite Life Cycle Model

The Army's **Composite Life Cycle Model** illustrates how events and transitions in three areas of a soldier's life (i.e., unit, personal work, and family) can pile up across time and areas, potentially overwhelming a service member. The model is part of the Army's Health Promotion and Risk Reduction Campaign (U.S. Army, 2010). A greatly simplified rendition of this model is shown in Figure 12.1.

The stressors associated with the unit level in Figure 12.1 are predeployment, deployment, and reintegration home. Personal work stressors shown include basic and initial training, transitioning to duty assignments (which probably include relocating to another state or overseas), testing for promotion, being promoting, experiencing a death of another soldier, and injury. Stressors that may occur within family life include marriages, birth of a child, financial challenges, relationship difficulties, birth of a second child, divorce, remarriage, co-parenting challenges, and parental illness. Such a visual rendition the ongoing transitions faced by soldiers and their families emphasizes the importance of readiness in each life cycle strand and the targeting of preventive interventions (e.g., predeployment programs, parenting education, financial literacy skills) at unit, service member, and family transition points (U.S. Army, 2010).

Resilience Building for Military Families

As noted earlier, resilience building for military families includes a focus on preventing distress or loss of positive functioning and a focus on providing resources and additional support if family members

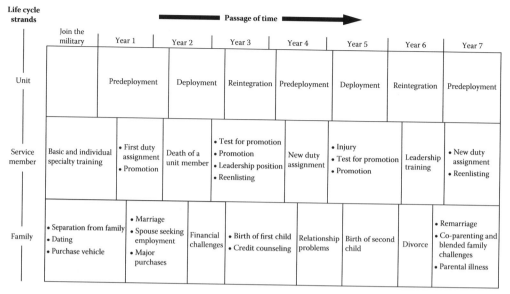

Figure 12.1 Simplified composite life cycle model. (Adapted from U.S. Army (2010). *Health promotion, risk reduction and suicide prevention report 2010*. Retrieved from http://www.army.mil/-news/2010/07/28/42934-army-health-promotion-risk-reduction-and-suicide-prevention-report/index.html.)

experience distress, or severe or persistent distress or loss of functioning (Westphal & Woodward, 2010). Chapter 9 describes established military family programs, and Chapter 11 provides examples of recent resilience programming geared toward families. Resilience programming may be targeted toward all military families (i.e., **universal preventive interventions**), toward those who may be at higher risk for developing distress or loss of functioning (i.e., **selected preventive intervention**), or toward individuals who are exhibiting early signs of distress or loss of functioning (i.e., **indicated preventive interventions**) (Mrazek & Haggerty, 1994).

Predeployment programs and reintegration programs following return from deployment are examples of universal preventive interventions because almost all military families will experience a deployment. Predeployment programming for families of individual augmentees might be considered selected prevention intervention because these families experience separation from the service member when other families in the same unit do not and thus may be expected to experience greater stress. Many family programs (e.g., New Parent Support Program, FOCUS, Strong Bonds, Yellow Ribbon Reintegration events, financial readiness workshops) and services (e.g., child care, DoD schools, transition assistance program, spouse employment) reviewed in other chapters may be considered universal, selected, and indicated preventive interventions because they can simultaneously serve families experiencing no, some, or a great deal of stress. If distress is too great or functioning too impaired, indicated preventive interventions such as family therapy, substance abuse counseling, or family advocacy may be needed.

The DoD Report to Congressional Defense Committees (DoD, 2010n) includes a complete list of military family readiness programs and activities currently provided by the DoD and the Departments of the Army, Navy, Marine Corps, and Air Force. This report also outlines action plans for the next 5 years to reduce overlaps in programs; link them to readiness, recruitment, and retention; evaluate current and recommended programs; improve program marketing, particularly for the Reserve Component; further develop behavioral health to improve access, education, and availability; develop a Family Readiness Clearinghouse for families, service providers, and communities (described in Chapter 10); expand child care capacity for those distant from a military installation; build partnerships with educational institutions and community organizations; and build the capacity of communities to support military families.

DIRECTION FOR PROVIDING CARE

Clinical practice guidelines are tools to inform practitioners' decision making when working with a client or patient who is experiencing physical or psychological health problems. Evidence-based practice guidelines on postdeployment health, mild traumatic brain injury (mTBI), and mental health issues (e.g., depression, substance use) are found at a VA/DoD website (http://www.healthquality.va.gov/index.asp). Treatment options for PTSD and TBI can also be accessed at http://www.dcoe.health.mil/ForHealthPros.aspx.

Recommendations in the practice guidelines are based on a critical review of epidemiological, diagnostic, prognostic, and treatment studies. The strength of the recommendation is indicated based on the quality and consistency of the evidence. When ambiguous or conflicting evidence or scientific data are lacking, recommendations are based on clinical experience and do not indicate the strength of recommendation (The Management of Concussion/mTBI Working Group, 2009).

This section begins with a model for helping others immediately following a traumatic event. Then treatment information for service members with a TBI or PTSD and their family members is addressed. This section ends with a discussion on caregiving.

Psychological First Aid

Psychological First Aid (PFA) is a way of helping children, adolescents, adults, and families immediately following a traumatic event to "reduce distress, assist with current needs, and promote adaptive functioning, not to elicit details of traumatic experiences and losses" (Brymer et al., 2006, p. 8). This model does not assume that experiencing a traumatic event will automatically result in mental health problems or persistent difficulties. Rather, it assumes that persons will exhibit a range of early behavioral, physical, psychological, and spiritual reactions. Some of these reactions may interfere with effective coping; PFA may help survivors positively manage distress and assist in recovery.

PFA is based on five evidence-informed intervention principles recommended by an international panel of experts who study and treat those exposed to disaster and mass violence studies (Hobfoll et al., 2007). These principles are offered to guide and inform prevention and early to mid-term intervention efforts following traumatic events. These principles are to promote: "1) a sense of safety, 2) calming, 3) a sense of self- and community efficacy, 4) connectedness, and 5) hope" (Hobfoll et al., 2007, p. 284). From these five principles emerge the core PFA actions that trained PFA workers perform; these actions are listed in Box 12.1.

Panel members included representatives of the American Red Cross, the National Center for Posttraumatic Stress Disorder, the National Child Traumatic Stress Network, and the Center for the Study of Traumatic Stress, and other organizations. Many organizations have incorporated these principles into their programs and publications (Benedek & Fullerton, 2007). PFA is used in many settings by a variety of helping professionals, including first responders, emergency health-care workers, school crisis response teams, and those who work in disaster relief organizations (Brymer et al., 2006). Just as we can learn and apply basic first aid procedures in response to physical trauma (e.g., CPR, techniques to stop bleeding, insure optimal body temperature, prevent infection), we can learn to apply first aid procedures after psychological trauma. Learning basic *physical* first aid means we can try to stop blood loss while we wait for an ambulance or to clean and apply antibacterial medication to a cut rather than making a doctor's appointment. Likewise, tools to promote *psychological* wellness can be applied immediately after experiencing a highly stressful situation or a traumatic event. Just as nonmedical personnel may administer first aid for a physical trauma, PFA is designed to be administered by non–mental healthcare professionals who have received appropriate training in order to protect and promote psychological health and well-being (Brymer et al., 2006).

Military and civilian mental health and family support professionals, chaplains, and medical personnel also are using PFA when responding to the psychosocial needs of others who have

BOX 12.1 BEST PRACTICES

CORE ACTIONS OF PSYCHOLOGICAL FIRST AID

- Contact and Engagement: To respond to contacts initiated by survivors, or to initiate contacts in a nonintrusive, compassionate, and helpful manner.
- Safety and Comfort: To enhance immediate and ongoing safety, and provide physical and emotional comfort.
- Stabilization: To calm and orient emotionally overwhelmed or disoriented survivors.
- Information Gathering: To identify immediate needs and concerns, gather additional information, and tailor Psychological First Aid interventions.
- Practical Assistance: To offer practical help to survivors in addressing immediate needs and concerns.
- Connection with Social Supports: To help establish brief or ongoing contacts with primary support persons and other sources of support, including family members, friends, and community helping resources.
- Information on Coping: To provide information about stress reactions and coping to reduce distress and promote adaptive functioning.
- Linkage with Collaborative Services: To link survivors with available services needed at the time or in the future.

Source: Information compiled from Brymer, M., Jacobs, A., Layne, C., Pynoos, R., Ruzek J., Steinberg, A., … Watson, P. (2006). *Psychological first aid: Field operations guide* (2nd ed., p. 19). National Child Traumatic Stress Network and National Center for PTSD. Retrieved from http://www.ptsd.va.gov/professional/manuals/psych-first-aid.asp. With permission.

experienced a traumatic event. Using PFA procedures, the Navy and Marine Corps implemented Combat and Operational Stress First Aid (COSFA) to guide early interventions with individuals who have experienced a traumatic event; it is expected to be adapted for use with Navy and Marine Corps families (Nash et al., 2011).

Civilians may obtain training in PFA from state organizations (e.g., department of human services) and local chapters of the American Red Cross (which also has training specifically on coping with deployments). Prior to seeking training in PFA, consider your comfort level with working with highly distressed individuals in a variety of settings and unpredictable settings, being assigned non–mental health-related tasks (e.g., serving meals, cleaning the floor), collaborating with professionals from diverse fields, and providing support to individuals with diverse backgrounds (e.g., ethnicity, culture, religion, developmental levels). Also consider whether your health and responsibilities at work and with family allow you to be away should you decide to volunteer or work with an agency that sends PFA workers to disaster areas for a period of time (Brymer et al., 2006).

Traumatic Brain Injury

The optimal treatment of TBI requires tailored coordination of care for the unique needs of each service member or veteran (Jafee et al., 2009). Service members with TBI may receive care in a variety of health-care settings, in particular if they are eventually discharged from the military. Throughout their treatment they receive care at military treatment facilities, the VA, and civilian health-care systems. TBI, particularly moderate and severe TBI, affects cognitive abilities such as understanding and negotiating complex situations, language comprehension, memory, concentration, and judgment. These cognitive effects may translate into missing appointments, failure to take medications, and an inability to drive or take public transportation. TBI can also result in negative behavioral symptoms such as aggression, outbursts, irritability, and disinhibition resulting in confusion, discomfort, or fear in others, including treatment providers unfamiliar with TBI (Jafee et al., 2009).

Persons with TBI may be unable to live independently. Consequently, family members become caregivers, advocates, and managers to insure service members and veterans with TBI receive the care they need. In Box 12.2 a caregiver shares what she has learned as she takes this unexpected and unwanted path. The vital role played by family members in treatment was acknowledged by the Management of Concussion/mTBI Working Group (2009) that noted "early education of patients and their families is the best available treatment for concussion/mTBI and for preventing/reducing the development of persistent symptoms" (p. vi).

During treatment and recovery, doctors, nurses, and other professionals look to the caregiver for feedback on how the service member is progressing as injuries can differ from person to person and so treatment effects can differ. Ideally, care is family-centered; that is, the service member, family, and medical personnel work as a team.

BOX 12.2   TIPS FROM THE FRONTLINE

A CAREGIVER'S REFLECTIONS

On July 8th of 2010, my husband of 32½ years fell 8 feet down a trap door, landing on a concrete floor. He sustained serious head injuries and was in a coma for 4 weeks. Although his TBI was not from military combat, he is retired from the U.S. Air Force, so the VA figures prominently in his rehabilitation. Here's what I am learning as a caregiver that might be useful to pass on to others:

- *Ask questions.* Ask all medical and rehabilitation staff until you receive the information you seek. No questions are stupid because your life has been altered forever.
- *Use resources.* Search for others who have experienced what you have. For a few weeks I avoided the Internet, terrified of what I'd find. But knowledge is power, so ask medical staff for recommendations. Useful sites: the Defense and Veterans Brain Injury Center at http://www.dvbic.org, the Centers for Disease Control and Prevention at http://www.cdc.gov/TraumaticBrainInjury/index.html, an initiative from the Office of the Surgeon General at http://www.traumaticbraininjuryatoz.org, and the Brain Injury Association at http://www.biausa.org.
- *Advocate.* Doing what I have needed to do means I'm a stronger, more confident, and more empowered advocate. Before, some situations would have had me quivering in my shoes. No more. When dealing with health insurance companies, the VA, or an employer, I have followed this advice: be polite, be pleasant, but be persistent. Someone may try to discourage you, especially if you're a woman. Speak to the supervisor. Say, "This is unacceptable." But don't go looking for a fight. Pick your battles; save energy for what matters. Your family member doesn't have a private room? Unless a roommate is disrupting recovery and rehabilitation, let it go.
- *Each TBI is different.* Doctors, websites, and books describe what you MAY expect and what MAY happen. But persons progress at their own rate and have different deficits, depending on the area of the brain injured.
- *Use what the military and DoD offer.* The VA has a Polytrauma System of Care for TBI rehabilitation. Had I known earlier, I would have made every effort to get my husband placed there sooner; his progress would have been faster and better. The VA has pilot programs your loved one may qualify for, military liaisons who will work on a plan of care, and psychologists who stand ready to support you. In my experience, most civilian social workers only know about local facilities in their county and not about VA

resources. If using a civilian facility, visit many and choose one acceptable to YOU. If it doesn't participate with your health insurer, ask why. Perhaps it can be changed. It never, ever, hurts to ask!

- *Now is not the time to rock the "I'm independent, I can handle anything, and I'm proud of it" attitude.* Because the fact is, no, you really can't. If you're lucky, family will help. Many friends will be thrilled to help, and you'll be surprised and touched. Consider friends' strengths and use them: computers, electronics, medical, financial, and home repair. Some can take in the mail and keep an eye on the house. Some listen. Friends prop me up and dust me off when I fall, and gently shove me forward with their words and their confidence in me when I sometimes have none, and give me the strength to continue to cope. Saints and martyrs are boring; don't join that club!
- *Some friends will disappear.* My social life has taken a hit, and it makes me very sad. A few friends continue to include me and I'm grateful.
- *Make multiple copies of your loved one's Durable Power of Attorney and Medical Power of Attorney.* You'll need them for banks, financial companies, hospitals, and other institutions. If you don't have these documents, get an attorney to guide you. Use any legal help offered through the military.
- *Look for coping mechanisms, ways to help deal with what is and to let go of what was.* I continue to look. There are days I can take anything thrown at me. Other days, I cry more tears than I ever thought possible. I'm angry my husband injured himself. Then there's frustration, sadness, grief, depression, and embarrassment. I'm tired of taking care of all the problems. I have trouble focusing sometimes and staying on task.
- *I miss having someone love me.* My friends are absolutely wonderful, but they don't kiss me goodnight. I miss my husband before I'm even out of the parking lot of the facility where he's living and cry for the first few miles. My head spins: Will he ever be able to come back home to live? Will he need supervision?
- *Well-meaning persons say puzzling things.* For instance:
  - "Maybe this was a sign that your husband needed to slow down." Really? Sustaining a TBI is a radical way to do it.
  - "Take care of yourself and stay strong, so you can take care of your husband." Seriously? How about the concept of taking care of me, because I'm worthy of it on my own, and because I'm a decent, valuable human being, worthy of staying healthy, strong and sane for ME?
- *I'm a married widow who can't "move on."* I grieve for the life after retirement we looked forward to. My hope is someday we have a semblance of that life. As my husband's colleague told me, "Watching a person with a TBI heal and progress is like watching white paint dry." He's right. I can't commit to certain things; I can't plan too far ahead. Our lives are in limbo.
- *I don't know how much of my husband will come back.* Because of his TBI, my husband has become unable to show his usual love and affection. Some has come back, but it's different. When he says mean things to me, my brain tells me it's the TBI. My heart, however, can't seem to remember and it hurts. It hurts a lot.
- *It's normal to grieve for the person who was.* Part of me will always grieve for the husband I knew, the best friend I've lived with and loved for over 30 years. A different version of that person has appeared. I'm hoping, with time, more of the person I knew will come back. It's happened some already; I pray it will continue.

Glyni Fenn
Wife and Advocate

As Glyni Fenn notes above, human service professionals must know civilian, DoD, and VA resources inside and outside of their area, region, or state in order to best serve service members, veterans, and their families. A number of professionals can be involved in the care of service members and veterans with TBI. Point of contact case management team members can include: a primary care manager who provides clinical care and refers to specialists; a nurse or nurse practitioner medical care case manager at the military treatment facility or VA Polytrauma Center; a nonmedical care manager to help with the disability systems and transitions between health-care systems (e.g., from the DoD to the VA); the DoD recovery care coordinator (for mild to serious TBI) or the DoD/VA federal recovery care coordinator (for severe to catastrophic TBI) to coordinate medical personnel, Wounded Warrior program staff, federal health-care teams, and community resources; the Defense and Veterans Brain Injury Center (DVBIC) regional care coordinator to insure care from injury to rehabilitation to reentry; and the TRICARE managed care support case managers to coordinate care within the TRICARE system. For service members, their nonmedical case manager is called one of the following depending upon the branch of service: the Army Wounded Warrior Case Manager, the Wounded Warrior Program Case Manager (Air Force), the Navy Safe Harbor Program Case Manager, and the Wounded Warrior Regiment Case Manager (Marine Corps). For veterans, their nonmedical case manager may be called the OEF/OIF Program Manager Liaison, the Transition Patient Advocate, or the VA Liaison (Center of Excellence for Medical Multimedia, 2011).

Studies of military families with a service member with a TBI are limited, so we need to consider what has been learned from studies of civilian families. These studies have highlighted the relationship between family members' positive coping and the injured person's process of recovery. In addition, family members (e.g., parents, spouses, and siblings) report assuming care for the injured loved one out of love, deep compassion, and an ethical responsibility (Jumisko, Lexell, & Soderberg, 2007).

Research over the past 30 years indicates that family members experience a great deal of stress, even a decade or more postinjury. Families with young children, financial problems, and minimal social support are more vulnerable to stress. The injured person's cognitive, emotional, and behavioral problems are experienced as more problematic for family members than physical problems. The stress associated with the unrelenting task of being their loved one's champion and primary caregiver in cases of moderate and severe TBI may result in depression, anxiety, and other stress reactions. As a result, marital or relationship partners may seek divorce or relationship dissolution (Verhaeghe, Defloor, & Grydonck, 2005).

Family members' coping strategies may be considered adaptive (e.g., accomplishing important tasks, identifying new roles, seeking social support) or maladaptive (e.g., using alcohol or medication as means of denial or escape). Coping strategies are influenced by the severity of the injury. For example, family members may be more likely to withdraw from social contact if their loved one's behavior is socially inappropriate.

Family members often find receiving social support and assuming important roles previously undertaken by the loved one can reduce the experience of stress (Verhaeghe et al., 2005). While families learn more effective ways to cope over time, educational information and social support can enhance their coping. Family members want clear and accurate information about TBI; details about treatment plans, prognosis, course of recovery, and possible worse and best scenarios; and strategies on how to care for their loved one (Griffin, Friedemann-Sánchez, Hall, Phelan, & van Ryn, 2009).

A family-focused treatment initiated in recent years for those with a TBI and their family members includes **multifamily group treatment**. This treatment is a combination of individual sessions and group education workshops and sessions. Content includes information about TBI, family and relationship issues, problem-solving cognitive difficulties, self-identity issues, family responses and adjustment, and coping strategies for families (Perlick et al., 2011).

TBI may be accompanied by other injuries (e.g., damage to tissue, bones, eyes; chronic pain; PTSD), requiring intensive hospital stays and rehabilitation. Long-term treatment of these polytraumas may result in emotional strain for families. Families support their loved one through a long course of medical treatment and rehabilitation; interact with the bureaucracy of the DoD and VA; and spend significant amounts of time away from their homes and/or daily lives as they participate in their loved one's care. In addition, those with polytrauma due to combat, versus veterans suffering an injury after separating from the military, tend to be in the early years of marriage and tend to have young children. VA clinicians have used both the theory of ambiguous loss and medical family therapy employing cognitive-behavioral, narrative, and family systems approaches to support these families (Collins & Kennedy, 2008).

As part of the National Defense Authorization Act of 2007, Congress mandated the development of a specific family caregiver curriculum for those providing care to a service member or veteran with TBI. A result of this mandate is the curriculum *Traumatic Brain Injury: A Guide for Caregivers of Service Members and Veterans*. Useful for both family members and those who work with them, the curriculum is found on the website, Traumatic Brain Injury: The Journey Back Home (http:// www .traumaticbraininjuryatoz.org), a collaborative effort between the Defense Health Board and the Center of Excellence for Medical Multimedia (2011; an initiative from the Office of the Surgeon General).

The Journey Back Home website contains videos, interactive features, and materials for those with TBI and for family caregivers. The "Caregiver's Journey" portion of the website contains videos of caregivers describing their journeys, illustrating common reactions of family members and service members and the tasks they face. A video series of family caregiver meetings with a social worker cover topics such as managing the physical and cognitive effects of TBI, problem solving, advocating, taking care of self, helping children cope, addressing family needs, transitioning home, obtaining help with caregiving, addressing everyday issues, moving forward, and having hope. These sessions parallel content found in the caregiver guide available for download. The guide covers an introduction to TBI, the effects of TBI and how to help, becoming a caregiver, and navigating services and benefits. Templates can also be downloaded to help with recording notes on physical, cognitive, behavioral, and communication effects; family needs; children; legal matters; problem solving; and progress on recovery. Other materials available for download include worksheets, assessments, and descriptions of TRICARE and the VA systems. TBI survivors, experienced caregivers, treatment experts, and a family caregiver advisory board developed the materials (Defense and Veterans Brain Injury Center and the TBI Family Caregiver Advisory Panel, 2010).

Posttraumatic Stress

In this section, we review some of the therapeutic treatments for individuals diagnosed with PTSD. Then we consider the implications of PTSD for family members and support available for them.

Treatments for Posttraumatic Stress   Posttraumatic stress is considered to be a spectrum of reactions to a trauma: acute stress reactions, combat-operation stress reactions, acute stress disorder, and PTSD (The Management of Post-traumatic Stress Working Group, 2010). Those who survive a trauma may experience only some of the reactions, while others may experience the entire spectrum (the spectrum is described in Chapter 7). The goal is early intervention to increase the likelihood of preventing injuries such as PTSD.

Service members who exhibit acute stress reactions or combat operational stress reactions should be accessed and provided PFA and care of basic physical needs. Additional interventions may be warranted, such as psychotherapy and facilitation of spiritual and social support (The Management of Post-traumatic Stress Working Group, 2010).

For those diagnosed with PTSD treatment may consist of some or all of the following: evidence-based psychotherapy, medication, treatment of a concurrent substance use disorder, alternative care options (e.g., hypnosis to help manage pain, anxiety, or nightmares), management of specific pain, family therapy, and social and spiritual support. Relaxation techniques may help those who are physically tense or hyperreactive. Imagery rehearsal therapy (i.e., imagining in a relaxed state more pleasant and positive images in place of a nightmare) may reduce nightmares and difficulties related to sleeping (The Management of Post-traumatic Stress Working Group, 2010).

VA/DoD clinical guidelines strongly recommend the use of evidence-based practices in screening, therapeutic treatments, and medications. Recognizing PTSD early allows treatment to begin quickly, resulting in less impairment and less time suffering (The Management of Post-traumatic Stress Working Group, 2010). These treatments are briefly described below.

Cognitive-based therapy (CBT) includes learning about symptoms of PTSD, identifying thoughts and feelings associated with the trauma, identifying and challenging dysfunctional beliefs about the trauma (e.g., "I should have been able to … during the event," "I should have known…") that give rise to or sustain PTSD symptoms, and replacing these beliefs with more logical, functional, and reality-based beliefs. CBT is conducted in 12 sessions (The Management of Post-traumatic Stress Working Group, 2010).

Exposure therapy includes psychoeducation (e.g., learning about trauma reactions, PTSD, and symptoms) and exposure to the trauma-related stimuli. Specifically, an in vivo exposure has the person physically doing safe but feared stimuli that trigger symptoms in order of difficulty. For example, a veteran who avoids crowds because being in one when an IED exploded may be asked to first watch a crowd from a distance, then walk toward a small crowd, then stand and talk with someone near a crowd, and then walk through a crowd. Each step is repeated until it can be experienced with low emotional or physiological responses, and then the next step is approached. Imaginal exposure includes imagining the trauma and describing its physical and emotional details with a therapist in order to gain more control over feelings and thoughts about the trauma. Written exposure includes writing about the traumatic event and then reading what is written to the therapist. Treatment usually spans 8–15 sessions (Committee on Treatment of Posttraumatic Stress Disorder, 2008; The Management of Post-traumatic Stress Working Group, 2010).

Stress inoculation therapy (SIT) is a structured process that teaches anxiety management skills. Clients learn about stress, its prevalence, how to see perceived threats as problems to solve, and relaxation and breathing control to learn to better manage distress. Clients then move to practicing skills (e.g., emotion regulation, relaxation, assertiveness training, positive self-talk, thought stopping) and finally to applying the skills through such situations as role-playing of distressing situation or visualizing a situation. SIT is typically conducted in 8–12 sessions or over a 3–12 month time period (Meichenbaum, 1996; The Management of Post-traumatic Stress Working Group, 2010).

Eye movement desensitization and reprocessing (EMDR) desensitizes clients to the trauma-related memories that cause them distress by encouraging the recall of images and resulting emotions, identifying alternate understandings of the trauma experience, and challenging clients to consider these other understandings. The goal is to disable the distressing memories that work to maintain symptoms (The Management of Post-traumatic Stress Working Group, 2010).

Family Interventions

Most service members, including those who experience combat, do not develop PTSD. However, when it does occur, PTSD has implications for family members as well as service members. Family members become extremely concerned when they see their loved one exhibiting symptoms of PTSD: reexperiencing the trauma (e.g., flashbacks, nightmares, exaggerated emotions, and physical actions), avoiding contact and engaging in emotional numbing (e.g., loss of interest, detached, restricted emotion), and showing increased arousal (e.g., difficulty sleeping, outbursts of anger, hypervigilance, exaggerated startle response). They may feel afraid, unsure how to help, and worried about the person's safety (The Management of Post-traumatic Stress Working Group, 2010).

Research on couples and families from prior wars and across multiple countries has documented effects of PTSD not only on the service members and veterans but also on family relationships. Wives have reported feeling tense, anxious, depressed, lonely, confused, and burdened by caregiving (Dekel, Goldblatt, Keidar, Solomon, & Polliack, 2005). Couples in which a trauma-exposed veteran has PTSD are at greater risk of relationship distress, violence, and divorce than those couples who do not. Severe PTSD symptoms, particularly emotional numbing, negatively affect marital adjustment for both male and female veterans (Dekel & Monson, 2010). Families may experience rigidity in functioning, violence, low cohesion, and high conflict; may scapegoat the person with PTSD; and may restrict intimacy, self-expression, and personal openness (Dekel et al., 2005).

Researchers and clinicians are attempting to identify the mechanisms by which stress reactions, including PTSD, are transmitted from a traumatized person to another person. The process is not clearly understood; however, evidence exists that suggests multiple mechanisms probably contribute (Dekel & Monson, 2010).

One mechanism by which stress reactions are transmitted may be the empathy felt by the caregiver for the trauma survivor. This empathy may encourage overidentification with the survivor to the point of assuming the survivor's stress reactions. Second, perceived burden and chronic stress of caregiving on emotional and physical health, social life, and financial well-being may lead to stress reactions. Third, adaptation to traumatic stress may depend upon the interaction of individual functioning, couple functioning (e.g., nurturance, communication, conflict), and previous unresolved stress (Dekel & Monson, 2010).

Fourth, behaviors (e.g., not expressing emotions, limited self-disclosure) that are used to avoid situations, memories, or emotions related to the trauma can be detrimental to relationship satisfaction. Cognitive processes (e.g., interpreting other's behaviors negatively) can also maintain relationship and family difficulties. They may have shattered assumptions about safety and difficulty understanding the behavior of a person with PTSD. Finally, living with a traumatized person may be experienced as an ambiguous loss in which the person is physically but not psychological present. If the ambiguity becomes immobilizing, it can lead to stress reactions (Dekel & Monson, 2010).

When compared to the focus placed on individual treatment for PTSD, discussion of treatment and support of family caregivers has been minimal. Until recently, most treatment options have been primarily geared toward the individual with PTSD and emerged from the goal of helping the person with PTSD by decreasing relationship stress or increasing family support of the trauma survivor (Dekel & Solomon, 2007). For example, family members, typically partners, can be included in individual sessions with their loved one or group education sessions with other families.

However, it is becoming clear that the effects of PTSD on families call for a more systemic approach to care and treatment (Erbes, Polusny, MacDermid, & Compton, 2008). Evidence suggests including a partner in treatment can benefit the partner and relationship functioning and improve PTSD symptoms (Monson, Fredman, & Adair, 2008). In acknowledgement of the need of services for veterans and for family members, the VA is training its clinicians in behavioral family therapy and multifamily group psychoeducation, both evidence-based interventions (Makin-Byrd, Gifford, McCutcheon, & Glynn, 2011). Veterans with PTSD most likely will welcome such family participation in treatment. In one study, a majority of veterans who were receiving PTSD treatment considered PTSD to be a source of family stress, wanted their families to be more involved in their PTSD treatment, and wanted guidance on how to communicate with their family members (Batten et al., 2009).

Family members have indicated wanting assistance directly for their own sake and not just as a caregiver for someone else. They want help with reducing their stress levels. Toward this end they would prefer a partners-only group, cultural and leisure activities to counteract feelings of isolation, and individual therapy for themselves (Lyons, 2007). In addition, support for family members needs to extend beyond an initial diagnosis of PTSD to acknowledge life cycle changes, stages of PTSD, and the strengths family members bring to their caregiving. Barriers to participation (e.g., child care, transportation, service member's or veteran's objections) need to be lowered (Dekel & Solomon, 2007).

Multiple sources of information about stress responses and PTSD have recently been developed for family members. The VA has materials for download, including explanations of PTSD, descriptions of treatment options, and video discussion of stress responses in women (http://www.ptsd.va.gov/public/index.asp). For those who wish for more in-depth information, a free online course, PTSD 101, is found at http://www.ptsd.va.gov/professional/ptsd101/ptsd-101.asp. The DCoE for Psychological Health and Traumatic Brain Injury launched the Real Warriors Campaign to reduce stigma about seeking psychological services and encourage awareness and help-seeking behaviors (http://www.realwarriors.net). Families are part of this campaign. Through the website, they are provided information on how to support their service member and care for themselves. Recommendations include taking time for oneself, using clear communication, maintaining healthy habits, being positive and patient, asking for help, and seeking services.

In response to a mandate by Congress, the http://www.afterdeployment.org website was developed to address problems and concerns experienced by service members and their families following deployment. The After Deployment website offers assessments, online workshops, videos, and links to more information including a blog on PTSD and Pentagon Channel videos on service members overcoming PTSD.

The DoD and the nonprofit organization Screening for Mental Health launched Military Pathways®, a screening program for family members and service personnel in both the Active and Reserve components. These anonymous mental health and alcohol self-assessments are found at https://www.militarymentalhealth.org/Welcome.aspx.

CAREGIVING

One clear lesson emerging from OIF and OEF is that providing quality care for injured service members and veterans requires providing quality care for their families. This lesson was strongly noted by the Workgroup on Intervention with Combat Injured Families, a group of military and civilian clinicians and researchers from family trauma, psychiatry, and military medicine convened by the Center for the Study of Traumatic Stress in 2007 (Cozza, 2009b). This workgroup developed a set of principles to (1) guide research and interventions to assist families and their functioning, and (2) improve communication about combat injury within and among health care, family, and community settings (Cozza, 2009b).

Families of service members are greatly affected when their service member is injured. Even minimal injuries from which a service member fully recovers bring worry and concern, while life-threatening and extensive injuries can permanently reorganize how families function as members are propelled into caregiving and care-receiving roles. For example, the service member or veteran faces developing an identity that incorporates the injury or injuries while establishing or maintaining a relationship with a partner or an adult daughter or son. Meanwhile, spouses or parents who work full time may have to change to a part-time job or forego paid employment altogether in order to provide daily care for a wife, husband, daughter, or son injured while on active duty.

Caregivers may be spouses, significant others, parents, children, extended family members, and friends who are committed to sharing life with their service members and veterans. Caregivers can find their lives consumed by the numerous tasks and demands. They may spend hours each day providing personal care (e.g., bathing, dressing, feeding) to their loved one, orchestrating multiple doctor and rehabilitation appointments each week, completing and organizing necessary paperwork, and advocating on behalf of their loved one and themselves as they seek services.

A study of the economic impact of caregiving commissioned by the Joint Department of Defense and Department of Veterans Affairs Wounded, Ill, and Injured Senior Oversight Committee found that 57% of caregivers provided at least 10 hours of care per week, 75% quit work or took time away from school or work, a third made new child care arrangements, and 11% changed housing or location. In addition, 37% had unmet financial obligations, and 41% acquired new financial obligations. The percent of caregivers having financial obligations correlated with the hours of caregiving provided each week. Some caregivers lost their jobs if their time away from work exceeded that allowed by the Family Medical Leave Act. Losing a job also meant for some losing access to health insurance, such as parents of a service member (Christensen et al., 2009).

The Workgroup on Intervention with Combat Injured Families developed principles of care to guide human service professionals as they assist military families and to improve communication (Cozza, 2009b). It is important to know these principles of care as they can guide the work of not only military but civilian professionals, providers, organizations, and communities as they offer appropriate care and services to military families from the Active and Reserve Components and families of veterans (Gutierrez & Brenner, 2009; Thomas et al., 2010). These principles are summarized in Box 12.3.

BOX 12.3   BEST PRACTICES

CARING FOR FAMILIES OF SERVICE MEMBERS WITH VISIBLE AND INVISIBLE COMBAT INJURIES

When providing care and services to families of those injured, military and civilian providers, professionals, organizations, and communities should strive to:

- Apply principles of psychological first aid, that is, attend to families' safety and comfort, give information and practical assistance, and connect families to community resources in order to encourage recovery.
- Provide family-focused medical care for the injured by relieving family distress, supporting parental functions and parenting effectiveness, and providing guidance on how to talk with children about combat injuries.
- Reinforce the resilience of families and address possible problems that require further help and support.
- Offer effective injury communication that is timely, contains appropriate and accurate information, addresses family members' anxiety, and sustains hope, from the time of notification through rehabilitation.
- Tailor services and care to the family's changing needs through treatment and rehabilitation, recognizing the family's strengths and anticipating future needs.
- Understand children's responses vary by age and gender and recognizes how distress, need for care, and ability to communicate vary by age.
- Reach beyond professional boundaries to foster collaboration and coordination of services among the family and military and civilian health-care resources and treatment.
- Respect the traditions of military families and a family's background (e.g., culture, language, composition, ethnicity, and religion).
- Help families to access care and address barriers to service, including educating communities about the needs of families.
- Be knowledgeable about and provide educational materials that address challenges faced by families.

Source: Information compiled from Cozza, S. J. (Ed.) (2009b). *Proceedings of the workgroup on intervention with combat injured families, December 11–12, 2007.* Bethesda, MD: Center for the Study of Traumatic Stress. Retrieved from http://www.cstsonline.org/resources/resource-94_ workgroup_intervention_combat_injured_families.

Central to providing quality care to families of an injured service member is communication. **Injury communication** is an important process to understand, and the accompanying skills are key to successfully supporting families. Injury communication refers to providing and delivering information related to the injury to families and to the impact on family members' capacity to understand and use the information provided. Injury communication begins with the notification of the family about injury of the service member and continues throughout the treatment process and rehabilitation. The goal throughout this process is to promote injury recovery and family function and health (Cozza, 2009b).

It is helpful to think about injury communication across relationships, developmental ages, and time. Sharing information about an injury and its implications for family life occurs with the person injured, as well as with a partner, parents, children, extended family members, health-care providers, friends, and other supportive people (e.g., chaplains, priests, pastors, community resources). Injury communication occurs between and among these people, and the ease with which one person speaks to another may differ. For example, parents able to speak with their son or daughter who is injured about the injury may find it difficult to talk with their grandchild, or a spouse able to explain the injury to a school-age child may falter when explaining it to a teenager (Cozza, 2009b).

Effective injury communication requires an approach sensitive to a person's developmental and cognitive abilities. Young children who easily gauge the emotional environment require simple yet straightforward descriptions of what has happened to a parent, a sibling, a grandparent, or whoever was injured (Cozza, 2009b).

Injury communication occurs across time. The information family members want and need to know immediately upon notification of injury to their service member differs from the information they and the service member will need to know for successful participation in treatment. A transition back home will require yet other information, for example, how to negotiate community resources or how to respond to strangers' questions about the injury (Cozza, 2009b).

In addition to injury communication, families may need support adapting to the loss of a person as he or she once was. Living and caring for someone with TBI or PTSD can be experienced as an ambiguous loss as the person may be physically but not psychologically present or not psychological present in the same way as before the injury (Betz & Thorngren, 2006; Boss, 2006; Landau & Hissett, 2008). This stressor of ambiguity can become unmanageable and immobilizing and, therefore, traumatizing to family members. However, family members can experience the stressor of ambiguity, although chronic, as manageable (Boss, 2006). While self-care techniques are important, Boss (2006) argues that they are not enough when loss is an ambiguous one. Recognition of an ambiguous loss and the ambiguities it brings (e.g., now both a spouse and a caregiver, uncertain what each day will bring) are important in making the loss manageable. Box 12.4 lists additional points that can assist family members in normalizing their experiences and living with ambiguities (Boss, 2006).

Caregivers may experience stress reactions as they confront loneliness, worry, injury of their loved one, and loss. Stressed caregivers have had a sense of a just world, connections to others,

---

BOX 12.4   BEST PRACTICES

POINTS TO SHARE WITH FAMILIES EXPERIENCING AMBIGUOUS LOSS

- Resilience and health are more common than we think
- Find meaning
  - Make sense of situation/event
  - Lack of meaning harms health
  - Maybe but not necessarily through spiritual/religious beliefs
- Work at accepting an imperfect situation
  - Requires flexibility
  - Living well despite imperfect absence and presence
- Connect with others
  - Join familiar and trusted communities of friends and family
- Rebuild identities and roles
  - Form a new understanding of oneself as a partner, family member, and community member
  - Intentionally reconstruct family roles, boundaries, and rules
  - Create or modify rituals and celebrations
- Normalize ambivalence
  - Acknowledge conflicting feelings and emotions
  - Respect different ways of managing ambivalence

Source: Information compiled from Boss, P. (2006). *Loss, trauma, and resilience: Therapeutic work with ambiguous loss.* New York, NY: W. W. Norton.

identities, beliefs about themselves and others, and relationships disrupted (Boss, 2006; Cozza, 2009b; Dekel & Monson, 2010). It is easy for caregivers to use most of their energy and time providing physical and emotional care to their loved one and being the advocate for the individual and family. It is important that practitioners encourage and facilitate self-care for caregivers in order to prevent burnout. Caregivers may benefit from exercise, good nutrition, adequate sleep, regular and extended time away from caregiving, social support including someone who will listen who is nonjudgmental, accepting emotional reactions as normal, valuing their own needs and interests, and prioritizing what is important (including their own well-being) and letting other time and energy demands fall off the list (Dekel et al., 2005).

Extensive physical and psychological injuries usually mean that service members or veterans will need to rely on family members to assist them during treatment and recovery. Family members—spouses, parents, partners, siblings, adult children, aunts, and uncles—are the champions for their injured service member, working on behalf of their loved one. Most commonly, a spouse or a parent will be the daily caregiver and advocate. Regardless of who is the main caregiver (or caregivers), ultimately this person functions best if surrounded by a cadre of family members, friends, and neighbors who can provide practical support (e.g., respite care, child care, help with household chores or repairs) and social/emotional support (e.g., listening, friendship, trips to movies, a meal out). Social support protects against negative stress reactions following a trauma (Brewin, Andrews, & Valentine, 2000), so those who work with military and veteran families can prompt caregivers not only to accept such support but to actively develop it.

DEATH

As noted in Chapter 8, little research exists on military families who have experienced the death of a service member. However, personal accounts such as the one written by Joanne Steen and research on loss from literature on civilians suggest multiple points to consider when working with families whose service member has died.

Voices From the Frontline

A WIFE TALKS ABOUT THE DEATH OF HER HUSBAND

My husband, a Navy pilot, was killed when the helicopter he was flying exploded in midair. None of the seven crewmen onboard survived. As a military wife-made-widow, I searched for resources to understand the chaos of emotion, thought, and feeling which was brewing within me and found no written resource in the civilian sector that adequately described the complexity of military loss. My homegrown survival group of military widows and widowers was able to identify with the criteria for traumatic grief, as originally presented by Prigerson et al. (1999), to a limited degree. Yet, these criteria fell short of defining either the full depth of a military death in the line of duty in times of peace or war, or our complicated reactions to this death.

Most military deaths are traumatic, and the remains are often unviewable, comingled, or nonrecoverable. Many military deaths occur in hostile theaters of operation, on deployments, and in off-site training exercises, making the scene of the death unreachable to surviving family members. Suicides by military service members are often disenfranchised, resulting in deprived grief and recognition in the surviving families. Surviving spouses and dependent children usually live at a duty station, placing them great distances from family and friends. Surviving parents are dispersed throughout the country, and most often lack the connection or availability to military installations. In our post–September 11th environment, military deaths are publicized in the media, yet often reduced to a 30-second sound bite, which is perceived as minimizing the loss in the eyes of surviving family members.

Service to country and commitment to duty further complicates a military death. Common symbols of our country, such as the American flag, become powerful reminders of a military death to a loved one.

It's safe to say surviving military families live out the ultimate sacrifice of their loved ones each and every day, in big and small ways that go unnoticed or unacknowledged. It takes years for a surviving military family to fully accept the reality of their profound loss.

Joanne M. Steen
Coauthor of Military Widow: A Survival Guide (2006)

First, resilience is more common than not, and most individuals adapt to a loss without professional intervention or grief counseling (Bonanno, 2004); however, understanding the process of grief can help individuals cope with a loss (Bonanno & Mancini, 2008; Bonanno et al., 2002). Second, yearning for the one who has died is a predominant emotion during the time when grieving is more intense (Shear & Mulhare, 2008). Third, individuals and families differ in grief responses and length of time to accept a death to the point of thinking of the loss and experiencing the reminders of the person without overwhelming distress (Bonanno et al., 2002).

Fourth, rather than seeing bereavement as a process through stages, researchers are considering the "states" of bereavement (Prigerson & Maciejewski, 2005) and are looking at factors that may help or hinder a process of recovery (Wright et al., 2006). In Western societies, bereaved persons typically experience **acute grief** during which time she or he yearns for the loved one daily, feels deep sadness, struggles with the finality of the loss, is preoccupied with memories and thoughts of the loved one, and has diminished interest in ongoing life (Shear & Mulhare, 2008). Acute grief typically becomes **integrated grief** in which bereaved persons comprehend the death, are not preoccupied by thoughts and memories, and have interest in life.

Fifth, evidence from studies of bereaved civilian spouses indicates that sudden and traumatic loss, such as from combat or military service in general, may be associated with continuing distress years after the loss (Wright et al., 2006). They may experience **complicated grief** in which they experience prolonged yearning and other symptoms such as disbelief or bitterness over the loss, numbness, a sense life is empty, and an inability to move forward with plans (Bonanno, Rennicke & Dekel, 2005; Prigerson & Maciejewski, 2005). They may feel guilty about not preventing the death or suffering, believe it is wrong to enjoy life when the loved one cannot, and feel angry or disappointed with others or with the unfairness of life. At the same time, they may avoid reminders that the loved one is dead. Persons experiencing complicated grief may experience depression, PTSD, or both; may engage in reckless behaviors; may have sleep disruptions; and may have thoughts of suicide (Shear & Mulhare, 2008).

Those who experience complicated grief may benefit from cognitive and behavioral therapy (Bonanno et al., 2002). Modified interpersonal psychotherapy, based on attachment theory and using strategies from cognitive-behavioral therapy for PTSD, has been initially tested with promising results for those who stayed in the treatment (Shear & Mulhare, 2008).

In addition to individual therapy, other intervention strategies have been proposed for coping with a traumatic loss because they promote adaptive processes associated with family resilience: belief systems, organizational patterns, and communication (Walsh, 2007). These key processes of family resilience were introduced in Chapter 5.

Applied to grieving families, belief systems that promote family resilience include arriving at a meaning for the loss that brings comfort. The military's ceremonial recognition and rituals convey honor of and respect for those who die while carrying out their duties. This public acknowledgement of sacrifice of a military member's life in selfless service to others and showing reverence, respect, and gratitude to family members offer specific ways for families to ascribe meaning to their loss (Wright et al., 2006). However, it must be recognized that families or individual family members may differ in the extent to which they find such public rituals helpful. Some family members may see rituals as something to endure while others see them as a source of comfort (Steen & Asaro, 2006).

Organizational patterns such as the use of formal and informal supports are another key process in promoting adjustment to a traumatic loss. Support can come from military leaders when they formally acknowledging the contributions of those who have died and through the assistance of the Army's Casualty Assistance Officer, the Navy or Marine Corps Casualty Assistance Calls Officer, or the Air Force Casualty Assistance Representative. Military family groups and friends can provide critical emotional and practical support initially and subsequently (Wright et al., 2006).

Self-help books such as Steen and Asaro's (2006) *Military Widow: A Survival Guide,* and the organizations Gold Star Mothers, Gold Star Wives, Military Families United, and Tragedy Assistance Program for Survivors offer compassion and guidance on practical and emotional matters.

Human service professionals can assist family members to identify additional sources of formal support (e.g., religious groups, child and youth programs, self-help groups, and health-care providers) and informal support (e.g., colleagues at work, church members, neighbors) and examine ways to locate such support, such as initiating conversations, self-disclosure, becoming involved in a group or club, and volunteering (Huebner et al., 2009; Mancini et al., 2005).

When grieving, open communication and productive problem-solving processes can also encourage positive coping by families. Families benefit from clear and consistent messages about the death of their service member; however, they often need patience as information can be delayed as details are verified (Steen & Asaro, 2006). Additionally, they can benefit from recognizing that individuals within the same family may express their grief differently and that there is no "right" way to grieve (Bonanno, 2004).

Months into their bereavement, military families may sense a change in their relationship with their loved one's unit or with the military in general. While the military "takes care of its own" with casualty assistance, funeral rituals, and initial daily contact by unit and/or family readiness group members, families may feel bewildered when the telephone calls and visits taper off and when they realize military functions such as promotions or holiday parties pass by without an invitation. They may feel abandoned by the military. However, unit life moves on as individuals transfer and deployments occur (Steen & Asaro, 2006). While they might not be involved in the day-to-day life of their loved one's last unit, families may continue a connection with the military through participation in local or national events that recognize their loved one's service and sacrifice and in military rituals on national holidays.

Steen and Asaro (2006) acknowledge that going through grief is not pain-free and it encompasses all aspects of life. They encourage those who have lost a loved one to talk with those who will listen and acknowledge grief. They suggest learning more about grieving the death of a military service member and emphasize, "the life skills you developed as a military [family] will help you cope with military" bereavement (p. 14).

Empirical and clinical studies of military families over the past 70 years have added to our knowledge of family functioning during stressful situations such as war and following traumatic events such as injury and death (MacDermid Wadsworth, 2010). Those who work in military and civilian communities can support military families by using resilience-related practices that promote positive coping strategies.

SUMMARY

- The military is building a culture that recognizes the centrality of psychological health to mission readiness and supports resilience-related practices for service members and families.
- Each of the services has implemented combat operational stress control programs. Military members are being trained to recognize the signs and symptoms of impaired psychological health that are often visible in behaviors, cognitive functioning, and affect; learn that seeking help for such an injury is as wise as seeking help for a physical wound; and know how to seek help for themselves, a buddy, or someone in their command when signs and symptoms are present.
- The Real Warriors Campaign, launched in 2009 by the DCoE for Psychological Health and Traumatic Brain Injury, provides educational information about and video examples

of service members seeking care for psychological health issues and continuing successful military and civilian careers.

- Stress and trauma can overwhelm service personnel and their family members, resulting in stress reactions, injury, and illness.
- PFA is a way of helping children, adolescents, adults, and families immediately following a traumatic event.
- The effects of trauma can extend beyond the person who directly experienced it to family members.
- Central to providing quality care to families of injured service members is communication. *Injury communication* is an important process to understand, and the accompanying skills are key to successfully supporting families.
- TBI treatment requires tailored coordination of care for the unique needs of each service member. Service members with TBI may receive care in a variety of health-care settings, in particular if they are eventually discharged from the military: military treatment facilities, the VA, and civilian health-care systems.
- PTSD has implications for the family members as well as the service personnel. Multiple sources of information about stress responses and PTSD exist for family members. The http://www.afterdeployment.org website was developed to address problems and concerns experienced by service members and their families following deployment.
- Little research exists on bereaved military families. However, research on civilians indicates most bereaved persons experience acute grief and eventually integrated grief. Traumatic loss appears to increase the possibility of complicated grief in which the bereaved experience prolonged yearning and other symptoms.

EXERCISES

1. Identify the organizations closest to you that offer PFA training. Explore whether you can talk with volunteers or staff members who received and used this training. If it is possible to talk with them, explore where and when they used the training. Consider whether you would be an appropriate candidate for PFA training.
2. Study and evaluate the content found on one of the following websites: the Journey Back Home (http://www.traumaticbraininjuryatoz.org), the Real Warriors Campaign (http://www.realwarriors.net), and After Deployment (http://www.afterdeployment.org). If possible, discuss the content found on the website with a member of a military family.
3. If you live near an Army installation, interview one or more service providers (e.g., family readiness program manager) about how they are using the Composite Life Cycle Model.
4. Create a handout that lists web-based resources available for National Guard and Reserve families.

13

Serving Military Families

In Chapter 13, you will

- Meet Ashley Armand, a senior majoring in family studies, and Stephen Fountain, a graduate student, who are working with or plan to work with veterans, service members, and their families
- Examine career paths that lead to serving military families
- Consider the importance of compassion satisfaction and compassion fatigue
- Discover practices and ways to promote self-care to encourage compassion satisfaction
- Identify the settings where you might apply what you learn in this book

Meet

Ashley Armand, Senior, Family Studies Student

I took a military family life course as a stepping stone to working with military families. I want to work with military families whose service member has a TBI. I have learned that a TBI can change who people are and how they act. My goal is to work in an organization that studies and treats TBI. A TBI places a great deal of stress on families, and I want to focus on how we can best support them. If there are enough people out there who support military families, their issues will become normal in our society. Military families will be better off. All families will be better off.

Stephen Fountain, Graduate Student in Student Affairs

I have a lot of military in my extended family. My grandfather served in the Korean War and was promoted to Colonel. It couldn't have been easy, especially because of all he had to go through being black. My uncle and half-sister have served, too. The course on family life and the military allowed me to better understand things about my family and myself. Learning about what people in the military may endure helps me understand why some may be hesitant to speak about their experiences. However, if those of us in a helping profession demonstrate we are compassionate and trustworthy, veterans may confide in us if they need support. For example, I heard about a veteran who slept with a gun under his pillow and a knife under his bed because he felt he needed those things to protect his life. He found faculty and staff on campus to support his adjustment and is successfully completing his degree.

My Master's degree will be in education with a focus on student affairs and development. I currently work with student organizations on campus. Insights from this class are helping me today and will help me with my career in the future to better understand what veterans experience in the college setting.

INTRODUCTION

As Ashley Armand and Stephen Fountain, you may be in school studying and planning for a career working with service members and military families. Or you may have an established career and find you have the opportunity to work with military families. In prior chapters, you were introduced to numerous military and civilian agencies and organizations that serve military families. You read results from many studies on military families and read about policies that recognize the opportunities and challenges of military family life. It is now your turn to take this information with you on your own career path or in your future work with service members and military families.

In this chapter, we examine some of the obvious and not-so-obvious careers that offer a way to serve military families, either directly or indirectly. These career paths are illustrated through stories shared by working professionals. You may be surprised about the myriad ways you can apply your knowledge of military families. In addition, we note the paths to take if you wish to work directly with military families by describing the federal and contract paths and listing online job search sites. Finally, we emphasize the satisfaction that comes with working with military families and ideas for maintaining this satisfaction as you continue in your career.

THE MANY PATHS TO SERVING MILITARY FAMILIES

There are many paths that allow us to serve military families. No matter what path you take, expect the unexpected in your work. You may find yourself traveling to a military installation in a country you never imagined visiting, or being lowered down to the deck of a ship from a helicopter to give presentations to sailors on their way home from a deployment. You may discover renewed excitement and satisfaction in work you have been doing for more than 25 years as you and a military family celebrate their resilience. Or find yourself humbled and inspired by a child who draws a picture of herself and her mommy holding hands across an ocean. Like many of the people you have met in this book, you may find yourself questioning your assumptions about the military and gaining new insights into what is meant by resilience, commitment, and honor. As you serve military families, you will likely find that your life, too, is being enriched.

The Researcher Path

Deborah Gibbs, MSPH and Senior Health Analyst at RTI International, shares the path she took to working in support of military families:

"I think that the key to finding satisfying work is in making a match between an issue that you care about and your skills and temperament. I can imagine the process working in reverse, that is, someone who starts with their skills, then finds the issue on which they'll use those skills. And then, of course, you hope that such work is available and reasonably compensated!

"Child welfare and issues affecting vulnerable women and families are such issues for me. I've done some direct service work, enough to know that I wasn't particularly good at it. The tasks that I was drawn to involved synthesizing information and answering interesting questions. I became a researcher and am now focusing some of my work on military families.

"There are trade-offs to make when choosing a career: knowing that you made a difference in one person's life, versus hoping to make a difference in a lot of lives; and working face to face or remotely from the people affected. These are just two examples of the choices we make."

The Writer Path

"My first job was heading the Bank Street Infant and Family Center where I worked with babies, toddlers, families, and teachers," explains Amy Dombro, a coauthor of this book. "This was in the mid-70s when infant/toddler child care programs were new. Our program was a model. As I talked with student teachers and visitors about what we did and why, I discovered that conveying information simply so that it can be easily understood and used by others is more difficult than it seems. That led me to begin writing—with, for, and about children, families and teachers—which I've been doing ever since.

"Four years ago, Lynette Fraga, then Director of Military Projects at ZERO TO THREE, offered me the chance to write a series of brochures for military families about supporting their babies and toddlers with deployment and separation. 'I don't know one person in the military,' I said to her. 'You know about and respect families,' she said. 'Most important you know how to listen.' With her encouragement, I agreed to do the project.

"By the next year, as the optempo increased, we started work on Honoring Our Babies and Toddlers: Supporting Young Children Affected by a Military Parent's Deployment, Injury or Death for professionals and two accompanying guides for families (download copies at http://www.zeroto-three.org/about-us/funded-projects/military-families/honoring-our-babies-and-toddlers.html).

"While writing these guides, I met Shelley, a coauthor of this book. Over a brownie during a break in the meeting, I shared with her that I felt awkward talking with people in uniform and military family members. 'They are from a different culture,' I explained. 'And many of them have had experiences I can't even imagine.' 'They know what they know,' she said. 'You know what you know. It will take all of us to support military families. So don't hesitate to bring what you do best to the table.'

"Soon after our conversation, I wrote the part of the guides that I am most proud of: charts in the voices of babies and toddlers to show professionals and family members what children under three may experience during deployment and when a parent is injured or dies. It is a strategy I have used in my writing before. Shelley's insight had reminded me I did have something to offer military families and freed me to do so.

"Most recently while working on this book, I have had the opportunity to talk with many service members and families serving our country. I've learned about myself, commitment, integrity, and coping in difficult times. All of these people are sacrificing to protect me and my family. I plan to continue using my skills as a writer to thank and support them."

The Video Producer Path

Kristin Westbrook, Creative Director, Science Applications International Corporation (SAIC), explains how she began her work supporting service members and their families. "We use video to engage reluctant audiences in the military. We are training what people want to hear about least of all: casualty notification and assistance, sexual assault prevention, and suicide prevention.

"We totally stumbled on this work. I had worked with an ad agency before that produced high-level national TV commercials. My husband, Wayne, a member of our team, is a cinematographer. He's brilliant at lensing, that is the use of lenses in filming. He understands light.

"The Air Force Academy rape scandal in 2003 put us all to the test. Congress demanded that the Air Force tell Congress what they were going to do to change the culture. The Air Force wanted a top-notch course with a dramatic scenario; as luck would have it, the division of SAIC supporting this customer was on the same floor as our division and knew our work.

"Recently we've been focusing on suicide prevention. Suicide is a mystery that may never be solved. Everyone working in this field is a pioneer, trying to figure this out. We've been talking with lots of families who have honored us by sharing their stories. Each talks about how service members who kill themselves 'unplug' or 'disconnect'; the challenge is trying to reach them.

"This work gives us a chance to serve. Working with military families, we are part of something bigger. It's an amazing feeling. Military families are inspiring. The deep respect that I now have for people in the military came gradually. Not because it wasn't deserved from the people I met right off the bat. It's that I came from a parallel peacenik universe.

"I guess that's the beauty of life—making new connections and relationships. Thanks to service members, their families, and this experience, I feel like I'm just hitting my stride as a producer and I will do whatever I can to support them."

The Veteran Supporting Other Veterans Path

Perhaps you are a veteran who wants to support other veterans. This desire may lead you to apply for a job in higher education, as it did for Welby Alcantara, Veterans Affairs Coordinator, City College of New York, who describes, "Coming back to the civilian world you can feel like an immigrant who doesn't speak the language or know the culture. You spend months being trained so that when you hit combat, you do what you have to do without a pause. Thinking is minimal.

"After being told where to go, what to eat, who your friends are, and what to do, you get out and even choosing what socks to put on can be an issue. When you are in Iraq or Afghanistan, you have a rifle or sidearm right there. You feel empowered. When you come back, you don't feel safe.

"Veterans are coming back stressed out. They need help. Their families need help, too. The ones who speak up are doing OK. It's the quiet ones who won't share some of their pain. They are the ones I fear for.

"That's why lots of us are leading and taking part in many new programs today. We know if we don't do something, lots of other vets are going to fall through the cracks. I don't see my work with vets who are students as a job. It's like they are my brothers and sisters. When I help another vet, it is like helping myself.

"Vietnam vets are stepping up, too. They are taking the watch cap and doing the right thing. They see a younger version of themselves and are determined that the way they were treated when they returned home is not going to happen again. That's why you have all those people at the airports to welcome people home. It means a whole lot."

Welby Alcantara's assistant, Aarian Oliver, who is also a veteran, adds, "Most vets and their families didn't know what they were getting into when they joined the military. I was a medic. Depression was a big thing for service members and their spouses. We'd have many on base who were 'frequent flyers' to the ERs for treatment.

"People who were in the military know what others experience. That's why we can and want to support one another. It doesn't mean that if you weren't in the military you can't be effective. But for us … we're a family. When I see these new student vets come in, it's like Welby and I are their granddads."

The Family Member to Family Readiness Manager Path

As Robin Berry, who you met in Chapter 11, explains, "I'm a military spouse and the mother of a son. My now former husband deployed two times. Our family's experience has turned out to be helpful in my work today. It gave me some understanding into what other military families might be experiencing and prompted me to think about what extended family members and community members might experience as they support or try to support military families.

"When my husband deployed in 2003, we found that a lot of people did not know how to respond to us. It's not a surprise. We were the only military family that any of us knew. But it was a challenge. Everyone in our family started helping out. My brother-in-law took over caring for the pool, a job my husband usually did. We felt that everyone was helping so much we were reluctant to ask for more help when it was really needed.

"Yet, some close friends stopped asking me to go bowling or play cards because they thought it would be a burden for me to have to make child care arrangements. We had always done these activities as couples, and it was awkward now that I was on my own.

"I had to change jobs, so I was not working evenings and weekends and could be home with our son. That left me in a new work situation with new colleagues who did not know me or my family situation.

"At church, the sermons said we should all be at peace. I agree with that, but they made it sound like going to war is a really bad thing. When you have someone in your family deployed, you do not want to hear that. So we felt isolated from church.

"After working as an Airman and Family Readiness Manager for nearly 10 years, I believe that most of the support and resources military families need is relationship-based. I learned early on that family members and service members had to be able to trust me. Going to work with military families and/or those who support them requires knowing the military culture or being open to learning about it. Only then can we adapt what we know from our own experiences and education to support military families."

The Educator Path

Into the foreseeable future, there will be a need for coordinated and sustainable services to support military families. With this need in mind, Karen Blaisure, one of the coauthors of this book, created a course titled *Family Life and the Military* where she teaches. "Within a few years of 9/11 and the deployment of large numbers of Reserve Component members, it was evident that our family studies and child development undergraduate and graduate students would need to understand the experiences of military families. We began offering a one-credit weekend course that developed after a few years into a three-credit course. Along with studying issues of relocation, spouse employment, and education of children, we want students to learn about the impact of deployment and combat deployment on family life. We want our graduates prepared to interact sensitively and practically with military families in their current work and in their future careers in child development, social service, and education. We also wanted to highlight job opportunities for working primarily with military families."

Hearing Karen's presentation about the course at a conference, Tara Saathoff-Wells, another coauthor of this book, created a similar course, *Military Family Life*, at her university. As she explains, "I felt students needed a safe space to address academic issues, personal issues, and career issues related to the military. They needed a place they could explore their feelings about the war, about the troops, about things they see in the media, and about experiences they may have or hear about with family members or friends in the military.

"Also, we had a lot of students expressing interesting in working with military families as career options. They were given websites to explore and that's about it. I wanted them to have more. This course gives students a chance to explore career options in the civilian and military worlds."

Alisha Cederberg enrolled in the course on family life and the military for both personal and professional reasons. Alisha, a graduate student and financial services specialist recounts, "My husband was in the Air Force for 2 years. It's been frustrating for him getting others to accept that his years of service counted for something. The class has given me a framework to understand more of what he is experiencing as well as what veterans and military spouses I work with on campus experience. I think of one student whose wife was deployed. Now a single parent, he thought he'd have to withdraw from school. We talked about ways he might be able to organize his time so that he could take a course online, continue to get financial aid, and not totally stop attending the university."

SUPPORTING MILITARY FAMILIES IN YOUR COMMUNITY

In every community, every day, we can find concrete ways to show our military families respect and gratitude .... You don't have to come from a military family, have a base in your community, or be an expert in military issues to make a difference. Every American can do something.

Michelle Obama and Jill Biden (2010)

You may encounter civilians who wonder what they can do to show their appreciation and support for military families. Supporting the services provided by the organizations noted in other chapters is one way to show appreciation. Joining a group or participating in their service projects are other ways, as is joining military family members who are sending boxes to their loved one.

Voices From the Frontline

REFLECTIONS FROM A WIFE AND MOM

My husband and daughter are both soldiers currently deployed. Last time they were in two different countries. Caitlin ended up on the border of Kuwait and Iraq—one of 60 women in a 600-person deployment. Charlie was a chaplain in Ramadi, Iraq.

This time they are both at Bagram Airfield Base in Afghanistan. With flat rate boxes, I can put stuff in the same box for both of them. The box I'm packing today is a bunch of stuff Caitlin put aside before she left for training.

I send odds and ends. Charlie needed vitamins and tea. I forward their magazines. Send snacks. I just sent Charlie a cap from North Hero, Vermont. It's sunny over there.

They are on a 5-year rotation. Having gone through deployment before, you know you can do it. Last time when people asked, "Are you OK?" I would need to admit, "No, I'm not." This time I thought I really needed to be working with the military families to make it through this. So, in January 2008, I started working as a Family Readiness Support Assistant. Supporting other families helps me.

Barbara Purinton
Military Wife, Mother, Family Readiness Support Assistant

Since 9/11, numerous groups have formed for the purpose of finding a way to contribute or to support those who are acting on behalf of the United States. Many of these groups have chosen projects to demonstrate their support for service members and their families. To find these groups, talk with others in your community. Check on the Internet. You will find organizations small and large, local and national that support military families with activities including:

- Quilt making
- Sewing pillowcases
- Adopt a soldier/unit/platoon programs
- Remodeling of homes for wounded warriors
- After-school and summer activities for children of military families
- Putting together and sending of care packages
- Purchasing calling cards troops can use to call home
- Writing and sending thank you cards and poems
- Providing motorcycle escorts at funerals

Examples of occasional or unexpected interactions with military families are endless. They may be as simple as being a K-12 teacher where a child in your classroom has a parent who is a member of the Reserve Component and has been called up for deployment overseas. Perhaps that child's family is the only family in town undergoing activation and deployment. You may participate in programs such as Big Brothers/Big Sisters and be a "big" for a child with a deployed parent. For others, you may live and work near a large installation where the cycle of deployment is part of everyday life, and you can see ways in which the larger community adapts to the changes with large numbers of people entering and leaving on different assignments.

Here are other suggestions of how you might support military family members from some of the people you have met in this book:

- *"Be respectful, not intimidated by uniforms and jargon. Always remember where military families come from and what they care about: the same places and things as you and your family." Joyce Wessel Raezer, Executive Director, National Military Family Association.*

- *"Say, 'Thank you!' when you see a service member or military family.* As civilians we can choose our beliefs and actions about war. Our soldiers don't have a choice. They lifted their right hand and said they will support and defend our country and they have to go. We as family have no choice either," *Sabrina Behari, Military Family Member.*
- *"Ask, 'What can I do to support you?'* Don't go out looking to solve a big problem or to do therapy. Something as simple as inviting an at-home parent for a cup of coffee while your kids play together or taking a child to soccer practice every Thursday afternoon can be a life-preserver and make all the difference." *Chris Sullins, former Army Reserve, Combat Stress Prevention Officer.*
- *"Find a way to listen.* Not being in the military may not be a hindrance. You just have to be open to get to know someone and discover how to make a connection," *Ted Cravens, Army Reserve Combat Stress Prevention Officer.*
- *"Know there are things you may not know—or will ever know.* They say you can't understand someone until you walk a mile in their shoes. Sometimes service members and families have unique experiences and we can't follow their footsteps. That doesn't mean you can't be there for them," *Rhonda Thomlinson, Military Family Member.*
- *"Be familiar with resources available to military families.* This knowledge allows you to be able to help families connect to services in your community. At the same time, these resources can also help you learn more about the military and military families," *Rick Campise, Col, USAF, BSC, Commander, 559th Medical Group.*
- *"Make it clear to your representative in Congress that supporting the military is important.* We require a standing military to keep our country free and that costs money. Service members are not paid a lot for what they do," *Marianne Blackburn "Mimi" Drew, Rear Admiral (LH), USN (Retired).*

One final thought about supporting military families: there is nothing too small you can do to support a service or family member. As we were working on this book in the home of coauthor Colonel Angela Pereira and her husband Major Tony Vargas, coauthor Shelley MacDermid Wadsworth explained that her mother was working with a group of other women to make small cloth bags that would be filled with toiletries and sent to troops overseas. Hearing that, Angela said, "I think I have some of those. They were sent to us in Abu Ghraib." She ran upstairs and returned with three small bags. "I still treasure these little cloth bags someone sent to us in Iraq," she explained. "They were like gold. There was a central location where things sent to us were put. You could go through and find what you needed. I found these there. They held small bottles of care products like shampoo and conditioner. Hair conditioner in desert conditions is an amazing thing. But more than that, there was heart in these bags. They are pretty and so different from the world I was in." Years later, the memories caused her eyes to fill with tears as she continued, "They were made with love. Someone was saying, 'We know you are out there. We care about you.'"

CAREERS

Some of you may want to pursue career options within the military community. One option is to join a branch of the military and specialize in your training and education as a human services or healthcare professional, such as a social worker, a psychologist, physical therapist, or a nurse. If you have already graduated from college, you may investigate the option of Officer's Candidate School as a way to join the Active or Reserve Component.

There are civilian options as well. Civilians who work in DoD or one of the service branches may be hired as government employees, and their pay follows a set pay scale. A government position requiring someone with a bachelor's degree would likely be listed as a General Schedule (GS) grade of 7 or 9. A position that requires a master's degree in a mental health profession would likely be a GS-11 grade. The base pay scale for GS positions can be found online (U.S. Office of Personnel Management, n.d.). The DoDEA hires civilian employees for many jobs on and off military installations, in many career fields including teachers.

For-profit companies and not-for-profit organizations also hire civilians to fill social service or behavioral health positions needed by the military. These companies or organizations are typically awarded a contract with the DoD for a set number of years, and they hire employees to carry out the required work of the contract. It is common to have military personnel, GS workers, and contractors working together on military installations.

A number of human service organizations and agencies exist in each of the service branches and their titles may be slightly different across branches. These positions may be GS or contract positions and include such titles as family life consultants; family life and education specialists; work/life consultants; social services support specialist; child development center directors and staff; substance abuse counselors; domestic violence counselors; early childhood, primary, secondary and/or special educator within the DoD school system; relocation specialists; new parent support home visitors; medical social worker; family therapists; child and youth program specialists; recreation staff; and guidance counselors.

The Veterans Health Administration also hires professionals in medical and behavioral health. Vet Centers are staffed by mental health professionals such as social workers and psychologists and have recently established marriage and family therapy positions.

Job postings for civilians can be found on the list of websites that follows. It is recommended that you check these sites regularly as positions may only be open for a few weeks. Follow application directions carefully to ensure that your application is processed correctly and for the positions in which you are interested.

- Jobs are listed at http//www.usajobs.gov by government agency and area of focus, and it includes links for DoDEA, and the Department of the Air Force and Army.
- Army Civilian Personnel Online is a site specific to the U.S. Army (http://cpol.army.mil).
- The Department of Veterans Affairs site lists career opportunities, particularly health-related opportunities (http://www.vacareers.va.gov).
- The Department of the Navy's civilian personnel recruitment site lists civilian positions within the Navy and the Marine Corps (https://chart.donhr.navy.mil).
- The following organizations hire contractors to serve in various capacities; information on their hiring processes is available on their individual websites. Contracts are awarded for a set number of years at the conclusion of which the contracts are put up for bid again. The same or another organization may be awarded the contract.
  - Serco (http://www.serco-na.com)
  - Ceridan (http://www.ceridian.com)
  - Choctaw Archiving (http://www.choctawarchiving.net)
- Positions for military spouses are listed by military installation or job search category at http://jobsearch.spouse.military.com.

PROMOTING COMPASSION SATISFACTION

As the professionals in this chapter and throughout this book confirm, most individuals who work with and on behalf of military families find their work highly satisfying. In general, such satisfaction is common among helping professionals. The term **compassion satisfaction** refers to this type of powerful satisfaction, fulfillment, and joy of helping others and seeing small and large transformations in their lives (Radey & Figley, 2007).

The work of helping others, however, is not without its own stress. Ochberg (n.d.) described the process as follows:

> We do our job and we do it well and we feel gratified—even blessed. [We …] hear the story told with such intensity, or we hear similar stories so often, or we have the gift and curse of extreme empathy and we suffer …. We tire … we aren't ourselves … from too much caring and too little self-caring. (para. 2, 5)

Military and civilian helping professionals from medicine, family support, behavioral and social health, and faith communities may experience the process described by Ochberg. As they provide direct care of service members, they see life-threatening injuries, both visible and invisible, and perhaps a seemingly endless number with these injuries. Military corpsmen, medics, nurses, doctors, and chaplains often provide their caregiving in theatre and under life-threatening conditions. Other professionals and volunteers who work with, study, and support service members may also experience stress (Bride & Figley, 2009).

Compassion stress is used to refer to a natural outcome of experiencing another's suffering, great or small, and wanting to relieve it. Signs of compassion stress include feelings of confusion, helplessness, and isolation (Figley, 1995). To reduce the likelihood of experiencing compassion stress, it is important that helping professionals practice positive self-care, adopt a positive attitude, and avail themselves of resources that can help mitigate the stress.

However, prolonged exposure to compassion stress can lead to **compassion fatigue** that is a state of short-term "exhaustion and dysfunction, biologically, physiologically, and emotionally" (Figley, 1995, p. 2). Prior unresolved trauma, uncontrolled work stressors, poor self-care, and work dissatisfaction can contribute to the experience of compassion fatigue (Figley, 1995).

Compassion fatigue differs from **burnout** (i.e., feeling long-term exhaustion, a decreased interest in work, and dissatisfaction with the work environment) in that the former includes the aspect of caregiving in the context of another person's experience of trauma (Bride & Figley, 2009). The effects of compassion fatigue may mirror the effects of being directly exposed to a traumatic event: distressing emotions, functional impairment, hyperarousal, avoiding reminders of the trauma, and intrusive thoughts and images of the trauma, including nightmares (Bride & Figley, 2009).

Radey and Figley (2007) proposed a conceptual model to explain how compassion satisfaction develops among helping professionals. First, we respond to the situation with the right amount of assistance that is neither too little nor too much. Second, expressing gratefulness, appreciation, and liking helps us to see more possible ways to respond effectively to a situation: "positivity widens the range of thoughts and actions (e.g., play, explore, cooperate, interact, greet) and generates greater flexibility and innovation" in contrast to expressing negativity that limits creative solutions (Radey & Figley, 2007, p. 209).

The next component in this model of how compassion satisfaction develops is **self-care**, that is taking action to be healthy through such steps as exercise, proper nutrition, self-reflection, interaction with family and friends, and taking time away from work. Organizations are important in promoting self-care of employees and can do so by providing a welcoming and warm environment in which to work; supervision, adequate benefits, and staff training; and limiting and diversifying caseloads (Radey & Figley, 2007).

This model suggests that combined with a caring workplace, the use of wise judgment, positivity, and self-care will result in helpers experiencing compassion satisfaction. Compassion satisfaction is shown by high morale and delivering high-quality services (Radey & Figley, 2007). Compassion satisfaction adds to positive fulfillment and encourages us to flourish as we provide "care within an optimal range that connotes goodness, flexibility, learning, growth, and resilience in the face of work demands. Flourishing caregivers provide highly competent and compassionate care while retaining high morale and work satisfaction" (Radey & Figley, 2007, p. 208).

In Box 13.1, we include suggestions for increasing the likelihood of experiencing compassion satisfaction when working with individuals and families who have experienced traumatic events. These suggestions, which are organized into categories developed by Radey and Figley (2007), include ideas offered and recommended by others. You and your colleagues may wish to add other suggestions to this list. It is particularly important to implement these suggestions when first noticing signs of compassion stress, in order to lessen the possibility of the stress developing into compassion fatigue.

BOX 13.1   BEST PRACTICES

PROMOTING COMPASSION SATISFACTION AND
PREVENTING COMPASSION FATIGUE

Increase or Maintain a Positive Attitude Toward Clients and Toward Life

- Practice gratitude (e.g., begin and end each day noting something to be grateful for)
- Express appreciation to others for who they are or what they have done
- Express enthusiasm
- Remember receiving another's compassion
- Focus on the good being done
- Accept that one person cannot fix everything
- Reinforce others for taking care of themselves

Increase Resources to Manage Stress

- Connect concepts and skills learned in classroom with "real life"
- Take continuing education courses
- Know personal limits, set boundaries, and say "no" when it is possible
- Seek mentoring
- Talk with someone you trust
- Normalize reaching out for help
- Add touches to the workplace, so it is more comfortable and soothing (e.g., comfortable chair, calming photographs or mementos)
- Participate in a nonwork activity that recharges and energizes
- Visit places that nourish one's soul
- Accept the love of a pet, the song of a bird, the beauty of a flower

Increase Self-Care

- Set and meet personal goals to increase or maintain self-care (e.g., proper nutrition, exercise, meditation)
- Reflect on quality of care provided to clients and level of self-care at that time
- Obtain adequate rest and sleep, follow healthy eating guides, exercise, meditate
- Drink water to avoid dehydration
- Take short breaks during work and practice deep breathing
- Notice when hungry, angry, lonely, or tired and respond appropriately
- Avoid alcohol, nonprescription medications, smoking, sugar, and caffeine
- Spend time with family and friends who restore rather than deplete energy
- Participate in or begin team meetings that provide opportunity to give and receive social support.

Compiled from Boss (2006), Brymer et al. (2006), Hirsch and Engel (2008), Radey and Figley (2007), and U.S. Department of Veterans Affairs (2010b).

Finally, the Green Cross Academy of Traumatology (n.d.) has recognized the importance of self-care. Members of this international nonprofit organization are mostly licensed mental health-care providers who provide crisis and trauma counseling, assessment, and referral following a traumatic event. They also offer education, training, and consultation about responding to traumatized individuals and families. This organization emphasizes the centrality of self-care in provision of competent assistance. Members are required to abide by standards of self-care as part of ethical practice and acknowledgement of a universal right to wellness (http:// www.greencross.org).

Military families look to knowledgeable, compassionate, and competent professionals for guidance during times of challenge and for direction in enjoying and maximizing the benefits of military life. As you complete your education, seek training, and begin or continue working, consider the importance of doing all you can to encourage positive attitudes, the use of resources, and self-care for yourself and for your colleagues. In so doing, you also benefit those you serve: military families.

SUMMARY

- There are many career paths that offer a way to serve military families, either directly or indirectly. Researchers, writers, video producers, family members, veterans, education specialist, and many other professionals have all found applications for their skills that benefit military members and families.
- Colleges and universities have recently begun to develop courses to prepare individuals to interact sensitively and practically with military families in their current work and in their future careers.
- Civilians can show their appreciation and support for military families by supporting organizations that serve military families, joining groups formed to support or honor military families or participating in their service projects, and showing respect and appreciation in daily encounters with military members and families.
- There are many options for pursuing a career within the military community: joining a branch of the military and specializing as a human services or health-care professional, as a government employee in a helping profession, or as an employee of a private company or organization that has been awarded a contract with the DoD to provide civilians to fill social service or behavioral health positions needed by the military.
- Job postings for civilians who want to work as a government employee can be found on the websites of the individual organizations and agencies that provide services to military families.
- Most individuals who support and care for military families find their work satisfying, and they experience compassion satisfaction. However, helping others and experiencing another's suffering can be emotionally challenging and can lead to compassion stress, which, if not addressed, can result in compassion fatigue, that is, short-term physical and emotional exhaustion and dysfunction.
- To enhance their compassion satisfaction and deliver high quality services, helping professionals can judge the appropriate response to another's situation to avoid overresponding or underresponding, express positivity, practice self-care, and develop or find a caring workplace.

EXERCISES

1. Using one of the online job search sites listed in this chapter, identify at least one position for which you qualify or will qualify based on your education, training, and experience. Study the basic requirements, and the knowledge, skills, and abilities necessary for each job. Prepare the required application materials for one of the positions.
2. Research the titles for human services professionals in each of the service branches.
3. Brainstorm how workers in a range of careers could encounter military families. How would they know someone comes from a military family? What might they do to invite military family members to identify themselves?
4. Develop attainable self-care goals that include at least one of each of the following components: exercise, better nutrition, self-reflection (e.g., meditation, prayer), interaction with family and friends, and taking time away from work on a regular basis.

Acronyms

AAFES   Army and Air Force Exchange Service
ACU   Army Combat Uniform
AER   Army Emergency Relief
AFAS   Air Force Aid Society
AFQT   Armed Forces Qualifying Test
AFSC   Air Force Specialty Codes
AFW2   Air Force Wounded Warrior Program
AW2   Army Wounded Warrior Program
AWOL   Absent Without Leave
BUMED   U.S. Navy's Bureau of Medicine and Surgery
CACO   Casualty Assistance Calls Officer
CAO   Casualty Assistance Officer
CAR   Casualty Assistance Representative
CDCs   Child Development Centers
CHEA   Council for Higher Education Accreditation
CNO   Casualty Notification Officer
CO   Commanding Officer
CONUS   Within the continental or contiguous United States
COSC   Combat Operational Stress Control
COSFA   Combat and Operational Stress First Aid
CSF   Comprehensive Soldier Fitness
DADT   Don't Ask, Don't Tell
DCoE   Defense Centers of Excellence for Psychological Health and Traumatic Brain Injury
DDESS   Department of Defense Domestic Dependent Elementary and Secondary Schools
DeCA   Defense Commissary Agency
DEERS   Defense Enrollment and Eligibility Reporting System
DoD   Department of Defense
DoDDS   Department of Defense Dependents Schools
DoDEA   Department of Defense Education Activity
DSM IV   Diagnostic and Statistical Manual IV
DUSD/MCFP   Office of the Deputy Under Secretary of Defense (Military Community and Family Policy)
EFMP   Exceptional Family Member Program
EMDR   Eye movement desensitization and reprocessing
ESGR   Employer Support of the Guard and Reserve
FAP   Family Advocacy Program
FCC   Family Child Care
FMLA   Family and Medical Leave Act
FOB   Forward Operating Base
FOCUS   Families OverComing Under Stress
FRG   Family Readiness Group
GAT   Global Assessment Tool
GS   General Schedule
H2H   Heroes to Hometowns
HA/DR   Humanitarian Assistance/Disaster Response
IA   Individual Augmentee(s)

IAVA   Iraq and Afghanistan Veterans of America
IBA   Interceptor Body Armor
IED   Improvised explosive device
JFSAP   Joint Family Support Assistance Program
KIA   Killed in Action
MCEC   Military Child Education Coalition
MCM   Manual for Courts-Martial
MCX   Marine Corps Exchange
MEDEVAC or MEDIVAC   Medical evacuation
MFLC   Military and Family Life Counselor
MFRI   Military Family Research Institute at Purdue University
MHAT   Mental Health Advisory Team
MIA   Missing in Action
MOS   Military Occupational Specialty
MOS   Military OneSource
mTBI   Mild Traumatic Brain Injury
MWR   Morale, Welfare and Recreation
NEC   Navy Enlisted Classification system
NEX   Navy Exchange
NICoE   National Intrepid Center of Excellence
NMCRS   Navy-Marine Corps Relief Society
NPSG   New Parent Support Program
OCONUS   Outside of the continental or contiguous United States
OEF   Operation Enduring Freedom
OIF   Operation Iraqi Freedom
OMK   Operation: Military Kids
OND   Operation New Dawn
OPTEMPO   Operational Tempo
PCS   Permanent Change of Station
PDHRA   Post-Deployment Health Reassessment
PFA   Psychological First Aid
POW   Prisoners of War
PREP   Prevention and Relationship Enhancement Program
PTSD   Posttraumatic stress disorder
PX or BX   Post Exchange or Base Exchange
RESPECT-Mil   Re-Engineering Systems of Primary Care Treatment in the Military
ROTC   Reserve Officer Training Corps
RWW   Returning Warrior Workshop
SAC   School-Age Care Programs
SAIC   Science Applications International Corporation
SIT   Stress inoculation therapy
SOC   Service Member's Opportunity College
SOMK   Speak Out for Military Kids
SVA   Student Veterans of America
SWAN   Service Women's Action Network
TAPS   Tragedy Assistance Program for Survivors
TBI   Traumatic Brain Injury
TDY or TAD   Temporary duty
UCMJ   Uniform Code of Military Justice
USAFRICOM   U.S. Africa Command
USCENTCOM or CENTCOM   U.S. Central Command
USDA   U.S. Department of Agriculture

USERRA Uniformed Services Employment and Reemployment Rights Act
USEUCOM U.S. European Command
USJFCOM U.S. Joint Forces Command
USNORTHCOM U.S. Northern Command
USPACOM U.S. Pacific Command
USSOCOM U.S. Special Operations Command
USSOUTHCOM U.S. Southern Command
USSTRATCOM U.S. Strategic Command
USTRANSCOM U.S. Transportation Command
VA Department of Veterans Affairs
VBA Veterans Benefits Administration
VETS Veterans Employment and Training Services
VFW Veterans of Foreign Wars
VHA Veterans Health Administration
WWR Marine Corps Wounded Warrior Regiment

Glossary

Accessions: Individuals accepted into the military, also called recruits.

Accompanied tour: A military assignment to an overseas location that includes the service member's family.

Active Component: The portion of the U.S. military forces comprised of full-time active duty members in the Army, Navy, Marine Corps, and Air Force.

Acute grief: During bereavement, the process of yearning for the loved one daily, feeling deep sadness, struggling with the finality of the loss, being preoccupied with memories and thoughts of the loved one, and having diminished interest in ongoing life.

Acute stress disorder: Symptoms that begin within 4 weeks of exposure to a traumatic event and last up to 1 month; an individual may exhibit anxiety and have impaired functioning in one area of life (e.g., work, family); symptoms may include reexperiencing the trauma (through dreams, flashbacks, reoccurring thoughts), avoiding stimuli (e.g., locations, smells, sounds, people) that may be reminders of the event, detachment from others, and emotional numbing.

Acute stress reaction: Temporary symptoms in response to a traumatic event (e.g., disorientation, agitation, anxiety, confusion) that usually disappear in hours or days.

Acute stressor: A short-term stressful event or situation (e.g., a child having difficulties with a friend).

Adaptive coping strategies: Approaches used by families to stabilize and maintain balance in the family system that promote individual growth and development and improve family functioning.

Adult dependents: Family members who are a parent, grandparent, former spouse, sibling, disabled older child, or any other individual who is claimed by the service member as a dependent.

Allowance: A set dollar amount that is paid to service members in addition to their basic monthly pay that is designed to at least partially compensate for the costs of items considered necessary for the service member.

Ambiguous loss: Loss characterized by lack of closure or clear understanding of the extent of the loss (e.g., there is no verification of a loved one's death or no certainty that he or she will return or be same as he or she used to be); boundary ambiguity may be experienced as an ambiguous loss.

Ambiguous loss theory: Part of the work in family stress theory that focuses specifically on understanding family events/crises that are not always resolvable, which mean that families face the challenges of finding meaning in their circumstances and being able to live and grow despite ongoing ambiguity, being resilient in the face of uncertainty.

Ambiguous stressor: A stressor characterized by limits to knowing what happened and/or what the outcomes might be.

Applicants: Individuals who apply to enter the military.

Armed Forces of the United States: All of the components of the Army, Navy, Air Force, Marine Corps, and Coast Guard when it augments the Navy.

Base: The Air Force and Navy term for a military installation.

Baseline data: In research, data provided at a beginning point in a research project or by compiling the results of several studies so that future data collected can be compared to beginning data to assess change and continuity.

Battle Rattle: Military slang for protective armor used in combat; also referred to as IBA or Interceptor Body Armor.

Being stressed: The state of someone who experiences tension created by a mismatch in his or her abilities and/or resources to meet the demands of a situation.

Beneficiary: Someone eligible to use or access a military-related benefit, such as shopping at stores on a military installation or accessing TRICARE health-care coverage.

Bipolar disorder: A psychological health disorder characterized by mood swings that range from depression to feeling euphoric and energetic.

Boundary ambiguity: An unclear perception of who is in and who is out of the family, created by having a family member "present" physically but not psychologically or present psychologically but not physically.

Buffer: In spousal communication processes, appraising a situation as being a group problem but deciding to take responsibility for solving it individually, instead of as a couple.

Burnout: A state of long-term exhaustion, a decreased interest in work, and dissatisfaction with the work environment.

Camp: The Marine Corps term for a military installation.

Caregiver burden: The increased sense of responsibility and stress that a caregiver experiences in attending to the needs and welfare of another person.

Caregivers and Veterans Omnibus Health Services Act: A federal law that provides assistance to caregivers of veterans injured in the line of duty or training on or after September 11, 2001.

Casualties: Individuals who have died or have been wounded while serving.

Casualty Assistance Calls Officer: A Navy or Marine Corps representative who notifies a service member's designated next of kin when there is a death of a sailor or marine, provides information, and assists the family with funeral or memorial services, filing paperwork for benefits and entitlements, and relocation.

Casualty Assistance Officer: An Army representative who provides information and assists the family with funeral or memorial services, filing paperwork for benefits and entitlements, and relocation when there is a death of a soldier.

Casualty Assistance Representative: An Air Force Corps representative who notifies a service member's designated next of kin when there is a death of an airman, provides information, and assists the family with funeral or memorial services, filing paperwork for benefits and entitlements, and relocation.

Casualty Notification Officer: An Army representative, often accompanied by a military chaplain and/or organization commander, who notifies a service member's designated next of kin when there is a death of a soldier.

Chain of command: The highly structured line of authority and responsibility, which designates who is in charge of what and whom and along which orders are passed.

Chief of Staff: The most senior ranking officer of a branch of the military service, who is responsible for the readiness of personnel, among numerous other responsibilities.

Child development centers: Facilities found on most military installations that provide daytime, business day child care for infants to 5-year-olds.

Chronic stressor: A stressful longer-term event or situation (e.g., an ongoing health issue).

Cognitive-based therapy: In the treatment of PTSD, cognitive-based therapy includes learning about symptoms of PTSD, identifying thoughts and feelings associated with the trauma, identifying and challenging dysfunctional beliefs about the trauma, and replacing these beliefs with more logical, functional, and reality-based beliefs.

Cohorts: In research, a cohort consists of new enrollees who join the study at the same time where the research design calls for multiple points of new enrollments.

Combat and operation stress: The physical, mental, and emotional symptoms (e.g., anxiety, hyperarousal, fatigue, depression, concentration problems) that extend beyond 4 days after a traumatic event.

Combat Operational Stress Control: An overarching principle that guides military leaders as they develop regulations and policies on how to address the physical, cognitive, emotional, and/or behavioral stress symptoms that service members experience as a result of combat or other military operations and to keep stress within an acceptable range; policies and programs emphasize enhancing resilience and performance through prevention and early interventions with individuals and families who experience psychological injury.

Combat operational stress reactions: The physical, cognitive, emotional, and/or behavioral stress symptoms as a result of combat or as result of other operations; these reactions may be experienced for just a few hours or days or may persist for weeks, months, or longer.

Combat stress reactions: The expected reactions of service members who have experienced stressful events while in combat, including emotional, intellectual, physical, and/or behavioral reactions.

Combat-injured families: The spouses, children and stepchildren, parents, ex-spouses, siblings, and other extended relations of an injured service member.

Commissary: Tax-free grocery stores located on military installations and reserved for use by military beneficiaries.

Communal coping: When appraisal of a problem and actions taken to resolve the problem are seen as group responsibilities, communal coping acknowledges that individuals are nested within groups, such as marital dyads and family systems, and that the other members of the group are likely to be affected when one or more members are distressed.

Community capacity: The collective ability of a community to address community needs and to confront situations that threaten the safety and well-being of community members.

Compassion fatigue: A state of short-term physical, physiological, and emotional exhaustion that can result after a prolonged period of experiencing other's suffering; prior unresolved trauma, uncontrolled work stressors, poor self-care, and work dissatisfaction can contribute to the experience of compassion fatigue.

Compassion satisfaction: The satisfaction, fulfillment, and joy of helping others and seeing small and large transformations in their lives that is common among helping professionals.

Compassion stress: A natural outcome of experiencing another's suffering, great or small, and wanting to relieve it; signs of compassion stress include feelings of confusion, helplessness, and isolation.

Complicated grief: During bereavement, the process during which the bereaved experience prolonged yearning and other symptoms such as disbelief or bitterness over the loss, numbness, a sense that life is empty, and an inability to move forward with plans.

Composite Life Cycle Model: A conceptual model used by the U.S. Army to illustrate how events and transitions in three areas of a soldier's life (i.e., unit, personal work, and family) relate to each other across time, family development, and career milestones.

Comprehensive Soldier Fitness: A strength-based program rooted in positive psychology and designed to enhance soldier, family, and civilian worker resilience and performance through a confidential personal assessment, online training, and unit training.

Compromising: Making family and individual efforts to achieve balance within a new community.

Conservation of Resources: A theory used to understand ways that people seek out, invest, and protect resources they find valuable in coping with stressful events; it postulates that people invest in resources that they perceive to be valuable and useful, which are in turn shaped by family, community, and culture; when resources are lost or threatened, stress results and people will try to conserve (maintain) the resources they have.

Consolidating: When a family unit and its individual members unite in their group efforts and support individual efforts to make modifications to the family's operating system so that the family can better cope with stressors.

Constituents: In research, people and organizations that can benefit from the knowledge gained, as well as any sponsors of the research.

Coping: A variety of efforts to overcome challenges or difficulties.

Core concept: A principle that guides military leaders as they develop regulations and policies and that sets standards and expectations that leaders are to support.

Council of State Governments: A nonprofit, nonpartisan organization for state governments.

Cross-sectional: In research, studies designed to collect data from a group at a single point in time.

Cumulative stressor: A stressful event or situation that contributes to the current situation, creating a pileup of stressors.

Defense Enrollment and Eligibility Reporting System: A programs that verifies those who are eligible for military-based services and benefits; each eligible person is enrolled into this system so that he or she can be identified as a family member or legal dependent when interacting with the military community.

Defense of Marriage Act: A federal act passed in 1996 that explicitly states that marriage at the federal level is only recognized if it occurs between one man and one woman and reaffirms that individual states are not compelled to recognize same-sex marriages that occurred in a different state.

Deficits model: A family development model based on identifying the factors families lack that are associated with unhealthy development.

Demilitarized Zone: A buffer zone between North Korea and South Korea.

Department of Defense: The federal department tasked with national security and supervising the U.S. Armed Forces.

Department of Veterans Affairs: A U.S. presidential cabinet-level position comprised of the Veterans Benefits Administration, the Veterans Health Administration, and the National Cemetery Administration, which provide medical care and other federal benefits to eligible veterans and their family members.

Deployment: The movement of military forces, equipment, and logistical support to an area of military operations.

Developmental regression: The inability to maintain developmental gains and revert back to earlier behaviors, particularly in very early childhood.

Diagnostic and Statistical Manual IV: The American Psychiatric Association's publication that lists mental health disorders and their symptoms.

Don't Ask, Don't Tell: DoD Directive 1304.26, a federal law prohibiting gays and lesbians from serving in the U. S. Armed Forces; under this directive, the military could not ask recruits about their sexual orientation and military members were not obligated to disclose if they were gay or lesbian because that knowledge would be grounds for their discharge from the military.

Dual-military marriages: Marriages in which a military member in one branch of service is married to a military member in the same or different branch of service.

Dyadic research: Research in which data is gathered from both members of a couple; a typical method of studying shared and nonshared perceptions the couple has about their life and marriage.

Emotional cycle of deployment model: An evolving six-stage model highlighting structural and emotional issues that families may encounter before, during, and after deployment.

Emotion-focused coping: Individual cognitive and behavioral strategies used to regulate one's distress.

Endstrength: The total number of military personnel required by the Armed Forces or a branch of the Armed Forces, taking into account recruitment, retention, death, and retirements and other separations.

Exchange: A shopping facility on a military installation that provides durable goods, merchandise, and services for military beneficiaries, including restaurants and businesses such as hair salons; large exchanges are similar to civilian department stores.

Explicit norm: An overtly stated expectation; in the military, an explicit norm is wearing a uniform on duty, while in a family an explicit norm may be a set bedtime for children.

Exposure therapy: In the treatment of PTSD, a model that includes psychoeducation (e.g., learning about trauma reactions, PTSD, and symptoms) and exposure to the trauma-related stimuli; in vivo exposure to a feared stimulus is used to gradually reduce the symptoms that are triggered by the stimulus by keeping the person safe and teaching him or her to use relaxation techniques to reduce the impact of the stimulus.

External locus of control: An individual's generalized expectations that they have little or no control over events that are affecting them.

Extrafamilial: Outside the family system.

Eye movement desensitization and reprocessing: In the treatment of PTSD, a model used to desensitize clients to the trauma-related memories that cause them distress by encouraging the recall of images and resulting emotions, identifying alternate understandings of the trauma experience, and challenging clients to consider these other understandings; the goal is to disable the distressing memories that trigger the symptoms.

Family and Medical Leave Act: A federal law that offers eligible employees of covered employers job-protected, unpaid leave of up to 12 workweeks for care of seriously ill family members, to attend to their own serious health condition, or upon the birth or adoption of a child.

Family Care Plan: A firm arrangement for the care of children during deployment, including a determination of who will care for the member's child or children during deployment and other absences; arrangements to provide financial, medical, and logistical support for the children's well-being; name and consent to the plan of any noncustodial parent who will not be the caregiver during the service member's absence; and designation of a temporary caregiver in case of incapacity or death of the service member while permanent custody is established.

Family child care providers or child development providers (Navy): Individuals certified to provide child care to children from infancy to 12 years of age in their homes on military installations; family child care homes may offer daytime, evening, nighttime, and weekend hours.

Family coherence: Satisfaction with interpersonal connections and dynamics among family members.

Family of creation: The family system created through partnering and/or parenting.

Family resilience framework: An expanded model of family resilience that examines key processes involved in family resiliency and resources that families draw upon to help manage and reduce stress and cultivate resiliency and positive growth, including family belief systems, family organizational patterns, and family communication processes.

Family separation allowance: Payment made to service members who are required to be away from their permanent duty station for more than 30 continuous days.

Family stress: An upset in the equilibrium, or steady state, of a family, which requires that the family makes adjustments in order to maintain or regain a sense of coherence.

Family stress theory: A body of theoretical work that describes family system experiences of crises (both normative and nonnormative) and the ways in which the family identifies resources, challenges, and strengths in coping strategies and coordinates efforts to maintain or regain coherence and resilience.

Family-of-origin relationships: Relationships with parents or siblings or others with whom one grew up

First-time birthrate: A statistic calculated as the number of births of a first child per 1000 women, ages 15–44 in the civilian population.

Gearing up: Preparing personnel and gear for deployment by issuing personal gear and equipment, obtaining and preparing uniforms, going to medical appointments, completing legal and financial paperwork, participating in any additional unit or individual training, and preparing unit equipment for transportation.

General Stress and Coping Theory: Principles used to explain and/or understand internal aspects of coping (cognitions and emotions).

Generalize: In research, to be able to apply what is learned from the study to everyone all the time.

Gulf War I: The term used for U.S. military operations in the Persian Gulf from 1990–1991, also known as Operation Desert Storm or the Persian Gulf War.

Hardiness: A personality trait that allows an individual to cope with stress and catastrophe effectively.

Implicit norm: An implied expectation; in the military an implicit norm is showing respect for all military service members and veterans, while in a family an implicit norm is how affection is shown.

Inactive National Guard: National Guard personnel who are required to muster only once a year with their unit.

Indicated preventive interventions: Resilience programming targeted toward individuals who are exhibiting early signs of distress or loss of functioning.

Individual augmentee: A service member who is temporarily assigned to another command, deploys with the new command, and returns to his or her parent command upon completion of the deployment.

Individual Ready Reserve: Personnel who have served as active duty or in the selected reserve and still have time remaining on their military service obligation.

Individuals-nested in families-nested in social settings: An ecological model that centers individuals within their family and larger social settings (neighborhood, religious setting, school/work) and highlights how individuals need meaningful connections with others in order to access and build resources for healthy living.

Injury communication: Providing and delivering information related to the injury to families and to the impact on family members' capacity to understand and use the information provided.

Integrated grief: During bereavement, the process during which bereaved persons comprehend the death, are not preoccupied by thoughts and memories, and have interest in life.

Interfacing: When a family and its individual members interact with or operate within the larger social contexts of work, community, and school groups.

Intergenerational trauma: The transmission of secondary trauma to children.

Interstate Compact on Educational Opportunities for Military Children: An agreement among states on how to handle educational issues that often vary across states, such as enrollment, placement, eligibility, and graduation requirements.

Intimate terrorism: Violence usually perpetrated by men and based upon a motivation to dominate a spousal relationship through violent force and control.

Joint Chiefs of Staff: The senior officers of their respective services who are military advisors to the President, the Secretary of Defense, and the National Security Council.

Judicial due process: Due process of law; the principle that the government must respect all of the legal rights that are owed to a person, including witnesses, a jury, a pretrial hearing, formal notification of the charges, free legal representation, and a speedy trial.

Land navigation: Using a map and compass travel from one place to another.

Land-grant university: A university established in each state on land granted to the state by the federal government to make education more accessible to the working class and to teach agriculture, engineering, sciences, and military tactics; to conduct research; and to provide extension services.

Longitudinal: In research, a term describing studies that collect data at multiple points in time, allowing researchers to follow people over time.

Magical thinking: Making incorrect assumptions about cause and effect (e.g., "If I wish hard enough, my Daddy will be OK.").

Meaning-focused coping: Individual cognitive and behavioral strategies used to reframe and give different meaning to a stressful event or situation.

Mental Health Advisory Team: A research team established by the Office of the U.S. Army Surgeon General to examine behavioral health of service members and behavioral health care in OIF and OEF.

Military brat, Air Force brat, Army brat, Navy brat, or Marine Corps brat: A positive and affectionate term claimed by military children to refer to themselves and others growing up in the military.

Military departments: The Department of the Army, the Department of the Navy (which includes the Marine Corps), and the Department of the Air Force; each is responsible for organizing, training, and equipping its personnel.

Military installations: Facilities owned or leased and operated by the military.

Military operational specialty: An assigned military job or occupation.

Military sexual trauma: Sexual trauma experienced while in active service.

Motivation to serve: Reasons for serving in the military.

National Cemetery Administration: A branch of the VA responsible for national and state veterans' cemeteries, as well as headstones, markers, and presidential memorial certificates.

National Defense Authorization Act: A federal law that is passed by Congress every year to grant the Department of Defense funds to operate and specific guidance on how to spend those funds.

Neural plasticity: Flexibility in the development of neural connections that responds to early experiences and deprivations, starting the lifelong process of "tailoring" the brain to the person with all his or her personal, social, and environmental experiences.

Nonnormative stressors: Family life stressors that do not occur to most families and are unexpected (e.g., a child with a terminal illness); nonnormative stressors unique to military families are the injury or death of a family service member by friendly fire or missing in action.

Nonvolitional stressor: A stressful event or situation that is imposed upon the person/family (not wanted or chosen).

Normative stressors: Family life stressors that occur for most families and at expected times, such as life cycle transitions (e.g., birth of a child, death of an aged grandparent) and developmental changes (e.g., children going to school).

Norms: Expectations about how to act in a situation; can be explicitly stated or implicitly understood.

Operation Enduring Freedom: U.S. military actions in Afghanistan that began in October 2001.

Operation Iraqi Freedom: U.S. military actions in Iraq that began in March 2003 and ended in August 2010, when the name for continuing operations was changed to Operation New Dawn.

Operation New Dawn: U.S. military action in Iraq that began in September 2010.

Operational tempo or optempo: The frequency and intensity of military operations or missions.

Overall birthrate: A statistic calculated as the total number of births per 1000 women, ages 15–44 in the civilian population, which includes first, second, third, and all subsequent births.

Parental efficacy: Parents' availability and effectiveness in caring for their children.

Permanent Change of Station: A relocation of a service member's work affiliation from one unit or duty station to another; service members may request their duty preference but the assignment is determined by the needs of the branch of service.

Personally Procured Transportation Move: A "do it yourself" move (versus a government arranged move).

Pileup of stressors: An occurrence of overlapping demands on an individual, family, or other system.

Post: The Army term for a military installation.

Posttraumatic stress: A spectrum of emotional, physical, and behavioral reactions to a trauma, many of which may not be experienced by an individual exposed to trauma.

Posttraumatic stress disorder: An anxiety disorder that may occur following a traumatic event (e.g., threat of death, threat of death of another, or threat of physical, sexual, or psychological integrity) with symptoms that persist more than 1 month after the traumatic event.

Problem-solving coping: Individual cognitive and behavioral strategies used to address the problem creating a stressful event or situation.

Propensity to serve: Interest or plans to serve in the military.

Prospective: In research, studies that start in the present and continue into the future to see what experiences are linked to physical and psychological health outcomes late in life.

Protective factors: Skills and resources that individuals and families can draw upon to help them cope with adversity.

Psychobiological stress research: Research that integrates neurobiological research with psychosocial research to include physiological measures of stress, such as cortisol, serotonin, and dopamine levels; autonomic response systems, including respiration and perspiration rates and eye dilation; and MRI brain scans, as well as self-reports on stressful events and circumstances.

Psychological First Aid: A way of helping children, adolescents, adults, and families immediately following a traumatic event to help reduce their stress level, ensure that their current needs are met, and encourage adaptive functioning.

Public stigma: Prejudice and discrimination against those with psychological disorders.

Purple: A term indicating that an activity or a program includes all branches of the U.S. Armed Forces.

Rank: An achieved military status, representing a level of responsibility and attainment of knowledge, expertise, and leadership skills.

Ready Reserve: One of the three components of the Reserve Component that includes the selected reserve, the Individual Ready Reserve, and the Inactive National Guard.

Rear detachment: Military personnel who remain at the home installation when there is a deployment of the unit to combat or to another military operation.

Recovery trajectory: The process of recovery over time from illness or injury with expected advances, setbacks, and potential changes in abilities; a concept used in the medical and rehabilitative fields.

Reserve Component: The portion of the U.S. military forces comprised of the Ready Reserve, Standby Reserve, and Retired Reserve.

Resilience: A process of positive adaptation and growth after experiencing an adverse event/circumstance; resilience can be measured by several outcome indicators and is influenced by a blend of risk and protective factors.

Resilience Continuum: An evidence-based model that describes indicators of psychological health for individuals, families, and commands and refocuses responsibility for promoting psychosocial health on everyone in the system.

Restructuring: Making modifications to the family's current operating system in the areas of roles, family rules, patterns of interaction and communication, and goals so that the family can cope with stressors.

Retired Reserve: One of the three components of the Reserve Component that includes those reserve officers and enlisted who receive retired pay or are eligible for retired pay but are not 60 years old or over, not members of the Ready or Standby Reserves, and have not chosen to be discharged.

Risky behaviors: Actions that heighten threats to an individual's health, safety, or emotional well-being, including alcohol and other drug misuse, disordered eating, increased risk-taking, and both sexual and nonsexual aggression.

Roles: A group of norms that govern a situation; similar to "parts" played by actors on stage or in a movie.

School-age care programs: Before and after-school programs located on many military installations that provide activities and supervision of school-age children of military families.

Scope: In research, how broad a research question is and how widely it can be generalized (applied to populations outside of participants who have been included in the study).

Secondary traumatization: The indirect exposure to trauma due to interactions with the traumatized person that begins to affect the well-being of the persons around the individual.

Secretary of Defense: A presidential cabinet member who oversees national security agencies and the Department of the Army, the Department of the Air Force, and the Department of the Navy (which includes the Marine Corps).

Selected preventive intervention: Resilience programming targeted toward those who may be at higher risk for developing distress or loss of functioning.

Selected reserve: Reservists in the Army, Navy, Marine Corps, Air Force, and Coast Guard, and members of each state's Air and Army National Guard.

Self-care: Actions taken to be physically and emotionally healthy through such steps as exercise, proper nutrition, self-reflection, interaction with family and friends, and taking time away from work.

Self-efficacy: The extent to which persons believe that they can meet a goal or expectation.

Self-stigma: Internalization of the public's biases against those with psychological illnesses.

Sense of self: How one views one's self and abilities; a self-definition of who one is.

Separation: A term often used by family members refer to time apart from their service member; spouses may also use the word to indicate a break in a romantic relationship.

Separation from the military: Being released from active duty, discharged from military obligations, and transferred to the reserves or retired list.

Shoppettes: Convenience stores located on military installations and reserved for use by military beneficiaries.

Situational couple violence: Couple violence that tends to be much more gender symmetrical (both men and women engage in violent action) and is linked with particular couple conflicts unique in the relationship of the couple.

Squad tactics: Strategies used by a small unit of service members to achieve a goal.

Standby Reserve: One of the three components of the Reserve Component that includes personnel temporarily not in the Ready Reserves due to a hardship or disability or due to being designated as having civilian employment critical to national security.

Stigma: In psychological health, negative associations about psychological health disorders or the treatment of psychological health problems, and/or the belief that there are negative connotations associated with having a psychological health problem.

Strengths-based model: A family development model that identifies and builds on families' existing strengths to encourage healthy development.

Stress: Both a process and a state of being brought about when a person's appraisal of a situation or context results in a judgment of a mismatch in his or her abilities and/or resources to meet the demands of the situation.

Synergizing: Coordinating all family system and individual member's efforts to consolidate various change efforts within the family system.

Theory of mind: A limit in the ability to understand things from another person's point of view.

"Total" institution: An organization or a company that rewards and promotes based on performance and that has complete influence in an individual's daily experiences on and off the job.

Traumatic brain injury: A blow or jolt to the head or penetration of the head by an object, disrupting brain function.

Unaccompanied tour: An assignment to an overseas location where the family is not authorized to travel with and remain with the service member because the assignment area is deemed to be politically unstable, dangerous, or lacking in support services for families.

Unified Command Plan: An annual review with possible modification of the mission or jurisdiction of the unified commands.

Unified Commands: Two or more military departments working under a single commander to conduct operations in support of a continuing defense or combat mission in a region or an ongoing functional mission; there are currently six unified combatant commands with specific missions in regions throughout the world.

Uniform Code of Military Justice: Part of the U. S. Code of law that regulates the conduct of personnel in the uniformed services.

Uniformed Services: The Army, Navy, Marine Corps, Air Force, Coast Guard, Public Health Service Commissioned Corps, and the National Oceanic and Atmospheric Administration's Commissioned Officer Corps; the first five are Armed Services, and the last two are Noncombatant Uniformed Services.

Uniformed Services Employment and Reemployment Rights Act: A federal law that prohibits employers from discriminating on the basis of an employee's consideration of joining the military or an employee's current or past military service.

Universal preventive interventions: Resilience programming targeted toward all military families.

Vet centers: Counseling facilities open to all veterans who served in a combat theatre or anywhere during times of armed hostilities and to their family members; they offer individual and group counseling, family therapy related to military issues, sexual trauma counseling, employment and substance abuse assessment and referral, screening and referral for medical issues, and outreach and education.

Veterans Benefits Administration: A branch of the VA responsible for managing education benefits, disability compensation, pensions, burial allowances, vocational rehabilitation, home loans, life insurance, and survivors' benefits for eligible veterans and their families.

Veterans Health Administration: An integrated health-care system that provides medical care to eligible veterans and includes hospitals, community-based outpatient clinics, community living centers, long-term care facilities, and readjustment counseling centers.

Violent resistance: The partner's (usually female) actions to resist against an attempt by a spousal partner to control her actions and opportunities.

Volitional stressor: A stressful event or situation that was wanted or chosen (such as taking steps to change one's marital status).

Warrant Officer: A military member who is designated an officer through a warrant (a specific authorization) as opposed to an officer who is designated through a commission; usually, Warrant Officers are technical experts or specialists with a specific set of skills.

References

Ackerman, R., DiRamio, D., & Garza Mitchell, R. L. (2009). Transitions: Combat veterans as college students. In R. Ackerman & D. DiRamio (Eds.), *Creating a veteran-friendly campus: Strategies for transition and success* (pp. 5–14). San Francisco, CA: Jossey-Bass.

Adler, A. B., & Dolan, C. A. (2006). Military hardiness as a buffer of psychological health on return from deployment. *Military Medicine, 171*, 93–98.

Adler-Baeder, F., Pittman, J. F., & Taylor, L. (2005). The prevalence of marital transitions in military families. *Journal of Divorce and Remarriage, 44*, 91–106.

Air Force Aid Society (2010). *Air Force Aid Society: The official charity of the U.S. Air Force.* Retrieved September 9, 2010 from http://www.afas.org.

Air Force Times (2010). Family centers. Retrieved August 24, 2010 from http://www.airforcetimes.com/benefits/family_resources/online_hbml10_milfam_familycenters/.

Alexander, C. (2010, September). *The shock of war.* Retrieved from http://www.smithsonianmag.com/history-archaeology/The-Shock-of-War.html.

Allen, E., & Markman, H. (2010). *Marital functioning and intervention for U.S. Army couples.* Presented at the 2010 International Research Symposium on Military Families, Indianapolis, IN.

Allen, E. S., Rhoades, G. K., Stanley, S. M., & Markman, H. J. (2010). Hitting home: Relationships between recent deployment, posttraumatic stress symptoms, and marital functioning for army couples. *Journal of Family Psychology, 24*, 280–288.

American Psychiatric Association (2000). *Diagnostic and Statistical Manual of Mental Disorders, Fourth Edition, Text Revision (DSM-IV-TR).* Arlington, VA: Author.

American Red Cross (2011). *A brief history of the American Red Cross.* Retrieved from http://www.redcross.org/museum/history/brief.asp.

Ames, G. M., & Cunradi, C. (2004). Alcohol use and preventing alcohol-related problems among young adults in the military. *Alcohol Research in Health, 28*, 252–257.

Army Emergency Relief (2002). *Helping the Army take care of its own.* Retrieved November 30, 2011 from http://www.aerhq.org.

Aronson, R. (2005). The soldier's heart (R. Aronson, Director). In D. Fanning (Executive Producer), *Frontline.* Boston: WGBH.

Badr, H., Barker, T. M., & Milbury, K. (2011). Couples' psychosocial adaptation to combat wounds and injuries. In S. MacDermid Wadsworth & D. Riggs (Eds.), *Risk and resilience in U.S. military families* (pp. 213–233). New York, NY: Springer Science.

Barker, L. H., & Berry, K. (2009). Developmental issues impacting military families with young children during single and multiple deployments. *Military Medicine, 174*, 1033–1040.

Bathalon, G. P., McGraw, S. M., Sharp, M. A., Williamson, D. A., Young, A. J., & Friedl, K. E. (2006). The effect of proposed improvements to the Army Weight Control Program on female soldiers. *Military Medicine, 171*, 800–805.

Batten, S. V., Drapalski, A. L., Decker, M. L., DeViva, J. C., Morris, L. J., Mann, M. A., & Dixon, L. B. (2009). Veteran interest in family involvement in PTSD treatment. *Psychological Services, 6*, 184–189.

Beardslee, W. R., & Wheelock, I. (1994). Children of parents with affective disorders: Empirical findings and clinical implications. In W. R. Reynolds & H. F. Johnston (Eds.), *Handbook of depression in children and adolescents* (pp. 463–479). New York, NY: Plenum.

Beekley, M. D., Byrne, R., Yavorek, T., Kidd, K., Wolff, J., & Johnson, M. (2009). Incidence, prevalence, and risk of eating disorder behaviors in military academy cadets. *Military Medicine, 174*, 637–640.

Bell, N. S., Amoroso, P. J., Yore, M. M., Smith, G. S., & Jones, B. H. (2000). Self-reported risk-taking behaviors and hospitalization for motor vehicle injury among active duty Army personnel. *American Journal of Preventative Medicine, 18*, 85–95.

Benedek, D. M., & Fullerton, C. S. (2007). Translating five essential elements into programs and practice: Commentary on "Five essential elements of immediate and mid-term mass trauma intervention: Empirical evidence" by Hobfoll, Watson et al. *Psychiatry, 70*, 345–349.

Betz, G., & Thorngren, J. M. (2006). Ambiguous loss and the family grieving process. *The Family Journal: Counseling and Therapy for Couples and Families, 14*, 359–365.

Bicksler, B. A., & Nolan, L. G. (2009). *Recruiting an all-volunteer force: The need for sustained investment in recruiting resources—An update.* Arlington, VA: Strategic Analysis. Retrieved from the Department of Defense Personnel and Readiness website: http://prhome.defense.gov/MPP/ACCESSION%20POLICY/reports.aspx.

Blaisure, K. R., & Arnold-Mann, J. (1992). Return and reunion: A psychoeducational program aboard U.S. Navy ships. *Family Relations, 41,* 178–185.

Bonanno, G. A. (2004). Loss, trauma, and human resilience: Have we underestimated the human capacity to thrive after extremely aversive events? *American Psychologist, 59,* 20–28.

Bonanno, G. A., & Mancini, A. D. (2008). The human capacity to thrive in the face of potential trauma. *Pediatrics, 121,* 369–375.

Bonanno, G. A., Rennicke, V., & Dekel, S. (2005). Self-enhancement among high-exposure survivors of the September 11th terrorist attach: Resilience or social maladjustment? *Journal of Personality and Social Psychology, 88,* 984–998.

Bonanno, G. A., Wortman, C. B., Lehman, D. R., Tweed, R. G., Haring, M., Sonnega, J., … Nesse, R. M. (2002). Resilience to loss and chronic grief: A prospective study from preloss to 18-months postloss. *Journal of Personality and Social Psychology, 83,* 1150–1164.

Booth, B., Segal, M. W., Bell, D. B., with Martin, J. A., Ender, M. G., Rohall, D. E., & Nelson, J. (2007). *What we know about Army families: 2007 update.* Retrieved from the U.S. Army Morale, Welfare, and Recreation website: http://www.army.mil/cfsc/research.htm.

Boss, P. (1987). Family stress. In M. B. Sussman & S. K. Steinmetz (Eds.), *Handbook of marriage and the family* (pp. 695–723). New York, NY: Plenum Press.

Boss, P. (2001). Definitions: A guide to family stress theory. In P. Boss (Ed.), *Family stress management* (2nd ed., pp. 39–70). Thousand Oaks, CA: Sage.

Boss, P. (2006). *Loss, trauma, and resilience: Therapeutic work with ambiguous loss.* New York, NY: W. W. Norton.

Boss, P. (2007). Ambiguous loss theory: Challenges for scholars and practitioners. *Family Relations, 56,* 105–111.

Bowen, G. L., Mancini, J. A., Martin, J. A., Ware, W. B., & Nelson, J. P. (2003). Promoting the adaptation of military families: An empirical test of a community practice model. *Family Relations, 52,* 33–44.

Boyce, W. T., & Chesterman, E. (1990). Life events, social support and cardiovascular reactivity in adolescence. *Journal of Developmental and Behavioral Pediatrics, 11,* 105–111.

Boyko, E. J., Jacobson, I. J., Smith, B., Ryan, M. A. K., Hooper, T. I., Amoroso, P. J., … Smith, T. C. for the Millennium Cohort Study Team. (2010). Risk of diabetes in U.S. military service members in relation to combat deployment and mental health. *Diabetes Care, 33,* 1771–1777.

Bray, R. M., Spira, J. L., Williams, J., & Lane, M. E. (2010). Substance use and mental health issues among single service members: Findings from the 2008 DoD survey of health related behaviors. In *Proceedings from 2010 International Research Symposium on Military families.* Indianapolis, IN: RTI International.

Brewin, C. R., Andrews, B., & Valentine, J. D. (2000). Meta-analysis of risk factors for posttraumatic stress disorder in trauma-exposed adults. *Journal of Consulting Clinical Psychology, 68,* 748–766.

Bride, B. E., & Figley, C. R. (2009). Secondary trauma and military veteran caregivers. *Smith College Studies in Social Work, 79,* 314–329.

Britt, T. W., Davison, J., Bliese, P. D., & Castro, C. A. (2004). How leaders can influence the impact that stressors have on soldiers. *Military Medicine, 169,* 541–545.

Britt, T. W., Greene-Shortridge, T. M., Brink, S., Nguyen, Q. B., Rath, J., Cox, A. L., … Castro, C. A. (2008). Perceived stigma and barriers to care for psychological treatment: Implications for reactions to stressors in different contexts. *Journal of Social and Clinical Psychology, 27,* 317–335.

Bruner, E. F. (2005). *Military forces: What is the appropriate size for the United States?* CRS Report RS21754. Washington, DC: Congressional Research Service, Library of Congress.

Brymer, M., Jacobs, A., Layne, C., Pynoos, R., Ruzek J., Steinberg, A., … Watson, P. (2006). *Psychological first aid: Field operations guide* (2nd ed.). National Child Traumatic Stress Network and National Center for PTSD. Retrieved from the National Center for PTSD website: http://www.ptsd.va.gov/professional/manuals/psych-first-aid.asp.

Bureau of Medicine & Surgery, Deployment Health Directorate (2008). *Operational stress control: Conserving the force.* Retrieved from the Navy and Marine Corps Public Health Center website: http://www.nmcphc.med.navy.mil/healthy_living/psychological_health/stress_management/operandcombatstress.aspx.

Burrell, L. M. (2006). Moving military families: The impact of relocation on family well-being, employment, and commitment to the military. In C. A. Castro, A. B. Adler, & T. W. Britt (Eds.), *Military life: The psychology of serving in peace and combat: The military family* (Vol. 3, pp. 39–63). Westport, CT: Praeger Security International.

Burrell, L. M., Adams, G. A., Durand, D. B., & Castro, C. A. (2006). The impact of military lifestyle demands on well-being, Army, and family outcomes. *Armed Forces & Society, 33*, 43–58.

Burton, T. E., & MacDermid Wadsworth, S. (2011, May). *Evaluation of a multimedia intervention for children and families facing multiple military deployments.* Presented at the Annual Convention of the American Psychological Society, Washington, DC.

Calhoun, P. S., Beckham, J. C., & Bosworth, H. B. (2002). Caregiver burden and psychological distress in partners of veterans with chronic posttraumatic stress disorder. *Journal of Traumatic Stress, 15*, 205–212.

Caregivers and Veterans Omnibus Health Services Act of 2010, Pub. L. No. 111–163, 124 Stat. 1130 (2010).

Carlton, J. R., Manos, G. H., & Van Slyke, J. A. (2005). Anxiety and abnormal eating behaviors associated with cyclical readiness testing in a Naval hospital active duty population. *Military Medicine, 170*, 663–667.

Carroll, E. B., Robinson, L. C., Orthner, D., Matthews, W., & Smith-Rotabi, K. (2008). Essential life skills for military families: Mobilizing the cooperative extension system in NC. *Journal of Family and Consumer Sciences, 100*, 52–57.

Casey, G. W., Jr. (2011). Comprehensive soldier fitness: A vision for psychological resilience in the U.S. Army. *American Psychologist, 66*, 1–3.

Castaneda, L. W., & Harrell, M. C. (2008). Spouse employment: A grounded theory approach to experiences and perceptions. *Armed Forces and Society, 34*, 389–412.

Castaneda, L. W., Harrell, M. C., Varda, D. M., Hall, K. C., Beckett, M. K., & Stern, S. (2008). *Deployment experiences of Guard and Reserve families: Implications for support and retention.* Santa Monica, CA: RAND Corporation.

Center of Excellence for Medical Multimedia (2011). *Traumatic brain injury: A guide for caregivers of service members and veterans.* Retrieved from http://www.traumaticbraininjuryatoz.org/Caregivers-Journey.aspx.

Centers for Disease Control and Prevention (2010). *Facts about traumatic brain injury.* Retrieved September 29, 2010 from the BrainLine.org website: http://www.brainline.org/content/2008/07/facts-about-traumatic-brain-injury.html.

Chambers, J. W., II. (1999). Conscription. In J. W. Chambers, II, F. Anderson, L. Eden, J. T. Glatthaar, R. H. Spector, & G. K. Piehler (Eds.), *The Oxford Companion to American military history* (pp. 180–182). New York, NY: Oxford University Press.

Chandra, A., Lara-Cinisomo, S., Jaycox, L. H., Tanielian, Han, B., Burns, R. M., & Ruder, T. (2011). *Views from the homefront: The experiences of youth and spouses from military families* (Technical Report). Santa Monica, CA: RAND Corporation.

Chandra, A., Martin, L. T., Hawkins, S. A., & Richardson, A. (2010). The impact of parental deployment on child social and emotional functioning: Perspectives of school staff. *Journal of Adolescent Health, 46*, 218–223.

Charney, D. S. (2004). Psychobiological mechanisms of resilience and vulnerability: Implications for successful adaptation to extreme stress. *American Journal of Psychiatry, 161*, 195–216.

Chartrand, M. M., Frank, D. A., White, L. F., & Shope, T. R. (2008). Effect of parents' wartime deployment on the behavior of young children in military families. *Archives of Pediatrics and Adolescent Medicine, 162*, 1009–1014.

Chawla, N., & MacDermid Wadsworth, S. (2011, May). *A multimedia intervention for families of wounded veterans: A randomized study.* Presented at the Annual Convention of the American Psychological Society, Washington, DC.

Chief of Naval Operations (n.d.). *Navy family ombudsman program manual: Serving our families around the world.* Washington, DC: Navy Installations Command.

Commander, Navy Region Mid Atlantic (n.d.). Child development homes. Retrieved December 7, 2011 from http://www.cnic.navy.mil/CNRMA/FleetFamilyReadiness/SupportServices/Families/ChildYouthPrograms/ChildDevelopmentHomes/index.htm.

Child Life Council (2010). *Child Life Council Fact Sheet.* Retrieved from http://www.childlife.org/About/

Christensen, E., Hill, C., Netzer, P., Farr, D., Schaefer, E., & McMahon, J. (2009). *Economic impact on caregivers of the seriously wounded, ill, and injured.* Alexandria, VA: CAN. Retrieved from http://www.cna.org/documents/D0019966.A2.pdf.

Christenson, W., Taggart, A. D., & Messner-Zidell, S. (2009). *Ready, willing, and unable to serve.* Retrieved from the Mission: Readiness website: http://cdn.missionreadiness.org/NATEE1109.pdf.

Cohen, J. A., Mannarino, A. P., Gibson, L. E., Cozza, S. J., Brymer, M. J., & Murray, L. (2006). Interventions for children and adolescents following disasters. In E. C. Ritchie, P. J. Watson, & M. J. Friedman (Eds.), *Interventions following mass violence and disasters* (pp. 227–256). New York: Guilford.

Cohen, S. P., Brown, C., Kurihara, C., Plunkett, A., Nguyen, C., & Strassels, S. A. (2010). Diagnosis and factors associated with medical evacuation and return to duty for service members participating in Operation Iraqi Freedom or Operation Enduring Freedom: A propsective cohort study. *The Lancet, 375*, 301–309.

Collins, R. C., & Kennedy, M. C. (2008). Serving families who have served: Providing family therapy and support in interdisciplinary polytrauma rehabilitation. *Journal of Clinical Psychology, 64*, 993–1003.

Combat Operational Stress Control (2007). *COSC continuum & decision matrix.* Retrieved December 7, 2011 from the Marine Corps Community Services website: http://www.usmc-mccs.org/cosc/coscContMatrix-Marines.cfm?sid=ml&smid=6&ssmid=1.

Committee on Gulf War and Health (2008). *Gulf War and health: Physiologic, psychologic, and psychosocial effects of deployment-related stress* (Vol. 6). Washington, DC: The National Academies Press.

Committee on the Initial Assessment of Readjustment Needs of Military Personnel, Veterans, and Their Families; Board on the Health of Selected Populations; Institute of Medicine (2010). *Returning home from Iraq and Afghanistan: Preliminary assessment of readjustment needs of veterans, service members, and their families.* Washington, DC: National Academies Press. Retrieved from http://www.nap.edu/catalog/12812.html.

Committee on Treatment of Posttraumatic Stress Disorder (2008). *Treatment of posttraumatic stress disorder: An assessment of the evidence.* Washington, DC: The National Academies Press.

Congressional Budget Office (2011). *Analysis of Federal Civilian and Military Compensation.* Retrieved from http://www.cbo.gov/doc.cfm?index=12042&zzz=41511.

Cook, B. J., & Kim, Y. (2009). *From soldier to student: Easing the transition of service members on campus.* Washington, DC: American Council on Education. Retrieved from http://www.acenet.edu/Content/NavigationMenu/ProgramsServices/MilitaryPrograms/index.htm.

Cooper, J. (1999). Militia and National Guard. In J. W. Chambers, II, F. Anderson, L. Eden, J. T. Glatthaar, R. H. Spector, & G. K. Piehler (Eds.), *The Oxford companion to American Military History* (pp. 440–443). New York, NY: Oxford University Press.

Cornum, R., Matthews, M. D., & Seligman, M. E. P. (2011). Comprehensive soldier fitness: Building resilience in a challenging institutional context. *American Psychologist, 66*, 4–9.

Corporate Facts: Walmart by the Numbers (2010). Retrieved from http://walmartstores.com/pressroom/FactSheets/.

Corrigan, P. (2004). How stigma interferes with mental health care. *American Psychologist, 59*, 614–625.

Council of State Governments (2008). *Interstate compact on educational opportunity for military children: Legislative resource kit.* Retrieved from http://www.csg.org/programs/policyprograms/NCIC.aspx#militarychildren.

Coyne, J. C., & Smith, D. A. F. (1994). Couples coping with a myocardial infarction: Contextual perspective on patient self-efficacy. *Journal of Family Psychology, 8*, 43–54.

Cozza, S. J. (2009a, September). *Military children and families: Supporting health and managing risk.* Presented at the DoD Joint Family Readiness Conference, Chicago, IL.

Cozza, S. J. (Ed.). (2009b). *Proceedings of the workgroup on intervention with combat injured families, December 11–12, 2007.* Bethesda, MD: Center for the Study of Traumatic Stress. Retrieved from http://www.cstsonline.org/resources/resource-94_workgroup_intervention_combat_injured_families

Cozza, S. J., Chun, R. S., & Polo, J. A. (2005). Military families and children during operation Iraqi freedom. *Psychiatric Quarterly, 76*, 371–342.

Cozza, S. J., & Guimond, J. M. (2011). Working with combat-injured families through the recovery trajectory. In S. MacDermid Wadsworth & D. Riggs (Eds.), *Risk and resilience in U.S. military families* (pp. 259–277). New York, NY: Springer Science.

Cozza, S. J., Guimond, J. M., McKibben, J. B. A., Chun, R. S., Arata-Maiers, T. L., Schneider, B., ... Ursano, R. J. (2010). Combat-injured service members and their families: The relationship of child distress and spouse-perceived family distress and disruption. *Journal of Traumatic Stress, 23*, 112–115.

Crow, J. R., & Myers-Bowman, K. S. (2011). "A fear like I've never felt": Experiences of parents whose adult children deployed to combat zones. *Marriage and Family Review, 47*, 164–195.

Cunningham, M., Henry, M., & Lyons, W. (2007). *Vital mission: Ending homelessness among veterans.* Washington, DC: National Alliance to End Homelessness, Homelessness Research Institute.

Dalack, G. W., Blow, A. J., Valenstein, M., Gorman, L., Spinner, J., Marcus, S., ... Lagrou, R. (2010). Working together to meet the needs of Army National Guard soldiers: An academic-military partnership. *Psychiatric Services, 61*, 1069–1071.

Daniel, L. (2010, September 2). *Military child development centers rates change.* The Dolphin. Retrieved from http://www.dolphin-news.com/.

Davis, M. C., Leucken, L., & Lemery-Chalfant, K. (2009). Resilience in common life: Introduction to the special issue. *Journal of Personality, 77*, 1637–1644.

de Burgh, H., White, C., Fear, N., & Iversen, A. (2011). The impact of deployment to Iraq or Afghanistan on partners and wives of military personnel. *International Review of Psychiatry, 23*, 192–200.

Dedert, E. A., Green, K. T., Calhoun, P. S., Yoash-Gantz, R., Taber, K. H., Mumford, M. M., … Beckham, J. C. (2009). Association of trauma exposure with psychiatric morbidity in military veterans who have served since September 11, 2001. *Journal of Psychiatric Research, 43*, 830–836.

Defense and Veterans Brain Injury Center (2009). *TBI & the military.* Retrieved September 29, 2010 from http://dvbic.gbkdev.com/TBI---The-Military.aspx.

Defense Centers of Excellence (n.d.). *DCoE resilence continuum.* Retrieved December 7, 2011 from http://www.dcoe.health.mil/ForHealthPros/Resources.aspx.

Defense Centers of Excellence (2010a). *The Defense Centers of Excellence for Psychological Health and Traumatic Brain Injury.* Retrieved October 8, 2010 from http://www.dcoe.health.mil.

Defense Centers of Excellence (2010b). *How we do it: Promoting resilience, recovery, and reintegration.* Retrieved December 7, 2011 from http://www.dcoe.health.mil/HowWeDoIt.aspx.

Defense Centers of Excellence (2010c). *National Intrepid Center of Excellence (NICoE).* Retrieved October 25, 2010 from http://www.dcoe.health.mil/ComponentCenters/NICoE.aspx.

Defense Commissary Agency (2010). *The Defense Commissary Agency: About us.* Retrieved November 30, 2011 from http://www.commissaries.com.

Defense Manpower Data Center (2009). *2008 survey of active duty spouses: Tabulations of responses* (Report No. 2008-041). Arlington, VA: Author. Retrieved from the Department of Defense Personnel and Readiness website: http://prhome.defense.gov/MCFP/docs/2008%20Military%20Spouse%20Survey.pdf.

Defense Manpower Data Center (2011a). *Active duty military strength report for March 31, 2011.* Retrieved from http://siadapp.dmdc.osd.mil/personnel/MILITARY/miltop.htm.

Defense Manpower Data Center (2011b). *Global War on Terrorism by reason code October 7, 2001 through May 31, 2011.* Retrieved from http://siadapp.dmdc.osd.mil/personnel/CASUALTY/gwot_reason.pdf.

Defense Manpower Data Center (2011c). *Global War on Terrorism: Casualties by military service component—active, guard and reserve.* Retrieved from http://siadapp.dmdc.osd.mil/personnel/CASUALTY/gwot_component.pdf.

Defense Manpower Data Center (2011d). *Global War on Terrorism: Operation Enduring Freedom by casualty within service October 7, 2001 through May 31, 2011.* Retrieved from http://siadapp.dmdc.osd.mil/personnel/CASUALTY/wotsum.pdf.

Defense Manpower Data Center (2011e). *Global War on Terrorism: Operation Iraqi Freedom by casualty within service March 19, 2003 through May 31, 2011.* Retrieved from http://siadapp.dmdc.osd.mil/personnel/CASUALTY/oif-total.pdf.

Defense Manpower Data Center (2011f). *Global War on Terrorism: Operation New Dawn by casualty within service September 1, 2010 through May 31, 2011.* Retrieved from http://siadapp.dmdc.osd.mil/personnel/CASUALTY/ond-total.pdf.

Defense and Veterans Brain Injury Center (DVBIC) and the TBI Family Caregiver Advisory Panel. (2010). *Traumatic brain injury: A guide for caregivers of service members and veterans.* Retrieved from http://www.traumaticbraininjuryatoz.org.

Defense of Marriage Act (2011). Retrieved July 5, 2011 from DOMAWatch: http://www.domawatch.org/about/federaldoma.html.

Dekel, R., Goldblatt, H., Keidar, M., Solomon, Z., & Polliack, M. (2005). Being a wife of a veteran with post-traumatic stress disorder. *Family Relations, 54*, 24–36.

Dekel, R., & Monson, C. M. (2010). Military-related post-traumatic stress disorder and family relations: Current knowledge and future directions. *Aggression and Violent Behavior, 15*, 303–309.

Dekel, R., & Solomon, Z. (2007). Secondary traumatization among wives of war veterans with PTSD. In C. R. Figley & W. P. Nash (Eds.), *Combat stress injury: Theory, research, and management* (pp. 137–157). New York, NY: Routledge.

Dekel, R., Solomon, Z., & Bleich, A. (2005). Emotional distress and marital adjustment of caregivers: Contribution of level of impairment and appraised burden. *Anxiety, Stress, and Coping, 18*, 71–82.

Department of Defense (2004). *Task force report on care for victims of sexual assault.* Washington, DC: Author.

Department of Defense (2008a). *The foundations of care, management and transition support for recovering service members and their families.* Washington, DC: Author.

Department of Defense (2008b). *Report to Congress on the comprehensive policy improvements to the care, management and transition of recovering service members (NDAA Section 1611 and 1615).* Washington, DC: Author. Retrieved from http://prhome.defense.gov/WWCTP/Reports.aspx.

Department of Defense (2009). *DoD 101: An introductory overview of the Department of Defense.* Retrieved from http://www.defenselink.mil/pubs/dod101/dod101.html.

Department of Defense (2010a). *Child care: Overview.* Retrieved November 30, 2011 from the Military HOMEFRONT website: http://www.militaryhomefront.dod.mil/tf/childcare.

Department of Defense (2010b). *Community resources: Understanding and using your military exchange.* Retrieved August 31, 2010 from the Military OneSource website: http://www.militaryonesource.com/ MOS/FindInformation/Category/Topic/Issue/Material.aspx?MaterialTypeID=9&MaterialID=14580.

Department of Defense (2010c). *Counseling: Overview.* Retrieved November 30, 2011 from the Military HOMEFRONT website: http://www.militaryhomefront.dod.mil/portal/page/mhf/MHF/ MHF_HOME_1?section_id=20.80.500.124.0.0.0.0.0.

Department of Defense (2010d). *Dealing with deployment: The Navy Family Ombudsman Program.* Retrieved August 27, 2010 from the Military OneSource website: http://www.militaryonesource.com/MOS/ FindInformation/Category/Topic/Issue/Material.aspx?MaterialTypeID=9&MaterialID=14818.

Department of Defense (2010e). *Department of Defense names new directorate to support guard and reserve members, their families and employers.* Retrieved October 4, 2010 from the Business Wire website: http://www.businesswire.com/news/home/20100726006549/en/Department-Defense-Names-Directorate-Support-Guard-Reserve.

Department of Defense (2010f). *Domestic abuse.* Retrieved November 30, 2011 from the Military HOMEFRONT website: http://www.militaryhomefront.dod.mil/portal/page/mhf/MHF/ MHF_HOME_1?section_id=20.40.500.137.0.0.0.0.0.

Department of Defense (2010g). *Domestic abuse: Benefits and allowances.* Retrieved November 30, 2011 from the Military HOMEFRONT website: http://www.militaryhomefront.dod.mil/tf/domesticabuse/benefits.

Department of Defense (2010h). *GI Bill transferability has arrived.* Retrieved October 5, 2010 from http:// www.defense.gov/home/features/2009/0409_gibill.

Department of Defense (2010i). *Joint Family Support Assistance Program (JFSAP).* Retrieved October 4, 2010 from the Military HOMEFRONT website: http://www.militaryhomefront.dod.mil/sp/jfsap.

Department of Defense (2010j). *Military HOMEFRONT.* Retrieved November 30, 2011 from the Military HOMEFRONT website: http://www.militaryhomefront.dod.mil/mcfp.

Department of Defense (2010k). *Military OneSource.* Retrieved August 25, 2010 from the Military OneSource website: http://www.militaryonesource.com/MOS/About.aspx.

Department of Defense (2010l). *MWR: Overview.* Retrieved November 30, 2011 from the Military HOMEFRONT website: http://www.militaryhomefront.dod.mil/tf/mwr.

Department of Defense (2010m). *New parent support program: Overview.* Retrieved August 27, 2010 from the Military HOMEFRONT website: http://www.militaryhomefront.dod.mil/portal/page/mhf/MHF/MHF_ HOME_ 1?section_id=20.40.500.420.0.0.0.0.0.

Department of Defense (2010n). *Plans for the Department of Defense for the support of military family readiness: Report to the Congressional Defense Committees pursuant to Section 1781b of Title 10, United States Code.* Retrieved from the Military HOMEFRONT website: http://www.militaryhomefront.dod.mil/12038/ ProjectDocuments/MilitaryHOMEFRONT/Reports/2010 Report to Congress NDAA Sec 581.pdf.

Department of Defense (2010o). *Special Needs/EFMP.* Retrieved August 25, 2010 from the Military HOMEFRONT website: http://www.militaryhomefront.dod.mil/portal/page/mhf/MHF/MHF_ DETAIL_1?section_id=20.40.500 .570.0.0.0.0.0&current_id=20.40.500.570.500.20.0.0.0.

Department of Defense (2010p). *Yellow Ribbon Program: For those who serve, and those who support.* Retrieved October 4, 2010 from the Yellow Ribbon Program website: http://www.yellowribbon.mil.

Department of Defense (2011a). *A survivor's guide to benefits: Taking care of our own families.* Washington, DC: Author. Retrieved from the Tragedy Assistance Program for Survivors website: http://www.taps.org/ resources.aspx?id=1108.

Department of Defense (2011b). *Unified Command Plan.* Retrieved from http://www.defense.gov/home/ features/2009/0109_unifiedcommand.

Department of Defense. (2011c). *Update to the report on assistance to local educational agencies for defense dependents education.* Washington, DC: Author. Retrieved from http://www.militaryk12partners.dodea .edu/resources.cfm?colId=references_id=20.20.60.70.0.0.0.0.0.

Department of Defense Education Activity (2009). *DoDEA facts!* Retrieved from http://www.dodea.edu/home/ about.cfm?cId=facts.

Department of Defense Education Activity (2010a). *About DoDEA.* Retrieved November 30, 2011 from http:// www.dodea.edu.

Department of Defense Education Activity (2010b). *DoDEA announces 2010 SAT results.* Retrieved November 30, 2011 from http://www.dodea.edu/pressroom/releasesDisplay.cfm?prId=20100920.

Department of Defense Education Activity (2010c). *DoDEA students continue positive performance on the TerraNova 3 multiple assessments.* Retrieved from http://www.dodea.edu/pressroom/releasesDisplay. cfm?prId=20100928_2.

Department of Defense Education Activity (2011). *DODEA educational partnership.* Retrieved November 30, 2011 from http://www.militaryk12partners.dodea.edu/studentsAtTheCenter/about/about-dofdea.html.

Department of Defense (n.d.). Organizational chart. Retrieved November 29, 2011 from http://www.defense. gov/orgchart/.

Department of Defense-State Liaison Office (2010). *The interstate compact on educational opportunities for military children: An overview.* Retrieved from http://www.mic3.net/pages/resources/resources.aspx.

Department of Defense Task Force on Mental Health (2007). *An achievable vision: Report of the Department of Defense task force on mental health.* Falls Church, VA: Defense Health Board.

Department of the Army (2000). *Family readiness handbook* (USARC Regulation 608-1). Fort McPherson, GA: Department of the Army.

Department of the Army (2006a). *Army regulation 614-100: Officer assignment policies, details, and transfers.* Washington, DC: Author.

Department of the Army (2006b). *Combat and operational stress control* (Field manual No. 4-02.51). Washington, DC: Author.

Department of the Army (2009). *Army regulation 614-200: Enlisted assignments and utilization management.* Washington, DC: Author.

Department of the Army (2010). *Health promotion, risk reduction and suicide prevention report.* Washington, DC: Author.

Department of Veterans Affairs. (2009). *Welcome to the GI bill web site.* Retrieved October 5, 2010 from http://www.gibill .va.gov/post-911/post-911-gi-bill-summary

Deployment Health Clinical Center (n.d.). *Definition of deployment.* Retrieved from http://www.pdhealth.mil/ guidelines/annoC.asp.

Deployment Health Clinical Center (2010a). *Military Pathways®.* Retrieved October 8, 2010 from http://www .pdhealth.mil/mhsa.asp.

Deployment Health Clinical Center (2010b). *RESPECT-Mil.* Retrieved October 8, 2010 from http://www .pdhealth.mil/respect-mil.

Di Nola, G. M. (2008). Stressors afflicting families during deployment. *Military Medicine, 173,* v–vii.

Dirkzwager, A. J. E., Bramsen, I., Ader, H., & van der Ploeg, H. M. (2005). Secondary traumatization in part-ners and parents of Dutch peacekeeping soldiers. *Journal of Family Psychology, 19,* 217–226.

Dobreva-Martinova, T. Villeneuve, M., Strickland, L., & Matheson, K. (2002). Occupational role stress in the Canadian forces: Its association with individual and organizational well-being. *Canadian Journal of Behavioral Sciences, 34,* 111–121.

Donnelly, J. (2010). *Rising military suicides.* Retrieved August 16, 2010 from the Congress.org website: http:// www.congress .org/news/2009/11/25/rising_military_suicides.

Drummet, A. R., Coleman, M., & Cable, S. (2003). Military families under stress: Implications for family life education. *Family Relations, 52,* 279–287.

Duckworth, J. (2003). The military culture. *Family Therapy Magazine, 2*(4), 12–17.

Duncan, P. M., Garcia, A. C., Frankowski, B. L., Carey, P. A., Kallock, E. A., Dixon, R. D., & Shaw, J. S. (2007). Inspiring healthy adolescent choices: A rationale for and guide to strength promotion in primary care. *Journal of Adolescent Health, 41,* 525–535.

Educator's Guide to the Military Child During Deployment. (n.d.). Retrieved December 4, 2011 from http:// www2.ed.gov/about/offices/list/os/homefront/homefront.pdf

Employer Support of the Guard and Reserve (2009). *About ESGR.* Retrieved November 30, 2011 from http:// esgr.org/site/AboutUs.aspx.

Ender, M. G. (Ed.) (2002). *Military brats and other global nomads: Growing up in organization families.* Westport, CT: Praeger Security International.

Ender, M. (2006). Voices from the backseat: Demands of growing up in military families. In T. W. Britt, A. B. Adler, & C. A. Castro (Eds.), *Military life: The psychology of serving in peace and combat: The military family* (Vol. 3, pp. 138–166). Westport, CT: Praeger Security International.

Engel, C. C., Oxman, T., Yamamoto, C., Gould, D., Barry, S., Stewart, P., ... Dietrich, A. J. (2008). RESPECT-Mil: Feasibility of a systems-level collaborative care approach to depression and post-traumatic stess disorder in military primary care. *Military Medicine, 173,* 935–940.

Engel, R. C., Gallagher, L. B., & Lyle, D. S. (2010). Military deployments and children's academic achievement: Evidence from Department of Defense education activity schools. *Economics of Education Review, 29,* 7–82.

Erbes, C. R., Polusny, M. A., MacDermid, S., & Compton, J. S. (2008). Couple therapy with combat veterans and their partners. *Journal of Clinical Psychology, 64,* 972–983.

Faber, A. J., Willerton, E., Clymer, S. R., MacDermid, S. M., & Weiss, H. M. (2008). Ambiguous absence, ambiguous presence: A qualitative study of military reserve families in wartime. *Journal of Family Psychology, 22,* 222–230.

Family Medical Leave Act Regulations: A Report on the Department of Labor's Request for Information; Proposed Rule, 72 Fed. Reg. 35550 (2007).

Fear, N. T., Jones, M., Murphy, D., Hull, L., Iversen, A. C., Coker, B., … Wesslely, S. (2010). What are the consequences of deployment to Iraq and Afghanistan on the mental health of the UK armed forces? A cohort study. *Lancet, 375*, 1783–1797.

Ferrier-Auerbach, A. G., Kehle, S. M., Erbes, C. R., Arbisi, P. A., Thuras, P., & Polusny, M. A. (2009). Predictors of alcohol use prior to deployment in National Guard soldiers. *Addictive Behaviors, 34*, 625–631.

Figley, C. R. (Ed.) (1995). *Compassion fatigue: Coping with secondary traumatic stress disorder in those who treat the traumatized.* New York, NY: Brunner/Mazel.

Figley, C. R., & McCubbin, H. I. (Eds.) (1983). *Stress and the family: Coping with catastrophe* (Vol. 2). New York, NY: Brunner/Mazel.

Finkel, L. B., Kelley, M. L., & Ashby, J. (2003). Geographic mobility, family, and maternal variables as related to the psychosocial adjustment of military children. *Military Medicine, 168*, 1019–1024.

Fisher House Facts (n.d.) Retrieved December 7, 2011 from http://www.fisherhouse.org/about/index.html.

Flake, E. M., Davis, B. E., Johnson, P. L., & Middleton, L. S. (2009). The psychosocial effects of deployment on military children. *Journal of Developmental and Behavioral Pediatrics, 3*, 271–278.

Fogel, A. (2010). *Infancy: Infant, family, & society* (5th ed.). Cornwall-on-Hudson, NY: Sloan Publishing.

Folkman, S., & Moskowitz, J. T. (2007). Positive affect and meaning-focused coping during significant psychological stress. In M. Hewstone, H. A. W. Schut, J. B. F. De Wit, K. Van Den Bos, & M. S. Stroebe (Eds.), *The scope of social psychology: Theories and applications. Essays in honor of Wolfgang Stroebe* (pp. 193–208). New York, NY: Psychology Press.

Force Health Protection & Readiness Policy & Programs (2007). *The post-deployment health reassessment: Safeguarding the health of those who protect us.* Retrieved from http://fhp.osd.mil/pdhrainfo.

Friedl, K. E., Grate, S. J., & Proctor, S. P. (2009). Neuropsychological issues in military deployments: Lessons observed in the DoD Gulf War Illnesses research program. *Military Medicine, 174*, 335–346.

Friedman, M. J. (2004). Acknowledging the psychiatric cost of war. *New England Journal of Medicine, 351*, 75–77.

Gade, P. A., Tiggle, R. B., & Schumm, W. R. (2003). The measurement and consequences of military organizational commitment in soldiers and spouses. *Military Psychology, 15*, 191–207.

Gambardella, L. C. (2008). Role-exit theory and marital discord following extended military deployment. *Perspectives in Psychiatric Care, 44*, 169–174.

Garber, A. K., Boyer, C. G., Pollack, L, M., Chang, Y. J., & Shafer, M. (2008). Body mass index and disordered eating behaviors are associated with weight dissatisfaction in adolescent and young adult female military recruits. *Military Medicine, 173*, 138–145.

Garcia, R. (2009). *Veteran center handbook for student veterans.* Retrieved from http://www.studentveterans.org/resourcelibrary.

Gates, G. (2010). *Lesbian, gay, and bisexual men and women in the US military: Updated estimates.* Retrieved from the Williams Institute Military Issues Studies at UCLA School of Law website: http://www3.law.ucla.edu/williamsinstitute/publications/Policy-Military-index.html.

Gawande, A. (2004). Casualties of war: Military care for the wounded from Iraq and Afghanistan. *New England Journal of Medicine, 351*, 2471–2475.

Gewirtz, A. H., Erbes, C. R., Polusny, M. A., Forgatch, M. A., & DeGarmo, D. S. (2011). Helping military families through the deployment process: Strategies to support parenting. *Professional Psychology: Research and Practice, 42*, 56–62.

Gewirtz, A. H., Polusny, M. A., DeGarmo, D. A., Khaylis, A., & Erbes, C. R. (2010). Posttraumatic stress symptoms among National Guard soldiers deployed to Iraq: Associations with parenting behaviors and couple adjustment. *Journal of Consulting and Clinical Psychology, 78*, 599–610.

Gibbs, D. A., Martin, S. L., Kupper, L. L., & Johnson, R. E. (2007). Child maltreatment in enlisted soldiers' families during combat-related deployments. *Journal of the American Medical Association, 298*, 528–535.

Global Security (2005). *Marine divisions.* Retrieved from http://www.globalsecurity.org/military/agency/usmc/mardiv.htm.

Goff, B. S. N., Crow, J., Reisbig, A. M. J., & Hamilton, S. (2007). The impact of individual trauma symptoms of deployed soldiers on relationship satisfaction. *Journal of Family Psychology, 21*, 344–353.

Goffman, E. (1959). *The presentation of self in everyday life.* New York, NY: Doubleday.

Goldenring, H., & Cohen, E. (1988). Getting into adolescents' heads. *Contemporary Pediatrics, 5*, 75–90.

Goldstein, J. & Kenney, C. (2001). Marriage delayed or foregone? New cohort forecasts of first marriage for US women. *American Sociological Review, 66*, 506–519.

Goodenough, W. (1981). *Culture, language, society.* Menlo Park, CA: Benjamin Cummings Publishing.

Goodspeed, M. H. (2003). *U.S. Navy: A military history.* Washington Navy Yard, DC: Navy Historical Foundation.

Gorman, G. H., Eide, M., & Hisle-Gorman, E. (2010). Wartime military deployment and increased pediatric mental and behavioral health complaints. *Pediatrics, 126*, 1058–1066.

Gorman, L. A., Fitzgerald, H. E., & Blow, A. J. (2010). Parental combat injury and early child development: A conceptual model for differentiating effects of visible and invisible injuries. *Psychiatric Quarterly, 81,* 1–21.

Graham, I. (2010, July 30). *DoD childcare fees will soon change.* Retrieved from the DoD Live website: http://www.dodlive.mil/index.php/2010/07/dod-childcare-fees-will-soon-change/.

Granado, N. S., Smith, T. C., Swanson, G. M., Harris, R. B., Shahar, E., Smith, B., … Ryan, M. A. K. for the Millennium Cohort Study Team (2009). Newly reported hypertension after military combat deployment in a large population-based study. *Hypertension, 54,* 966–973.

Greden, J. F., Valenstein, M., Spinner, J., Blow, A., Gorman, L. A., Dalack, G. W., Marcus, S., & Kees, M. (2010). Buddy-to-buddy, a citizen soldier peer support program to counteract stigma, PTSD, depression, and suicide. *Annals of the New York Academy of Sciences, 1208,* 90–97.

Greenberg, N., Langston, V., & Jones, N. (2008). Trauma Risk Management (TRiM) in the UK Armed Forces. *Journal of the Royal Army Medical Corps, 154,* 123–126.

Green Cross Academy of Traumatology (n.d.). *Standards of care: Standards of self care guidelines.* Retrieved from http://www.greencross.org/index.php?option=com_content&view=article&id=184&Itemid=124.

Griffin, J. M., Friedemann-Sánchez, G., Hall, C., Phelan, S., & van Ryn, M. (2009). Families of patients with polytrauma: Understanding the evidence and charting a new research agenda. *Journal of Rehabilitation Research and Development, 46,* 879–892.

Griffith, J. (2005). The Army National Guard soldier in post-9/11 operations: Perceptions of being prepared for mobilization, deployment, and combat. *Journal of Political and Military Sociology, 33,* 161–178.

Griffith, J. (2008). Institutional motives for serving in the U.S. Army National Guard: Implications for recruitment, retention, and readiness. *Armed Forces & Society, 34,* 230–258.

Griffith, J. (2009). After 9/11 what kind of reserve soldier? Considerations given to emerging demands, organizational orientation, and individual commitment. *Armed Forces & Society, 35,* 214–240.

Gutierrez, P. M., & Brenner, L. A. (2009). Helping military personnel and recent veterans manage stress reactions. *Journal of Mental Health Counseling, 31,* 95–100.

Hagedoorn, M., Kuijer, R., Buunk, B., DeJong, G., & Wobbes, T. (2000). Marital satisfaction in patients with cancer: Does support from intimate partners benefit those who need it the most? *Health Psychology, 19,* 274–282.

Haglund, M. E. M., Nedstadt, P. S., Cooper, N. S., Southwick, S. M., & Charney, D. S. (2007). Psychobiological mechanisms of resilience: Relevance to prevention and treatment of stress-related psychopathology. *Development and Psychopathology, 19,* 889–920.

Hamilton, B. E., Martin, J. A., & Ventura, S. J. (2010). *Births: Preliminary data for 2009.* National Vital Statistics Reports, 59 (3). DHHS Publication No. (PHS) 2011–1120. Retrieved from the Centers for Disease Control and Prevention website: http://www.cdc.gov/nchs/nvss/birth_products.htm.

Hansen, F. R. (2000). *American history teacher's book of lists.* San Francisco, CA: Jossey-Bass. Retrieved from http://www.teachervision.fen.com/us-history/resource/5669.html.

Hardy, L., Arthur, C. A., Jones, G., Shariff, A., Munnoch, K., Isaacs, I., & Allsopp, A. J. (2010). The relationship between transformational leadership behaviors, psychological, and training outcomes in elite military recruits. *The Leadership Quarterly, 21,* 20–32.

Harrell, M. C., Lim, N., Castaneda, L. W., & Golinelle, D. (2005). *Working around the military: Challenges to military spouse employment and education.* Santa Monica, CA: RAND Corporation. Retrieved from http://www.rand.org/pubs/monographs/MG196.html.

Harrison, J., & Vannest, K. J. (2008). Educators supporting families in times of crisis: Military reserve deployments. *Preventing School Failure, 52*(4), 17–23.

Headquarters, Department of the Army (2006). *Combat and operational stress control* [Field manual 4-02.51 (FM 8-51)]. Washington, DC: Author. Retrieved from http://www.fas.org/irp/doddir/army/fm4-02-51.pdf.

Heubner, A. J., Mancini, J. A., Bowen, G. L., & Orthner, D. K. (2009). Shadowed by war: Building community capacity to support military families. *Family Relations, 58,* 216–228.

Hill, R. (1949). *Families under stress: Adjustment to the crises of war separation and reunion.* New York, NY: Harper & Brothers.

Hill, R. (1958). Generic features of families under stress. *Social Casework, 49,* 139–150.

Hirsch, M. D., & Engel, E. J. (2008). *Coping with compassion fatigue.* Retrieved from the Military OneSource website: http://www.militaryonesource.com/MOS/FindInformation/Category/Topic/Issue/Material.aspx?MaterialID=13616&MaterialTypeID=9&NoCookieCTI=1.

Hobfoll, S. E. (1989). Conservation of resources: A new attempt at conceptualizing stress. *American Psychologist, 44,* 513–524.

Hobfoll, S. E. (1998). *Stress, culture and community: The psychology and philosophy of stress.* New York, NY: Plenum Press.

Hobfoll, S. E., Dunahoo, C. A., & Monnier, J. (1995). Conservation of resources and traumatic stress. In J. R. Freedy & S. E. Hobfoll (Eds.), *Traumatic stress: From theory to practice* (pp. 29–47). New York, NY: Plenum Press.

Hobfoll, S. E., Horsey, K. J., & Lamoureux, B. E. (2009). Resiliency and resource loss in times of terrorism and disaster: Lessons learned for children and families and those left untaught. In D. Brom, R. Pat-Horenczyk, & J. D. Ford (Eds.), *Treating traumatized children: Risk, resilience, and recovery* (pp. 150–163). New York, NY: Routledge/Taylor & Francis.

Hobfoll, S. E., Watson, P., Bell, C. C., Bryant, R. A., Brymer, M. J., Friedman, M. J., … Ursano, R. J. (2007). Five essential elements of immediate and mid-term mass trauma intervention: Empirical evidence. *Psychiatry, 40*, 283–315.

Hogan, P. F. & Seifert, R. F. (2010). Marriage and the military: Evidence that those who serve marry earlier and divorce earlier. *Armed Forces & Society, 36*, 420–438.

Hoge, C. W., Auchterlonie, J. L., & Milliken, C. S. (2006). Mental health problems, use of mental health services, and attrition from military service after returning from deployment to Iraq or Afghanistan. *Journal of the American Medical Association, 295*, 1023–1032.

Hoge, C. W., Castro, C. A., Messer, S. C., McGurk, D., Cotting, D. I., & Koffman, R. L. (2004). Combat duty in Iraq and Afghanistan, mental health problems and barriers to care. *New England Journal of Medicine, 351*, 13–22.

Hoge, C. W., Clark, J. C., & Castro, C. A. (2007). Commentary: Women in combat and the risk of post-traumatic stress disorder and depression. *International Journal of Epidemiology, 36*, 327–329.

Hoge, C. W., McGurk, D., Thomas, J. L., Cox, A. L., Engel, C. C., & Castro, C. A. (2008). Mild traumatic brain injury in U.S. soldiers returning from Iraq. *New England Journal of Medicine, 358*, 453–463.

Homes for Our Troops I (2009). *Homes for Our Troops: Building specially adapted homes for our severly injured veterans.* Retrieved from http://www.homesforourtroops.org.

Hooper, T. I., Debaky, S. F., Bellis, K. S., Kang, H. K., Cowan, D. N., Lincoln, A. E., & Gackstetter, G. D. (2006). Understanding the effect of deployment on the risk of fatal motor vehicle crashes: A nested case-control study of fatalities in Gulf War era veterans, 1991–1995. *Accident Analysis and Prevention, 38*, 518–525.

Hosek, J., Kavanagh, J., & Miller, L. (2006). *How deployments affect service members.* Santa Monica, CA: RAND Corporation. Retrieved from http://www.rand.org/pubs/monographs/MG432.html.

Huebner, A. J., & Mancini, J. A. (2005). *Adjustments among adolescents in military families when a parent is deployed.* Final report to the Military Family Research Institute and Department of Defense Quality of Life Office. Retrieved from the Military Family Research Institute website: http://www.mfri.purdue.edu/content/reports/Adjustments%20among%20605.pdf.

Huebner, A. J., Mancini, J. A., Bowen, G. L., & Orthner, D. K. (2009). Shadowed by war: Building community capacity to support military families. *Family Relations, 58*, 216–228.

Huebner, A. J., Mancini, J. A., Wilcox, R. M., Grass, S. R., & Grass, G. A. (2007). Exploring uncertainty and ambiguous loss. *Family Relations, 56*, 112–122.

Hutchinson, J. W., Greene, J. P., & Hanson, S. L. (2008). Evaluating active duty risk-taking: Military home, education, activity, drugs, sex, suicide, and safety method. *Military Medicine, 173*, 1164–1167.

Institute of Medicine (2010). *Returning home from Iraq and Afghanistan: Preliminary assessment of the readjustment needs of veterans, service members, and their families.* Washington, DC: The National Academies Press. Retrieved from http://www.nap.edu/catalog/12812.html.

Intrepid Fallen Heroes Fund (2010). *Intrepid fallen heroes fund—About IFHF.* Retrieved from http://www.fallenheroesfund.org/About-IFHF.aspx

Intrepid Sea, Air & Space Museum. (2008). *National Intrepid Center of Excellence officially dedicated at National Naval Medical Center.* Retrieved from http://www.intrepidmuseum.org/LatestNews/June-2010/National-Intrepid-Center-of-Excellence-Officially-.aspx.

Jacobson, I. G., Ryan, M. A. K., Hooper, T. I., Smith, T. C., Amoroso, P. J., Boyko, E. J., … Bell, N. S. for the Millennium Cohort Study Team (2008). Alcohol use and alcohol-related problems before and after military combat deployment. *Journal of the American Medical Association, 300*, 663–675.

Jacobson, I. G., Smith, T. C., Smith, B., Keel, P. K., Amoroso, P. J., Wells, T. S., … Ryan, M. A. K. for the Millennium Cohort Study Team (2009). Disordered eating and weight changes after deployment: Longitudinal assessment of a large US military cohort. *American Journal of Epidemiology, 169*, 415–427.

Jafee, M. S., Helmick, K. M., Girard, P. D., Meyer, K. S., Dinegar, K., & George, K. (2009). Acute clinical care and care coordination for traumatic brain injury within the Department of Defense. *Journal of Rehabilitation Research and Development, 46*, 655–666.

Johnson, J. (2010, August). Brain injury info. *Military Officer, 46.*

Johnson, M. (2009). Differentiating among types of domestic violence: Implications for healthy marriages. In E. H. Peters & C. M. Kamp Dush (Eds.), *Marriage and family: Perspectives and complexities* (pp. 281–297). New York, NY: Columbia University Press.

Joint Chiefs of Staff (n.d.). *Joint Chiefs of Staff.* Retrieved from http://www.jcs.mil/.

Joint Mental Health Advisory Team 7 (2011). *Joint Mental Health Advisory Team 7 (J-MHAT 7) Operation Enduring Freedom 2010 Afghanistan,* report. Falls Church, VA: Office of The Surgeon General of the Army.

Joint Service Committee on Military Justice (2008). *Manual for courts-martial, United States.* Washington, DC: Department of Defense.

Jones, E., & Wessely, S. (2003). "Forward psychiatry" in the military: Its origins and effectiveness. *Journal of Traumatic Stress, 16,* 411–419.

Joseph, A. L., & Afifi, T. D. (2010). Military wives' stressful disclosures to their deployed husbands: The role of protective buffering. *Journal of Applied Communication Research, 38,* 412–434.

Jumisko, E., Lexell, J., & Soderberg, S. (2007). Living with moderate or severe traumatic brain injury: The meaning of family members' experiences. *Journal of Family Nursing, 13,* 353–369.

Kang, H., Dalager, N., Mahan, C., & Ishii, E. (2005). The role of sexual assault on the risk of PTSD among Gulf War veterans. *Annals of Epidemiology, 15,* 191–195.

Karney, B. R., & Crown, J. S. (2007). *Families under stress: An assessment of data, theory, and research on marriage and divorce in the military.* Santa Monica, CA: RAND Corporation. Retrieved from http://www.rand.org/pubs/monographs/MG599.html.

Karney, B. R. & Crown, J. S. (2011). Does deployment keep military marriages together or break them apart? Evidence from Afghanistan and Iraq. In S. MacDermid Wadsworth & D. Riggs (Eds.), *Risk and resilience in U.S. military families* (pp. 23–45). New York, NY: Springer.

Kelley, M. L., Doane, A. N., & Pearson, M. R. (2011). Single military mothers in the new millennium: Stresses, supports, and effects of deployment. In S. MacDermid Wadsworth & D. Riggs (Eds.), *Risk and resilience in U.S. military families* (pp. 343–363). New York, NY: Springer Science.

Kelley, M. L., Schwerin, M. J., Farrar, K. L., & Lane, M. E. (2007). A participant evaluation of the U.S. Navy Parent Support Program. *Journal of Family Violence, 21,* 301–310.

Kelly, J. & Johnson, M. P. (2008). Differentiation among types of intimate partner violence: Research update and implications for interventions. Family Court Review, 46, 476–499.

Kelty, R. Kleykamp, M. & Segal, D. R. (2010). The military and the transition to adulthood. *The Future of Children, 20,* 181–207.

Kennedy, J. E., Jaffee, M. S., Leskin, G. A., Stokes, J. W., Leal, F. O., & Fitzpatrick, P. J. (2007). Posttraumatic stress disorder and posttraumatic stress disorder-like symptoms and mild traumatic brain injury. *Journal of Rehabilitation Research & Development, 44,* 895–920.

Kessler, R. C., Berglund, P., Demler, O., Jin, R., Merikangas, K. R., & Walters, E. E. (2005). Lifetime prevalence and age-of-onset distributions of DSM-IV disorders in the National Comorbidity Survey Replication. *Archives of General Psychiatry , 62,* 593–602.

Khoshaba, D. M., & Maddi, S. R. (1999). Early experiences in hardiness development. *Consulting Psychology Journal, 51,* 106–116.

Killgore, W. D., Cotting, D. I., Thomas, J. L., Cox, A. L., McGurk, D., Vo, A. H., … Hoge, C. W. (2008). Post-combat invincibility: Violent combat experiences are associated with increased risk-taking propensity following deployment. *Journal of Psychiatric Research, 42,* 1112–1121.

Kim, P. Y., Thomas, J. L., Wilk, J. E., Castro, C. A., & Hoge, C. W. (2010). Stigma, barriers to care, and use of mental health services among active duty and National Guard soldiers after combat. *Psychiatric Services, 61,* 582–588.

Klesges, R. C., Haddock, C. K., Lando, H., & Talcott, G. W. (1999). Efficacy of forced smoking cessation and an adjunctive behavioral treatment on long-term smoking rates. *Journal of Consulting and Clinical Psychology, 67,* 952–958.

Knox, J., & Price, D. H. (1999). Total force and the new American military family: Implications for social work practice. *Families in Society, 80,* 128–136.

Kuehn, B. M. (2009). Soldier suicide rates continue to rise: Military, scientists work to stem the tide. *Journal of the American Medical Association, 299,* 1111–1113.

Kushner, D. (1998). Mild traumatic brain injury: Toward understanding manifestations and treatment. *Archives of Internal Medicine, 158,* 1617–1624.

Landau, J., & Hissett, J. (2008). Mild traumatic brain injury: Impact on identity and ambiguous loss in the family. *Family, Systems, & Health, 26,* 69–85.

Lapp, C. A., Taft, L. B., Tollefson, T., Hoepner, A., Moore, K., & Divyak, K. (2010). Stress and coping on the home front: Guard and Reserve spouses searching for a new normal. *Journal of Family Nursing, 16,* 45–67.

Lauder, T. D., & Campbell, C. S. (2001). Abnormal eating behaviors in female Reserve Officer Training Corps cadets. *Military Medicine, 166*, 264–268.

Lauder, T. D., Williams, M. V., Campbell, C. S., Davis, G., Sherman, R., & Pulos, E. (1999). The female athlete triad: Prevalence in military women. *Military Medicine, 164*, 630–635.

Laurence, J. (2006). Poultry and patriotism: Attitudes toward the U.S. military. In T. W. Britt, A. B. Adler, & C. A. Castro (Eds.), *Military life: The psychology of serving in peace and combat: Military culture* (Vol. 4, pp. 211–228). Westport, CT: Praeger Security International.

Lavee, Y., McCubbin, H. I., & Olson, D. H. (1987). The effect of stressful life events and transitions on family functioning and well-being. *Journal of Marriage and the Family, 49*, 857–873.

Lazarus, R. S., & Folkman, S. (1984). *Stress, appraisal, and coping.* New York, NY: Springer.

Leskin, G. A. (2010). *FOCUS project: Program adaptations.* Presented at the Navy and Marine Corps Combat & Operational Stress Control Conference 2010, San Diego, CA.

Lester, P., Leskin, G., Woodward, K., Saltzman, W., Nash, W., Mogil, C., ... Beardslee, W. (2011). Wartime deployment and military children: Applying prevention science to enhance family resilience. In S. MacDermid Wadsworth & D. Riggs (Eds.), *Risk and resilience in U.S. military families* (pp. 149–173). New York, NY: Springer.

Lester, P., Mogil, C., Saltzman, W., Woodward, K., Nash, W., Leskin, G., ... Beardslee, W. (2011). Families overcoming under stress: Implementing family-centered prevention for military families facing wartime deployments and combat operational stress. *Military Medicine, 176*, 19–25.

Lester, P., Peterson, K., Reeves, J., Knauss, L., Glover, D., Mogil, C., ... Beardslee, W. (2010). The long war and parental combat deployment: Effects on military children and at-home spouses. *Journal of the American Academy of Child & Adolescent Psychiatry, 49*, 310–320.

Library of Congress (2009). *Uniform Code of Military Justice legislative history.* Retrieved from http://www.loc.gov/rr/frd/Military_Law/UCMJ_LHP.html.

Lincoln, A., Swift, E., & Shorteno-Fraser, M. (2008). Psychological adjustment and treatment of children and families with parents deployed in military combat. *Journal of Clinical Psychology, 84*, 984–992.

Lindstrom, K. E., Smith, T. C., Wells, T. S., Wang, L. Z., Smith, B., Reed, R. J., ... Ryan, M. A. (2006). The mental health of U.S. military women in combat support occupations. *Journal of Women's Health, 15*, 162–172.

Lipari, R. N., & Lancaster, A. R. (2003). *Armed Forces 2002 sexual harassment survey* (DMDC report No. 2003-026). Arlington, VA: Defense Manpower Data Center.

Little, R. D., & Hisnanick, J. J. (2007). The earnings of tied-migrant military husbands. *Armed Forces and Society, 33*, 547–570.

Litz, B. T. (2005). *A brief primer on the mental health impact of the wars in Afghanistan and Iraq: A National Center for PTSD fact sheet.* Boston, MA: National Center for PTSD.

Litz, B. T., Orsillo, S. M., Friedman, M., Ehlich, P., & Batres, A. (1997). Posttraumatic stress disorder associated with peacekeeping duty in Somalia for U.S. military personnel. *American Journal of Psychiatry, 154*, 179–184.

Logan, K. V. (1987). The emotional cycle of deployment. *U.S. Naval Proceedings, 113*, 43–47.

Lundquist, J. H. (2004). When race makes no difference: Marriage and the military. *Social Forces, 83*, 731–757.

Lundquist, J. H. (2006). The Black-White gap in marital dissolution among young adults: What can a counterfactual scenario tell us? *Social Problems, 53*, 421–441.

Lundquist, J. H. (2008). Ethnic and gender satisfaction in the military: The effect of a meritocratic institution. *American Sociological Review, 73*, 477–496.

Lundquist, J. H., & Smith, H. L. (2005). Family formation among women in the U.S. military: Evidence from the NLSY. *Journal of Marriage and Family, 67*, 1–13.

Luthar, S. S. (2006). Resilience in development: A synthesis of research across five decades. In D. C. Cicchetti (Ed.), *Developmental psychopathology: Risk, disorder, and adaptation* (2nd ed., Vol. 3, pp. 739–795). Hoboken, NJ: John Wiley and Sons.

Lyle, D. S. (2006). Using military deployments and job assignments to estimate the effect of parental absences and household relocations on children's academic achievement. *Journal of Labor Economics, 24*, 319–350.

Lyons, J. A. (2007). The returning warrior: Advice for families and friends. In C. R. Figley & W. P. Nash (Eds.), *Combat stress injury: Theory, research, and management* (pp. 311–324). New York, NY: Routledge.

Lyons, R. F., Mickelson, K. D., Sullivan, M. J. L., & Coyne, J. C. (1998). Coping as a communal process. *Journal of Social and Personal Relationships, 15*, 579–605.

MacDermid, S. M., Samper, R., Schwarz, R., Nishida, J., & Nyaronga, D. (2008). *Understanding and promoting resilience in military families.* West Lafayette, IN: Military Family Research Institute.

MacDermid, S. M., Weiss, H. M., Green, S. G., & Schwarz, R. L. (2007). *Military members on the move.* West Lafayette, IN: Military Family Research Institute.

MacDermid Wadsworth, S., Pagnan, C., & Seidel, A. (2010, November). *Coming home after war: A longitudinal study of U.S. reservists and their families.* Paper presented at the Annual Conference of the National Council on Family Relations, Minneapolis, MN.

MacDermid Wadsworth, S. M. (2010). Family risk and resilience in the context of war and terrorism. *Journal of Marriage and Family, 72,* 537–556.

MacDermid Wadsworth, S. M., & Southwell, K. (2011). Military families: Extreme work and extreme 'work-family.' *The Annals of the American Academy of Political and Social Science, 638,* 163–183.

Maddi, S. R., Kahn, S., & Maddi, K. L. (1998). The effectiveness of hardiness training. *Consulting Psychology Journal, 50,* 78–86.

Maguen, S., Vogt, D. S., King, L. A., King, D. W., & Litz, B. T. (2006). Posttraumatic growth among Gulf War I veterans: The predictive role of deployment-related experiences and background characteristics. *Journal of Loss and Trauma, 11,* 373–388.

Makin-Byrd, K., Gifford, E., McCutcheon, S., & Glynn, S. (2011). Family and couples treatment for newly returning veterans. *Professional Psychology: Research and Practice, 42,* 47–55.

Malia, J. A. (2006). Basic concepts and models of family stress. *Stress, Trauma, and Crisis, 9,* 141–160.

Managed Health Network Government Services (2010a). *MFLC Joint Family Support Assistance Program (JFSAP).* Retrieved from https://www.mhngs.com/app/programsandservices/jfsap.content.

Managed Health Network Government Services (2010b). *Military & Family Life Consultant (MFLC) program.* Retrieved from https://www.mhngs.com/app/programsandservices/mflc_program.content.

Mancini, J. A., Bowen, G. L., & Martin, J. A. (2005). Community social organization: A conceptual linchpin in examining families in the context of communities. *Family Relations, 54,* 570–582.

Marshall, T. C., Jr. (2011, July 22). Obama commends military for handling of law's repeal. *American Forces Press Service.* Retrieved from the Department of Defense website http://www.defense.gov/news/newsarticle.aspx?id=64781.

Martin, J. A., & McClure, P. (2000). Today's active duty military family: The evolving challenges on military family life. In J. A. Martin, L. N. Rosen, & L. R. Sparacino (Eds.), *The military family: A practice guide for human service providers* (pp. 3–23). Westport, CT: Praeger Security International.

Martin, J. A., Rosen, L. N., & Sparacino, L. R. (2000). *The military family: A practice guide for human service providers.* Westport, CT: Praeger Security International.

Martinez, G. M., Chandra, A., Abma, J. C., Jones, J., & Mosher, W. D. (2002). Fertility, contraception, and fatherhood: Data on men and women from Cycle 6 (2002) of the National Survey of Family Growth. National Center for Health Statistics. *Vital Health Stat* 23(26). Retrieved from http://www.cdc.gov/nchs/data/series/sr_23/sr23_026.pdf.

Mathews, T. J., & Hamilton, B. E. (2009). *Delayed childbearing: More women are having their first child later in life. NCHS Data Brief, 21.* National Center for Health Statistics. Retrieved from the Centers for Disease Control and Prevention website: http://www.cdc.gov/nchs/data/databriefs/db21.pdf.

McCarroll, J. E., Fan, Z., & Bell, N. S. (2009). Alcohol use in non-mutual and mutual domestic violence in the U.S. Army: 1998–2004. *Violence and Victims, 24,* 364–379.

McCarroll, J. E., Fan, Z., Newby, J. H., & Ursano, R. J. (2008). Trends in US Army child maltreatment reports: 1990–2004. *Child Abuse Review, 17,* 108–118.

McCarroll, J. E., Ursano, R. J., Liu, X., Thayer, L. E., Newby, J. H., Norwood, A. E., & Fullerton, C. S. (2000). Deployment and the probability of spousal aggression by U.S. army soldiers. *Military Medicine, 165,* 41–44.

McCarroll, J. E., Ursano, R. J., Newby, J. H., Liu, X., Fullerton, C. S., Norwood, A. E., & Osuch, E. A. (2003). Domestic violence and deployment in U.S. Army soldiers. *Journal of Nervous and Mental Disease, 191,* 3–9.

McCleland, K. C., Sutton, G. W., & Schumm, W. R. (2005). Marital satisfaction before and after deployments associated with the Global War on Terror. *Psychological Reports, 103,* 836–844.

McCubbin, H. I., Joy, C. B., Cauble, A. E., Comeau, J. K., Patterson, J. M., & Needle, R. H. (1980). Family stress and coping: A decade review. *Marriage and Family, 42,* 125–141.

McCubbin, H. I., & Patterson, J. M. (1983a). The family stress process: The Double ABCx model of adjustment and adaptation. In H. L. McCubbin, M. B. Sussman, & J. M. Patterson (Eds.), *Advances and development in family stress theory and research* (pp. 7–37). New York, NY: Haworth.

McCubbin, H. I., & Patterson, J. M. (1983b). Family transitions: Adaptation to stress. In McCubbin & Figley (Eds.), *Stress and the family: Coping with normative transitions* (Vol. 1, pp. 5–25). New York, NY: Brunner/Mazel.

McFarland, M. (2005). Military cultural education. *Military Review, 85*(2), 62–69.

McFarland, B. H., Kaplan, M. S., & Huguet, N. (2010). Self-inflicted deaths among women with U.S. military service: A hidden epidemic? *Psychiatric Services, 61,* 1177.

McFarlane, A. C. (2009). Military deployment: The impact on children and family adjustment and the need for care. *Current Opinion in Psychiatry, 22,* 369–373.

McLagan, M. & Sommers, D. (2008). Lioness (M. McLagan & D. Sommers, Directors). In S. J. Fifer (Executive Producer), *Independent Lens*. San Francisco: ITVS.

McMichael, W. H. (2008). *DoD approves more accompanied tours in Korea*. Retrieved from http://www.armytimes.com/news/2008/12/military_korea_assignments_121008w/.

McNulty, P. A. F. (2008). Reunification: The silent war of families and returning troops. *Federal Practitioner, 25*(10), 15–20.

Meichenbaum, D. (1996). Stress inoculation training for coping with stressors. *The Clinical Psychologist, 49*, 4–7.

Mental Health Advisory Team V (2008). *Mental Health Advisory Team (MHAT) V Report*. U.S. Army Surgeon General. U.S. Army Medical Department.

Mental Health Advisory Team VI (2009). *Operation Iraqi Freedom 07-09*. Retrieved from the U. S. Army Medical Department website: http://www.armymedicine.army.mil/reports/mhat/mhat_vi/mhat-vi.cfm.

Mental Health America (2010a). *Operation Healthy Reunions: A program of Mental Health America*. Retrieved from the Operation Healthy Reunions website: http://www.nmha.org/reunions.

Mental Health America (2010b). *Welcome to Mental Health America*. Retrieved from http://www.mental-healthamerica.net/.

Miles, D. (2007, July 13). *Severely wounded troops find meaningful ways to continue serving*. Retrieved November 30, 2011 from the Department of Defense website: http://www.defense.gov/news/newsarticle.aspx?id=46714.

Military Advantage (2010). *Benefits: Military child care*. Retrieved November 30, 2011 from the Military.com website: http://www.military.com/benefits/resources/family-support/child-care.

Military Community & Family Policy (2009). *About Military Community & Family Policy*. Retrieved from http://apps.mhf.dod.mil/pls/psgprod/f?p=OC_PORTAL:Article:1865350021332336::::COHE:250644.

Military Interstate Children's Compact Commission (2011, November 8). MIC3: Month of the military family letter. Retrieved November 21, 2011 from http://www.mic3.net/.

Monson, C. M., Fredman, S. J., & Adair, K. C. (2008). Cognitive-behavioral conjoint therapy for posttraumatic stress disorder: Application to Operation Enduring and Iraqi Freedom veterans. *Journal of Clinical Psychology, 64*, 958–971.

Moore, B. A., & Reger, G. M. (2007). Historical and contemporary perspectives of combat stress and the Army combat stress control team. In. C. R. Figley & W. P. Nash (Eds.), *Combat stress injury: Theory, research, and management* (pp. 161–181). New York, NY: Routledge.

Morris, A. S., & Age, T. R. (2009). Adjustment among youth in military families: The protective roles of effortful control and maternal social support. *Journal of Applied Developmental Psychology, 30*, 695–707.

Morse, J. (2006). *The new emotional cycles of deployment*. Retrieved from the Force Health Protection & Readiness Policy & Programs website: http://deploymenthealthlibrary.fhp.osd.mil.

Mrazek, P. J., & Haggerty, R. J. (Eds.). (1994). *Reducing risks for mental disorders: Frontiers for preventive intervention research*. Washington, DC: National Academy of Sciences.

Naimi, T. S., Brewer, R. D., Mokdad, A., Denny, C., Serdula, M. K., & Marks, J. S. (2003). Binge drinking among U.S. adults. *Journal of the American Medical Association, 289*, 70–75.

Nash, W. P., Westphal, R. J., Watson, P. J., & Litz, B. T. (2011). Combat and Operational Stress First Aid: Responder Training Manual. Washington, DC: U.S. Navy, Bureau of Medicine and Surgery.

National Child Traumatic Stress Network (2008a). *Traumatic grief in military children: Information for families*. Los Angeles, CA & Durham, NC: National Center for Child Traumatic Stress. Retrieved from http://www.nctsn.org/nccts/nav.do?pid=ctr_top_military.

National Child Traumatic Stress Network (2008b). *Traumatic grief in military children: Information for medical providers*. Los Angeles, CA & Durham, NC: National Center for Child Traumatic Stress. Retrieved from http://www.nctsn.org/nccts/nav.do?pid=ctr_top_military.

National Conference of State Legislatures (2011). Retrieved June 30, 2011 from http://www.ncsl.org/default. aspx?tabid=16430

National Defense Authorization Act for Fiscal Year 2010. Pub. L. No. 111-84, 123 Stat. 2190 (2009).

National Defense Authorization Act of 2008, Pub. L. No. 110-181, §532 (2008).

National Guard (2009) *About the National Guard*. Retrieved from Posttraumatic stress disorder http://www.ng.mil/About/default.aspx

National Healthy Marriage Resource Center (2010). *Marriage and divorce in the National Guard and Reserves: A fact sheet*. Retrieved from http://www.healthymarriageinfo.org/resource-detail/index. aspx?rid=3132

National Highway Traffic Safety Association (2010). *2009 Traffic safety facts: A compilation of motor vehicle crash data from the fatality reporting system and the general estimates system*. Retrieved from http://www-nrd.nhtsa.dot.gov/cats/listpublications.aspx?Id=E&ShowBy=DocType.

National Military Family Association (2006). *Report on the cycles of deployment: An analysis of survey responses from April–September, 2005*. Alexandria, VA: Author. Retrieved from http://www.militaryfamily.org/publications/reports/.

National Military Family Association (2007). *Education & the military spouse: The long road to success.* Alexandria, VA: Author. Retrieved from http://www.militaryfamily.org/publications/reports/.

National Military Family Association (2010). *We serve, too: A toolkit about military teens.* Retrieved from http://www.militaryfamily.org/publications/teen-toolkit/.

National Security Council (n.d.). Retrieved from the White House website: http://www.whitehouse.gov/administration/eop/nsc.

Naval Inspector General (n.d.). *What is administrative separation from naval service?* Retrieved from http://www.ig.navy.mil/complaints/Complaints%20%20(Admin%20Separations).htm.

Navy Personnel Command (n.d.). *Deployment support program: Desk guide.* Retrieved from http://www.public.navy.mil/surfor/cds9/Documents/CDS9_Deployment_Support_Program_Desk_Guide.pdf.

Navy Personnel Command (2010). *Navy safe harbor—Wounded, ill, and injured support.* Retrieved from http://www.npc.navy.mil/CommandSupport/SafeHarbor.

Navy-Marine Corps Relief Society (2010). *Navy-Marine Corps Relief Society.* Retrieved November 30, 2011 from http://www.nmcrs.org

Newby, J. H., McCarroll, J. E., Ursano, R. J., Fan, Z., Shigemura, J., & Tucker-Harris, Y. (2005). Positive and negative consequences of a military deployment. *Military Medicine, 170,* 815–819.

Newby, J. H., Ursano, R. J., McCarroll, J. E., Liu, X., Fullerton, C. S., & Norwood, A. E. (2005). Post deployment domestic violence by U.S. Army soldiers. *Military Medicine, 170,* 643–647.

Obama, M., & Biden, J. (2010, September 3). Michelle Obama, Jill Biden: The troops need us. *USA Today.* Retrieved from http://www.usatoday.com/news/opinion/forum/2010-09-03-column03_ST3_N.htm.

Ochberg, F. M. (n.d.). *When helping hurts.* Retrieved from the Gift From Within website: http://www.giftfrom-within.org/html/helping.html.

Office of Applied Studies (2005, November 10). *Alcohol use and alcohol-related risk behaviors among veterans.* Retrieved August 17, 2010 from the Substance Abuse and Mental Health Services Administration website: http://www.oas.samhsa.gov/2k5/vetsAlc/vetsAlc.htm#link_group_1.

Office of the Assistant Secretary of Defense for Reserve Affairs (2005). *Reserve component categories of the reserve components of the Armed Forces.* Washington, DC: Author. Retrieved from http://ra.defense.gov/documents/publications/RC101%20Handbook-updated%2020%20Sep%2005.pdf.

Office of the Assistant Secretary of Defense for Reserve Affairs (2007). *Commander's family readiness toolkit.* Washington, DC: Author.

Office of the Assistant Secretary of Defense for Reserve Affairs (2010a). *Family readiness.* Retrieved December 7, 2011 from Office of the Assistant Secretary of Defense—Reserve Affairs website: http://ra.defense. gov/programs/fepp/family.html.

Office of the Assistant Secretary of Defense for Reserve Affairs (2010b). *Guard and reserve family readiness programs toolkit.* Retrieved August 27, 2010 from http://ra.defense.gov/documents/toolkit/Commanders%20Toolkit%200328.pdf.

Office of the Assistant Secretary of Defense for Reserve Affairs (2010c). *Office of the Assistant Secretary of Defense—Reserve Affairs.* Retrieved August 24, 2010 from http://ra.defense.gov/.

Office of the Deputy Under Secretary of Defense (Military Community and Family Policy) (2005). *2004 demographics: Profile of the military community.* Washington, DC: Author. Retrieved from http://www.militaryhomefront.dod.mil/portal/page/mhf/ MHF MHF_DETAIL_0?current_id=20.20.60.70.0.0.0.0.0.

Office of the Deputy Under Secretary of Defense (Military Community and Family Policy) (2006). *2005 demographics: Profile of the military community.* Washington, DC: Author. Retrieved from http://www.militaryhomefront.dod.mil/portal/page/mhf/MHF/MHF_DETAIL_0?current_id=20.20.60.70.0.0.0.0.0.

Office of the Deputy Under Secretary of Defense (Military Community and Family Policy) (2007). *2006 demographics: Profile of the military community.* Washington, DC: Author. Retrieved from http://www.militaryhomefront.dod.mil/portal/page/mhf/MHF/MHF_DETAIL_0?current_id=20.20.60.70.0.0.0.0.0.

Office of the Deputy Under Secretary of Defense (Military Community and Family Policy) (2008). *2007 demographics: Profile of the military community.* Washington, DC: Author. Retrieved from http://www.militaryhomefront.dod.mil/portal/page/mhf/MHF/MHF_DETAIL_0?current_id=20.20.60.70.0.0.0.0.0.

Office of the Deputy Under Secretary of Defense (Military Community and Family Policy) (2009a). *2008 demographics: Profile of the military community.* Washington, DC: Author. Retrieved from http://www.militaryhomefront.dod.mil/portal/page/mhf/MHF/MHF_DETAIL_0?current_id=20.20.60.70.0.0.0.0.0.

Office of the Deputy Under Secretary of Defense (Military Community & Family Policy) (2009b). *Report of the 2nd quadrennial quality of life review.* Washington, DC: Department of Defense. Retrieved from http://www.militaryhomefront.dod.mil/portal/page/mhf/MHF/MHF_DETAIL_0?current_id=20.20.60.70.0.0.0.0.0.

Office of the Deputy Under Secretary of Defense (Military Community and Family Policy) (2010). *2009 demographics: Profile of the military community.* Washington, DC: Author. Retrieved from http://www.militaryhomefront.dod.mil/portal/page/mhf/MHF/MHF_DETAIL_0?current_id=20.20.60.70.0.0.0.0.0.

Office of the Law Revision Counsel (2008). *Uniform Code of Military Justice.* United States Code. Washington, DC: Author.

Office of the President of the United States (2011). *Strengthening our military families.* Washington, DC: The White House.

Office of the Secretary of Defense Sexual Assault Prevention and Response Office (2010). *Department of Defense fiscal year 2009 annual report on sexual assault in the military.* Arlington, VA: United States Department of Defense.

Office of the Under Secretary of Defense, Personnel and Readiness (n.d.). *Population representation in the military services: Fiscal year 2009 report.* Retrieved from http://prhome.defense.gov/MPP/ACCESSION%20 POLICY/poprep.aspx.

Office of the Under Secretary of Defense, Personnel and Readiness. (2009a). *Military Morale, Welfare, and Recreation (MWR) programs* (DoD Instruction 1015.10). Washington, DC: Author.

Office of the Under Secretary of Defense, Personnel and Readiness. (2009b). *Monthly basic pay table for 2009.* Retrieved from http://militarypay.defense.gov/pay/bp/01_activeduty.html.

Office of the Under Secretary of Defense for Personnel and Readiness. (2010). *Military Community & Family Policy mission statement.* Retrieved August 24, 2010 from http://prhome.defense.gov/MCFP/.

Okie, S. (2005). Traumatic brain injury in the war zone. *New England Journal of Medicine, 352,* 2043–2047.

Oram. (n.d.). *Operation: Military Kids Hero Packs.* Retrieved from the 4_H Military Partnerships website: http://www.4-hmilitarypartnerships.org/DesktopDefault.aspx?tabid=130.

Orthner, D. K. (2002). *SAF IV survey report: Relocation adjustment among Army civilian spouses.* Prepared for the U.S. Army Community and Family Support Center. Chapel Hill, NC: University of North Carolina.

Orthner, D. K., & Rose, R. (2009). Work separation demands and spouse psychological well-being. *Family Relations, 58,* 392–403.

Owens, B. D., Kragh, J. F., Jr., Wenke, J. C., Macaitis, J., Wade, C. E., & Holcome, J. B., (2008). Combat wounds in Operation Iraqi Freedom and Operation Enduring Freedom. *Journal of Trauma, 64,* 295–299.

Ozbay, F., Johnson, D. C., Dimoulas, E., Morgan III, C. A., Charney, D. S., & Southwick, S. (2007). Social support and resilience to stress: From neurobiology to clinical practice. *Psychiatry, 4,* 35–40.

Park, N. (2011). Military children and families: Strengths and challenges during peace and war. *American Psychologist, 66,* 65–72.

Parker, M. W., Call, V. R. A., Dunkle, R., & Vaitkus, M. (2002). "Out of Sight" but not "Out of Mind": Parent contact and worry among senior ranking male officers in the military who live long distances from parents. *Military Psychology, 14,* 257–277.

Parrish, K. (2010, December 22). Cheers, applause accompany "Don't Ask" repeal signing. *The American Forces Press Service.* Retrieved from the Department of Defense website: http://www.defense.gov/news/newsarticle.aspx?id=62216.

Parsons, T., & Bales, R. F. (1956). *Family socialization and interaction process.* Abingdon, UK: Routledge.

Pellerin, C. (2011, January 7). Gates outlines "Don't Ask" repeal process. *American Forces Press Service.* Retrieved from the Department of Defense website http://www.defense.gov/news/newsarticle. aspx?id=62370.

Perconte, S. T., Wilson, A. T., Pontius, E. B., Deitrick, A. L., & Spiro, K. J. (1993). Psychological and war stress symptoms among deployed and non-deployed reservists following the Persian Gulf War. *Military Medicine, 158,* 516–521.

Perlick, D. A., Straits-Tröster, K., Dyck, D. G., Norell, D. M., Strauss, J. L., Henderson, C., … Cristian, A. (2011). Multifamily group treatment for veterans with traumatic brain injury. *Professional Psychology: Research and Practice, 42,* 70–78.

Perri, T. J. (2008). The economics of US civil war conscription. *American Law and Economics Review, 10,* 424–454.

Peterson, C., Park, N., & Castro, C. A. (2011). Assessment for the U.S. Army Comprehensive Soldier Fitness Program: The global assessment tool. *American Psychologist, 66,* 10–18.

Pflanz, S. & Sonnek, S. (2002). Work stress in the military: Prevalence, causes, and relationship to emotional health. *Military Medicine, 162,* 643–648.

Pierce, P. F. (2010, April). Work-family conflict among deployed military women. Invited presentation at the 2010 *International Research Symposium of the Military Family.* Research Institute at Purdue, Indianapolis, IN.

Pietrzak, R. H., Johnson, D. C., Goldstein, M. B., Malley, J. C., Rivers, A. J., Morgan, C. A., & Southwick, S. M. (2009). Psychological resilience and postdeployment social support protect against traumatic stress and depressive symptoms in soldiers returning from Operations Enduring Freedom and Iraqi Freedom. *Depression and Anxiety, 26,* 745–751.

Pietrzak, R. H., Johnson, D. C., Goldstein, M. B., Malley, J. C., Rivers, A. J., Morgan, C. A., & Southwick, S. M. (2010). Psychosocial buffers of traumatic stress, depressive symptoms, and psychosocial difficulties in veterans of Operations Iraqi Freedom and Enduring Freedom: The role of resilience, unit support, and postdeployment social support. *Journal of Affective Disorders, 120,* 188–192.

Pincus, S. H., House, R., Christenson, J., & Adler, L. E. (2001). The emotional cycle of deployment: A military family perspective. *Army Medical Department Journal, 4/5/6,* 15–23.

Pollock, D. C., & Van Reken, R. E. (2001). *Third culture kids: The experience of growing up among worlds.* Yarmouth, ME: Intercultural Press.

Polusny, N. A., Erbes, C. R., Murdoch, M., Arbisi, P. A., Thuras, P., & Rath, M. B. (2011). Prospective risk factors for new-onset post-traumatic stress disorder in National Guard soldiers deployed to Iraq. *Psychological Medicine, 41,* 687–698.

Pomper, K., Blank, H., Duff Campbell, N., & Schulman, K. (2005). *Be all that we can be: Lessons from the military for improving our nation's child care system.* Washington, DC: National Women's Law Center. Retrieved from http://www.nwlc.org/resource/be-all-we-can-be-lessons-military-improving-our-nations-child-care-system-2004-follow.

Prigerson, H. G., & Maciejewski, P. K. (2005). A call for sound empirical testing and evaluation of criteria for complicated grief proposed for DSM-V. *Omega, 52,* 9–19.

Prigerson, H. G., Shear, M. K., Jacobs, S. C., Maciejewski, P. K., Davidson, J. R., Rosenheck, R., ... Zisook, S. (1999). Consensus criteria for traumatic grief. A preliminary empirical test. *British Journal of Psychiatry, 174,* 67–73.

Radey, M., & Figley, C. R. (2007). The socialpsychology of compassion. *Clinical Social Work, 35,* 207–214.

Radford, A. W. (2009). *Military service members and veterans in higher education: What the new GI Bill may mean for postsecondary institutions.* Washington, DC: American Council on Education. Retrieved from http://www.acenet.edu/Content/NavigationMenu/ProgramsServices/MilitaryPrograms/serving/index.htm.

Ramsberger, P. F., LeGree, P. & Mills, L. (2003). Evaluation of the Buddy Team Assignment Program. *United States Army Research Institute for the Behavioral and Social Sciences.* Alexandria, VA.

Reivich, K. J., Seligman, M. E. P., & McBride, S. (2011). Master resilience training in the U.S. Army. *American Psychologist, 66,* 25–34.

Renshaw, K. D., Rodrigues, C. S., & Jones, D. H. (2008). Psychological symptoms and marital satisfaction in spouses of Operation Iraqi Freedom veterans: Relationships with spouses' perceptions of veterans' experiences and symptoms. *Journal of Family Psychology, 22,* 586–594.

Rentz, E. E., Marshall, S. W., Loomis, D., Casteel, C., Martin, S. L., & Gibbs, D. A. (2007). Effect of deployment on the occurrence of child maltreatment in military and nonmilitary families. *American Journal of Epidemiology, 165,* 1199–1206.

Riddle, J. R., Smith, T. C., Smith, B., Corbeil, T. E., Engel, C. C., Wells, T. S., ... Blazer, D. for the Millennium Cohort Study Team (2007). Millennium Cohort: The 2001–2003 baseline prevalence of mental disorders in the U.S. military. *Journal of Clinical Epidemiology, 60,* 192–201.

Robinson, M. E., Teyhen, D. S., Wu, S. S., Dugan, J. L., Wright, A. C., Childs, J. D., ... George, S. Z. (2009). Mental health symptoms in combat medic training: A longitudinal examination. *Military medicine, 174,* 572–577.

Roff, P. (2009, May 28). *Congress must help military vote [web log message].* U.S. News and World Report. Retrieved from http://www.usnews.com/blogs/peter-roff/2009/05/28/congress-must-help-military-vote.html.

Rosen, A., Walter, G., Casey, D., & Hocking, B. (2000). Combating psychiatric stigma: An overview of contemporary initiatives. *Australasian Psychiatry, 8,* 19–26.

Rosen, L. N., Durand, D. B., & Martin, J. A. (2000). Wartime stress and family adaptation. In J. A. Martin, L. N. Rosen, & L. R. Sparacino (Eds.), *The military family: A practice guide for human service providers* (pp. 123–138). Westport, CT: Praeger Security International.

Rowe, E. L., Gradus, J. L., Pineles, S. L., Batten, S. V., & Davison, E. H. (2009). Military sexual trauma in treatment-seeking women veterans. *Military Psychology, 21,* 387–395.

Ruscio, A. M., Weathers, F. W., King, L. A., & King, D. W. (2002). Male war-zone veterans' perceived relationships with their children: The importance of emotional numbing. *Journal of Traumatic Stress, 15,* 351–357.

Saltzman, W. (2010). *FOCUS project: Program overview and outcomes.* Presented at the Navy and Marine Corps Combat & Operational Stress Control Conference 2010, San Diego, CA.

Saltzman, W., Lester, P., Beardslee, W., & Pynoos, R. (2008). *FOCUS project for military families: Training manual.* Retrieved from the Health Affairs website: http://content.healthaffairs.org/content/24/2/499.full.html.

Sampson, R. (1995). Unemployment and imbalanced sex ratios: Race-specific consequences for family structure and crime. In M. B. Tucker & C. Mitchell-Kernan (Eds.), *The decline in marriage among African Americans: Causes, consequences, and policy implications* (pp. 229–254). Thousand Oaks, CA: Sage.

Sanchez, R. P., Bray, R. M., Vincus, A. A., & Bann, C. M. (2004). Active duty and reserve/guard personnel of U.S. military. *Military Psychology, 16,* 19–35.

San Diego Fleet & Family Support Center (2010). *Ombudsman.* Retrieved August 27, 2010 from http://www.cnrsw.navy.mil/fsc/ombudsman.asp.

Sandweiss, D. A., Slymen, D. J., LeardMann, C. A., Smith, B., White, M. R., Boyko, E. J., ... Smith, T. C. for the Millennium Cohort Study Team (2011). The effects of preinjury psychiatric status and injury severity on postdeployment posttraumatic stress disorder. *Archives of General Psychiatry, 68,* 496–504 .

Sayer, N. A., Noorbaloochi, S., Frazier, P., Carlson, K. F., Gravely, A., & Murdoch, M. (2010). Reintegration problems and treatment preferences among recent veterans: New directions for trauma research. *Psychiatric Services, 61,* 589–597.

Sayers, S. L., Farrow, V. A., Ross, J., & Oslin, D. W. (2009). Family problems among recently returned military veterans referred for a mental health problem. *Journal of Clinical Psychiatry, 70,* 163–170.

Scott, D. L. (2010). War-related deaths in the family. In N. B. Webb (Ed.), *Helping bereaved children: A handbook for practitioners* (3rd ed.) pp. 147–164). New York: Guildford Press.

Seelig, A. D., Jacobson, I. J., Smith, B., Hooper, T. I., Boyko, E. J., Gackstetter, G. D., ... Smith, T. C. for the Millennium Cohort Study Team (2010) Sleep patterns before, during, and after deployment to Iraq and Afghanistan. *Sleep, 33,* 1615–1622.

Segal, D. R., & Segal, M. W. (2004). America's military population. *Population Bulletin, 59*(4). Washington, DC: Population Reference Bureau.

Segal, M. W. (1986). The military and the family as greedy institutions. *Armed Forces & Society, 13,* 9–38.

Selective Service System. (2009) *Who must register.* Retrieved from http://www.sss.gov/FSwho.htm.

Serafino, N. M. (2004). *Peacekeeping and related stability operations: Issues of U.S. military involvement.* Washington, DC: Congressional Research Service, Library of Congress.

Servicemembers Opportunity Colleges (n.d.). *Military bill of rights.* Retrieved November 30, 2011 from http://www.soc.aascu.org/socconsortium/PublicationsSOC.html.

Servicemembers Opportunity Colleges (n.d.). *SOC consortium guide 2009–2011* (Vol. 1). Washington, DC: Author. Retrieved from http://www.soc.aascu.org/socconsortium/PublicationsSOC.html.

Shear, M. K., & Mulhare, E. (2008). Complicated grief. *Psychiatric Annals, 38,* 662–670.

Sheppard, S. C., Malatras, J. W., & Israel, A. C. (2010). The impact of deployment on U.S. military families. *American Psychologist, 65,* 599–609.

Smith, B., Ryan, M. A. K., Wingard, D. L., Patterson, T. L., Slymen, D. J., & Macera, C. A. for the Millennium Cohort Study Team (2008). Cigarette smoking and military deployment: A prospective evaluation. *American Journal of Preventive Medicine, 35,* 539–546.

Smith B., Wong, C. A., Smith, T. C., Boyko, E. J., Gackstetter, G. D., & Ryan, M. A. K. for the Millennium Cohort Study Team (2009). Newly reported respiratory symptoms and conditions among military personnel deployed to Iraq and Afghanistan: A prospective population-based study. *American Journal of Epidemiology, 170,* 1433–1442.

Smith, L. K., & Sarkar, M. (2008). *Making quality child care possible: Lessons learned from NACCRRA's military partnership.* Arlington, VA: National Association of Child Care Resources & Referral Agencies. Retrieved from http://www.naccrra.org/publications/naccrra-publications/publications/LesnsLrnd%20Rprt-m2.pdf.

Smith, S. D. (2006, August 31). *Military coordinates effort to help wounded troops return to work.* Retrieved November 30, 2011 from the Department of Defense website: http://www.defense.gov/News/NewsArticle.aspx?ID=660.

Smith, T. C., Jacobson, I. G., Smith, B., Hooper, T. I., & Ryan, M. A. (2007). Validation of occupation and prevalence of exposures in Millennium Cohort Study. *International Journal of Environmental Health Research, 17,* 271–284.

Smith, T. C., Wingard, D. L., Ryan, M. A. K., Kritz-Silverstein, D., Slymen, D. J., & Sallis, J. F. for the Millennium Cohort Study Team (2008). Prior assault and posttraumatic stress disorder after combat deployment. *Epidemiology, 19,* 505–512.

Smith, T. C., Wingard, D. L., Ryan, M. A., Kritz-Silverstein, D., Slymen, D. J., & Sallis, J. F. (2009). PTSD prevalence, associated exposures, and functional health outcomes in a large, population-based military cohort. *Public Health Reports, 124,* 90–102.

Solomon, Z., Zur-Noah, S., Horesh, D., Zerach, G., & Keinan, G. (2008). The contribution of stressful life events throughout the life cycle to combat-induced psychopathology. *Journal of Traumatic Stress, 21,* 318–325.

Stahre, M. A., Brewer, R. D., Fonseca, V. P., & Naimi, T. S. (2009). Binge drinking among active duty military personnel. *American Journal of Preventative Medicine, 36*, 208–217.

Stanley, S. M., Blumberg, S. L., & Markman, H. J. (1999). Helping couples fight for their marriages: The PREP approach. In R. Berger & M. Hannah (Eds.), *Handbook of preventive approaches in couple therapy* (pp. 279–303). New York, NY: Brunner/Mazel.

Steen, J. M., & Asaro, M. R. (2006). *Military widow: A survival guide.* Annapolis, MD: Naval Institute Press.

Strengthening Our Military Families (2011). Washington, DC: The White House. Retrieved from the Department of Defense website: http://www.defense.gov/home/features/2011/0111_initiative/.

Suicide Risk Management & Surveillance Office (2008). *Army Suicide Event Report (ASER): Calendar year 2007.* Tacoma, WA: Army Behavioral Health Technology Office.

Suls, J., Green, P., Rose, G., Loundsbury, P., & Gordon, E. (1997). Hiding worries from one's spouse: Associations between coping via protective buffering and distress in male post-myocardial infarction patients and their wives. *Journal of Behavioral Medicine, 20*, 333–349.

Sussman, N. (2006). In session with Dennis S. Charney, M. D.: Resilience to stress. *Primary Psychiatry, 13*, 39–41.

Tanielian, T., & Jaycox, L. H. (Eds.) (2008). *Invisible wounds of war : Psychological and cognitive injuries, their consequences, and services to assist recovery.* Santa Monica, CA: RAND Corporation.

Tan, M. (2009, December 20). A million soldiers deployed since 9/11. *Army Times.* Retrieved May 20, 2010, from http://www.armytimes.com/news/2009/12/army_deployments_121809w/.

Tang, C.-Y., & MacDermid Wadsworth, S. (2010). Time and workplace flexibility: 2008 national study of the *changing workforce.* New York: Families and Work Institute.

Teachman, J. D., & Tedrow, L. (2008). Divorce, race and military service: More than equal pay and equal opportunity. *Journal of Marriage and Family, 70*, 1030–1044.

Tejada-Vera, B., & Sutton, P. D. (2010). Births, marriages, divorces, and deaths: Provisional data for 2009. *National Vital Statistics Reports* (Vol. 58, No. 25). Hyattsville, MD: National Center for Health Statistics.

The American Legion (2010). *Heroes to hometowns.* Retrieved from The American Legion: http://www.legion.org/heroes.

The Management of Concussion/mTBI Working Group (2009). *VA/DoD clinical practice guideline for management of concussion/mild traumatic brain injury.* Retrieved from the Department of Veteran's Affairs website: http://www.healthquality.va.gov/.

The Management of Post-traumatic Stress Working Group (2010). *The VA/DoD clinical practice guideline for the management of post-traumatic stress: VA/DoD evidence based practice.* Retrieved from the Department of Veteran's Affairs website: http://www.healthquality.va.gov/Post_Deployment_Health_PDH.asp.

The Military Health System (2010a). *Health care in the MHS.* Retrieved November 30, 2011 from http://www.health.mil/About_MHS/Health_Care_in_the_MHS.aspx.

The Military Health System (2010b). *The military health system: Frequently asked questions.* Retrieved November 30, 2011 from http://www.health.mil/About_MHS/FAQs.aspx.

Thomas, J. L., Adler, A. B., Wittels, P., Ennes, R., & Johannes, B. (2004). Comparing elite soldiers' perceptions of psychological and physical demands during military training. *Military Medicine, 169*, 526–530.

Thomas, J. L., Wilk, J. E., Riviere, L. A., McGurk, D., Castro, C. A., & Hoge, C. W. (2010). Prevalence of mental health problems and functional impairment among active component and National Guard soldiers 3 and 12 months following combat in Iraq. *Archives of General Psychiatry, 67*, 614–623.

Tick, E. (2005). *War and the soul.* Wheaton, IL: Quest Books.

Tollefson, T. T. (2008). Supporting spouses during a military deployment. *Family & Community Health: The Journal of Health Promotion & Maintenance, 31*, 281–286.

TRICARE Management Activity (2010a). *National Guard and reserve members and their families.* Retrieved November 30, 2011 from http://www.tricare.mil/mybenefit/home/overview/Eligibility/WhoIsEligible/NationalGuardAndReserveAndFamilies.

TRICARE Management Activity (2010b). *TRICARE covered services: Psychotherapy.* Retrieved November 30, 2011 from http://www.tricare.mil/mybenefit/jsp/Medical/IsItCovered.do?kw=Psychotherapy.

TRICARE Management Activity (2010c). *What is TRICARE?* Retrieved November 30, 2011 from http://www.tricare.mil/mybenefit/home/overview/WhatIsTRICARE?status=Retired+Service+Member&country=United+States&zipCode=21078&plan=US+Family+Health+Plan+%28USFHP%29.

Tyler, M. (2002). The military teenager in Europe: Perspectives for health care providers. In M. Ender (Ed.), *Military brats and other global nomads: Growing up in organization families* (pp.25–34). Westport, CT: Praeger Security International.

United Nations (1995). *Mission readiness and stress management.* New York, NY: Office of Human Resources Management. Retrieved from http://www.un.org/Depts/OHRM/stress.htm.

U.S. Air Force (n.d.). *Air Force mission.* Retrieved Decemeber 7, 2011 from http://www.af.mil/main/welcome .asp.

U.S. Air Force (2010). *Air Force wounded warrior.* Retrieved from http://www.woundedwarrior.af.mil/.

U.S. Army (n.d.). *The Army values.* Retrieved December 7, 2011 from http://www.army.mil/values/.

U.S. Army (2010). *Health promotion risk reduction suicide prevention report 2010.* Retrieved from http:// usarmy.vo.llnwd.net/e1/HPRRSP/HP-RR-SPReport2010_v00.pdf.

U.S. Army Garrison Baumholder (2008). *Baumholder Directive 420-1: Military quarters handbook.* Baumholder, Germany: U.S. Army Garrison.

U.S. Army Human Resources Command (2010). *Frequently asked questions.* Retrieved from https://www.hrc .army.mil/site/Active/TAGD/CMAOC/CMAOCPages/cmaocfaq.htm#8.

U.S. Army Installation Management Command (2010). *The Army family covenant: Keeping the promise.* Retrieved from http://www.imcom.army.mil/hq/afc.

U.S. Army Medical Department (2010a). *Army wounded warrior program.* Retrieved from http://www.aw2 .army.mil/.

U.S. Army Medical Department (2010b). *Resilience training.* Retrieved from https://www.resilience.army.mil.

U.S. Census Bureau (2008). *Table FG6. One-parent unmarried family groups with own children under 18 by marital status of parents: 2008.* Retrieved from http://www.census.gov/population/www/socdemo/hh-fam/ cps2008.html.

U.S. Census Bureau, Current Population Survey (2010). *Annual Social and Economic Supplement. Table PINC-04.* Retrieved from http://www.census.gov/hhes/www/cpstables/032010/perinc/new04_001.htm.

U.S. Coast Guard (2010). *Missions.* Retrieved from http://www.uscg.mil/top/missions.

U.S. Department of Agriculture (2011). Extension. Retrieved November 23, 2011 from http://www.csrees.usda.gov/ qlinks/extension.html.

U.S. Department of Agriculture & Department of Defense Partnership (2010). *Extension and military collaboration.* Retrieved from http://militaryfamilies.extension.org/mission/.

U.S. Department of Labor (2009). *Uniformed services employment and reemployment rights act of 1994: Fiscal year 2008 annual report to congress.* Washington, DC: Author. Retrieved from http://www.dol.gov/vets/ programs/userra/main.htm.

U.S. Department of Labor, Bureau of Labor Statistics (2011). *Employment situation of veterans: 2010.* Washington, DC: Author. Retrieved December 6, 2011 from http://www.bls.gov/news.release/vet.nr0 .htm.

U.S. Department of Labor (2010, February). *Fact sheet #28A: The family and medical leave act: Military family leave entitlements.* Washington, DC: Author. http://www.dol.gov/whd/fmla/finalrule.htm.

U.S. Department of Veterans Affairs (n.d.). *VA history in brief.* Washington, DC: Author. Retrieved from http:// www.va.gov/opa/publications/archives/docs/history_in_brief.pdf.

U.S. Department of Veterans Affairs (2010a). *Federal benefits for veterans, dependents and survivors: 2010 edition.* Washington, DC: U.S. Government Printing Office. Retrieved from http://www.va.gov/opa/ publications/benefits_book.asp.

U.S. Department of Veterans Affairs (2010b). *Working with trauma survivors: What workers need to know.* Retrieved from http://www.ptsd.va.gov/professional/pages/working-with-trauma-survivors.asp.

U.S. Department of Veterans Affairs (2011a). *FY 2012 budget submission: Summary volume, volume 1 of 4.* Washington, DC: Author Retrieved from http://www.va.gov/budget/products.asp.

U.S. Department of Veterans Affairs (2011b). *Vet Centers.* Retrieved from http://www.vetcenter.va.gov/ index.asp.

U.S. Marine Corps (n.d.-a). *Combat operational stress continuum for families.* Retrieved August 27, 2010 from http://www.usmc-mccs.org/cosc/coscContMatrixFamily.cfm?sid=ml&smid=6&ssmid=2.

U.S. Marine Corps (n.d.-b). *The values that define a marine.* Retrieved December 7, 2011 from http://www .marines.com/main/index/making_marines/culture/traditions/core_values.

U.S. Marine Corps (2010). *Wounded warrior regiment.* Retrieved from http://www.woundedwarriorregiment.org.

U.S. Navy. (n.d.-a). *The stress continuum.* Retrieved December 7, 2011 from http://www.nmcphc.med.navy.mil/ downloads/stress/stress_continuum_trifold.pdf.

U.S. Navy. (n.d.-b) *The United States Navy: Honor, courage, commitment.* Retrieved December 7, 2011 from http://www.navy.mil/navydata/navy_legacy_hr.asp?id=193.

U.S. Office of Personnel Management (n.d.). *Salaries and wages.* Retrieved from http://www.opm.gov/ oca/11tables/index.asp.

Vaishnavi, S., Rao, V., & Fann, J. R. (2009). Neuropsychiatric problems after traumatic brain injury: Unraveling the silent epidemic. *Psychosomatics, 50,* 198–205.

Verhaeghe, S., Defloor, T., & Grypdonck, M. (2005). Stress and coping among families of patients with traumatic brain injury: A review of the literature. *Journal of Clinical Nursing, 14,* 1004–1012.

Vogt, D. S., Pless, A. P., King, L. A., & King, D. W. (2005). Deployment stressors, gender, and mental health outcomes among Gulf War I veterans. *Journal of Traumatic Stress, 18*, 272–284.

Vythilingam, M. (2010, May 20). *Combat operational stress control (COSC): An integral part of force health protection.* Presented at the Naval Center Combat and Operational Stress Control Conference 2010. Retrieved from http://www.med.navy.mil/sites/nmcsd/nccosc/coscConference/Pages/2010/cosc-Conference2010MediaDay3.aspx.

Walker, A. J. (1985). Reconceptualizing family stress. *Journal of Marriage and the Family, 47*, 827–837.

Wallace, A. E., Sheehan, E. P., & Young-Xu, Y. (2009). Women, alcohol, and the military: Cultural changes and reductions in later alcohol problems among female veterans. *Journal of Women's Health, 18*, 1347–1353.

Walsh, F. (2002). A family resilience framework: Innovative practice applications. *Family Relations, 51*, 130–137.

Walsh, F. (2003a). Changing families in a changing world: Reconstructing family normality. In F. Walsh (Ed.), *Normal family processes: Growing diversity and complexity* (pp. 3–26). New York, NY: Guildford Press.

Walsh, F. (2003b). Clinical views of family normality, health, and dysfunction: From deficit to strengths perspective. In F. Walsh (Ed.), *Normal Family Processes: Growing diversity and complexity* (pp. 27–57). New York, NY: Guildford Press.

Walsh, F. (2003c). Family resilience: A framework for clinical practice. *Family Process, 42*, 1–18.

Walsh, F. (2007). Traumatic loss and major disasters: Strengthening family and community resilience. *Family Process, 46*, 207–227.

Warden, D. (2006). Military TBI during the Iraq and Afghanistan wars. *Journal of Head Trauma Rehabilitation, 21*, 398–402.

Warner, C. H., Appenseller, G. N., Warner, C. M., & Greiger, T. (2009). Psychological effects of deployments on military families. *Psychiatric Annals, 39*, 56–63.

Washington State University Extension (2009). *What is a land-grant college?* Retrieved from http://ext.wsu.edu/documents/landgrant.pdf.

Watkins, S. J., & Sherk, J. (2008). *Who serves in the U.S. military? The demographics of enlisted troops and officers.* Retrieved from the Heritage Foundation website: http://www.heritage.org/research/reports/2008/08/who-serves-in-the-us-military-the-demographics-of-enlisted-troops-and-officers.

Weber, E. G., & Weber, D. K. (2005). Geographic relocation frequency, resilience, and military adolescent behavior. *Military Medicine, 170*, 638–642.

Wells, T. S., LeardMann, C. A., Fortuna, S. O., Smith, B., Smith, T. C., Ryan, M. A., … Blazer, D. (2010). A prospective study of depression following combat deployment in support of the wars in Iraq and Afghanistan. *American Journal of Public Health, 100*, 90–99.

Werner, M. J., Walker, L. S., & Greene, J. W. (1994). Screening for problem drinking among college freshmen. *Journal of Adolescent Health, 15*, 303–310.

Wertsch, M. E. (1991). *Military brats: Legacies of childhood inside the fortress.* New York, NY: Harmony Books.

Westat. (2010). *Support to the DoD comprehensive review working group analyzing the impact of repealing "Don't Ask, Don't Tell,": Findings from the surveys* (Vol. 1). Rockville, MD: Author. Retrieved from the Department of Defense website: http://www.defense.gov/home/features/2010/0610_gatesdadt/.

Westphal, R. J. & Woodward, K. R. (2010). Family fitness. *Military Medicine, 175*, 97–102.

Whiteman, S., & Barry, A. E. (2010, April). *Operation diploma: Profiles of student veterans attending college.* Presented at the Military Family Research Institute's 2010 International Research Symposium on Military Families, Indianapolis, IN.

Wiens, T., W., & Boss, P. (2006). Maintaining family resiliency before, during, and after military separations. In C. A. Castro, A. B. Adler, & T. W. Britt (Eds.), *Military life: The psychology of serving in peace and combat: The military family* (Vol. 3, pp. 13–38). Westport, CT: Praeger Security International.

Willerton, E., MacDermid Wadsworth, S., & Riggs, D. (2011). Introduction: Military families under stress: What we know and what we need to know. In S. MacDermid Wadsworth & D. Riggs (Eds.), *Risk and resilience in U.S. military families* (pp. 1–20). New York, NY: Springer.

Willerton, E., Samper, R., & MacDermid, S. M. (2008). *Support for casualty assistance officers.* Purdue University: Military Family Research Institute. Retrieved from http://www.mfri.purdue.edu/content.asp?tid=2&id=8.

Willerton, E., Schwarz, R. L., MacDermid Wadsworth, S. M., & Oglesby, M. S. (2011, August). Military fathers' perspectives on involvement. *Journal of Family Psychology, 25*, 521–530.

Williams, J., Jones, S. B., Pemberton, M. R., Bray, R. M., Brown, J. M., & Vandermaas-Peeler, R. (2010). Measurement invariance of alcohol use motivations in junior military personnel at risk for depression or anxiety. *Addictive Behaviors, 35*, 441–451.

Wilsnack, S. C., & Wilsnack, R. W. (1995). Drinking and problem drinking in U.S. women: Patterns and recent trends. *Recent Developments in Alcoholism, 12*, 29–60.

Wilson, S. R., Wilkum, K., Chernichky, S. M., MacDermid Wadsworth, S., & Broniarczyk, K. M. (2011). Passport towards success: Description and evaluation of a program designed to help children and families reconnect after a parents' military deployment. *Journal of Applied Communication Research, 39*, 225–251.

Wolfe, J., Erickson, D. J., Sharkansky, E. J., King, D. W., & King, L. A. (1999). Course and predictors of posttraumatic stress disorder among Gulf War veterans: A prospective analysis. *Journal of Consulting and Clinical Psychology, 67*, 520–528.

Woodruff, S. I., Conway, T. L., & Edwards, C. C. (2000). Increasing response rates to a smoking survey for U.S. Navy enlisted women. *Evaluation and the Health Professions, 23*, 172–181.

Woodruff, T., Kelty, T., & Segal, D. R. (2006). Propensity to serve and motivation to enlist among American combat soldiers. *Armed Forces & Society, 32*, 353–366.

Wright, K. M., Burrell, L. M., Schroeder, E. D., & Thomas, J. L. (2006). Military spouses: Coping with the fear and the reality of service member injury and death. In C. A. Castro, A. B. Adler, & T. W. Britt (Eds.), *Military life: The psychology of serving in peace and combat: The military family* (Vol. 3, pp. 64–90). Westport, CT: Praeger Security International.

Wright, K. M., Cabrera, O. A., Bliese, P. D., Adler, A. B., Hoge, C. W., & Castro, C. A. (2009). Stigma and barriers to care in soldiers postcombat. *Psychological Services, 6*, 108–116.

Zellman, G. L., Gates, S. M., Moini, J. S., & Suttorp, M. (2009). Meeting family and military needs through military child care. *Armed Forces & Society, 35*, 437–459.

ZERO TO THREE (2009). *Honoring our babies and toddlers: Supporting young children affected by a military parent's deployment, injury or death.* Washington, DC: Author.

ZERO TO THREE (2011). *Coming Together Around Military Families®.* Retrieved from http://www.zerotothree.org/about-us/funded-projects/military-families/.

Zvonkovic, A. M., Solomon, C. R., Humble, A. M., & Manoogian, M. (2005). Family work and relationships: Lessons from families of men whose jobs require travel. *Family Relations, 54*, 411–422.

Author Index

Subject Index

A

ABCx Model, 92–93, 98
Academics, deployment on children, 68
Accessions, 21
Accompanied tour, 35
ACE Military Guide to the Evaluation of Educational Experiences in the Armed Services, 191
Active Component, 60, 152
    members, 4
    respondents, 24
Active duty, 42–44, 106
    personnel, 107
        by branch of service, 25
    service members, 109
Acute grief, 231
Acute stress disorder, 127
Acute stress reaction, 127
Adaptive coping strategies, 95
Adolescents, in combat-injured families, 151
Adult dependent category, 152
AER, *see* Army Emergency Relief
AFAS, *see* Air Force Aid Society
Air Force, 141
Air Force Academy, 237
Air Force Aid Society (AFAS), 164
Air National Guard, 44–45, 60
Alcohol
    misuse, 114
    and substance use/abuse, 132
Allowances, 106
Ambiguous loss, 49
Ambiguous loss theory, 96–97
American Red Cross, 182–183
Anxiety disorder, 127
Applicants, 21
Armed Forces of the United States, 5–7
Armed Forces Qualifying Test (AFQT), 21
Armed Services YMCA, 183
Army Emergency Relief (AER), 163
Army Family Covenant, 198–199
Army National Guard, 44–45, 60
Army, Navy, Air Force, and Marine
        Corps Reserves, 45
Army's Resilience Training program, 208–209
Assistant Secretary of Defense for Reserve
        Affairs, 161

B

Baseline data, 113
Basic Allowance for Housing (BAH), 106
Battle Buddies, 104
Battlemind Training, 208
Behavioral problems, in children, 70
Beneficiary, 12
Binge drinking rates, 114
Bipolar disorder, 210

Birthrate, 109
Blue Star Organizations, 183
Boundary ambiguity, 49
Buddy-to-Buddy program, 189
Buffer stressful information, 145
Burnout, 243

C

Caregiver, 221–222, 226, 227–230
Caregiver burden, 142
Caregivers and Veterans Omnibus Health Services
        Act of 2010, 180
Casualties, 56
Casualty Assistance Calls Officer (CACO), 56
Casualty Assistance Officer (CAO), 56
Casualty Assistance Representative (CAR), 56
Casualty Notification Officer (CNO), 56
CBT, *see* Cognitive-based therapy; Combat
        Brigade Team
Chain of command, 3, 9–12
Charity organizations, 163–164
Chief of Staff, 3
Child care, 62–64, 171–172
Child development centers (CDCs), 62
Children in DoDEA schools, 65
Civilian organizations, 181
Civil War, 181
Clearinghouse on Military Family Readiness, 188
Coercive controlling violence, 149
Cognitive-based therapy (CBT), 225
Cognitive processes, 226
Cohesion, 118
Cohorts, 111
Cold War, 5
Combat and Operational Stress First Aid (COSFA), 220
Combat Brigade Team (CBT) spouses, 143
Combat deployments, 67, 130, 134–136
Combat-injured families, 149–152
Combat operational stress control (COSC), 215–217
Combat operational stress reactions, 215
Combat stress, 127
Combat stress reactions (CSRs), 126
Coming Together Around Military Familie⁽ᵐ⁾ (CTAM⁽ᵐ⁾),
        77, 189
Commissary, 106, 172
Communal coping, 145
Community capacity, 176
Community, sense of, 41–42
Compassion fatigue, 243
Compassion satisfaction, 242–245
Compassion stress, 243
Complicated grief, 231
Composite life cycle model, 217
Comprehensive resources for military families, 161–163
Comprehensive soldier fitness (CSF), 214
Compromising, 96
Conceptual model, of resilience and risk, 44

An environmentally friendly book printed and bound in England by www.printondemand-worldwide.com

This book is made entirely of sustainable materials; FSC paper for the cover and PEFC paper for the text pages.

#0019 - 220915 - C0 - 254/178/17 - PB - 9780415880664